DATE DUE

After Freedom Summer

NEW PERSPECTIVES ON THE HISTORY OF THE SOUTH

UNIVERSITY PRESS OF FLORIDA

Florida A&M University, Tallahassee
Florida Atlantic University, Boca Raton
Florida Gulf Coast University, Ft. Myers
Florida International University, Miami
Florida State University, Tallahassee
New College of Florida, Sarasota
University of Central Florida, Orlando
University of Florida, Gainesville
University of North Florida, Jacksonville
University of South Florida, Tampa
University of West Florida, Pensacola

University Press of Florida
Gainesville · Tallahassee · Tampa · Boca Raton
Pensacola · Orlando · Miami · Jacksonville · Ft. Myers · Sarasota

After
Freedom Summer

How Race Realigned Mississippi Politics,
1965–1986

Chris Danielson

John David Smith, series editor

The publication of this book is made possible in part by a grant
from Montana Tech of the University of Montana.

16 15 14 13 12 11   6 5 4 3 2 1

LIBRARY OF CONGRESS CATALOGING-IN-PUBLICATION DATA
Danielson, Chris.
After Freedom Summer : how race realigned Mississippi politics, 1965–1986 /
Chris Danielson.
p. cm.
Includes bibliographical references and index.
ISBN 978-0-8130-3738-7 (acid-free paper)
1. African Americans—Mississippi—Politics and government—20th century.
2. African American politicians—Mississippi—History—20th century.
3. Political participation—Mississippi—History—20th century. 4. Mississippi
Freedom Project—Influence. 5. Mississippi—Politics and government—1951–
6. Mississippi—Race relations—History—20th century. 7. Mississippi—Race
relations—Political aspects—History—20th century. I. Title.
E185.93.M6D235 2011
305.8009762—dc23
2011018996

University Press of Florida
15 Northwest 15th Street
Gainesville, FL 32611-2079
http://www.upf.com

Dedicated to the two people who more than anyone else made this book possible—my seventh-grade history teacher, Jamie Cone, and my mother.

Contents

Figures

Acknowledgments

NUMEROUS PEOPLE HAD a hand in the shaping and direction of this manuscript, and I apologize in advance for any omissions. Thanks go to Charles Eagles, Charles Ross, Robert Haws, and John Winkle at the University of Mississippi. I would also like to thank the faculty of the Department of History and Art History, especially Barbara Brookes and Russell Johnson, for their suggestions. John Boles and Randall Hall, as well as the rest of the staff of the *Journal of Southern History* deserve thanks for their editorial comments on the article that I drew from this manuscript, which in turn influenced the entire work. The staffs at the J. D. Williams Library and the Law Library at the University of Mississippi, as well as at Special Collections at Clemson University and the Gerald R. Ford Presidential Library, were all a great help. A special thanks to Mattie Abraham and the staff at Special Collections at Mississippi State University. Working in the MSU archives with such a friendly and helpful staff is always a pleasure.

My employer, Montana Tech of the University of Montana, has generously supported this project, through the actions of Associate Vice Chancellor Joseph Figueira and Dean Douglas Coe. Thanks also go to all the interviewees who took time out of their schedules to talk to me.

The two people who are most responsible for this project, aside from myself, I have saved for last. One is Coach Jamie Cone, my seventh-grade Texas History teacher at Miller Intermediate in Pasadena, Texas, who sparked my love for history and set me on the long road to academia and scholarship. The other is my mother, Nancy, who supported and encouraged me even when I doubted myself and always felt I was following the right path for my career and life. Without her love and support none of this would have been possible.

After Freedom Summer

Introduction

ON MARCH 14, 1977, Fannie Lou Hamer died at a hospital in Mound Bayou, Mississippi. Hamer, who had been suffering from breast cancer and diabetes, had largely been out of high-profile civil rights activities since the early 1970s. This included an unsuccessful run for the state Senate in 1971, an extension of her activities with the Mississippi Freedom Democratic Party in the 1960s. Hamer's death drew major media coverage and attracted aging civil rights figures to her memorial service, including former congressman Andrew Young whom President Jimmy Carter had recently appointed to be the U.S. ambassador to the United Nations, and Aaron Henry, head of the state National Association for the Advancement of Colored People (NAACP).[1]

The gathering of African-American dignitaries, many now in positions of power, served as a reminder of the significant changes brought by the civil rights movement and the black enfranchisement created by the Voting Rights Act of 1965, now twice renewed by the time of Hamer's passing. Yet other less public changes were also evident in Mississippi, the state long regarded as the most recalcitrant on civil rights due to its history of violence and white political resistance going back to Reconstruction. Ten days before Hamer's death, Governor Cliff Finch, who had overseen the final integration of the state Democratic Party in 1976, signed into law a bill abolishing the State Sovereignty Commission. Some changes were symbolic ones, such as Gov. William Waller proclaiming (but not attending) Medgar Evers Day in 1973 on the anniversary of the civil rights leader's assassination. Hamer herself had been honored with a commemorative day in her hometown of Ruleville in 1976. Others were more tangible, namely the elections of Unita Black-well and Violet Leggette as the first two black women mayors in Mississippi, and the appointment of Robert Clark, one of only four black state legislators, to become the first black committee chairman in the twentieth century. Clark's leadership as head of the House Education Committee would play a major role in bringing about a significant reform of the state's public education system in 1982.[2]

These advances obviously did not come without struggle, but the fight for black political empowerment continued well after the post-1965 era. In 1977, most state legislators were elected from white-majority multimember districts created by a nearly all-white legislature, a system which largely prevented the election of black candidates. No black sheriffs had held office since Reconstruction, and black county supervisors were underrepresented. The state's largest city, Jackson, had an all-white city commission, and African Americans did not hold any major state offices, state Senate positions, or U.S. House seats. Black political underrepresentation was largely due to state and local gerrymandering and vote dilution, and black voters and civil rights attorneys still actively contested it in the 1970s.

Despite these barriers, many studies of the civil rights era give the impression that significant white resistance to black voting ended with the 1960s and neglect the period of the new black politics of the later civil rights years. Yet in the state of Mississippi, white hostility did not quickly dissipate. Mississippi, which fought desegregation more fiercely than other southern states in the "classical" phase of the civil rights era, continued this resistance into the post-1965 period.[3] The state's opposition to integration became more sophisticated and legalistic and was expressed through a variety of vote-dilution mechanisms. Civil rights activists and black voters in the post-1965 period utilized the federal government and courts to defeat these schemes and turn black suffrage into tangible and recognizable black political power in state and local governments.

This monograph examines the continuing centrality of race in Mississippi politics, specifically the development of black politics and the resulting white response in the years after the Voting Rights Act of 1965, or the latter phase of the "long civil rights movement."[4] While the violence of the 1960s had largely passed by the 1970s, the basic issues of political access were still being contested in Mississippi on the state and local levels. As the direct action of the civil rights movement shifted to black political access, the movement in many ways reverted back to its pre-*Brown* focus on legal activism, a tactic used widely by the NAACP, as Timothy Minchin as shown.[5] This institutionalizing of the movement was not only due to federal civil rights legislation but also in response to what Joseph Crespino called the "subtle and strategic accommodation" of white conservatives to the federal government's civil rights demands.[6] The state's opposition to integration became more sophisticated and was expressed through a variety of vote-dilution mechanisms, which slowed the development of black political power and led civil rights activists to continue appeals to the federal government, culminating in the renewal of the expanded Voting Rights Act of 1982.

These changes were part of the broader development of suburban political conservatism in the 1970s, as Matthew Lassiter and Kevin Kruse have shown.[7] Civil rights activists consolidated their gains and made new advancements through existing electoral channels, but so too did white politicians in Mississippi abandon their earlier massive resistance and fight in the courthouses and city halls against their old foes with more subtle means. State and local governments' efforts to dilute the black vote and keep black men and women out of elective office slowed the development of black politics in the post-1965 era. Despite electoral barriers, black candidates for office waged campaigns and developed black political power on the municipal, county, and state levels. This fight also involved long campaigns of litigation against vote dilution, and much of the later civil rights struggle mirrored the early, legalistic focus of the NAACP.

This post-1965 struggle is also part of the rise of a black political elite in Mississippi, itself part of what Manning Marable said occurred nationally as protest gave way to political access in the 1970s. Yet this access, he reminds his audience, was limited to the black elite and widened class divisions in black America. In Mississippi and elsewhere, a small number of black elected and appointed officials were brought into state and local governments, but little change came to the state's impoverished black working class. Marable viewed this as the "retreat" of the second Reconstruction, succinctly declaring that "nothing fails like success."[8]

While it may be tempting in the age of Obama to dismiss Marable's analysis as unwarranted pessimism, his views were echoed by other scholars of black political power. Steven Lawson, in his study of the effects of the Voting Rights Act, highlighted the limited ability of black officeholders to remedy class and racial discrimination. Rather than focus on black class divisions like Marable, Lawson instead cited gerrymandering and other forms of vote dilution as impediments to full equality. Kenneth Andrews, in his sociological study of the Mississippi civil rights movement and its legacy, also focuses on the white response to black mobilization as a check on black progress, concluding that such a response as well as limited resources meant that "movements rarely, if ever, get everything they want." When in 2010 the Mississippi Delta suffers from an infant mortality rate ten times that of Iran, one is easily reminded of the limits of the franchise.[9]

This is not a story of unified white resistance anymore than it is one of unqualified black progress. The Democratic and Republican parties responded to the new black politics with strategies that alternated between soliciting black and conservative white voters. The enfranchisement of black voters altered Mississippi's gubernatorial campaigns and eventually helped realign the state towards the Republican Party as white voters changed their allegiances. Meanwhile, the Democratic Party establishment continued to utilize methods of vote dilution such as legislative malapportionment, county and congressional redistricting, and at-large municipal elections. These vote dilution schemes were repeated throughout the South, with Mississippi often continuing its resistance after other states had abandoned theirs. This phase of resistance in Mississippi ended up being merely a delaying action by state officials, since all of the voting schemes were eventually overturned with successful lawsuits by local Mississippians. The extended and strengthened Voting Rights Act of 1982, in particular, eventually swept away the last of these barriers. Federal pressure, as it had in the 1960s, finally forced changes.

While economic issues such as social class and suburbanization and cultural issues such as gun control contributed to the political realignment of white Mississippians towards the Republican Party, race still remained the primary reason for the electoral shift. Dan Carter and others have persuasively shown the central role that race played in the political realignment of the South in the wake of the civil rights movement. Recent scholars such as Matthew Lassiter, Byron Schafer and Richard Johnston have emphasized class and suburban development in the political realignment of the South and argue that race has been exaggerated by earlier scholars. To them, partisan realignment is rooted in whites' economic, not racial identification. Kevin Kruse, in his study of Atlanta, gives more attention than the previous scholars to the role of race in political realignment, and like Joseph Crespino he illuminates the shifting tactics and strategies of white resistance. Jere Nash and Andy Taggart's work has also argued against the new focus on economic considerations and instead identified race as a factor, albeit one subsumed into other cultural issues. Jason Sokol avoids classifications and instead emphasizes continuity and change in the varieties of accommodations southern whites made to the empowerment of African Americans. He eschews a race-based approach in partisan realignment, however, when discussing shifts of the southern middle class to the GOP.[10]

This new scholarship focusing on class and other non-racial issues is generally not applicable to Mississippi. Race was the major factor behind the New Right shift of Mississippi's white electorate to the GOP, and realignment occurred because of growing white dissatisfaction with black political empowerment and continued activism. What Lassiter, Kruse, and others miss by their focus on suburban areas such as Charlotte and Atlanta is that Mississippi was (and still largely is) a heavily rural Sunbelt state. Attempts to generalize the entire South based upon the studies of suburbs do not provide a complete picture of the region when most suburbanization in 1970s Mississippi was limited to Jackson. The addition of Mississippi also complicates the suburban homogeneity of the Sunbelt model. C. Vann Woodward aptly critiqued the entire use of the term "Sunbelt" and linking the history of the South and the Southwest.[11] While many new Republican votes in the 1970s did come from suburbanizing areas like Jackson, the GOP's right wing clearly focused its attention on pursuing rural and small-town George Wallace Democrats and in doing so saw segregationist whites as a natural constituency. The economic conservatism of the Mississippi GOP, while attractive to middle- and upper-income suburbanites, would not attract populist-leaning rural whites to the degree racial appeals would. It is well-known to both scholars of the civil rights movement and laymen that Mississippi, in the words of Neil McMillen, was the most "race-haunted" of the southern states.[12] The haunting extended to political realignment and partisan identification as well, and not even the civil rights movement and the political changes wrought by the Voting Rights Act could exorcise that ghost from the state's political life.

For examples of the central role of race in Mississippi party politics, one need only look at some of the major state political events of the

1970s. The slow acceptance of black Mississippians into the political life of the state opened new opportunities and access to power for black Mississippians, but the biracial coalition the Democratic Party forged in the 1970s also forced black candidates to accept limits to keep white segregationists from defecting to the state Republicans. Only continued legal activism and the threat of black spoilers, the latter made real by Charles Evers's 1978 Senate bid, kept the Democrats from completely appeasing the white elements of the party and reverting to the past. The presence of black voters also had a national effect as well. The divisions within the state Republican Party over pursuing black voters influenced national politics, specifically the ideological splits in the national GOP between moderates like Gerald Ford and conservatives like Ronald Reagan.

Some of the stories herein have been covered in varying degrees by other scholars, but this is the first work to include them all in one volume and add additional research as well. This book provides wide-ranging coverage of race and the role it played in state politics and the political realignment of Mississippi. It extends chronologically into the 1980s, and unlike more quantitative, sociological approaches like Kenneth Andrews's study, this study takes a qualitative approach.[13] Also, issues like the various schemes of vote dilution used by the state have not been extensively covered in many earlier works. The fullest treatment is Frank Parker's *Black Votes Count*, which devoted two chapters to vote dilution cases.[14] Some black voter struggles, such as the efforts to elect a black congressman or the dismantling of discriminatory county redistricting, have only been covered briefly or not at all. There have been some detailed local studies of the post–civil rights era and black political participation, namely Emilye Crosby on Claiborne County and J. Todd Moye on Sunflower County, but not of broader state coverage.[15] While not attempting to be a "total history" of the development of African-American politics in Mississippi, major events such as the election of Mike Espy in 1986 as well as local political developments such as the early administration of Charles Evers in Fayette are covered and woven into the broader narrative of Mississippi's political and racial changes.

1 Black Politics in Mississippi to 1965

BLACK POLITICIANS in Mississippi reached their highest level of power shortly after the Reconstruction Acts enfranchised the freedmen. The political gains of African Americans during Reconstruction, known as the "heroic age" of black Mississippians, did not outlast the 1870s.[1] White violence and intimidation during and after the return of white Democratic rule in 1875 forced a sharp decline in black political offices and voting, and most black men lost the vote completely with the ratification of the Constitution of 1890. While the white electorate widened with the enfranchisement of women under the 19th Amendment in 1920, black women—as well as men—gained nothing. Black Mississippians would not return to the active political life of the state until after World War II, when black veterans and emboldened civil rights organizations slowly expanded black voting. Despite the best efforts of civil rights groups in the 1950s and early 1960s, violent white resistance and economic coercion stymied massive black voter registration and led advocates of black suffrage in Mississippi to push for strong backing from the federal government. The Kennedy administration, responding to pressures from civil rights activists in the South, began the first steps to bring back the franchise to African Americans in the Magnolia State.

Black voting and political participation in Mississippi began with congressional passage of the Reconstruction Act of 1867. The Act enfranchised the freedmen and facilitated the development of black political power in the defeated Confederacy. Majority-black Mississippi and South Carolina became the two states with the highest number of black officeholders during Reconstruction. By the end of the Reconstruction period, five black men in Mississippi had held the office of secretary of state, and one each had served terms as lieutenant governor and state superintendent of education. Black legislators went to Jackson, but they did not secure a majority in the legislature as they had in the Palmetto State. On the county level, voters elected fifteen black sheriffs and took control of the boards of supervisors in the state's black belt. Many black men also served in law enforcement and county offices, although disproportionately in lesser positions. Three black men also served in the U.S. Senate and one, John Lynch, held a seat in the House of Representatives. Hiram Revels and Blanche K. Bruce served in the Senate and were the only black men in the Senate until the election of Edward Brooke of Massachusetts in 1966. Although whites continued to control most statewide offices and black politicians never achieved a majority in the state government or Republican Party, the presence of black politicians represented a major advance in a short period of time, and showed what black agency combined with federal civil rights enforcement could do.[2]

The expansion of black political power triggered a violent backlash from white Mississippians. Beginning in 1874, armed whites organized to threaten and kill black voters and officeholders. During the statewide elections in 1875, white violence and electoral fraud against black and white Republicans secured Democratic control of the legislature, which then forced the resignation of Republican Governor Adelbert Ames. Many elected black officials resigned to avoid murder at the hands of vigilantes.[3]

The First Mississippi Plan in 1875, as the Democratic "redemption" came to be known, did not entirely eliminate blacks from the state's political life, but black voting sharply declined, and, as Neil McMillen has noted, intimidation and violence meant most black men had stopped voting by the time of the constitutional convention of 1890. Despite the decline in black political participation, white politicians in Mississippi still feared potential black dominance, and many black men still remained registered, if not actually voting. White Democrats felt especially threatened by the Republican-controlled Congress and the administration of President Benjamin Harrison. The so-called Force Bill, which would have allowed federal intervention on behalf of disfranchised black voters, had just failed in Congress by one vote. In response, white delegates gathered in the summer of 1890 to create a new state constitution. The delegates moved to eliminate forever their anxieties about black electoral power by permanently disfranchising nearly all black Mississippians. The provisions of the new constitution, such as the poll tax, the "understanding clause," and the list of disqualifying crimes, codified an already existing state of disfranchisement and purged blacks from the voter registration rolls. Black men who insisted on pressing for the ballot risked death at the hands of white lynch mobs. While black Mississippians played a major role in the state Republican Party and even elected a few of their own to the state legislature as late as 1898, the 1890 convention officially curtailed most black political activity.[4] Succeeding presidential administrations often acquiesced to local white pressure and phased out many of the remaining federal positions held by black Mississippians, further weakening the black-controlled state GOP. Mound Bayou, which had no white residents, contained the only elected black officials in the state. Isaiah Montgomery founded the town as an experiment in black self-sufficiency, so its all-black municipal government represented an anomaly rather than the norm in Mississippi politics.[5]

White supremacy remained unchallenged well into the twentieth century. The administrations of governors like James Vardaman and Theodore Bilbo combined populist agendas with racial demagoguery even after black residents had long lost access to the ballot.[6] Despite the rigidity of Jim Crow, hints of change began to appear in the Magnolia State by the 1930s. New Deal programs helped to lay the grounds for future black political activism. One example occurred in Holmes County, where a Farm Security Administration (FSA) program gave low-interest loans to sharecroppers to buy land the government acquired from bankrupt plantation owners. As a result the program created a small, independent base of black landowners relatively free from the economic pressures of whites. The black farmers who bought land under the FSA program would form the core of the civil rights movement in the county in the 1960s.[7]

The economic and social upheavals of World War II finally produced conditions conducive for black activism. The wartime experiences of the 85,000 black Mississippians who served in the armed forces made some of them less willing to accept segregation. Some returning black veterans joined the Mississippi Progressive Voters' League, a voter registration organization that had 5,000 members by 1947. Fear and intimidation, along with the League's focus on registering the small black middle class, kept the number of black voters at no more than 7,000 by the 1948 presidential election. Within a few years the National Association for the Advancement of Colored People (NAACP), which had had a precarious existence in state since its appearance in 1918, took the lead in the limited civil rights activity of the period.[8]

Although black voter registration had increased to 22,000 by 1954, the white response to the U.S. Supreme Court's invalidation of school segregation in *Brown v. Board of Education* led to a sharp reversal. The Citizens' Councils, an organization of largely middle-class white segregationists that sprang up in the wake of *Brown* to oppose the ruling, used economic coercion and intimidation against blacks who registered to vote. Whites also tightened the voting laws by passing an amendment that stated that applicants had to write a "reasonable" interpretation of the state constitution for a registrar. The actions of the Councils and the new voting laws reversed earlier progress in black voter registration. By the end of 1955, only 12,000 blacks appeared on the state's voting rolls, a small increase from the 1940s. During the rest of the 1950s, civil rights campaigns unfolded in states such as Alabama, but hardening white resistance stymied its development in Mississippi.[9]

For much of the pre-1965 era, the Republican Party commanded the allegiance of black Mississippians through a politics of clientage, but this had changed by the middle of the century. The Mississippi Republican Party, barely existent and shut out of elected offices, did not provide any examples of leadership for civil rights activists during the 1950s. While a privileged group of upper-income African Americans known as the Black and Tans had controlled the party since the nineteenth century, many black Mississippians had deserted over the leadership's failure to oppose white supremacy. Most of the Black and Tans had little to do with the mass of black Mississippians and jockeyed for federal patronage and political favors from national Republicans. Perry Howard, a black lawyer and the national committeeman of the party from 1924 to 1960, did not even live or vote in Mississippi after 1920. This limited patronage was one of the few examples of black political involvement in pre-1965 Mississippi, but it involved very few black Mississippians. The party stayed under black control until 1956, when the Black and Tans had to share their convention seats with an all-white delegation known as the Lily Whites. In 1960, the Lily Whites won official recognition and made the state Republican Party an all-white party.[10]

With both the state Democratic and Republican parties either hostile or indifferent to African Americans, people like Medgar Evers of the state NAACP took the lead in promoting civil rights activity in 1950s Mississippi. Evers, a native of Decatur, Mississippi, joined the service during World War II and exemplified the black soldier who returned to the South determined to improve conditions. He and his brother Charles, also a veteran, began registering black veterans in Decatur, but white intimidation and hostility prevented the Evers brothers from actually voting. Medgar then attended Alcorn A&M College on the GI Bill, where he met and married Myrlie Beasley. While employed as an insurance salesman in Mound Bayou he began working for the NAACP and the Regional Council for Negro Leadership, an organization founded by T.R.M. Howard, a prosperous Mound Bayou physician and insurance salesman. In December 1954, the NAACP made him the state's first field secretary, and whites regularly made death threats against him.[11]

Evers helped create through affiliation with the national NAACP a new type of pre-1965 black politics, one built around civil rights activism and support from the national Democratic Party, which would transition into the post-1965 era. Still, Evers spent most of his time and resources in the 1950s investigating the murders of black Mississippians and reorganizing NAACP branches rather than registering black voters. He and Vera Pigee of Clarksdale did successfully organize youth chapters of the NAACP to prepare young black Mississippians to exercise the franchise. The chapters also helped politicize black youth, especially college students, who later conducted sit-ins of segregated public facilities such as libraries. The sit-ins and other direct action campaigns across the South in 1960 and 1961, especially the Freedom Rides, prompted the Kennedy administration to champion black suffrage as an alternative to direct action militancy and also to reward black voters for supporting Kennedy in the 1960 election.[12]

The Kennedy administration supported voter registration campaigns in the South through the Voter Education Project (VEP), a nonpartisan group formed in 1962 and devoted to black voter registration and the investigation of barriers to such activity. The White House hoped that supporting suffrage would defuse enthusiasm for sit-ins and other forms of direct action. The civil rights forces in Mississippi formed an umbrella group known as the Council of Federated Organizations (COFO), headed by Mississippi NAACP President Aaron Henry. Like Medgar Evers, Henry was a World War II veteran determined to bring racial change to Mississippi. A pharmacist involved with the Clarksdale NAACP, Henry first registered to vote after the war and became the first black person to vote in Coahoma County's Democratic primary. He incurred white hostility when he organized a push to desegregate Clarksdale's schools after the *Brown* decision. He became president of the state organization in 1960.[13]

Henry worked on voter registration with Robert Moses, an organizer in the Student Nonviolent Coordinating Committee (SNCC). Moses, a New York mathematics teacher, held a degree from Hamilton College and a master's in philosophy from Harvard. He soon developed contacts with prominent civil rights leaders like Bayard Rustin. With the backing of SNCC organizer Ella Baker, he went to Mississippi to help with the VEP.[14]

Henry and Moses used COFO to disburse VEP funds for voter registration. COFO activities in the early 1960s included voter registration drives in southwest Mississippi and Jackson, where the canvassers suffered arrests and violent reprisals. White violence and intimidation stymied the efforts, and the VEP registered fewer than 4,000 new voters in two years.[15]

Despite legal barriers and extralegal violence, the voter registration drives helped to raise black Mississippians' awareness of their right to vote. In rural areas not touched by the voter registration drives of the 1940s and 1950s, many black residents did not even know they could vote. Fannie Lou Hamer, a sharecropper from Ruleville who would later become the most prominent black woman in the Mississippi civil rights movement, said she was not even aware of the right to vote until SNCC volunteers arrived at the Sunflower County town in 1962. SNCC workers informed illiterate sharecroppers of their voting rights, although fear and coercion prevented many from exercising it.[16] Civil rights leaders soon made efforts to heighten the political consciousness of black Mississippians through a series of challenges to the all-white world of electoral politics.

Robert L. T. Smith, Sr. and Merrill Winston Lindsey launched one of the first efforts to educate black Mississippians about their political rights. In 1962, the two black NAACP members qualified for the congressional House races in the Democratic primary after the chairman of the state Democratic Executive Committee allowed their names to go on the ballot to avoid a lawsuit. Smith's and Lindsay's candidacies made them the first African Americans in Mississippi to run as Democrats for Congress. Smith, a Jackson grocer, ran in the fourth district, while Lindsey, a resident of Holly Springs, ran in the newly formed second

FIGURE 1. Rev. Robert L. T. Smith, Sept. 9, 1987. In 1962 Smith was one of the first African Americans to run for Congress as a Democrat in Mississippi. Unable to win since he ran before passage of the Voting Rights Act, his candidacy was emblematic of the symbolic "consciousness raising" campaigns such as the Freedom Vote, which predated black officeholding in the state. Willie J. Miller Papers, 501–589, Special Collections Department, Mitchell Memorial Library, Mississippi State University.

district. Both men were ministers and members of Mississippi's black middle class and less susceptible to economic pressure from whites. Robert Smith and his son had been active in sit-ins in Jackson, and the elder Smith had unsuccessfully sued the State Sovereignty Commission in 1959 over its funding of the Citizens' Councils.[17]

Smith broke an important color barrier in Mississippi by becoming the first black political candidate to buy airtime on a Mississippi television station and thus penetrate the state's news blackout on civil rights coverage. Smith ran as a Democrat pledged to the national party's support of civil rights and supported a wide array of federal programs that would help impoverished residents of the district. On the air, he denounced the "red flag of hatred and bigotry" used by "cunning men and predatory organizations who peddle hate with the use of our tax money." Myrlie Evers said Smith's televised appearance was "like the lifting of a giant curtain." The station received death and bomb threats from some white viewers and refused to sell Smith anymore airtime.[18]

The white congressional candidates and the state newspapers, with the exception of the black newspaper *The Jackson Advocate*, ignored the black men's campaigns. Lindsay and Aaron Henry, who served as his manager, ran a well-organized campaign with local offices in a number of counties in the second district. Like Smith, Lindsay pledged "unqualified support" for the Kennedy administration. The challengers had little chance of success and ran mainly to spur further registration and civil rights activity. The following year, Clinton C. Collins Sr. of Laurel continued Smith and Lindsay's efforts and conducted the only real election contest in 1963 by a black candidate. Collins, whom the State Sovereignty Commission had previously cleared for suspected civil rights activity, qualified as a Democratic candidate for justice of the peace in Jones County in the 1963 primary. His candidacy, like that of Smith and Lindsay the previous year, had no serious chance of success.[19]

COFO forces also organized a mock election in 1963. During the statewide general elections in 1963, Aaron Henry and Ed King, a white minister, ran for governor and lieutenant governor on a "Freedom Ballot Campaign." King, originally of Vicksburg, had returned to Mississippi in 1963 at the urging of Medgar Evers and accepted the chaplaincy of Tougaloo College, a black Methodist university in Jackson.[20]

The organizers of the mock election, known as the Freedom Vote, aimed to spread awareness about voter registration among black Mississippians. The campaign took place in the aftermath of Medgar Evers's assassination; Evers had been shot and killed outside his home in Jackson by a sniper on June 11, 1963, the night of President Kennedy's televised address endorsing federal civil rights legislation.[21]

The organizers and participants in the Freedom Vote boycotted the 1963 governor's race, which provided no real alternatives to Jim Crow for the few black Mississippians who met the strict requirements to vote. That November the Republican Party ran Rubel Phillips against the Democratic nominee, Lieutenant Governor Paul Johnson. Phillips tried to link Johnson to President Kennedy's proposed civil rights legislation but lost to the equally segregationist Johnson in a landslide. Most blacks who paid attention to the election instead took part in the Freedom Vote. Despite harassment, the mock election drew 83,000 votes, about four times the number of blacks registered in the state. COFO used the organizing efforts from the vote to expand its operations, and about 500 black Mississippians tried to vote in the real election as well by submitting affidavits as protest ballots against voter discrimination.[22]

In the summer of 1964, workers from SNCC and CORE organized Freedom Summer, a voter registration drive that utilized hundreds of white northern college students to register Mississippi blacks. The project garnered major national attention, especially after three civil rights workers (two of them white) disappeared near Philadelphia. While the murders of James Chaney, Mickey Schwerner, and Andrew Goodman remain the most famous event of Freedom Summer, volunteers performed many critical activities on the grassroots level. These events included the Freedom Schools set up by volunteers to educate black children. The schools, which served a vital if underappreciated role in the movement, encouraged black students to petition the federal government for civil rights enforcement and spurred political interest among older residents.[23]

In addition to voter registration and education, COFO workers established the Mississippi Freedom Democratic Party (MFDP), an integrated but mostly black organization that received little aid from the national Democratic Party. Barred from participating in the Regular (the segregationist white) Democrats' conventions and meetings, the civil rights workers set up their own separate system of meetings to elect delegates to challenge the seating of the all-white state delegation to the national Democratic Party convention in Atlantic City. Despite the MFDP's efforts, the challenge failed to unseat the regular delegation, and most of the non-MFDP civil rights activists accepted a compromise brokered by prominent white liberals in the national Democratic Party. The Atlantic City affair also created tensions between the MFDP and the NAACP because the NAACP and Aaron Henry backed the compromise, which some MFDP members saw as a betrayal.[24]

In the wake of the MFDP's defeat in Atlantic City, COFO activists mobilized for the fall elections. Instead of targeting the congressional races, COFO favored a lower-level approach and ran candidates in the 1964 elections of the Agricultural and Stabilization and Conservation

Service (ASCS) committees. The all-white county ASCS committees used acreage allotments and control of commodity production for price stabilization to discriminate against black farmers. COFO ran black farmers and sharecroppers as candidates in some heavily black counties but failed to win any positions on the committees. The intimidation did not prevent the MFDP from running ASCS candidates in the next election.[25]

The defeats for the civil rights workers continued in 1965. In January, the MFDP tried to unseat the state's congressional delegation on the grounds of voter exclusion, but the U.S. House of Representatives rejected the appeal. In the municipal elections in May 1965, two black candidates, Pinkie Pilcher and the Rev. Tobe Boykin, ran for office in Greenwood and Jonestown, respectively. Pilcher, a sixty-six-year-old widow and kindergarten teacher, qualified for the primary for the city commission. An active MFDP member, she had tried unsuccessfully to win a seat as a precinct delegate in Leflore County the previous year. Boykin and Pilcher still had to contend with a very low rate of black voter registration and lost their races. Poll workers turned Pilcher herself away from the polls because she did not have her poll tax receipts.[26]

By the summer of 1965, the civil rights forces had made some gains in Mississippi. A network of community organizers and activists, absent just a few years before, existed in many areas of the state. An interracial political party had organized with the hopes of re-creating a biracial democracy. Voter registration had increased, and the federal government under President Lyndon Johnson expressed a willingness to enforce civil rights laws and pass new legislation. In addition, the organizing and educational efforts, including symbolic efforts like the 1962 elections, had helped raise political awareness among some black Mississippians. In Holmes County, for example, the citizenship classes that SNCC conducted inspired a group of independent black farmers to travel to the county courthouse in Lexington and attempt to register to vote. In the words of Steven Lawson, the civil rights activists had "failed to destroy the tyranny of the registrars, [but] they did loosen the mental knot keeping blacks away from citizenship."[27]

The events of the 1950s and early 1960s can be viewed another way. With the failure of the challenges, the MFDP had no visible successes. Outside of the all-black town of Mound Bayou, no black person had yet been successfully elected to a public office in the state. The voter registration numbers told most of the story. While the VEP and COFO workers had increased black voter registration to pre-*Brown* levels by

1964, the total number of 28,500 voters represented only 6.7 percent of the state's black population. Mississippi's registration lagged behind all other southern states, even lower than the twenty percent black voter registration in neighboring Alabama.[28] White violence and resistance, along with the persistence of the "mental knot," continued to hamstring effective black political power.

The civil rights alliance also began to unravel. COFO dissolved early in 1965, largely over NAACP fears of competition with SNCC and the MFDP. The older, more conservative NAACP did not mesh well with the more militant MFDP, which sought an independent, black-controlled political organization. The rise of black power rhetoric in the MFDP alienated moderates like Aaron Henry, who saw such behavior as reverse racism. By 1965, Henry and Claude Ramsey, the white director of the state AFL-CIO, had created the Mississippi Democratic Conference (MDC) as an alternative to both the MFDP and the regular Democratic Party. The Regulars still refused to share any political power with black Mississippians, regardless of party affiliation.[29]

By the end of 1964, black politics in Mississippi had evolved from the narrow and limited patronage politics of the Black and Tan Republican era to a civil rights politics built around activism and linked to civil rights and labor organizations affiliated with the national Democratic Party. This development foreshadowed later federal intervention under the Voting Rights Act as well as black Mississippians' allegiance to the Democratic Party. To the local voter registration workers, such intervention was necessary because in the face of white resistance and the fragmenting civil rights efforts, they needed a more activist and direct intervention by the federal government to overcome Mississippi's white supremacy.

2 Plates of Silver, Plates of Mud

1965–1970

ON AUGUST 6, 1965, President Lyndon Johnson signed the Voting Rights Act into law. The act had passed over the opposition of numerous southern congressmen, including the entire delegation from Mississippi. During the first five years of its enforcement, the act helped black politics in Mississippi shift from symbolic actions to serious attempts to gain public office. While black Mississippians continued to wage high-profile political campaigns for offices they could not hope to win, most civil rights organizations in the state focused on registering voters and running black candidates in local races in heavily black areas of the state. During the major election campaigns of 1967 and 1969, black voters elected the first significant number of black public officials in the state since the nineteenth century. Civil rights organizations such as the NAACP and MFDP pursued strategies to turn civil rights organizing into tangible political gains. The NAACP focused on nominating and electing candidates in the Democratic primaries, while the MFDP rejected an association with segregationist Democrats and opted to support independent candidacies. The respective strategies produced the two most prominent black politicians of 1960s Mississippi. Robert Clark became the first black state legislator in the twentieth century when he won a seat from the MFDP enclave of Holmes County. Charles Evers, NAACP field secretary and successor to his slain brother, also assumed office as the mayor and head of an all-black town government in the biracial town of Fayette.

The MFDP favored a grassroots, bottom-up approach that aimed to empower black communities and create local leaders, a strategy born from their origins in SNCC organizing and voter registration campaigns. Yet the NAACP's top-down, bureaucratic "boss" approach, promoted by Charles Evers, Aaron Henry, and white moderates won out in the struggle for black political power in the 1960s. Ultimately, the NAACP strategy, with the backing of national Democrats, led to more black victories than the MFDP approach, and with the creation of the Loyalist Democrats, a more moderate alternative consisting of NAACP-backed civil rights leaders and white moderates, the MFDP faded from view. A host of other blacks, most elected as NAACP-backed Democrats, represented the first real political access for black Mississippians. Although most black candidates for office lost, enough won to establish the largest body of elected black officials since the nineteenth century. Some, like Osborne Bell in Marshall County and Howard Huggins in Holmes County, would later become the first black sheriffs in the twentieth century. Despite the stronger NAACP position, Mississippi black politics in the latter half of the 1960s lacked clear boundaries between the various civil rights organizations. The political organizing of NAACP-affiliated integrationists overlapped with MFDP-supported black independents and black power militants during the rebirth of black political activity in the Magnolia State.

The Voting Rights Act, which covered all or part of seven southern states, allowed for the creation of this first generation of black politicians in the late 1960s. It provided federal registrars and poll watchers and suspended the use of literacy tests for voting in the affected jurisdictions. During its first five years, it significantly increased black voter registration in the affected states. Mississippi's black voter registration rose from 6.7 percent of the black population to 59.8 percent by September 1967. However, the act did not fund voter education, so civil rights organizers bore the burden of educating prospective voters in the use of the ballot. The Justice Department did not dispatch federal examiners to all the counties, instead preferring voluntary compliance from state and local authorities. As late as March 1966, thirty counties, where less than twenty-five percent of the adult black population had been registered, still had not seen a single federal registrar. Sen. James Eastland's influence as chairman of the Senate Judiciary Committee prevented the arrival of a registrar in his native Sunflower County until nearly a year after the act went into effect.[1]

The reluctance of the Justice Department to deploy federal registrars on a wide scale limited but did not prevent an increase in new voters.

FIGURE 2. Charles Evers, field director of the Mississippi NAACP in the 1960s. The controversial brother of slain civil rights leader Medgar Evers, Charles Evers continued voter registration work in Mississippi after his brother's assassination in 1963. By 1968 he won election as mayor of the town of Fayette, but he alienated some civil rights activists with his authoritarian tactics and political dealmaking with white segregationists. William F. "Bill" Minor Papers, 80–166, Special Collections Department, Mitchell Memorial Library, Mississippi State University.

After three months, the number of black voters in the state had doubled to 57,000, with most of the growth in counties with federal registrars. Both the MFDP and the NAACP prepared for the 1966 and 1967 elections by registering new black voters, but the two organizations operated separately from each other after the dissolution of the COFO coalition in 1965. Henry and Ramsey, with newspaper editor and white moderate Hodding Carter, moved their political organizing beyond the Mississippi Democratic Conference, an organization of NAACP-backed civil rights activists and white moderates they established in 1965. The moderates took control of the state's Young Democratic clubs and established an NAACP-labor coalition that recognized the authority of the national Democratic Party over the segregationist regular Democrats. The interracial coalitionists, not the mostly black Freedom Democrats, won the recognition of the national Young Democrats.[2]

With the MFDP and the moderates openly split from each other by the end of 1965, the two sides followed their separate paths to elect officials in the 1966 and 1967 elections. The NAACP and the Freedom Democrats both focused on black-majority counties and registered voters and ran candidates for office, but the two groups' political strategies differed. The MFDP, as a separate political party, favored independent candidacies. The moderates, by contrast, ran candidates as members of the Democratic Party and in the party's primaries and worked with friendly whites. Whites such as Ed King continued to stay with the MFDP, but the few whites in Mississippi who favored civil rights generally preferred the more moderate NAACP. The NAACP under Charles Evers, its new field secretary, spent 1965 and 1966 organizing and registering voters in the southwestern river counties of Adams, Claiborne, Jefferson, and Wilkinson, while the Freedom Democrats concentrated on the Delta.

Like his brother Medgar, Charles Evers served in World War II and graduated from Alcorn College. Unlike his late brother, Charles Evers favored more worldly pursuits. He admitted that "Medgar chased civil rights . . . I chased girls, civil rights, and the dollar." He moved to Philadelphia in Neshoba County in 1951, but hostility from local whites over voter registration forced him to leave the state. He relocated to Chicago, and, unlike his brother, he ceased his civil rights activism and worked in assorted legal and illegal professions, including prostitution and numbers running, activities that would later become a political liability and shape his autocratic political style. The outspoken and bombastic

Charles could not have been more different from his quiet and soft-spoken brother, but they both brought considerable passion and energy to the civil rights movement in Mississippi. After he returned to the state for Medgar's funeral, he informed NAACP Executive Secretary Roy Wilkins that he intended to assume his brother's position as field secretary of Mississippi. Wilkins reluctantly agreed, and Evers quickly organized voter registration campaigns and new county branches of the NAACP in the southwestern counties. During the summer of 1966, Wilkins expanded Evers's authority by appointing him head of the NAACP's voter registration efforts in Mississippi.[3]

While Evers and other civil rights workers registered black voters for the upcoming elections, the state legislature passed a number of laws that diluted the growing black vote and hindered both the MDC-NAACP forces and the MFDP. The requirements allowed counties to switch to at-large voting, increased the qualifying requirements for independent candidates, and redrew state legislative districts to stack majority-black counties with majority-white counties. The legislators allowed some positions, such as school superintendents, to be appointed instead of elected positions.[4]

In the first elections since the enactment of the Voting Rights Act, the voters chose the state's congressional delegation for the 1966 midterm. The MFDP ran candidates in each of the five redrawn districts, including Ed King, the white chaplain of Tougaloo College and candidate for lieutenant governor in the 1963 Freedom Vote, who challenged John Bell Williams in the third district. Other candidates included Ralthus Hayes, a black Tchula farmer who had first tried to register to vote in 1963 after taking a SNCC voter education class, and the Rev. Clifton Whitley of Rust College in Holly Springs, who ran against Senator James Eastland.[5]

The MFDP candidates easily lost in the June primary. In the Senate race, Whitley drew about 34,000 votes to Eastland's 240,000. In the House races, only Ed King drew more than 10,000 votes. King, as the only white candidate in the election, possibly drew more black votes since he could not be as easily associated with black power militancy. King also benefited from Charles Evers's voter registration drives, and his overall vote total was twenty-one percent, several percentage points better than his black counterparts. King claimed he won five percent of the white vote and did not campaign in white neighborhoods during the election.[6]

The MFDP followed up the primary by running Whitley and two others as independents on the November ticket. White Democrats tried to keep the three candidates off the November ballot by citing new stringent requirements passed by the state legislature for independent candidates, but the black candidates successfully sued in federal court. Despite the court ruling, a black victory was still impossible since the districts were majority-white. At an October gathering in Jackson, MFDP organizers conceded defeat in the upcoming congressional election and instead focused their efforts on political education for the 1967, not 1966 elections.[7]

Some civil rights leaders refused to back the MFDP as well. Charles Evers gave his endorsement to Prentiss Walker, the Republican congressman challenging Sen. Eastland. Evers decided that Walker, a white Republican, stood a better chance of winning than a black independent who could not garner any significant white votes. Evers's animosity towards the MFDP played a role as well, with Evers trying to be the political boss and deliver the black vote. The endorsement split black support between Whitley and Walker and helped neither of them on Election Day.[8]

Prentiss Walker, despite the endorsement from Evers, represented the Lily White state Republican viewpoint and had no interest in the black vote. Walker, a chicken farmer and chair of the all-white GOP delegation to the 1960 presidential convention, had won a congressional seat during Sen. Barry Goldwater's sweep of Mississippi in the 1964 presidential election. Walker represented the white-majority, hill-country fourth district and did little to challenge segregation. Not only did he join his Democratic colleagues in opposing the Voting Rights Act, he contributed to a racial controversy in 1965 that drew national attention. When House Minority Leader Gerald Ford came to the state for a speech at the University of Mississippi, he accepted Walker's invitation to speak at a Republican luncheon in Natchez. Ford cancelled the Natchez appearance when Charles Evers threatened a mass march unless state GOP officials sold tickets to black Republicans, which drew an angry rebuke from Wirt Yerger, the chair of the state GOP.[9]

During the 1966 campaign, Walker tried to "outsegregate," in the words of state AFL-CIO chief Claude Ramsey, Sen. James Eastland. With black voter registration only just beginning on a wide scale, the black vote was not yet influential in statewide elections. As a Goldwater conservative and ardent states' rights supporter, Walker repeated what Rubel Phillips did in 1963 and appealed to white segregationists, but most white voters stayed with the even more reactionary Eastland. Only four counties went for Walker, including the black-majority counties of Claiborne and Jefferson, and Walker trailed in Wilkinson County by only fifty-nine votes. The boost for Walker in the southwest resulted from Charles Evers's endorsement, since black independent candidate Clifton Whitley drew more votes than Walker in black-majority counties like Holmes and Bolivar.[10]

Walker's archconservative views and indifference to black Mississippians represented the direction the Mississippi Republican Party had been heading since the end of Black and Tan rule. While the Republicans did not indulge in the crude racial demagoguery of Democrats such as Ross Barnett, they represented a growing demographic of suburban, white, conservative professionals across the South who had little interest in soliciting black votes. Like the rest of the emerging Sunbelt, Mississippi's suburban areas became the base of Magnolia State Republicanism. Wirt Yerger, an insurance salesman who served as the Mississippi party chairman until 1966, exemplified the new breed of southern Republicans. Yerger founded the Mississippi Young Republicans in 1956 when he won the chairmanship of the state party and played a key role in the overthrow of the Black and Tans. Segregationists harassed Yerger when President Eisenhower sent troops to Little Rock in 1957, but the experience did not give him much sympathy for civil rights. In 1961, after President Kennedy sent federal marshals to protect the Freedom Riders in Alabama, Yerger criticized Kennedy for violating states' rights. In the 1960s, he told the national Republican chairman the oft-repeated statement that he did not favor "writing off completely any vote [the black vote specifically], but I do think it is best to go hunting where the ducks are."[11]

In the era of low black voter registration, the GOP reasoned that the best "ducks" were white segregationists. The failed GOP candidacies in the 1960s showed the difficulty the white conservatives of the party had trying to convince white Democrats to leave the party of states' rights and segregation. A two-party system threatened to weaken white supremacy by dividing the white electorate. While white Mississippians voted overwhelmingly for Goldwater and his anti-civil rights platform in 1964, they did not reciprocate with state Republicans since their Democratic opponents had even more fervent commitments to Jim Crow.

The "Great White Switch" had occurred, as Earl and Merle Black labeled the shift of southern white voters to voting Republican in presidential elections, but party identification with the Democrats continued on the state and local level due to the continuing white dominance of the Mississippi Democratic Party.[12]

A unified white segregationist vote for the Democrats also hampered the MFDP congressional campaigns. The 1966 MFDP races, despite their slim chance of success, imitated earlier campaigns like the Freedom Vote by raising visibility for the party and encouraging the registration of black voters. Much of the visibility came from the efforts of the candidates and MFDP members themselves because the local media dismissed the efforts of the Freedom Democrats as "token opposition." Major papers did cover speeches by MFDP candidates such as Whitley, but they gave far more coverage to the Republican challengers because the GOP held its first primary in the state's history in Prentiss Walker's district.[13]

In November, all the MFDP candidates lost. Although registration of black voters had hit 117,000 by the end of the year, the failure of black voters to cast a united vote for the candidates contributed to the MFDP defeat in the congressional races. The black vote statewide split between Whitley and Prentiss Walker, and Walker could not attract enough white Democrats to seriously threaten Eastland.[14]

In various local races in 1966, black candidates in areas such as Holmes County who had MFDP affiliation sought offices along with non-MFDP black candidates. Tensions between the MFDP and NAACP clouded the races in Holmes County when the local NAACP President accused county FDP chair Ralthus Hayes of spreading misinformation about the NAACP. The two MFDP-backed candidates lost their races.[15]

The one exception to the black defeats in 1966 occurred in heavily black Jefferson County, where Robert Williams, an independent, challenged a white incumbent for seat on the county board of education. Williams, a minister, farmer, and NAACP member, ran in a majority-black ward. The NAACP had a stronger presence in Jefferson County, and their voter registration combined with the ward system proved critical to Williams's victory. Williams did not face the countywide elections that many other counties used for their school board elections, so most of the county's whites could not vote against him.[16]

Some areas of the state, notably Sunflower County, showed some potential for black politics, when a federal court took the unprecedented step of voiding an election on the grounds of white exclusion of black voters. Fannie Lou Hamer and other black residents of the towns in Sunflower County had filed a suit alleging that the county registrar unlawfully prevented them from voting in the 1965 municipal elections in Sunflower City, Moorhead, and several other towns. In 1966 the U.S. Fifth Circuit Court of Appeals in *Hamer v. Campbell* ruled unconstitutional the actions of the Sunflower County registrar. Judge John R. Brown and his associates limited the scope of the case by omitting the towns of Ruleville, Drew, Inverness, and Doddsville from the judgment but did order new elections for 1967 in Sunflower City and Moorhead.[17]

The MFDP also changed its strategy in 1967. That year, Mississippi held its first elections of all state and county offices since the Voting Rights Act became law. Despite the efforts of the MFDP in registering voters and raising political awareness through prominent races, the party still had no electoral victories. With the exception of the Agricultural and Stabilization and Conservation Service Committee elections and some scattered local races, the MFDP had conducted mostly symbolic statewide campaigns that had little chance of success. With the MFDP losing political viability, the party now shifted its full support to winning victories in more promising elections in black-majority counties and districts. Reapportionment played a role, too, since state legislative districts as well as many local offices were gerrymandered to break up black electoral majorities. The MFDP's focus on local races hoped to use black majorities to elect county officials in areas of heavy black concentration.[18]

Local FDPs ran black candidates in the 1967 elections, although some members questioned the strategy. At a Hinds County FDP meeting in February, some members, hoping for more "qualified" candidates, wanted the party to wait until the 1971 elections to make a serious effort at public office, but most of the members in attendance rejected that approach. Local FDPs established the necessary organization to mobilize black voters and get them to the polls. The Holmes County FDP sent out twenty precinct leaders and two hundred block captains to work as unpaid volunteers, with the block captains teaching new voters about registration and the voting process.[19]

While the MFDP stayed active in areas like Holmes and Hinds Counties and parts of the Delta, the NAACP continued to register voters in its own spheres of influence. The Coahoma County branch, under the leadership of Aaron Henry, backed seven black candidates in the 1967

FIGURE 3. Barbara Jordan and Aaron Henry. Clarksdale pharmacist and
NAACP President Aaron Henry represented, along with Evers, the moderate
wing of civil rights forces in 1960s Mississippi, opposing the Mississippi Freedom Democratic Party (MFDP) and working with white moderates to form
the Loyal Democrats to oppose the segregationist Regulars in 1970s state politics. William F. "Bill" Minor Papers, 80–227, Special Collections Department,
Mitchell Memorial Library, Mississippi State University.

primary. In the southwestern counties, Evers and the NAACP, buoyed
by the victory of Robert Williams the previous year, continued their
registration campaigns. Like the MFDP, Evers and Henry focused on areas of the state where their organization was the strongest and favored
running people for county offices over statewide campaigns.[20]

Despite the conflicts between the NAACP and MFDP, the organizations shared a desire to elect black candidates, and they put aside their
differences and informally agreed to work together towards that goal in
1967. The two groups intermingled to a considerable degree, and local
NAACP branches and FDPs conducted joint efforts in over half of the
primary races. Much like their earlier work with COFO, the two organizations operated in temporary umbrella groups such as the Mississippi
Voter Registration and Education League and Mississippians United to
Elect Negro Candidates.[21]

The presence of growing numbers of black voters also created a new phenomenon in modern Mississippi politics. White candidates, especially incumbents, began to solicit black ballots by offering services to black voters. From Port Gibson to Bolton and elsewhere, white county officials graveled roads in black neighborhoods and insured the prompt delivery of welfare checks, prompting an FDP newsletter to remark that "this kind of thing is a little late now, and . . . it should have been done all along."[22]

White officials, unused to asking black Mississippians for anything, found the transition created by the Voting Rights Act uncomfortable at best and unfathomable at worst. One white supervisor in Hinds County went to an FDP meeting in Bolton to ask for support, but he made few solid promises to the assembled crowd, and when he was asked about hiring blacks in the beat, he said that he employed "some niggers, er colored, I mean Negroes down there now." Realizing his blunder, the supervisor flushed red before the stunned audience. Attitudes like this meant the FDP generally put little faith in white candidates, with one paper in Hinds County declaring that "they promise a plate of silver and give us a plate of mud."[23]

The MFDP faced its first test of 1967 in the special election in Sunflower County. The court ordered an election in May for the voided 1965 municipal elections in Sunflower City and Moorhead. The MFDP ran an organized campaign with an all-black slate when no whites would run on an integrated ticket. Young black men headed the MFDP tickets in both towns. Twenty-one-year-old Otis Brown Jr., head of the county FDP, ran for mayor in Sunflower City. Brown, educated in the local Freedom Schools, previously served as a SNCC field secretary. In Moorhead, Jimmy Lee Douglass, a twenty-two-year-old grocery store worker, ran for mayor. Older black residents of the county, including two women, made up most of the FDP's alderman candidates. Outside support included the Delta Ministry, an ecumenical civil rights organization associated with the National Council of Churches and prominent figures such as Sen. Eugene McCarthy (D-Minn.), Stokely Carmichael, and Dick Gregory. The publicity generated by the court rulings meant that the state papers gave the municipal election significant attention. The MFDP faced an uphill battle because black voter registration in Sunflower County still lagged way behind white registration.[24]

The results of the MFDP campaigns did not please the party and indicated future problems for black candidates. The white candidates actively sought black votes in Sunflower City, which had a seventy per-cent black population. White intimidation, especially black fears of economic retaliation, also influenced the election. Despite the intense campaign and the presence of federal observers, the MFDP slate lost the special election by an average margin of seventy votes in Sunflower City and over one hundred in Moorhead, out of less than a thousand votes total. The white strategy worked, for the white candidates in Sunflower City successfully wooed enough black votes along with the minority white vote. One MFDP candidate summed up the main problem when she declared that "colored folks and whites voted for white folks . . . but white folks didn't vote for colored folks."[25]

The poor showing in Sunflower City and Moorhead did not bode well for the black NAACP candidates in the August Democratic primary. Seventy-six blacks in twenty-two counties, mostly ones with heavy black populations, ran in the primary. Most sought district or beat-level county offices like constable, justice of the peace, or supervisor, but some pursued countywide offices and state legislative seats.[26]

A heavy white turnout for the governor's race contributed to the de-feat of many of the black candidates and white moderates. The 1967 con-test featured a racially charged Democratic primary between U.S. Rep. John Bell Williams and State Treasurer William Winter. Williams was a hero to many whites for his open endorsement of Barry Goldwater in 1964, which cost him his seniority in Congress. The moderate Winter, a former state representative from Grenada, solicited black votes behind the scenes but publicly courted white segregationists before the Citi-zens' Councils. A unified black vote for the more moderate Winter did not materialize any more than it did for the MFDP in Sunflower County. Winter carried black-majority counties like Jefferson and Claiborne in the gubernatorial runoff, but in Wilkinson the "responsible Negro vote," in the words of the Fayette Chronicle, went for John Bell Williams. Most of the white vote in the primary went for Williams, who went on to face in November the Republican nominee Rubel Phillips, who had also run in 1963.[27]

The black victories in 1967 occurred in majority-black counties, where black registration and voting was the highest. The counties where black candidates won included Holmes, Bolivar, and Coahoma Counties in the northwest Delta, Marshall County on the Tennessee state line, and the southwestern counties of Jefferson, Claiborne, and Wilkinson. The per-centage of black residents in each county numbered sixty-seven percent or greater, an undeniable advantage for black candidates. The heavy black majorities overcame the lower rate of black voter registration that had hampered earlier efforts such as in Sunflower County. Successful black candidates needed either a high rate of black voter registration or a very high black majority population to offset white soliciting of the black vote and the almost universal turnout of the white minority.[28]

The most visible non-gubernatorial campaign of 1967 victory occurred in the MFDP enclave of Holmes County with Robert Clark. Clark, a schoolteacher, lost his job and left the county when he voiced his support for gradual desegregation of the public schools after *Brown*. He returned in 1961 to become the athletic director and business manager of Saints Junior College, a private school in Lexington where he directed the Migrant Farm Program, an Office of Economic Opportunity (OEO) program. His family's political roots dated to Reconstruction, when his grandfather, a former slave, chaired the Hinds County Republican Party. Clark's teaching and coaching experience made him popular among the black community in Holmes County. He held a bachelor's from Jackson State College and master's from Michigan State University, which gave him a higher educational level than most white or black residents of the county.[29]

Clark decided to run for office when the all-white school board in January 1967 rejected an adult education program for the county. Clark challenged J. P. Love, Holmes County's state representative and chair of the House Education Committee. Clark joined a slate of twelve MFDP-backed black independent candidates, and all skipped the Democratic primary.[30] Clark's personal style of campaigning helped him to win where other black candidates in the majority-black county failed. He ran an intensive campaign and went door-to-door soliciting votes in the county, careful to avoid any appearance of favoritism. He said that "if you go into a community and you can't make every house in that community, don't you stop at one." Contacts he had established as a teacher and coach gave him a personal connection with most of the black residents of Holmes County. The board of supervisors' refusal to fund the adult education program also ended up aiding Clark. A local black church conducted the program, and a number of the adults who learned to read from the classes signed Clark's petition for office. If a resident did not know Clark personally then he or she likely knew his family, for the Clarks had a long history of teaching in the county schools. Perhaps most important, he also lacked the aura of black power radicalism that had come to taint the MFDP by 1967 and had alienated conservative and middle-class black Mississippians. While he enjoyed MFDP support, the local press described Clark as having "never been a civil rights activist." His nonthreatening demeanor no doubt aided him when he attracted the black middle class in the county by setting up a campaign committee independent of the MFDP. The NAACP branch in Tchula, despite its antagonistic relationship with the MFDP, helped the Clark campaign as well.[31]

The economic position of some of Holmes County's black farmers also played a role in Clark's success. While Holmes County was at the time the fifth poorest county in the nation with the state's highest disparity of white and black median family incomes, the county did contain a core of about 800 black landowners, some with farms up to 2,000 acres in size. Robert Clark owned his own farm with his nephew in the community of Ebenezer. Clark's grandparents, once slaves on the farm, acquired the land after emancipation. Griffin McLaurin, a constable's candidate in the county, had lived on a farm that his parents had purchased under the Farm Security Administration (FSA) program in Mileston in 1940. More than one hundred black farmers owned land in the fertile Delta region of the county because of the FSA buyout program. Hartman Turnbow, an MFDP activist who tried to register to vote in 1963 with thirteen other black residents, lived on seventy acres of Delta land. Some of the farmers, insulated to a degree from white economic retaliation, became involved with the MFDP. The existence of a nucleus of independent, landowning black farmers in the county who supported the MFDP and other civil rights activists gave black independent politics an edge over other counties in the state.[32]

Even though the Holmes County FDP candidates ran as independents, black Holmes Countians still took an interest in the Democratic primary. When the black-controlled Holmes County Voters' League requested black poll watchers for the primary election, the County Democratic Executive Committee refused. The increase in black voters gave the county to Winter, even though Williams won the runoff on the statewide ballot.[33]

White incumbents in Holmes County, as elsewhere, began to promise jobs and favors in return for black support. Sheriff Calvin Moore and Circuit Clerk Henry McClellan recognized the reality of staying in office in a county with a three-to-one black-white ratio and a seventy-three percent black voter registration rate, so they openly solicited black votes in the general election. McClellan's wooing of black voters dramatically broke from his past behavior, which included a Justice Department suit in 1964 for voter discrimination. When the sheriff sought the vote of Howard Huggins, a black cab driver, Huggins asked if the sheriff planned on hiring any black deputies. Moore promised to hire Huggins after the election. Not all the white incumbents felt the need to campaign for the black vote. J. P. Love, Robert Clark's white opponent, did not, a decision he would rue.[34]

By November, the FDP slate had dropped to eleven candidates after the legislature's tighter rules for independent candidates disqualified one of them. On election day, nine of the black candidates lost, with only Robert Clark and Griffin McLaurin winning office. Clark beat Love by only 116 votes. While on the surface the defeats seemed like a blow to the Holmes County FDP, the fact that Clark was the only winner out of eight black legislative candidates in the entire state and the first black state legislator elected since the nineteenth century represented a significant change in post-1965 Mississippi. A major reason for Clark's victory was that his multimember district contained the two majority-black counties of Yazoo and Holmes, making it an overall sixty-five percent black district. Multimember legislative districts in Mississippi involved the creation of districts, sometimes from two or more counties, often by combining black-majority districts with white-majority ones to create white voting majorities. The voters elected the entire legislative delegation in their district on an at-large basis, making it impossible for a black candidate to win in the white-majority district. The other seven losing black legislative candidates in the 1967 election ran in white-majority multimember districts.[35]

The *Lexington Advertiser*, a Holmes County paper, noted that many black residents voted in significant numbers for white candidates, although areas of strong MFDP influence gave larger vote totals to the black candidates. Sheriff Calvin Moore fulfilled his promise and hired Huggins as a part-time deputy. Moore thanked a black audience for their support and confessed his responsibility for past discrimination, swearing that he would be "everybody's sheriff."[36]

Black political power also grew in the southwestern Mississippi counties. Unlike Holmes County, the NAACP and Charles Evers held sway in the counties of Claiborne, Jefferson, and Wilkinson. Evers ran a virtual political machine, handpicking noncontroversial candidates who possessed at least a high school education. Black candidates ran in all three counties, and although most of them lost due to black vote splitting, enough victories occurred for the region to provide the majority of the elected black officials in the state for 1967. The only countywide success for a black candidate in the area occurred in Claiborne County, where Geneva Collins won the election for chancery clerk. Collins, a schoolteacher, ran for the office while her husband Alexander won a justice of the peace post. Her husband had more involvement in the NAACP and civil rights organizing than she did, but she agreed to run when asked by local black leaders. A black candidate in each of the three counties won a seat on the powerful county boards of supervisors, and black men also won positions as constables and justices of the peace.[37]

In Claiborne and Jefferson, black Democratic candidates won and won more seats than MFDP candidates did elsewhere. Not all of the victors in the southwest were Democrats, however. In Wilkinson County, James Jolliff Jr., the youthful head of the county NAACP, ran as an independent and won a supervisor's seat. Jolliff was active in civil rights organizing, including the black self-defense organization Deacons for Defense.[38]

Most of the remaining wins by black candidates happened in Bolivar and Marshall Counties. Bolivar County had seen periodic civil rights campaigns in 1964 and 1965, such as a successful Freedom School in Shaw, but neither the MFDP nor the NAACP achieved the level of organization that they did in Holmes County or southwestern Mississippi. In 1967, five black independents ran for state and county offices. One of the candidates, a Shelby auto mechanic named Kermit Stanton, had lost his job when he took part in a school boycott earlier in the year and responded by running for supervisor. Although most of the black candidates lost their races, the school boycott provided the necessary mobilization for Stanton to win office. Stanton won because of the heavy black vote in all-black Mound Bayou, despite losing the other three boxes in the district.[39]

In Marshall County, several black candidates made bids for office as well. Marshall County contained mostly black Rust College, where Clifton Whitley, the 1966 MFDP Senate candidate, worked as a professor. The campus had been an organizing area for Freedom Summer volunteers in the summer of 1964. A local civil rights group called the Marshall County Citizens for Progress had organized pickets and boycotts of white businesses in Holly Springs in 1966. Although the FDP had an active branch in Holly Springs, it lacked the level of organization and influence of the Holmes County FDP.[40]

None of the black candidates in Marshall County ran for office in 1967 as independents but instead followed the NAACP strategy and ran in the regular Democratic primary. One of them, Osborne Bell, a public schoolteacher and funeral home director, ran for the countywide office of coroner and ranger. Bell apparently did not belong to the Citizens for Progress, so he may have been attractive to conservative blacks and possibly some whites too. His white opponent, Charles Owen, also lacked Bell's experience. Bell had served twelve years as a funeral home director and participated in inquests and worked with the Shelby County, Tennessee, medical examiner. Owen, by contrast, only cited his work at Kennedy Veterans Hospital in Memphis as his medical background. At the time of the election, Owen majored in medical technology at the University of Mississippi. Bell narrowly won the Democratic primary, and two other black men won posts for justice of the peace and constable in the county. All the black Democratic nominees won the general election that November. The constable and justice of the peace candidates both ran from the fourth district, and its heavily black precincts gave them a significant margin over their white opponents.[41]

The NAACP's approach of filing and running within the Democratic Party yielded more victories for black office seekers than the MFDP's independent party approach. Over sixty MFDP candidates ran, but only six won. No black sheriff candidates won, and only two candidates, Geneva Collins and Osborne Bell, won countywide elections. A total of twenty-two blacks won local offices, mostly minor posts such as justice of the peace and constable. Out of twenty-five black candidates backed by the NAACP, eleven won the Democratic primary, and all the primary victors later won the general election in November.[42]

One reason for the differing strategies—and successes—of the MFDP and NAACP has to do with what Charles Payne described as the authoritarian trend in southern black leadership, including pre-1960s Mississippi civil rights activists.[43] The MFDP rejected that approach, instead committing to local decision-making and organizing, a philosophy born from its roots in SNCC and Freedom Summer. SNCC organizers worked to build relationships with local people and carried this idea over to the creation of the MFDP. The precinct meetings that the party organized in 1964 reflected the anti-authoritarian model, electing a variety of people from the black community as delegates. This worked well in Holmes County, but that county was unique, part of the different movement culture that Emilye Crosby says existed in the Delta versus southwest Mississippi, a culture that included the large number of black landowners around Mileston. Robert Clark, while not an official member of the MFDP, used the SNCC-MFDP tradition of building local relationships as part of his intensive campaign in 1967, instead of a top-down approach like Evers utilized. As Payne has noted, other Delta counties did not have long-term successful FDPs. North of Holmes, Leflore County's FDP fell into internal squabbling and discord and ceased to be effective after 1965.[44]

This cross-class approach differed from the NAACP, whose leadership in Mississippi was drawn from the black middle class. Manning Marable argues that desegregation and black power were not just desires for political power but also a black workers' movement, and John Dittmer reported that the black workers, not the middle class, gave the most consistent support to civil rights efforts in pre-1960s Mississippi.[45] The MFDP reflected that working-class approach to black power through its involvement of working-class blacks and the work of activists, such as Fannie Lou Hamer who helped organize the short-lived Mississippi Freedom Labor Union (MFLU). The NAACP's authoritarian model often precluded local decision-making in which leaders such as Charles Evers picked candidates to run for office, a practice he utilized in his power base in Jefferson County. This tradition of "bossism" also meant that NAACP leaders were comfortable cutting deals with white segregationists in return for political power. Charles Evers, during the Natchez boycott in 1965, negotiated an agreement with white leaders in the city over the objections of the local FDP and prevented the FDP from debating or protesting the compromise. Even Aaron Henry worked in this manner, maintaining a personal relationship with Robert Patterson, founder of the Citizens' Council.[46]

The NAACP distrust of the MFDP and its willingness to cut deals with whites and undermine black working-class efforts was most vividly seen in the handling of the Child Development Group of Mississippi (CDGM). The CDGM was a Head Start program funded by the Office of Economic Opportunity (OEO) as part of the War on Poverty, although the program operated for its first year without any federal funds. Civil rights activists and local people initially ran the CDGM centers, taking to heart OEO director Sargent Shriver's call for "maximum feasible participation of the poor." Many of the MFDP-indentified activists in the CDGM tried to restrict the participation of the NAACP and the traditional black elite. After segregationist politicians like Sen. John Stennis attacked the CDGM for its civil rights activism, a new organization was chartered, Mississippi Action for Progress (MAP). MAP drew the support of white moderates as well as NAACP leaders like Henry and Evers. The MAP centers, unlike the CDGM centers, reflected the authoritarian NAACP approach, with most members appointed by local government or officials instead of being elected. Henry in particular embittered MFDP activists by openly siding with white critics of the CDGM, including segregationist state politicians. MAP, using federal dollars controlled by state and local authorities and not grassroots activists, eventually overwhelmed the defunded CDGM, just as the NAACP would gradually absorb and overshadow the MFDP.[47]

The increase in newly registered black voters not only affected local races but the gubernatorial race as well. Black voting created a major ideological cleavage in the Republican Party that would last for years, even as they made another bid for the governor's office that November. Since 1960, conservatives like Wirt Yerger had guided party philosophy. The ultraconservatives, or conservative ideologues, favored minimal-government economic philosophies that promoted an unregulated free market. Many of these conservatives were successful businessmen who would benefit from such policies. Much like the neobourbons, the rural conservatives who led resistance to school desegregation of the 1950s, they regarded programs that helped the poor and African Americans as government interference.[48] They favored soliciting white voters who had supported George Wallace but with coded (sometimes thinly) racial appeals, not economic populism.

With the enactment of the Voting Rights Act, the ideologues found their influence in the party contested by a progressive wing. The label "progressive" was relative to Mississippi since many of the more liberal Mississippi Republicans were still conservative by national standards. The progressives differed from the ideologues with their significant efforts at black voter outreach, which reflected a desire to build a biracial party based on economic development and growth. Although some of their leaders came from the business sector, as did the conservative ideologues, the progressives did not see government programs as being incompatible with economic growth. The progressives generally supported social programs that favored low-income, predominantly black Mississippians, as well as civil rights legislation.

In between these two factions were the less ideologically committed members of the party. Like the state GOP overall, they were reliably conservative but shifted as the situation demanded. These uncommitted members, or pragmatists, may have had sympathies with one faction or the other (usually the conservative ideologues) but focused on gaining political power and maintaining party unity, even if it meant at times compromising ideology. The pragmatists would eventually become a significant force in the party, holding both party leadership positions and the small number of elected offices Republicans won in the 1970s.

These divisions and philosophies did not mean that the ideologues were unaffected by or ignorant of the changes wrought by black enfranchisement. As Joseph Crespino has shown, conservative Mississippians accepted the reality of black suffrage and made a "subtle and strategic accommodation" to the reality of federal civil rights enforcement. This accommodation did not mean the ideologues gave up resistance, but it instead became part of the "conservative counterrevolution" that enshrined states' rights and white elite privilege in a nonracial discourse.[49] The ideologues gave lip service to black outreach but held it in far less esteem than their more moderate Republicans. These developments were replicated in other areas of the South and became part of the "silent majority" that developed from the suburban conservatism of the 1960s and 1970s.[50] The counterrevolution was by no means uncontested within the party, however. As Jason Sokol has demonstrated, the acceptance of the civil rights movement by whites was a contested process with no single vision.[51] In effect, the Voting Rights Act and the enfranchisement of black Mississippians created in the state GOP the same conservative-moderate split that divided the national Republican Party.

Rubel Phillips, who had failed to win the governorship in 1963, now tried to beat John Bell Williams in 1967. Unlike his 1963 campaign, he ran as a progressive and racial moderate. He endorsed racial change for economic reasons and cited Jim Crow as the reason for the state's underdevelopment. He also ran on a platform that called for increased education spending and a compulsory school attendance law. The Hinds County FDP rejected Phillips's altered stance and urged black voters to boycott the governor's election and vote only for black candidates and to "not be a sucker for any slickster white politician." The executive

FIGURE 4. Rubel Phillips campaigning, 1960s. Phillips, twice the failed Republican candidate for governor, represented the possibilities of political transformation that the black franchise could render in Mississippi. Phillips ran as a segregationist for governor in 1963, but by the time of his 1967 race, he became the first Mississippi gubernatorial candidate in the wake of the Voting Rights Act to break ranks and openly solicit black voters. Mississippi Republican Party Papers, 353–642, Special Collections Department, Mitchell Memorial Library, Mississippi State University.

committee of the state MFDP endorsed Phillips as more palatable than his segregationist opponent, but Phillips, conscious of the need for white votes, distanced himself from the mostly black organization. The MFDP endorsement allowed Williams to cast Phillips as a thrall of liberal national Republicans such as Nelson Rockefeller and Jacob Javits.[52]

Phillips's commitment to segregation was questionable in light of his past. During his term as Alcorn County clerk in the 1950s, he registered black voters in higher numbers than other Mississippi counties. Building on that history, in 1967 he became the first candidate in modern Mississippi to solicit black leaders through a mailing campaign. White voters in Mississippi may have begun to switch their party identification in national elections, but they had not done so in state elections since the Democratic Party still adhered to white supremacy. Phillips realized that a simple racist appeal would not win him the election, so he reached out to the new pool of black voters. He received less than thirty percent of the statewide vote, although he did well in some of the black-majority counties, and won majorities in some black precincts. However, his failure to take even strong-movement counties such as Holmes with an anti-segregation position foreshadowed the difficulty the Republican Party would have wooing black voters with moderate positions.[53]

Observers and historians of the 1967 elections split on how significant the elections were for black Mississippians. Some emphasize the positive by looking at Clark's election, while others stress the negative impact of the large number of defeated black candidates. Regardless of the high number of lost races, the election of twenty-two black officeholders, even though black voter registration remained lower than whites, represented a significant shift in Mississippi politics and clearly showed changes wrought by the Voting Rights Act. White politicians in counties with large numbers of black voters now made concessions to win black votes, a state of affairs that did not exist in 1963.[54]

The 1967 elections had barely ended when another major electoral contest materialized. In January 1968 at a meeting of black political and civil rights leaders in Jackson, Charles Evers announced his candidacy for a special election to the U.S. House to fill the third district seat in southwest Mississippi vacated by John Bell Williams. Evers had poor relations with the MFDP, but he still appointed MFDP members Lawrence Guyot and Ed King to key campaign positions and both waged a spirited campaign for him, and local FDP chapters mobilized their supporters for Evers. Charles Griffin of Utica, a longtime congressional assistant to Williams, and State Sen. Ellis Bodron of Vicksburg led the pack of six white candidates. Evers ran "as a Mississippian and not under party label" since the special election did not require a party nomination. The black newspaper the *Jackson Advocate*, which had frequently condemned civil rights demonstrators and curried favor with white segregationists, even gave Evers some support by criticizing the white candidates. The paper said in an editorial that "nothing discussed by the non-Negro candidates during the campaign, even in broadest generalities, gave any assurance to the Negro citizens of the state that the election of any one of the non-Negro candidates would help make the future better than the past."[55]

Evers ran a vigorous campaign in which he called for federal programs to combat unemployment and construct low-income housing. Griffin campaigned largely on his experience as a congressional aide, while Bodron appealed to the right wing with his denunciations of "communistically inspired mob violence" and calls to escalate the war in Vietnam. Evers led the field of seven candidates in the first election in March but won only thirty percent of the total vote. Evers faced Griffin in the runoff, but since only 70,000 of the district's 195,000 voters were black, an Evers victory seemed impossible. Despite the odds, Evers still campaigned for the runoff election. He called Griffin "a runabout flunky" of John Bell Williams, and at a speech at Mississippi College he urged the United States to abandon its "tragic and immoral" war in Vietnam.[56]

Although the white students at Mississippi College gave him a warm reception, major white support did not materialize for the civil rights leader. Evers won the support of the state's Young Democrats, but the lack of support from state AFL-CIO leader Claude Ramsey angered Evers. Both candidates advertised on television, and Griffin himself refrained from any racist appeals, although running in a majority white-district guaranteed his election. In March, he won over 87,000 votes to Evers's 43,000. Despite his loss, Evers credited himself with inspiring black Mississippians by running in a major state race and showing whites that the black vote mattered. "I stopped the nigger, nigger talk," he claimed.[57]

Despite the gains of 1967, white resistance did not fade in 1968. Newly elected black officeholders experienced continued harassment. In March 1968, a jury of ten whites and two blacks convicted James Jolliff Jr., the black supervisor in Wilkinson County, of obstructing two agents of the Alcoholic Beverage Control Division. The jury convicted him despite the testimony of six black witnesses that contradicted the agents' claims.[58]

Jolliff received aid from an organization that would play a critical role in expanding black political power in the coming years. The Lawyers Committee for Civil Rights Under Law (LCCRUL), a Washington, D.C.-based civil rights legal group with offices in Jackson, represented Jolliff. The LCCRUL had developed from President Kennedy's White House Conference on Civil Rights in 1963. With the backing of the American Bar Association, LCCRUL lawyers opened offices in Jackson in 1965 on Farish Street with fellow civil rights groups, the NAACP Legal Defense Fund and Lawyers' Constitutional Defense Committee (LCDC).

Although the LCCRUL initially had a formal relationship with the Mississippi State Bar, any civility between the two organizations had ended by late 1966. The state bar, composed of white Mississippi lawyers with little or no interest in civil rights cases, expected the LCCRUL to only provide defense counsel in civil rights cases. Instead, LCCRUL attorneys aggressively filed lawsuits against the state in federal court, including legal aid for the civil rights activities of Charles Evers and Alcorn State University students in Claiborne County. The state bar severed its relationship with LCCRUL in April 1967.[59]

Jolliff received a two-year suspended sentence and five years' probation in addition to being removed from office. The MFDP sharply criticized the conviction. LCCRUL appeals soon changed Jolliff's fortunes. The Mississippi Supreme Court reinstated the former NAACP leader to office and overturned his conviction on the grounds that the ABC agents acted illegally and without a warrant. While most black officeholders were not brought up on charges, white harassment took a myriad of forms. Outgoing white officials did what they could to make incoming black officials unable to perform their duties. Geneva Collins, the Claiborne County chancery clerk, found the clerk's office in shambles and many of the county records hidden when she took over. When political scientist Lester Salamon surveyed Mississippi's elected black officials from the 1960s elections, over half he spoke to complained that various forms of white obstructionism hindered their duties as officeholders.[60]

The state Democratic Party also blocked meaningful black participation from the delegate selection for the national convention in 1968. Although some white incumbents had reached out to black voters in the previous year's election, many of the county Democratic organizations still refused to share any power on even a token basis with blacks. The Holmes County Democratic Executive Committee tried to shut local blacks out of the May 1968 precinct meetings in Lexington through last-minute location changes, even barring Robert Clark in one instance. When some of the county's black citizens met and nominated their own interracial slate, the committee refused to seat the five black delegates. Black residents of the county responded with a boycott of white businesses. At least thirty counties in the state reported violations similar to Holmes County.[61]

The continued obstruction of black Mississippians by the state Democratic Party led to the creation of the Loyal Democrats of Mississippi to win national recognition over the segregationist regular party. As

Lyndon Johnson declined renomination for president and the pro-civil rights Robert F. Kennedy entered the presidential race, the rival factions of the MFDP and the NAACP-Young Democrats of Mississippi met in June and held precinct and county meetings to pick delegates to the national Democratic convention in Chicago. The two sides agreed to form the Loyal Democrats to challenge the seating of the all-white delegation at the convention. The two civil rights groups worked out a compromise that gave the MFDP minority status in the Loyalist delegation to Chicago. Charles Evers headed the delegation and Aaron Henry chaired the state convention, and they made sure that MFDP delegates, including moderate members like Robert Clark, were kept out of key positions. One pro-MFDP paper denounced the autocratic actions of the "NAACP goons," but most MFDP members accepted their party's junior status in the Loyalists. Clark did not speak bitterly of the 1968 convention and said he served as the liaison between the MFDP and the NAACP. He referred to Henry and Evers as "entirely different individuals" but called them both friends. Unlike the 1964 MFDP challenge, which was composed of SNCC stalwarts such as Robert Moses and Fannie Lou Hamer, moderates such as Aaron Henry and Hodding Carter led the 1968 faction. The interracial delegation won their seats at the national convention, whereas the segregationist regular Democrats were excluded.[62]

Mississippi voters selected delegates not just for Chicago that year but also voted for some local officials. The 1968 elections yielded some impressive gains in a few black-majority counties where black candidates won some seats on local boards. For the first time, black people now controlled county election commissions in Holmes, Claiborne, and Jefferson Counties. The election commissions, while not as powerful as the board of supervisors, did choose voting places and poll workers so a black-majority board could end the obstructionist practices of all-white boards towards black candidates and voters. Holmes County's new board, for example, instituted a fifty-fifty, black-white ratio for election officials in the county. Fifteen blacks won seats on the election commission boards and four on school boards, with most of the victories in Holmes, Claiborne and Jefferson Counties. The advances did not come easily, for the white-controlled county governments sometimes tried to block victorious candidates. In Marshall County, a black candidate for the election commission won his seat only after he sued to get a recount, which was decided in his favor over alleged clerical errors in counting the ballots.[63]

The gains on the election commissions, while significant, generated little publicity when compared to the elections the previous year. National events during 1968 also pushed local events out of the headlines. Despite the local election controversies and victories, the presidential campaign that year overshadowed all other political events in the state. Although Mississippi voted for segregationist George Wallace in 1968, the majority-black counties largely went for liberal, pro-civil rights Hubert Humphrey.[64]

In 1969, the state held its first regular municipal elections since the passage of the Voting Rights Act. Most towns and cities staggered their elections for mayors and aldermen with the gubernatorial elections, leading to a major election season every two years. Many of the municipalities operated under at-large forms of voting by which the entire electorate voted for all the seats on the board of aldermen rather than the ward system, which subdivided the city into districts where the voters elected only the representative in their ward. In 1962 the state legislature, with the intention of preventing the election of black aldermen, required the at-large form of government for all code charter cities. The at-large system effectively prevented blacks from gaining office in towns where they comprised a minority or slight majority, while a ward system could allow black aldermen to be elected from majority-black districts. Under the at-large system, the first municipalities in Mississippi to elect black aldermen were small, majority-black towns.[65]

The Bolivar County town of Shelby became one of the first towns in the state to elect a black alderman. In 1968, black residents of the town boycotted white merchants when the school board fired two black teachers. After four months, the boycott ended when the town government agreed to integrate the Shelby Chamber of Commerce and a white alderman resigned his seat on the city board of aldermen to leave an open seat for a black candidate to try and win. The town's black voters elected Robert Gray, a service station owner, to take the seat and become the first black man in Shelby's city government. Later, in 1970, a black schoolteacher won another seat on the board.[66]

A total of 148 black candidates ran in the municipal primary elections in 1969. While some all-black tickets lost, such as in Woodville in Wilkinson County, others won. In Friars Point in Coahoma County, Dan Ferguson, a black justice of the peace, ran for mayor and headed a ticket of several other black candidates. The election in Friars Point also produced one of Mississippi's first black-versus-black elections. Clay Walter, a black man unaffiliated with Ferguson, ran against one of Ferguson's allies for the post of town marshal. Ferguson, whom many voters perceived as a militant, could not muster widespread support among the majority-black electorate of the town, and he and his followers failed to win any seats. Walter won his race, indicating that many town voters, black and white, saw him as more acceptable than Ferguson.[67] Black municipal candidates also lost races in Holmes County, although Howard Huggins, the deputy sheriff whom Sheriff Calvin Moore had hired after the 1967 elections, ran as a Democrat and won a seat on the Municipal Democratic Executive Committee. The beginning of Huggins's eventual rise to sheriff owed directly to the growing influence of the black vote, since Moore had hired him because of a campaign promise. Huggins, who had the backing of the white power structure in the county, could command biracial support, which made him a palatable candidate to white voters.[68]

While black candidates won a majority on the board of aldermen in Jonestown in Coahoma County, the biggest victory came in Jefferson County where Charles Evers's victory in Fayette gave Mississippi its first black mayor of a biracial town since Reconstruction. Evers ran for mayor and his handpicked "Evers slate" ran for the board of aldermen and Municipal Executive Democratic Committee in the county seat of Jefferson County. He ran on a platform that called for improved city services and equal protection and representation in city government. He urged blacks to "come out and vote for the Negro race." Whites in Fayette tried to intimidate black voters in the impoverished town by telling them they would lose their welfare checks if Evers won.[69]

The NAACP voter registration drives paid off, and the 448 newly registered black voters gave Evers the margin to oust the eighteen-year incumbent mayor. Northern college students came to the town and drove voters on the day of the election, and civil rights lawyers helped watch polls. The entire slate won, and he and his victorious allies presided over an inauguration packed with celebrities and out-of-state politicians.[70]

As the only black candidate for mayor to win that year, Charles Evers's victory was especially noteworthy, and along with Clark's election to the state legislature in 1967 these were the two most visible signs of change in Mississippi as the 1960s closed. The black victories in 1969 all occurred in smaller majority-black towns and hamlets where the at-large system of voting did not dilute the black vote. While any victories, however small, had significance when compared to the elections of just four years ago, most of these victories came from the NAACP's top-down approach through an organizing tradition that used unelected leaders such as Evers and Henry, not the grassroots, locally democratic approach of the MFDP.

Some visible trends emerged in the first five years of the Voting Rights Act. Much of the energy and drive of the early candidates for office came out of the movement's organizing and activism, and the protest tactics of the movement worked in tandem with black political campaigns. The fight for political access, with its voter registration drives and congressional challenges, served as the main catalyst for black politics in Mississippi. With near-total disfranchisement prior to 1965, the state lacked the established systems of black political participation that existed in northern cities and even some southern states after the end of all-white primaries with the U.S. Supreme Court's 1944 decision in *Smith v. Allwright*.

The most common form of activism that occurred during early black political campaigns was the "selective buying" campaign, or boycott. Steven Lawson argued that black voters reduced the use of other forms of protest once they acquired the ballot. Even the title of his one of his essays, "From Boycotts to Ballots," suggests that older forms of protest fell by the wayside as suffrage expanded. Charles Evers's Natchez boycott, which remains one of the most famous of 1960s Mississippi, took place in 1965 before the widespread enfranchisement of the Voting Rights Act. One historian described the Natchez boycott as the last major mobilizing campaign of the Mississippi civil rights movement. Although not as frequently used as it once was, black people in post-1965 Mississippi never abandoned the boycott. It continued as a strong weapon that merged political and economic protest.[71]

Boycotts continued in towns smaller than Natchez as black voter registration grew, especially in majority-black communities where white merchants depended on black patronage. The boycotters primarily wanted access to political power, although the campaigns involved other issues, such as gaining full access to American consumer culture and the use of courtesy titles. Many of the 1960s boycotts arose out of political, not economic grievances. In Lexington, black residents in May 1968 launched a selective buying campaign against white merchants when the Holmes County Democratic Executive Committee shut black voters and officeholders out of its meetings. Only later did the Citizens' Committee, which organized the campaign, add consumer concerns like courtesy titles and equal pay. Charles Evers showed up to support the campaign and said that "dollars and [the] ballot are weapons Negroes must use to win rights."[72]

The lack of black electoral unity remained the greatest obstacle to the election of black officials in the early period of black politics in Mississippi. With the passage of the Voting Rights Act, white politicians feared the emergence of a unified black vote, but the elections in 1967 and 1969 indicated the elusiveness of the unified black vote. As one Mississippi journalist reported in 1967, "[T]he Negro vote is split among so many factions the threat of a solid vote for a statewide candidate doesn't exist." All the state Democratic candidates ran as segregationists, with none making a concerted effort to openly solicit the black vote. On the local level, where the black vote would have had the most influence, the majority of black candidates lost. MFDP member and historian Leslie McLemore, referring to the 1967 Holmes County and the Sunflower elections, cited the lingering effects of fear and the economic caste system as factors compelling blacks to vote for white candidates.[73]

Although intimidation may have been a factor in motivating black voters to support whites, local white incumbents who asked black voters for their support often received it. Many black voters may have made conscious decisions to support white supervisors after they graded roads and graveled driveways in black neighborhoods. Others may also have reasoned that white incumbents would have more influence, especially on a white-majority board, when it came to distributing funds and favors than a relatively powerless token-black member. Some black Mississippians also wanted public jobs in addition to an eleventh-hour delivery of services. James Jolliff declared that road repair was not enough to satisfy black demands and cited the lack of administrative positions for blacks as his reason for running for supervisor in Wilkinson County.[74] For a variety of reasons, the black vote in Mississippi fragmented. A white bloc vote, not a black one, emerged since few whites voted for black candidates.

The lack of black unity also underscored the shifting boundaries of black politics during the late 1960s. The civil rights movement nationwide in both Mississippi and the nation had radicalized and splintered after 1965. The immediate legacy of the rise of black power had been the divide and animosity between the NAACP and the MFDP. Aaron Henry denounced the separate course of the MFDP as "reverse racism," and Charles Evers declared, "[I]t would be wrong . . . to have all Negroes in public office down here." MFDP stalwarts like Fannie Lou Hamer responded in kind and criticized "Uncle Tom" NAACP leaders and white liberals. The 1967 elections and the creation of the Loyalist Democrats show that the two groups worked together more closely than their public disputes suggested. Many local organizers held overlapping or multiple memberships in civil rights groups. Leslie Burl McLemore, a student at Rust College who helped register black voters in the early 1960s, was a member of SNCC and an MFDP delegate to Atlantic City in 1964, while simultaneously serving as president of the campus NAACP chapter.[75]

The influence of black power on the MFDP did serve to alienate many of the more moderate elements of the civil rights community from the party. While the MFDP never expelled whites like SNCC did, its newsletters voiced increasingly controversial and anti-establishment rhetoric. MFDP papers ran editorials endorsing the creation of "shooting clubs" to protect the black community and referred to the U.S. military as the "Ku Klux Klan of Vietnam." The newsletters also highlighted class concerns by endorsing other civil rights campaigns such as the farm boycotts of the United Farm Workers and Dr. Martin Luther King Jr.'s Poor People's Campaign. Despite the militant and antigovernment tone of the MFDP, the party remained committed to electoral politics and the election of black people into state and local government. To the MFDP, black power still included voting power.[76]

The MFDP's expressions of black power seemed mild when compared to the actions of the black separatist group, the Republic of New Africa (RNA). The Detroit-born group called for a separate black nation composed of the states of Mississippi, Louisiana, Alabama, Georgia, and South Carolina. Members of the group set up their headquarters in the town of Edwards in Hinds County as the first phase in creating their cooperative and egalitarian utopia, where class, color, and sexual discrimination would be abolished and the state would control the means of production for the benefit of all its citizens. The RNA's outspoken black nationalism did not win it many friends in the civil rights community. Charles Evers publicly criticized the RNA when it tried to expropriate land from a black farmer in Hinds County, almost leading to a fistfight between him and RNA President Imari Obadale. Evers refused to say he was explicitly opposed to the RNA, just to the idea of separatism.[77]

The involvement of the RNA in state and local politics demonstrated the fluidity and overlap between civil rights and black power organizations in the early years of Mississippi's black politics. Despite its separatist nature, the RNA utilized electoral politics as a way to build support in the black community. Although the RNA did not organize as a political party or run candidates like the MFDP, they did maintain contacts with MFDP candidates. Bill Miller, the RNA's Minister of Justice, even served as an MFDP officer.[78]

While Evers publicly criticized black power, other civil rights activists and black politicians maintained connections to militant groups. Robert Clark was scheduled to appear at the RNA founding convention in Detroit in 1968, but he canceled after unfavorable publicity about the convention appeared in the Jackson newspapers. Clark also registered for but did not attend the National Black Economic Conference at Wayne State University in Detroit, where black militants issued a manifesto demanding reparations from white religious institutions. He publicly declared that he was not an RNA member and did not support their tactics, but he defended the right of people to join the organization. He said privately that Obadale was a friend, but that when the RNA publicly embraced separatism he parted ways with them. Clark's comments indicated that black power connections could hurt black candidates in the political arena. Otis Brown Jr., a former Stokely Carmichael aide who ran unsuccessfully for mayor of Sunflower in the 1967 court-ordered elections, did not invite Carmichael to speak and publicly distanced himself from the black power slogans of the SNCC leader.[79]

Other civil rights figures that had connections to black power groups like the RNA included Fred Banks, a young black attorney who worked with the NAACP Legal Defense and Education Fund and served as president of the Jackson branch of the NAACP. Banks, a Jackson native and graduate of Howard University, handled school desegregation cases for the Fund, but he took part in other, more controversial cases. Banks represented eleven members of the RNA who were tried for the shooting death of a Jackson policeman after a police and FBI raid on the RNA's Jackson headquarters. Banks also worked the other end of the civil rights spectrum when he provided legal services to Charles Evers's administration in Fayette.[80] Wilkinson County Supervisor James Jolliff also worked with militant black groups. Although he headed the county NAACP, Jolliff led the Woodville chapter of the Deacons for Defense in series of marches during a 1967 boycott.[81]

The muddled lines between nonviolence and violence during the civil rights movement also blurred the margins between black power and black politics in the late 1960s and early 1970s. The words and actions

FIGURE 5. Rep. Fred Banks. An NAACP lawyer operating
out of Jackson, Banks represented numerous civil rights
plaintiffs and in 1975 won a seat in the Mississippi State
Legislature after a court order created three single-member
districts for Hinds County. Along with Rep. Robert Clark of
Holmes County, Banks and his two colleagues were the only
black representation in the Mississippi House until 1980.
William F. "Bill" Minor Papers, 80–28, Special Collections
Department, Mitchell Memorial Library, Mississippi State
University.

of civil rights workers did not always conform to clearly demarcated lines separating the philosophies of strict nonviolence, self-defense, and retaliatory violence. Fannie Lou Hamer, who resigned from SNCC after disputes with black radicals in the organization, once endorsed violence to keep strikebreakers from a plantation during a tenant farmers' strike. "I don't believe in killing, but a good whipping behind the bushes wouldn't hurt them," she said of "the nervous Nellies and the Toms" who cooperated with white landowners. Charles Evers also did not shy from threats of violence and self-defense in his rhetoric. After a car bomb almost killed Natchez NAACP President George Metcalf, Evers told a crowd that "[I]f they do it anymore, we are going to get those responsible. We're armed, every last one of us, and we are not going to take it." Evers's comments about black residents including children arming themselves almost got him fired by NAACP head Roy Wilkins. In nearby Wilkinson County during a boycott in 1967, James Jolliff declared that "[W]e are going to have to bury those Negroes who have sold themselves out to the white people." Black self-defense groups such as the Deacons for Defense formed in Natchez, Port Gibson, Woodville, and other Mississippi towns. The Natchez Deacons in particular became known for their displays of weaponry.[82]

The most visible example of the overlapping of violence and nonviolence in Mississippi, as well as Evers's penchant for authoritarianism, occurred during the Port Gibson boycott conducted by him and his organization. In 1966, black residents of the Claiborne County town followed the movement plan laid out in Natchez and launched a boycott of the town's white-owned businesses. Unlike the short-lived boycotts the Evers organization conducted in Natchez and Fayette, the Port Gibson affair dragged on, and white merchants filed a lawsuit against the boycotters in 1969. Intimidation and threats of violence accompanied the boycott. The boycott organizers employed "enforcers" to ensure that black residents complied with the campaign. The enforcers, according to court testimony, bought weapons and ammunition and drilled in units they called "Black Hats," distinctive due to their black cowboy hats. Some were members of or took the name of the Deacons of Defense.[83]

The enforcers used social ostracism and public humiliation techniques such as reading the names of boycott breakers aloud at NAACP meetings. They also used more direct forms of intimidation such as warning and verbally harassing the violators. Blacks that broke the boycott even suffered property damage and vandalism, and at least one man was beaten for crossing the picket lines. Although violent acts occurred, none of the actions were ever directly linked to boycott organizers such as Evers. Evers encouraged such actions, although not against specific individuals and only in vague and nebulous terms. In a public speech in 1969, he warned violators that "they would be taken care of later" by him and his supporters and would experience "discipline" for breaking the boycott. He later admitted that he was aware of the violence and intimidation but denied taking any direct part in it.[84]

Evers's rhetoric created problems for him with the state and national NAACP. Aaron Henry said that the statements by Evers contradicted NAACP policy and that the organization had no official link to the boycott or knowledge of its activities. Evers's actions clashed with the official strict philosophy of nonviolence that characterized much of the civil rights movement's leadership. Charges of violence and intimidation frequently accompanied selective buying campaigns throughout the civil rights era. Martin Luther King Jr., in his retelling of the Montgomery bus boycott, denied white charges of the existence of "goon squads" and said no harassment took place as part of the campaign. Evers's speech, while flirting with violence, only hinted instead of incited. The Supreme Court, in a 1982 decision that dismissed the merchants' lawsuit, held that the First Amendment protected Evers.[85]

With the close of the decade, black politics in Mississippi had made its first appearance since the nineteenth century. The efforts of civil rights workers and especially the enforcement of the Voting Rights Act had registered thousands of black Mississippians and gave birth to the first viable black political campaigns of the twentieth century. While relatively few of the first black candidates won their contests, enough did to inspire and open the way for future aspirants. The changes wrought by black political participation largely took place within the existing one-party Democratic structure of the Magnolia State. The MFDP's independent approach yielded one highly publicized victory, the election of Robert Clark in Holmes County. Despite Clark's victory, most of the MFDP-affiliated candidates did not succeed when they ran as independents. The NAACP and a small number of white moderates and liberals pursued political access in the Democratic primaries. The decision to run black candidates as Democrats resulted in more victories than the independent approach. Charles Evers's election as the mayor of Fayette became the victory that heralded the success of the NAACP approach, but other, less publicized victories across the state showed its viability as well.

By 1970, black militancy and independent politics had begun to wane. The MFDP struggled after the 1968 Chicago convention to exist as an independent political party, but the Loyal Democratic coalition absorbed much of the MFDP organization. The MFDP's leadership either left the state or became preoccupied with other concerns, and the NAACP had more success electing black officeholders. The Loyalist Democrats, now recognized by the national party, effectively shut the Freedom Democrats out of all but token positions in the Loyalist organization. The MFDP faded into a series of county parties, with the Holmes County FDP the only one that maintained a long-term existence. The Loyalists shifted to political battles with the Regulars who controlled the party machinery in the state.[86] Meanwhile, the Voting Rights Act's tenure was ending. In the five years since its enactment, the act had brought notable change to Mississippi's politics. The state that had no elected black officials outside of Mound Bayou in the early 1960s sent thirty-five elected officials to Atlanta to attend the VEP's Southwide Conference of Black Elected Officials in December 1968. The number grew to ninety-five by March 1971. Although the majority of the black candidates in the 1967 statewide and 1969 municipal elections had lost, the election of blacks to even minor posts in the state marked a major development from the earlier years.[87] The gains showed the viability of the Loyalist route, but the era of independent politics in Mississippi had not completely ended. As the 1970s opened, black independent political and civil rights activism continued even as the number of black officeholders grew and the black electorate became further integrated into Mississippi's political culture.

3 Gubernatorial Fantasies and Gradual Gains

PRESIDENT RICHARD NIXON, despite his "Southern Strategy" to woo segregationist whites to the Republican Party, signed the Voting Rights Act into law for another five years in 1970 over the opposition of Mississippi's congressional delegation.[1] During the extension period, black Mississippians continued the trend established in the 1967 and 1969 elections and shifted away from statewide races that raised black consciousness and turned instead towards races in heavily black counties where candidates could actually win offices. The older methods of the 1960s did not completely disappear with the shift to electoral politics. Black candidates on the local level expanded and in some cases secured majority control of county governments and city halls, but also continued the use of high-profile, largely symbolic races. The most prominent symbolic race in the early 1970s was Charles Evers's 1971 gubernatorial bid, which attracted major publicity but produced few tangible gains. Away from the media glare of the Evers campaign, black candidates won municipal and county offices in areas with heavy African-American populations. The direct action and protest of the 1960s continued to exist alongside black political organizing, although mass protest did not have the same prominence it enjoyed in the prior decade.

Liberals and civil rights advocates had worried that the Nixon administration would abandon the Voting Rights Act when U.S. Attorney General John Mitchell proposed to expand the coverage of the act nationwide to take the focus off of the South. Mitchell also frightened civil rights activists with his proposal to replace section five preclearance and the automatic review of election laws with voluntary litigation by the Justice Department. After some debate, Congress in 1970 passed a five-year extension of the act that preserved section five and suspended literacy tests nationwide. President Nixon, who did not want to deepen national divisions in the wake of growing unrest on college campuses over the expansion of the Vietnam War into Cambodia, signed the extension into law.[2]

The gains of the civil rights forces did not mean the white political establishment in Mississippi had given up fighting black political power. The legislature revived open primary legislation, first passed in 1966 but vetoed by Gov. Paul Johnson who had called it "radical." The law abolished party primaries and the opportunity for a candidate to win the general election with a plurality and replaced them with an open, nonpartisan primary with a runoff for the top two vote-getters if no one received a majority. Increasing black voter registration since 1966 and the possibility of a white Republican splitting the unified white vote revived fears of a black candidate winning with a plurality. Although a unified black vote did not materialize in the 1967 elections, Charles Evers's unsuccessful run for Congress in 1968 raised concerns that a black candidate could win a plurality in the 1971 statewide elections. The legislature passed the law again in April 1970, and a federal lawsuit by Evers and others led to its suspension on section five preclearance in April 1971.[3]

Back in Mississippi, black officeholders continued to slowly increase their numbers, such as when voters in Shaw in Bolivar County elected their first black alderman. Media attention in 1970 ignored local races and focused on the town of Fayette and its all-black government. Major news outlets covered the political sweep of the town's offices, which Evers and his allies had conducted in 1969. *Life, Time, Newsweek*, and *The New Yorker* reported the election and his administration's efforts to improve Fayette to a national audience.[4]

Evers brought some notable reforms to the Jefferson County seat in his first two years as mayor. He and his allies on the city council quickly integrated the town's eight-man police force, but the last remaining white officer quit by the end of 1970. He also appointed Robert Vanderson, a black schoolteacher, as the chief of police and authorized him to enforce Evers's law and order dictums. Reflecting his penchant for authoritarian measures, Evers ordered a 1:00 A.M. curfew for town bars and a police crackdown down on public swearing, drunkenness and speeding. Evers and Vanderson's application of the law earned the mayor a grudging respect from whites and resentment from some black residents. After Evers received death threats from the Ku Klux Klan, he and the city council also passed a ban on carrying firearms in city limits.[5]

Evers's administration also improved municipal services, raising taxes to pay for needed sewer extensions, streetlights, and paved sidewalks in the black neighborhoods, services the white community already enjoyed. The town government also passed and enforced a compulsory school attendance law even though the state did not have mandatory schooling.[6] The average educational level for black children in Jefferson County was 4.8 years of school, compared to 10.3 years for whites. Black residents also lacked access to medical care. Eighty to ninety percent of the county's black population had never received any significant medical treatment, and the black infant mortality rate was twenty-five times the national average for African Americans. A new ambulance provided transportation for the indigent in the city and county, and Evers appointed a black doctor as director of city medical services, a position that included running the Medgar Evers Health Clinic and providing free or low-cost regular care. By 1971, more than fifty people, including poor whites, received treatment at the clinic every day.[7]

Evers saw economic development as his top priority. Two-thirds of the black residents of the town received welfare, and the lack of industry and a declining agricultural economy contributed to unemployment and underemployment. The county had the highest rate of poverty in the state, with fifty-eight percent of the county's families living below the poverty line. Evers used the personal connections he established as Mississippi's NAACP field secretary to attract investors. In 1970, Sen. Edward Kennedy (D-Mass.) arranged a meeting between his friend Evers and officials from the International Telephone and Telegraph Company (ITT). The contact led to a $150,000 plant for automobile electrical components that employed 150 people. More industry and a federally funded vocational school followed the next year. Evers's efforts to revitalize Fayette brought some support from the recalcitrant whites of the town. Marie Farr Walker, the editor of the *Fayette Chronicle* and a frequent critic of the mayor, admitted that "[H]e's really trying to get industry, and this town needs more jobs badly." According to *Business Week*, Walker put aside her bias against the mayor and even publicly appeared with him during the groundbreaking for the ITT plant.[8]

Evers also tried to improve local race relations but with few successes. Evers tried unsuccessfully to get white policemen to come to work for the town, soliciting officers from other municipalities. He also tried to promote social integration through cultural events. In November 1969, he established the Tony Lawrence Fayette Music Festival, a youth-oriented interracial concert aimed at exporting the Fayette movement to neighboring counties. As part of his effort to reach out to young people, Evers advertised the concert in countercultural papers like *Kudzu*. A flyer for the concert advertised an impressive list of participants, including Elvis Presley and the Rolling Stones, but neither appeared. About five thousand black and white people did show up to hear gospel singer Mahalia Jackson and other performers.[9]

While Evers and his allies secured some significant gains for Fayette and Jefferson County, events in and out of his control hindered his goals. The widespread and crushing poverty of the region remained the biggest barrier. Despite his desire to make black people self-sufficient, Evers recognized the necessity for public and private welfare to improve the plight of local residents, especially since he inherited an empty treasury. By July 1969, poor finances forced Evers to lay off street workers and suspend the paychecks of the town's policemen and municipal employees, and later he also cancelled Christmas bonuses. In December 1969, Charles Ramberg, a young white Georgetown law student working as an advisor to the mayor, noted that Evers realized that he needed to move fast against the town's poverty. "We got to fix the streets," Evers declared. "[We've been] in office five months and no industry, no jobs, no nothing. Just four little fire hydrants."[10]

Evers traveled to Washington, D.C., and used his connections to appeal for donations and secure aid from prominent politicians. The Medgar Evers Fund of New York collected donations to purchase goods and services for Fayette. The Fund financed the health clinic and a new communications system for the town's emergency and law enforcement services. A black policemen's organization in Philadelphia, Pennsylvania, donated a new police car, and the mayor of New York City provided a garbage truck. Almost eighty doctors, including specialists from Hurley Hospital in Flint, Michigan, worked in shifts at their own expense at the health clinic. Publishers donated books to the schools, and pharmaceutical manufacturers provided medicine for the clinic. Some of the biggest grants came from the federal government. The Department of Health, Education and Welfare (HEW) gave $130,000 to the medical clinic, and the Economic Development Administration sent a grant of $30,000. Some whites in Fayette scorned Evers's publicized pleas as "begging," but Evers brushed off the criticism.[11] In the long run, however, Evers's actions were not enough and did little to alleviate the poverty of black citizens in the county.

Evers also drew fire for other actions during his administration. After his election, Evers declared that he would remain involved in civil rights activities and that political office did not "include giving up my fight for freedom." With that in mind, he moved to commemorate his slain brother. White citizens protested when he erected a monument to Medgar Evers in Confederate Park alongside an existing statue of a Confederate soldier. He eventually had to move the statue of his brother after Marie Walker's newspaper reminded the mayor that the park was the property of the county and not the city. He moved it to city hall but pledged to move it back to the park when black voters "take over the courthouse." The event became even more publicized when local police arrested a former Klansman from Tupelo for threatening to kill the mayor over the statue controversy. Evers also clashed with the State Highway Department over some pro-racial equality road signs he placed outside the town's entrances. The highway patrol removed the signs because they violated the right-of-way of the highway.[12]

Evers claimed his tenure as mayor was an extension of his civil rights activities. That also meant his autocratic approach and determination to be the political boss. Evers saw his cause as a noble one, telling his friends that "Fayette has got to succeed. *Fayette is our Israel.* If we fail here, civil rights in America will suffer." Some black residents did not share his convictions, and Evers's community policing irritated some locals. When a judge fined black policeman William Lias for threatening the son of one of the aldermen, the board of aldermen suspended the officer. Evers ignored the board and reinstated Lias. When Lias then reportedly beat up a black man in his custody, a group of seventy-five to eighty black residents protested in front of Evers's businesses in downtown Fayette, but Evers refused to suspend Lias.[13]

Evers also feared that black officeholders would damage the Fayette movement by repeating the mistakes of white politicians through graft and corruption. When Deputy Mayor Ferd Allen tried to sell the city some property, he attempted to charge Evers $1,000 for the quarter acre of land. Evers scolded Allen for the inflated price and told him that "[W]e are the city fathers now. We can't be stealing and gouging like they always were. We can't have it like it was before—with one or two people with all the money." This statement from Evers was particularly ironic, given the evidence that Evers diverted black boycotters to his own businesses during the Natchez and Port Gibson boycotts.[14]

The continuing and pervasive racism of the region also hampered the Evers administration. In 1970, when white city attorney Martha Wood and black policeman Monroe Jenkins became romantically involved and wanted to marry and live openly in Fayette, Evers fired both of them. Wood and Jenkins then left Fayette. Marie Walker, usually eager to print negative stories on the mayor, bowed to southern mores about interracial sex and only mentioned that Evers relieved the two of duty and that "[I]f other newspapers want to make more of it, they can." Evers claimed that he fired them for breaking state anti-miscegenation laws, but their tryst was not illegal since the U.S. Supreme Court struck down all state bans on interracial marriage three years earlier in *Loving v. Virginia*. Evers also cited more credible concerns about their safety in a racially tense Mississippi town and bowed to strong prejudices that both blacks and whites held against interracial marriage by arguing that "public safety comes before personal rights."[15]

The most vivid example of Evers's strong-arming involved Marie Walker of the *Fayette Chronicle*. She represented much of the town's white segregationist sentiment and frequently criticized the mayor for his policies. In July 1970, *Business Week* quoted her on her thoughts on Evers's bringing new industry to Fayette. She questioned "whether niggers will work even if he gets industry here."[16] An ugly situation developed when Charles Ramberg gave a copy of the article to a local black resident, who then led a group of people down to the office of the *Chronicle* to confront Walker. Walker claimed the group threatened her and organized picketing of her office. Leaders of the group photographed and took the names of every white person entering the *Chronicle* office. The marchers also entered her office, stole copies of the newspaper, and ripped down a displayed Mississippi state flag and wiped their feet on it.[17]

Charles Ramberg and Alphonse Deal, a black policeman serving as Evers's bodyguard, observed the incidents but made no effort to stop them. The presence of Ramberg and Deal led Walker to charge that Evers orchestrated the entire attempt at intimidation. She filed a complaint with the Department of Justice and demanded a retraction from *Business Week*. In her weekly column, Walker asked Evers if he was "acting like a mayor, or are you acting like the Hitlers, Stalins, Khrushchevs?" The incident drew the attention of Loyal Democrat and Evers-ally Hodding Carter III, the editor of the *Delta-Democrat Times*, who denounced the attempt to silence Walker and asked Evers to oppose the boycott against her paper. Evers condemned those who entered Walker's office, but did not comment on the boycott itself.[18]

While no evidence exists that places Evers at the newspaper office or indicates he ordered the campaign against Walker, the presence of his top aides at the scene suggested his involvement or prior knowledge. The tactics of the marchers, including overt intimidation and the taking of names, strongly resembled Evers's boycotts in Natchez and Port Gibson. Such actions blurred the boundaries between nonviolent protest and violent action. The trespassing and destruction of property also echoed the intimidation and assaults during earlier boycotts. Evers apparently learned from the Port Gibson boycott and did not give a public speech that denounced Walker or tacitly encouraged reprisals as he did in Claiborne County. When Evers said that he would continue his civil rights activities as mayor, it seems that he also meant the authoritarian aspects as well.

Charles Evers and Marie Farr Walker had a relationship far more complex than a simple public feud and reflected Evers's Machiavellian history of close relationships with segregationist whites while publicly wearing the mantle of a civil rights activist. The two had a personal and economic partnership that they conducted outside of the public eye. Evers reminisced fondly about Walker in his 1997 autobiography and referred to her as "a dear friend of mine." He claimed that her husband, a lawyer, privately informed Evers of the activities in the white community. Marie Walker also had sold Evers some land. He laughed off her negative editorials and said he told her "[Y]ou write all them bad things about me but that's alright. Just keep my name in there. I need the press." Jason Berry, a young white man who worked for Evers in 1971, recalled the same conversation.[19]

Evers and Walker both benefited from their public disputes. Walker gave Evers the necessary press, while circulation of her paper increased outside Jefferson County. Evers recalled that "[E]ven white folks in other counties wanted to read the newspaper where the lady editor attacked the nigger mayor." Charles Ramberg, who helped instigate the anti-Walker demonstration, commented in a private memo about what he saw as the negative side of Evers's constant desire for publicity.

While he admitted the wisdom of Evers's dictum that "[Y]ou've got to have good publicity so people will know what you're doing," Ramberg speculated that such concerns "can be why CE [Evers] tolerates Marie Walker—the need for 'favorable treatment' from her rag—at least to put his articles."[20] What is unclear is the extent of the relationship between the two, including whether the two purposefully staged or exaggerated the incident for the publicity, but given Evers's history at the Natchez and Port Gibson boycotts, a political deal certainly seemed to be in place.

By 1971, Evers's ambitions for higher office began to overshadow events in Fayette. He announced that he would run as an independent candidate for governor during the statewide elections that year, making him the first black man to seek that office. Evers's political connections with national politicians and his media exposure meant guaranteed national news coverage of the race. By 1971, sixty-eight percent of the black electorate in the state had registered to vote, for a total of 307,000 black voters. Black candidates across the state filed to run for state and county offices. In June, Evers tried to convince other black office-seekers to follow his independent candidacy by asking all the black candidates in the state to run for office as independents, not Democrats. Despite the potential of the black vote, white voters still outnumbered black voters by a two-to-one margin.[21]

Since Mississippi governors could not succeed themselves, Democratic successors for John Bell Williams crowded the field. Two racial moderates, William Waller and Charles Sullivan, led the pack. Waller, a native of Lafayette County and former Hinds County District Attorney, had unsuccessfully tried to prosecute Byron de la Beckwith for the murder of Medgar Evers. Waller had alienated some black Mississippians when he defended a Klansman accused of murdering a civil rights worker in Hattiesburg. Waller's main opponent, Lieutenant Governor Charles Sullivan, was also a former district attorney, but he did not enjoy Eastland's backing because of a long political feud he had with the senator.[22]

Evers quickly drew controversy with some of his actions on the campaign trail. Though Evers ran as an independent, he urged black voters to support avowed segregationist Jimmy Swan in the Democratic primary. Swan, a country music singer from Hattiesburg, had finished a strong third in the 1967 gubernatorial primary. In both 1967 and 1971, he campaigned as an outspoken white supremacist and foe of school integration. Evers's endorsement drew widespread criticism, even from liberal allies such as Sen. Hubert Humphrey (D-Minn.) and Hodding Carter III. Evers defended his decision on the grounds that the reactionary Swan would be easier to defeat in the general election than a more moderate candidate like Sullivan or Waller. Evers viewed white moderates as the biggest threat to black politics in Mississippi. He told his press secretary Jason Berry that "[M]iddle-o'-the-roaders . . . won't be no different than John Bell [Williams]. They'll hire 'em a few Toms and say, 'Lookit us down here in ole Mississippi. We sho' 'nuf changin.'" However, his actions were a continuation of his attempts to become cozy with white segregationists, a tactic that would grow later in the decade.[23]

Evers's scheme to nominate Swan failed, but the attempt would not be the last time he supported a white segregationist. Sullivan received the backing of Aaron Henry, who said the fellow Clarksdalian had "turned the corner" on race. Other black voters backed Waller. Sullivan led the primary race with thirty-eight percent of the vote, Waller with thirty-one percent, and Swan with seventeen percent. Evers's influence carried weight in his home base of Jefferson County, which went narrowly for Swan, but black voters in neighboring counties did not comply and generally favored Sullivan. Sullivan won other black-majority counties, such as Marshall County and MFDP-stronghold Holmes County, and did well in his native Delta with both white and black voters.[24]

The 1971 primary contest illustrated the decline of overt race-baiting in state politics, but a quieter defense of segregation replaced it. Neither Sullivan nor Waller made racist appeals to white voters, and in a break from 1967 both men promised to put blacks in the state government. Yet, to avoid alienating white voters neither candidate appeared before black audiences and both defended the private school system that proliferated across the state with the desegregation of the public schools. Racial change was more evident on the local level. White candidates, including many incumbents with segregationist pasts, solicited black audiences with even more frequency than 1967. John William Powell, the third-most senior member of the state Senate, asked black parishioners in Fayette for their votes, and he won the county in August.[25]

Black candidates had mixed results in the primary, and some of them skipped it entirely. In areas like the southwestern river counties where Evers had the most influence, many black candidates heeded his call to bypass the Democratic primary. The entire slate of black candidates in Wilkinson County withdrew from the primary and refiled as independents. In other areas, some black candidates, especially incumbents, remained in the primary. In Marshall County, the incumbent black officials from the 1967 elections won reelection as Democrats.[26]

Evers claimed his high-profile campaign was a consciousness-raising exercise for black voters, and he received sympathetic national press coverage. Walter Gordon, a reporter for the *Baltimore Sun* covering the Evers campaign, described the intangible results of the race when the Fayette mayor made a stop in Mendenhall. "With voting in the November election expected to polarize around race, even Mr. Evers's most ardent supporters concede him no chance," Gordon wrote. "But he is proving something: that a black candidate for governor can march into Mendenhall."[27]

With the defeat of Swan in the primary, Evers had no realistic chance of winning the governor's race, especially with no Republican on the ballot to divide the white vote. White voter registration had been increasing as well after the enactment of the Voting Rights Act, mostly in response to increased black voter registration and political activity. By 1968 white registration had reached 91.5 percent, a more than twenty percent increase from pre-1965 numbers.[28]

Evers's checkered past and loose tongue also wounded him. Reporters forced him to discuss on television degrading comments he made about women in a *Playboy* interview. Unfavorable publicity followed the publication of his 1971 autobiography in which he confessed about his criminal past in Chicago. While his press secretary said that white liberals in Mississippi were the "most enraged" by the book, his accounts of womanizing, prostitution, and interracial sex alienated some African Americans as well. James Meredith, the first black graduate of the University of Mississippi, said that Evers's criminal background created a "lack of enthusiasm" among black voters. Despite the negative attention, Evers raised funds from numerous out-of-state supporters, such as Sen. Edmund Muskie (D-Maine) and Mayor John Lindsay of New York City.[29]

Evers's "boss style" of politics also hurt other black candidates in the races. Over 150 black candidates had filed by August, and 309 were on the ballot in November. While Evers requested black candidates join him in his independent candidacy, he gave them little in return. He promoted black candidates at rallies but gave few funds to them, which hurt counties that lacked the level of black political mobilization that existed in Holmes or Jefferson Counties. His use of television ads backfired, increasing his visibility and mobilizing a heavy turnout of white voters against him.[30]

Although some black candidates pursued independent candidacies to show solidarity with Evers, others ran for reasons that had little to do with the governor's race. Robert Clark, first elected to the state legislature in 1967 as an independent, also ran for reelection as one. He cited continuing black fears of voting as his reason for boycotting the Democratic primary. Many black voters in his district, especially in Humphreys County, voted for the first time in 1971. He said that white intimidation of black voters was still frequent and because of that "[I]t was too much at that time to get black folks to go to the polls twice."[31]

Evers did receive support from an unlikely source. Imari Obadele, the leader of the black nationalist group the Republic of New Africa (RNA), called for a united front of black Mississippians to turn out and vote for Evers and other black candidates for office. Obadele said that Evers's candidacy for governor was "the last chance Mississippi's white controllers will ever have to put this state, within their system, on a course toward a just, progressive, biracial society." The RNA president indicated that he did not think integration would come about and predicted that whites "would not take their last chance." He saw even moderate black leaders such as Evers, with whom he had clear personal and philosophical disagreements, as future leaders of New Africa because they had been chosen or supported by segments of the black community. Obadele said that Evers, Aaron Henry, Robert Clark, and "[A]ll others who are leaders among us because we have chosen them or because they serve us will continue to be leaders among us in our own nation."[32]

The RNA also made contacts with some of black candidates on the local level, showing the overlapping boundaries between black power militancy and black political power. Bill Miller, the RNA's Minister of Justice, and Obadele met with MFDP candidates in Sunflower County. Lee Dorothy Kimbrough, the MFDP candidate for chancery clerk in the county, best represented the interconnections between the various civil rights and black power groups. She maintained contacts with the RNA, was an MFDP candidate, and also worked with the NAACP and the National Council of Negro Women (NCNW). Obadele, at least in his public rhetoric, tried to create a black nationalist consciousness based on color instead of political ideology. His calls for unity at the ballot box did not differ significantly from the goals of Evers and the MFDP, although they did not share his ultimate goal of a separate black homeland.[33]

In November, Evers lost to Waller in a landslide. Evers received only twenty-two percent of over 780,000 votes. He only carried the MFDP enclave of Holmes County and Claiborne, Jefferson, and Wilkinson Counties, the three river counties in his regional power base. The only counties in which he ran competitively with Waller were the majority-black Delta counties. He pulled only about half of the black registered voters, and other black candidates also fared poorly. Black people won only fifty of the local races and lost all of the countywide races. Only eight out of seventy-four supervisor candidates won, and Robert Clark was the only legislative candidate to win. Aaron Henry and Fannie Lou Hamer also lost their legislative races. Many black voters, as in the 1967 elections, voted for white candidates, but poor organization also hampered many black candidates who relied on old-style civil rights tactics such as rallies and leaflets instead of building political machines and parties. One black minister called it "a civil rights hangover." Robert Clark, who barely won re-election, believed that many black candidates did not campaign intensely enough for the black vote. Illegal methods also stymied some of the black vote. The Delta Ministry estimated that fraud and intimidation of black voters hampered black candidates and cost them twelve races in five black-majority counties.[34]

The 1971 campaign showed the limits of black independent politics and the problems with Evers's go-it-alone strategy. Some losing candidates blamed him for the outcome of local contests. Cleve McDowell, a black lawyer from Drew, complained that "all the national money went into the more glamorous races that had no chance of winning." McDowell lost a legislative race in a multimember district in majority-black Sunflower County. James Meredith echoed McDowell and accused Evers of running for governor only to help the upcoming 1972 Democratic presidential campaign and in the process linking local black candidates to his doomed race.[35]

The independent approach also bore part of the blame for the black defeat. In a repeat of 1967 trends, seven black Democrats, over half of them in Marshall County, won election in the August primary and went on to win in November without any opposition. While more black independents won than black Democrats, the lack of white opposition in the general election to black Democrats suggested that party affiliation helped to elect black candidates if they could win the primary. Black independents won mostly in Evers's stronghold in Jefferson County and neighboring Claiborne County. In Claiborne County, blacks took nine offices, including circuit clerk, tax assessor, and coroner, while in Jefferson two supervisors along with five other blacks won office. Evers's failure to command a unified black vote in the general election showed the geographic limits of his appeal. Even in nearby Wilkinson County, the black independent slate lost, and only incumbent James Jolliff won reelection to his supervisor's seat.[36] While the number of black politicians in the state continued to grow, the high expectations raised by the Evers campaign left a feeling of disappointment after the numerous defeats.

Despite the widely publicized failure of Evers in 1971, blacks continued to expand their political power at the local level. Much of the growth occurred in the northwestern Delta counties of Bolivar and Coahoma, where blacks also made a few advances in county offices. Three black men won in the Mound Bayou–Shelby region of district three, which made the area the center of black political power in the county. One of the three was Kermit Stanton, the Shelby mechanic first elected supervisor in 1967, who easily defeated his white opponent. Two black independents elected justice of the peace and constable joined him.[37]

In neighboring Coahoma County, black people made some gains in 1971, although they lagged behind Bolivar County. Jimmie Barnes, a schoolteacher, became the first black supervisor in the modern history of the county. He and a black candidate for constable won as independents from the heavily black fourth district, and another black constable won reelection as a Democrat. Black candidates for countywide offices won majorities in Clarksdale's black neighborhoods but could not muster enough votes in the outlying county where high white turnout occurred. The few victories in Bolivar and Coahoma Counties still represented progress for black politics and put those two counties, with the exception of Holmes County, in the forefront of black political power in the Delta. Blacks candidates in other Delta counties, such as neighboring Tunica and Quitman Counties, failed to win a single race in 1971.[38]

The media spotlight moved away from Mississippi with the end of the gubernatorial campaign, allowing local black politics to expand quietly. Municipal elections during the 1970s significantly increased the number of black officeholders in small, black-majority towns. Charles Evers returned to Fayette and won reelection without opposition in 1973. Black candidates won in several small, majority-black towns of the Delta in the 1973 municipal elections, especially in Bolivar County. The voters of Pace, a hamlet of fewer than 700 people, elected an all-black board of aldermen. Robert Leflore, a twenty-eight-year-old Vietnam veteran and business management major at Delta State University, became the town's first black mayor and won by pledging to improve community services. "I've been a citizen of Pace all my life," he declared, "and there has not been anything done for the black community since I've been here." The even smaller village of Gunnison elected two black men to its board of aldermen, and in Winstonville, voters elected an all-black government. In Shelby, the largest of the towns, a new black alderman joined the two black incumbents.[39]

Black political power did not always progress smoothly, and sometimes came haltingly and suffered reverses. During the 1973 municipal elections in Shaw the only black alderman lost his seat in the Democratic primary. The only black candidate to make it to a runoff was Gregory Flippins, a mayoral candidate and a twenty-two-year old Internal Revenue Service Employee, but he lost as well. The alderman's race sparked controversy when Flippins filed a protest claiming that the proper number of votes had not been cast for each candidate. Mississippi law disallowed "single-shot" voting and required that voters cast a number of votes equal to the number of races on the ballot, which prevented a voter from skipping over a race. The town's Democratic Executive Committee threw the election out, but the ruling had little effect since the same five aldermen won election in the new primary. Shaw's government did not stay all-white for long. In 1974 the city clerk resigned, and Barbara Curry, a black woman who had lost the race the year before, won a special election to fill the seat.[40]

Direct protests by the black community complemented the battles at the polls in Shaw. In 1975 two white policemen shot and killed Sylvester Clark, a black man who allegedly fired at the officers. A group of black Shaw residents in turn demanded the termination of the two officers and the police chief. The presence of alcohol in Clark's bloodstream and conflicting witness accounts led to the exoneration of the two officers, but residents formed People United for a Better Community and called for a boycott of over twenty white- and Chinese-owned businesses in Shaw. The group's spokesman told the board of aldermen that the chief and all three full-time policemen had to resign for the boycott to end. The boycott prompted the aldermen to set up a biracial committee to address racial problems, and one alderman admitted publicly that the boycott campaign was "hurting quite a number of businesses in town." The threat of violence compounded the tense situation, including an intimidation effort by a group of whites with shotguns who rode through the black community.[41]

Although a special election put another black man on the board of aldermen, the real shift in power came during the 1977 municipal elections when Gregory Flippins defeated the incumbent mayor. Flippins joined three black men on the board of aldermen and secured control of the city government. In neighboring Shelby, Robert Gray, the first black person elected to the city government, won a full term as mayor in 1977. In a nod to racial problems in the city, Gray pledged to "bring about a better understanding between the black and the white races."[42]

Politics in Coahoma County centered not on hamlets but on the city of Clarksdale, which contained over half the county's population. The population distribution of Coahoma County meant that black political gains there differed from neighboring Bolivar County. Cleveland, Bolivar County's largest city, contained only about a fourth of the county's population, but Bolivar County had more residents than Coahoma County. Coahoma County did not contain as many of the small majority-black towns that Bolivar County had. Coahoma's politics, black and white, were more centralized, but in Bolivar it was dispersed amongst small municipalities.[43]

Although black candidates had lost in the 1969 municipal elections, white politicians in Clarksdale soon recognized the value of the black vote, and by 1973 they openly solicited black voters. The Republican and Democratic candidates and several white candidates for mayor of Clarksdale attended the Coahoma County NAACP's annual Freedom Fund Banquet in May 1973. A few days later, after Aaron Henry voiced his dissatisfaction with black underrepresentation at the Democratic primary, the Democratic Municipal Election Committee added twelve black poll workers and appointed some as managers.[44]

The 1973 election also yielded an important black victory. Henry Espy, a black school board trustee and 1969 candidate for the board of aldermen, unseated a white incumbent on the city commission. Espy, who hailed from a wealthy family of morticians, conducted what the local paper called an "intensive" campaign that won him black and white votes. The paper estimated that Espy won 700 to 800 white votes, the number he polled over an unsuccessful black contestant in another race.[45]

The elections did not end racial controversy, however. Aaron Henry charged that Wilson's opponent had race-baited Wilson by issuing campaign literature that questioned Wilson's position as vice president of the local NAACP. The mayor's race was also sullied by allegations from both candidates that black votes were either bribed or solicited improperly.[46]

In the surrounding county, black candidates made inroads, but not without direct protests and the threat of white violence. In Jonestown, incumbent mayor John Wing defeated his black opponent, James Shanks, by a 204/106 margin. When poll watchers discovered that the paper in the voting machine had been inverted and thus reversed the vote count in Wing's favor, a crowd of black residents surrounded the city hall and allowed no one to enter to tamper with the machine until FBI agents arrived the next morning. What the *Clarksdale Press Register* dubbed "a little Wounded Knee" ended peacefully when the FBI and the town election commission ruled in Shanks's favor, giving him and three black alderman candidates victory in the election. In Friars Point, Dan Ferguson, who had run in 1969, again lost his bid to become the first black mayor of the river town, but two black men won seats on the board of aldermen and another won election as town marshal. Friars Point would not elect a black mayor until 1977.[47]

By the close of the 1970s, blacks had made significant strides in municipalities in the Bolivar-Coahoma region of the northwestern Mississippi Delta. Black officeholders had majority control in ten town governments and won elected positions in Clarksdale and Cleveland. Other areas of the Delta had experienced some growth but generally only gained one or two elected aldermen in a town instead of a majority. Only Holmes County, with its FDP organization, had a similar base of elected black officials, although many of them were county officials and exerted more influence than municipal officials. The number of black mayors had also increased significantly since Charles Evers's victory in 1969. By 1977, the state had fourteen black mayors, more than any other state.[48]

Not all of the gains occurred in the Delta. In the early 1970s, one rising black politician emerged in the town of Bolton in Hinds County and showed some continuation of the MFDP's local grassroots tradition. Bennie Thompson began his career in Bolton and eventually became one of the most prominent black public officials in the county. Thompson was born and raised in Bolton and hailed from the town's small black middle class. Although his father died at an early age, his mother continued to work as a schoolteacher and maintained a car and home for her family. Thompson began his civil rights involvement as a teenager in the early 1960s when he was arrested during the sit-in movement in Jackson. He completed a degree in political science at Tougaloo College and served with SNCC. While at Tougaloo, the college administration disciplined him and Constance Slaughter, the student body president, for civil rights activities. After graduating in 1968, he worked as a public schoolteacher and decided to run for alderman in his native Bolton in 1969. The town had a population of less than eight hundred, with a sixty-six percent black majority, and easily fit into the emerging pattern of small, majority-black towns that black candidates targeted with grassroots political campaigns. The town's voters had also indicated the potential for local black candidates by giving a majority to Charles Evers in his 1968 congressional race.[49]

Thompson's initial foray into Bolton politics met considerable white resistance. He and two other black candidates hoped to integrate the board of aldermen and work with the white incumbents. When the three blacks won their seats, the remaining white officeholders greeted them with hostility, especially after the losing white candidates lost a federal suit to oust the newly elected aldermen. The town's white clerk told the black aldermen, "I'm not going to do a thing any of you niggers say." Thompson also charged that the local all-white draft board sought to remove him from office by denying his conscientious objector status.[50]

Despite the resistance, Thompson and his allies used their majority on the board to secure black residents needed services such as streetlights and paved roads. The city also agreed to integrate the three-man police force by hiring two black policemen. Thompson, like Evers, continued his civil rights activism while he served as alderman. In 1971, when reports of black residents beaten by the highway patrol reached Thompson's attention, he lobbied the FBI to investigate and then publicly criticized the federal agency when it refused to get involved. Later that year, Thompson won a seat on the state board of the American Civil Liberties Union (ACLU) and joined civil rights attorneys John Brittain and Frank Parker, who both sat on the board. The Mississippi ACLU worked on voter registration and a number of other race-related issues in the state. Thompson's civil rights background placed him outside the norm of the black elected officials in late 1960s Mississippi, since young civil rights activists did not win office as often as older, more conservative members of the traditional black elite.[51]

Since Bolton's whites rebuffed most of Thompson's gestures, he and his allies had decided by November 1972 to run an all-black slate for the board of aldermen and election commission. Reflecting his SNCC background of local organizing, Thompson and other black residents in Bolton organized a convention that selected candidates for office and put together a platform that pledged to establish improved municipal services. The all-black fourteen-member ticket, with Thompson running for mayor, attracted the support of prominent black Mississippians. Charles Evers and Robert Clark came into town to speak on behalf of the slate, and Earl Lucas, the mayor of Mound Bayou, also stumped for the candidates.

Like Robert Clark's 1967 election in Holmes County, Thompson and his supporters ran an intensive campaign based on personal contacts, contacting every black voter in the small town. The black campaigners went to the town's churches and met people on the street and canvassed neighborhoods, all in an effort to counter the problem of black vote-splitting, which had frequently defeated black slates elsewhere in the state. The lack of white incumbency also helped the black candidates. None of the white aldermanic candidates were incumbents except for the mayor, who ran for an alderman seat. The election passed without violence, but threatening phone calls made Thompson carry a gun for protection. The personal contacts and lobbying efforts by the candidates overcame any black inclinations to vote for whites, and the voters put all fourteen black candidates into office in May 1973. Thompson, at age twenty-five, became the mayor of Bolton.[52]

The new black administration moved to implement its reforms, especially after Bolton's small white community refused to cooperate with them. The board of aldermen first ordered the reassessment of all the property values and shifted the tax burden from poor black residents to white property owners. The reevaluation increased town tax revenues from $8,000 to $26,000 and the property tax base from $400,000 to $1.4 million. The board expanded the police force and other services, but the increased funds could not cover all the necessary services. Thompson procured garbage and fire trucks for the town but said that "[W]e begged . . . and I mean beg[ged]" for the vehicles. He also secured federal funds for other improvements, including a day care center, sewer construction, and new public housing. Thompson's ability to solicit federal grants became so renowned that some white mayors in the Delta approached him to ask for assistance with their own applications. He was not alone in this ability. Unita Blackwell, who became one of the first black women mayors in Mississippi after the town of Mayersville incorporated in 1976, helped secure federal funds for a water system, paved streets, and sewers in her first term.[53]

While Bolton and other small Delta towns experienced a rapid growth in black municipal officials during the 1970s, some southwestern river counties saw an increase in black political power on the county level. In 1971, black candidates in Claiborne, Jefferson, and Wilkinson Counties heeded Charles Evers's call to boycott the Democratic primary and run as independents. Even incumbent Democrats pursued independent candidacies. Most of these efforts came to naught, except for Jefferson County where Evers's machine held sway. African Americans won election or reelection to four constable or justice of the peace posts, but the most notable victory was the election of a second black supervisor.[54]

In neighboring Claiborne County, racial tensions still simmered over the Port Gibson boycott suit filed by the white merchants in 1969. Despite no black victories in the 1970 municipal elections, a stronger black presence existed in the county offices than in the neighboring counties. One of the officials, Geneva Collins, held the countywide office of chancery clerk. Her husband Alexander held a justice of the peace's post, and black men held a supervisor's seat and constable's post. Four black men also sat on the county election commission. In the 1971 elections, one of the black constables won election to become coroner and ranger. The victories were offset by the defeat of Alexander and Geneva Collins who both lost their reelection bids to white opponents.[55]

The losses seemed a reversal, but the defeats of the Collinses resulted from their personal attributes. Geneva Collins's haughty and superior attitude, apparently stemming from her privileged position as a light-skinned member of the town's black middle class, contributed to her defeat. Her husband, in turn, was haunted by rumors that he had undermined the Port Gibson boycott by secretly negotiating with the white merchants. Sheriff Dan McKay and Shelton Segrest, Geneva's white opponent, both made overtures to black voters. McKay also hired several black employees, which helped in his victory over Robert Butler, a former Deacon of Defense. Black candidates won the offices of circuit clerk and tax assessor and collector, two prominent victories that offset the defeat of the Collinses. The 1971 victories gave black officeholders a net gain, and they now held fourteen of the thirty-two Claiborne County offices.[56]

Black political power in the southwest still faced problems after the 1971 elections. Some black politicians created hardships for themselves. The political career of Wilkinson County Supervisor James Jolliff ended shortly after his 1971 reelection. Jolliff reached the peak of his influence in early 1972, when he and number of local civil rights activists won control of the regular Democratic Party at the county convention in February and sent an all-black slate of delegates to the state convention. The following month, a grand jury indicted Jolliff for embezzlement for misappropriating culvert and grader blades owned by the county. Jolliff pled guilty in October 1972 and was removed from office and given one year's probation and a five-year suspended sentence. Louis Gaulden, a black man and Jolliff's Democratic opponent in 1971, won the November election to replace him.[57]

White resistance to black officeholders, not corruption, still proved the more common problem facing the new black politicians. Evan Doss, the black tax assessor and collector for Claiborne County, experienced such obstacles when he took office following his 1971 election. Like Bennie Thompson and his allies in Bolton, Doss sought to reassess the regressive tax burden in the county. Lower-income, mostly black residents paid property taxes based on twenty-five percent of their value, while many higher-income white residents paid as low as ten percent. As Doss indicated, large landowners were paying the same amount in taxes as the farmer with a few acres. In early 1972, the majority-white board of supervisors cut his operating budget and ordered him to cease his assessment. When Governor Waller and the State Tax Commission refused to help Doss, he held a series of public meetings at the courthouse to rally public support for his actions and kept in regular contact with leaders in the black community. The budget cuts and insufficient staff led Doss to twice suspend car tag sales in the county during his first term.[58]

Trends of independent politics continued in southwest Mississippi. Despite the increasing shift of black office-seekers to the Democratic Party, some black incumbents ran and won as independents. In Claiborne County, twenty-one black candidates ran for office on a slate put together by the People's Association of Claiborne County, an organization of black residents. Much like Bennie Thompson and his allies in Bolton, the People's Association conducted an intensive effort to personally contact each black voter in the county several times before the election, and its members also held a drive to register voters under twenty-one. The effort yielded significant gains for the black candidates, with victories creating a three-to-two black majority. Black incumbents won reelection, and black candidates won the posts of county attorney and county superintendent of education. Dan McKay, who won reelection as sheriff, became the only white to hold countywide office. McKay defeated Bennie Knox, a black member of the county board of education. Geneva Collins, determined to win back her seat as chancery clerk, had run and refused to withdraw from the race against Stella Jennings, the black chancery clerk, and her white opponent despite worries she might split the black vote. The black voters of the county largely ignored Collins and reelected the incumbent. After the 1975 elections, blacks controlled a majority of Claiborne County offices.[59]

Whites could play the independent card, too. In Jefferson County, white candidates for countywide offices sometimes ran as independents and successfully solicited black votes because blacks had gained control of the Democratic Party machinery in the county. These circumstances led to the defeat in 1975 of black candidates for countywide offices in both Jefferson and Wilkinson Counties. More black victories came from the board of supervisor races, whose members were elected from districts instead of countywide. Two black Democrats won seats in the 1975 elections in Jefferson County to give blacks a four-to-one majority on the board.[60]

While the civil rights organizing of the local activists and the NAACP in southwestern Mississippi produced tangible political power by the mid-1970s, black politics followed a different path in Marshall County. To a greater degree than in the rest of the state, black political development in the northern county resembled the activism and organizing of the 1960s civil rights era. Protest marches and direct action, while never disappearing completely in other heavily black areas of the state, complemented the increase of elected black officials in Marshall County.

The United League of Marshall County, founded in 1970 by Alfred "Skip" Robinson and Henry Boyd Jr., embodied the continuance of black political protest and activism in the county. Robinson, a building contractor, and Boyd, a paralegal and former schoolteacher, had been active participants in civil rights activities in the county in the 1960s. Both men were Freedom Democrats who joined the Loyalists and also worked with North Mississippi Rural Legal Services (NMRLS), an Ox-ford-based legal aid group for the indigent. NMRLS had been formed by some University Of Mississippi law faculty in 1966 and received funding from the Office of Economic Opportunity (OEO). In the absence of a state-funded program for public defenders, the NMRLS provided cru-cial legal aid to the indigent, but its lawyers also filed civil-rights suits against the state and local governments. Irate School of Law officials then ended their association with the group, but it continued to receive funding from the OEO.[61]

Even before the formation of the United League, the two men drew the ire of local officials with their activism. Robinson and Boyd orga-nized boycotts and pickets of schools and local white merchants over school integration and other civil rights issues. The police chief of Holly Springs told a State Sovereignty Commission investigator in 1969 that he believed the two men were the source of all the "trouble" in the town.[62]

Robinson and Boyd formed the United League in 1970 to help with a food drive in Marshall County. They traveled to Boulder, Colorado, to solicit the aid of the Black Economic Union and its head, former football player Jim Brown. The city government of Boulder, along with Univer-sity of Colorado students and local residents, organized a drive to send food and clothing donations to Holly Springs. The public image of Holly Springs as "America's Biafra" prompted state and local officials, led by Governor John Bell Williams, to travel to Denver to protest to Colorado Governor John A. Love about the negative publicity. The fallout from the League's campaign did push State Senator George Yarborough, who owned the local newspaper *The South Reporter*, to ask for assistance in quickly bringing food stamps to the county. Yarborough feared that if the county did not act swiftly, Robinson and Boyd would receive credit for the program, and the county began a food stamp program the fol-lowing year.[63]

In 1971, the year following the food drive, the League shifted its at-tention towards voter registration. A number of black candidates ran for county offices that year. Unlike the southwestern counties, many of the black candidates ignored Charles Evers's call to skip the Democratic primary and run as independents. Black Democratic incumbents, like Coroner Osborne Bell, ran as Democrats and won reelection.[64]

The United League, unlike most of the black office seekers in the county, heeded Evers's advice and bypassed the primary to run several of its own candidates as independents in the November election. Robinson ran for sheriff, while George Caldwell, a League member and professor at Rust College, ran for a justice of the peace post. Henry Boyd ran for chancery clerk and made no effort to downplay his civil rights activities. He declared that he "did not mind being called an agitator; yet no one can truthfully call me an outside agitator." He called himself an "inside agitator" and said, "[E]very housewife knows what an agitator on a washing machine is. It is the gadget that beat[s] out the filth, the dirt and grime." He pledged to fight discrimination and ran on a platform of expanded social services and antipoverty programs.[65]

Although Skip Robinson claimed a League membership of 4,000, none of the black independent candidates won in November. The League's activism apparently could not overcome the advantage of having a Democratic Party affiliation. The still-young League also did not have the organization or political base of the Holmes County FDP or other more successful independent parties. The League's members did not do better during the next round of elections in 1973 when several ran as candidates in the municipal elections in Holly Springs.[66]

In July 1974, the League launched a campaign in the Marshall County town of Byhalia after white policemen shot and killed two black men. The League and a number of black Byhalia residents responded with a combination of economic and political protest. They demanded better customer service from local stores, employment of blacks at the post office, and representation on the city council. The League and local residents immediately launched a boycott of white Byhalia merchants to pressure the town government. George Yarborough, through his editorials in the *South Reporter*, condemned the boycott and warned the participants of the anti-boycott ruling from the Mississippi courts in the Port Gibson case. Yet the courts gave little relief to the businessmen, and the Fifth Circuit Court of Appeals sided with the boycotters.[67]

Blacks in Marshall County made further gains at the ballot box as the boycott stretched into the fall. When a vacancy opened in the district four county supervisor's seat, a black woman named Bernice Totten filed to run in the special election. The 53-year old grandmother and former MFDP member and Head Start worker enjoyed the endorsement of the United League. Henry Boyd called her "strictly a United League member" who enjoyed the organization's full support. Totten won the October election and became the first black supervisor in Marshall County's modern history.[68]

In October of 1974 the United League's leaders, perhaps emboldened by Totten's victory, widened the boycott to include Holly Springs. The League demanded a fifty-fifty racial split in the town's police force and other non-elected positions, more blacks in management positions, and the creation of a biracial commission. The boycott extended to the *South Reporter*, which had long been hostile to the League. The atmosphere in the county remained tense throughout 1974 and 1975. The League apparently employed the same tactics of intimidation that Charles Evers and his associates used in Port Gibson. One League member was arrested for beating a man who broke the boycott in Byhalia, and county law enforcement reported several shootings. Reports of white intimidation also surfaced, and both Robinson and Boyd claimed attempts were made on their lives during the boycott.[69]

By February 1975, the boycotters and the white business and political community reached a compromise. The mayor of Byhalia, at a meeting of over 200 people, announced the creation of a biracial committee that in turn appointed and established a series of committees to address racial and economic issues. The city government also integrated the police and fire departments.[70]

The boycott was barely resolved when the county prepared for the statewide elections in 1975. In an effort to halt the Democratic primary, the United League filed a lawsuit that claimed that county officials added the names of non-resident citizens to the voting rolls to dilute black votes. The suit charged that the four white supervisors and the county election officials and Circuit Clerk Edwin Callicutt "willfully, maliciously, and purposefully" padded the registration books. Callicutt called the charges "vicious lies." Supervisor Bernice Totten took the accommodationist path of Henry and Evers and asked Judge Orma Smith to add her name to the lawsuit as a defendant with her fellow white county officials. Smith dismissed the lawsuit before the primary election.[71]

The United League fielded only a couple of members in the Democratic primary. Its leaders opted to run as independents again despite the failure of this tactic in 1971. All the black incumbents won reelection in the Democratic primary, but the most contentious race was between two white opponents. Circuit Clerk Edwin Callicutt tried to use the United League to slander Lucy Carpenter, his opponent. He charged that she had the backing of the League, which was true since the League endorsed the more favorable white candidate in races where no black candidate ran.[72]

While the League had little luck electing its own members to office, it had an influence on the overall elections in the county. Carpenter beat Callicutt by 291 votes. She won in heavily black precincts like North Holly Springs, Marianna, and Chulahoma by significant margins over the incumbent. Carpenter went on to face a white independent opponent, Jack Clements, that November. He attacked Carpenter for her League endorsement and said that the League, which he called "the biggest political machine in the history of Marshall County," had dedicated three thousand votes to her. Carpenter easily defeated Clements, who did not win any significant number of white or black votes by attacking the League.[73]

The League could influence the outcome of the elections but still could not command enough votes to become a viable independent party. Skip Robinson and Henry Boyd ran respectively for sheriff and state representative and lost. The House race became particularly contested when Boyd challenged the victory of his opponent, Ralph Doxey, the twenty-five-year-old grandson of Wall Doxey, a former U.S. representative from Holly Springs who briefly served as U.S. Senator in the 1940s. Boyd charged voting irregularities, including missing or tampered votes in the North Holly Springs and Waterford boxes. He and the United League, with the help of North Mississippi Rural Legal Services, pressed a formal challenge to the seating of Doxey.[74]

In Jackson, the state House of Representatives heard the challenge and conditionally seated Doxey while it investigated the charges. The House special panel, which included recently elected black legislator Fred Banks of Jackson, decided that the challenged votes would not significantly change the outcome of the election. Banks pointed out that 815 votes were questionable, but Doxey won by 2,200 votes and therefore could be seated. Boyd charged election fraud, but the wide margin of his defeat indicated that he did not have a wide following among black voters. His lack of popularity may have been due in part to his financial troubles, which included problems with a black credit union. Boyd owed money to several local businesses and lending institutions, which led to garnishment of his wages.[75]

By 1975, the United League of Marshall County had established itself as a civil rights group that won clear victories through the use of direct action and economic boycotts. Its actions helped secure a food stamp program for the county and brought change to Byhalia in 1974. Its leaders' attempt to forge an independent political route met with less success, although they did influence the outcome of county elections. During the second half of the 1970s, the United League would reach beyond Marshall County and sponsor civil rights activism in other areas of the state.

Despite the highly publicized failure of Charles Evers in the 1971 gubernatorial race, black political power in Mississippi had continued to make gains on the county and municipal level. By 1975, black political power had become clearly concentrated in several areas throughout the state. In the Delta, Robert Clark continued to represent Holmes County and served as the de facto representative for all of black Mississippi. As the voters in small, majority-black towns in Bolivar and Coahoma Counties elected black mayors and boards of aldermen, the northwestern Delta began to develop as a center of municipal black officeholding. Southwest Mississippi used its solid base of voter registration and elected black officials from the 1960s to become the other major region of black political power. Black men and women in the river counties won control of boards of supervisors and countywide offices throughout the decade. Marshall County, where blacks had won victories in the 1967 state elections, also saw a growth in black representation and a continuance of civil rights protest in the 1970s.

The aforementioned areas, while not the only places of black officeholding, did have the greatest yields for black candidates. Black officeholders were scattered throughout the state by 1975, from Lowndes and Noxubee counties on the Alabama state line to Madison County north of Jackson to some county and municipal officials in Washington, Issaquena, and other Delta counties.[76] The centers of black political power remained the areas that had first experienced success in the elections of the 1960s. Developments on the state level in the 1970s, most notably the end of the schism in the state Democratic Party, also had a profound impact on the direction of black politics. The rise of black politicians in counties across the state, either as independents or members of the Democratic Party, would enter a new era after 1975 as the rival Regular and Loyalist factions of the state party came together with the administration of Governor Cliff Finch.

Fused but Not Healed

AFTER FEARING MISCEGENATION for much of their history, white Mississippi Democrats entered into their own interracial marriage in 1976. The political division between the integrated Loyalists and the virtually all-white Regulars continued to pose a problem for the state party. The Loyalists enjoyed national party recognition but very limited state power, with the reverse for the Regulars. The election of Gov. Cliff Finch in 1975 led to a union of the factions. Finch's base among rural whites and African Americans and his open endorsement by black leaders such as Charles Evers and Aaron Henry helped create the first significant biracial political coalition in the state since Reconstruction. The continued fighting between white and black Democrats in the newly unified party demonstrated the uneasiness of fusion even as the Democrats scored some impressive electoral and legislative victories. Before and after the fusion of the Democrats, the Mississippi Republican Party tried to exploit the racial fissures of the vulnerable Democrats by wooing black voters in the 1970s. The GOP reached out to disaffected voters of both races, although they had more success with conservative whites.

The rift between the Regular and Loyalist Democrats from the 1968 Democratic convention continued during and after the 1971 statewide elections. Governor William Waller showed his limits as a racial moderate when he rejected an invitation from Aaron Henry to meet and send a united delegation to the 1972 Democratic National Convention. Waller made gestures of reconciliation towards the Loyalists as the convention approached, mostly because he realized that the national party

FIGURE 6. Charles Evers and Gov. Cliff Finch (*center*). Finch, a Batesville lawyer, won election in 1975 and negotiated a fusion of the state's squabbling Loyalist and Regular Democrats into a biracial state party. At first a firm supporter of Finch, Evers broke with him by 1978 and launched an independent bid to succeed longtime U.S. senator James Eastland, an action which underscored the fragility of party fusion. William F. "Bill" Minor Papers, 80–180, Special Collections Department, Mitchell Memorial Library, Mississippi State University.

would not seat the Regulars without Loyalist participation. Many white Regulars still opposed a compromise with the Loyalists. Leon Bramlett, the Regulars' state chairman, echoed the sentiments of many white Democrats when he said he didn't "think any of those men would be interested in a union with the Loyalist group." Bramlett spoke about the state party's executive committee, but many lower-level party officials and delegates had the same views.[1]

With the impasse unresolved, the two factions met and chose presidential delegates separately for the 1972 convention. The national party's credentials committee rejected the Regular delegation because they had ignored party rules for delegate selection. After the 1968 convention, the national Democratic Party had adopted rules for state parties that required "affirmative steps to encourage minority group participation . . . in reasonable relationship to the group's presence in the population of the state." State Democratic parties had to choose at least three-fourths of the delegation in the congressional districts or at lower levels.

The Regulars did not follow this rule, and the credentials committee said that their appointment of two blacks and two women to their twelve-person delegation did not constitute "reasonable representation" of women and minorities. The Regulars, at Waller's urging, filed an unsuccessful lawsuit to block the Loyalists' seating, but the Loyalists, who had followed party guidelines, eventually won the seats.[2]

The Loyalist victory in 1972 further reinforced the 1968 victory of moderates like Aaron Henry over the remnants of the MFDP. The MFDP had two members on the Loyalist delegation, but Fannie Lou Hamer lost a race to fill the post of national committeewoman, which went to Pat Derian, a white associate and future spouse of Hodding Carter III. The moderate Loyalists dominated with Aaron Henry chairing the slate and Charles Evers as national committeeman. Old MFDP members like Hamer expressed disgust with the Loyalists but stayed with them nonetheless. While efforts at black independent politics would continue in Mississippi, the old Freedom Democrats' decision to stay with the Loyalists showed that most black politicians saw the Democratic Party as the most viable path to power.[3]

The split between the Loyalists and Regulars continued between the 1972 convention and the 1975 state elections. Waller made a few attempts at interracialism that distinguished him from his predecessors. He appointed the first black Mississippians to state boards and agencies and his staff, but African Americans still comprised less than six percent of state employees by the end of his term. He also established a minority advisory council and a state office to provide loans to black businesses. In a move to commemorate the fading activism of the civil rights era, the governor proclaimed Medgar Evers Day on the tenth anniversary of Evers's murder, yet some saw the decree as an attempt to deflect criticism for approving a work release for one of the murderers of Hattiesburg civil rights leader Vernon Dahmer. Waller also alienated black Mississippians by vetoing hospital funding bills for Quitman and Hinds Counties and Mound Bayou. A furious Aaron Henry told Waller that his actions harkened back to the abandonment of the freedmen under the Compromise of 1877 and said that blacks and poor whites "must finally, as hard as we have tried not to, accept you as our active enemy."[4]

Another group became increasingly visible on the state political scene in the period between the elections. The Mississippi Republican Party, although not yet victorious in any statewide elections, continued to run candidates and force incumbent Democrats to defend their seats in the general election. The ideological divisions in the party meant it still reacted ambivalently to the black electorate and alternated between attempting to win black voters, as Rubel Phillips had tried in 1967, and alienating them by opposing black interests. Clarke Reed, a Greenville businessman and farmer who had succeeded Wirt Yerger as party chairman in 1966, took a number of actions that upset black Mississippians and led to clashes between him and Fayette mayor Charles Evers. The two politicians sparred when Evers charged that the state GOP practiced racial discrimination when it recommended enumerators for the 1970 census, which Reed vigorously denied, although he did admit that some black-majority counties did not have any black enumerators at all.[5]

Black suspicions of the GOP did not end with the census. In 1971, Reed aided HEW's closure of a Head Start agency in Sunflower County that Fannie Lou Hamer had helped organize. Reed also used his influence with the Nixon administration to try to block approval of a HEW grant for a health program for Claiborne and Jefferson Counties, arguing that approval of the grant for the mostly black counties amounted to special consideration for Fayette, the only town in the state with an all-black government. "Why should whites be discriminated against?" he told the Washington Post. HEW overrode Reed's objections and approved the $131,000 grant.[6]

Despite Reed's actions, he fell firmly into the pragmatist wing of the party and lacked a strong conservative identity. He briefly belonged to the far-right John Birch Society in the late 1950s but later downplayed that incident as a youthful indiscretion and insisted that he had quit after one meeting. In 1968, he helped swing the presidential nomination to Richard Nixon at the Miami Beach national convention against the wishes of delegates such as Prentiss Walker who wanted to nominate California Governor Ronald Reagan. Reed swayed the right wing of the Mississippi GOP to Nixon by assuring them that Nixon would move slowly on school desegregation. The federal government denied funds to districts that had token integration under freedom-of-choice plans, and the state Republican Party backed the local districts.[7]

Reed's position as the chair of the Southern Association of Republican State Chairmen increased his political influence and thus his pragmatism. He had a warm relationship with Harry Dent, President Nixon's southern political strategist, and advised him on ways to increase GOP gains in the South. Reed had to deal with conservatives angry over school desegregation as well as attract black voters to craft a conservative but not racist image of the party. He told Dent to make sure that HEW's civil rights division did not answer any queries from white Mississippians "bitching" about school desegregation. "The letterhead alone makes the recipients see red and starts them screaming," he warned. Dent in turn advised Reed on black outreach and set up meetings with Reed and black Republicans.[8]

If the pragmatic Reed valued victory over ideological purity, that sentiment was not shared by Jackson-resident William "Billy" Mounger, the party's finance chairman. Mounger, an ideological conservative who held liberal Republicanism in contempt, amassed a fortune as an oil and gas developer. He represented the pro-business and antiregulatory outlook of the conservative ideologues. An avid admirer of Barry Goldwater, Mounger opposed "New Deal giveaways" and business regulation, although Mounger himself took advantage of benefits from the GI Bill of Rights. He called himself a "small-government Republican" and began raising money for the state party in the early 1960s.[9]

As a social conservative and devout Presbyterian, Mounger also spoke disparagingly of politically and theologically liberal Christian denominations. On racial matters, he cloaked his statements in the ostensibly nonracial rhetoric of states' rights. He was not a Ross Barnett demagogue or even a Wirt Yerger when it came to statements on race. Mounger even turned up in the State Sovereignty Commission files for lending his name to a statement opposing the violence accompanying the desegregation of the University of Mississippi in 1962. He also accepted the need for some integration when he named three black members to the Hinds County Republican Party Executive Committee. However, he defended states' rights despite the negative associations the phrase conjured, even to the point of insisting that the word "sovereign" be kept in the 1968 state party platform. He declared that northern pro–civil-rights Democrats "lacked any real understanding of the social pressures weighing down the southern states." He opposed civil rights enforcement, especially what he called the "Gestapo-like" ruling by the IRS denying tax-exempt status to racially exclusive private schools.[10]

GOP leaders showed their skittishness about interracialism by refusing to participate in the major state races in 1971. When Meridian businessman Gil Carmichael told GOP officials that he planned to run for lieutenant governor, they talked him out of the race for fear that white Mississippians would associate his candidacy and the Republican Party with Charles Evers's independent gubernatorial campaign. No GOP candidate for governor ran either, preventing a split in the white vote that might have elected Evers.[11]

Gil Carmichael emerged as the Republican standard-bearer of the 1970s and a leader of the progressive wing of the party. A wealthy Volkswagen dealer from Meridian, he described himself as a "progressive conservative" who championed economic development. In 1972, he challenged Senator Jim Eastland, but he had to overcome an unusual primary opponent first. James Meredith, the first African American to graduate from the University of Mississippi, also ran as a Republican, which led the state GOP to hastily back Carmichael. Carmichael easily won the nomination in a statewide primary that drew fewer than 24,000 votes. In the general election Carmichael assailed Eastland and the Democratic organization for the state's poverty and underdevelopment. Carmichael, who also served on the advisory committee to the U.S. Commission on Civil Rights, worked to reach two very different groups of voters. His campaign staffers contacted prominent black leaders and businessmen to try to garner black voters while also soliciting the aid of white supporters of segregationist politicians such as George Wallace. Carmichael had little help from the state GOP, which wanted him to run just to avoid the specter of a black maverick like Meredith winning the Republican nomination. The Meridian businessman did not even enjoy national support from the Nixon White House, which publicly snubbed him by excluding him from a Jackson rally headlined by Vice President Spiro Agnew.[12]

One of the chief Republican backers of the progressive Carmichael was, ironically, Billy Mounger. The party finance chairman did not like Carmichael and complained about his desire for publicity and "ingratitude." Unlike Wirt Yerger, who was suspicious of Carmichael's moderation, Mounger put more faith at this time in the Republican candidate and raised funds for him. Mounger believed that Nixon had treated Carmichael poorly at the Agnew rally and felt bound by party loyalty to his fellow Mississippian.[13]

Carmichael's campaign worried Eastland enough to force the aging Sunflower County planter to actively campaign. Eastland even reached out to black voters to counter Carmichael's efforts. Carmichael's visits to black college campuses in Mississippi alarmed Eastland enough to make him dispatch a representative to the campuses to speak for him. The arch-segregationist senator even ran ads in the state's black newspaper,

FIGURE 7. Gil Carmichael campaigning for governor. A Volkswagen dealer from Meridian, Carmichael unsuccessfully ran for governor as a Republican in 1975 and 1979. A leader of the state GOP's progressive wing, Carmichael tried and failed to win office by soliciting black voters, losing both his election bids and his broader vision of creating a biracial GOP. William F. "Bill" Minor Papers, 80–75, Special Collections Department, Mitchell Memorial Library, Mississippi State University.

FIGURE 8. Mississippi Republican Party leaders meet with Ronald and Nancy Reagan. From left to right, Clarke Reed, state party chairman; Billy Mounger, party finance chairman; Nancy Reagan; Ronald Reagan; Thad Cochran; and Gil Carmichael. Carmichael's progressive agenda for the Mississippi GOP was vigorously opposed by Mounger, the leader of the party's conservatives. In the middle, pragmatists like Reed and Cochran pursued strategies that sought electoral success at the occasional sacrifice of conservative doctrine, a compromise that Mounger was unwilling to concede. Mississippi Republican Party Papers, 353–188, Special Collections Department, Mitchell Memorial Library, Mississippi State University.

the *Jackson Advocate*. Eastland later complained that "that son of a bitch cost my friends a half million dollars" in the last month of the election.[14]

In November, Eastland won by a majority of 58.1 percent. Carmichael won only the majority-black counties of Claiborne and Kemper out of his total win of eleven counties. Despite increased black voter registration since the 1960s and the white supremacist history of James Eastland, Carmichael could not siphon significant numbers of black Loyalist Democrats into the Republican camp. The base of Carmichael's support still came from majority-white areas around his home county of Lauderdale.[15]

Other Republicans did have some success in winning black votes. Two Republicans, Thad Cochran and Trent Lott, ran for congressional seats in 1972. Lott, a Pascagoula lawyer who ran in the fifth district, did not make any significant bid for black votes. Unlike the other four districts, his district did not have a single county with a black majority. Cochran, a Jackson attorney who ran in the fourth district in southwestern Mississippi, took a different approach. Mounger said Cochran ran an "almost issueless" campaign, but the candidate actively campaigned for black votes, a strategy no doubt influenced by the forty-three-percent black population of the district and the black-majority counties of Claiborne, Jefferson, and Wilkinson. The district also had sizable black populations in Hinds, Copiah, and Amite Counties. Mounger had no quarrel with this strategy and raised the majority of Cochran's campaign funds. He said that Cochran "did not always do what we campaign officers suggested, but I felt he always listened to us," a habit he said Carmichael did not emulate.[16]

Cochran's strategy included hiring a black aide, which won some black votes, but the independent candidacy of Eddie L. McBride, a twenty-nine-year-old black minister, aided the Republican lawyer far more. McBride did not win a single county but received over 11,000 votes, while Cochran defeated white Democrat Ellis Bodron by a fewer than 6,000 vote plurality. A black spoiler clearly had more of an effect on the Republican victory than efforts to attract blacks to the GOP. Upper- and middle-class white suburbanites in Jackson, not African Americans, formed the base of Cochran's support in 1972 and in future elections. The "upwardly mobile new reactionaries," as some observers called them, gave Cochran Hinds County by a fifty-seven-percent majority. Bodron, however, was no moderate and, like most white Mississippi Democrats in this era, a former segregationist, so Cochran had an appeal to moderate whites as well in 1972. Cochran did have some pull with a minority of black voters. In his successful 1974 reelection, he polled large majorities in Amite and Copiah Counties, a near-majority in Wilkinson County and forty-two percent of the vote in Claiborne and Jefferson Counties.[17]

Another factor cannot be discounted in Cochran's successful 1972 campaign. Like most Republicans in Mississippi, he had once been a Democrat, but Cochran entered the 1972 race as a political neophyte. Mississippi had been under the Voting Rights Act for seven years, so the state's incumbent politicians were still adjusting to black voting.

FIGURE 9. Thad Cochran with unidentified women. Cochran, a Jackson attorney, first won election in 1972 to the U.S. House and then won the U.S. Senate in 1978. A longtime pragmatist on racial matters, Cochran became one of the few state Republicans to have some success with black outreach, but he still owed his most significant electoral victories to black spoilers who weakened his white Democratic opponents, such as Charles Evers's independent run in 1978. Mississippi Republican Party Papers, 353–152, Special Collections Department, Mitchell Memorial Library, Mississippi State University.

The transition placed veteran Democratic politicians such as U.S. Representatives Jamie Whitten and Sonny Montgomery in the awkward position of soliciting black votes despite their segregationist histories. Unlike them, a newcomer like Cochran was a political *tabula rasa*. As former MFDP member Leslie Burl McLemore pointed out, black people regarded it as "an act of decency" when a white politician like Cochran in the early 1970s spoke at a black forum. Cochran did just that when he accepted McLemore's invitation to come and speak at Jackson State College during his campaign. Cochran's actions thus "endeared" him to black people, for such an action "bestowed a certain level of humanity on black people" that other white politicians did not do at the time. Cochran and David Bowen, a Democratic congressman from the second district also first elected in 1972, benefited from the time and place of their successful bids. Bowen, like Cochran, represented a district with a large black plurality, and both congressmen became the first in Mississippi to hire black staffers. In 1972, such actions resonated with black Mississippians when memories of Freedom Summer and Medgar Evers were less than a decade old and reports of racial discrimination at the polls still plagued the state.[18]

Some black politicians recognized the realities of Republican power on the national level and tried to maintain friendly ties. Charles Evers met publicly with Nixon when the president visited Meridian in 1973. Evers utilized his contacts with the national GOP during President Gerald Ford's administration to protest racial and gender discrimination at the Army Corps of Engineers Waterways Experiment Station in Vicksburg.[19] Evers's actions, in keeping with his past history, seemed geared more for his own political influence than an attempt to make the GOP in Mississippi a biracial party since he stayed close to the Loyalist Democrats and endorsed Cliff Finch for governor.

The 1975 governor's election led to the healing of the divided Democratic Party before the GOP made significant gains in Mississippi. In a move supported by both Regulars and Loyalists as a way to bridge divisions, the legislature passed a bill in January that allowed voters to select seventy-five percent of the delegates for the national convention during the June 1976 congressional primaries.[20]

In the Democratic gubernatorial primary that August, Cliff Finch, a Batesville trial lawyer who had supported Ross Barnett in the early 1960s, defeated Lieutenant Governor William Winter. Finch had long shed his segregationist past and embraced a populist-style campaign for governor. Despite his $150,000 annual salary, he carried around a lunch pail with bologna sandwiches and reached out to the "forgotten people of the state" by working at a variety of blue-collar jobs during the campaign. Observers commented that the populist campaigning of Finch resembled that of Alabama Governor George Wallace, but, unlike Wallace, Finch openly sought black votes. Finch won the endorsement of Charles Evers and Aaron Henry, and at the same time received behind-the-scenes support from Klansmen and other segregationists. Henry and most black Democrats had supported Winter in the primary. Finch also hired Warner Buxton, the student body president at Jackson State College during the 1970 shootings, to serve on his staff.[21]

Finch likely campaigned for black support because his opponents did the same. Henry Jay Kirksey, a sixty-year old black cartographer and former MFDP member, opposed Finch with an independent campaign that drew little support from the state's black political leaders. Kirksey, a plaintiff in a suit challenging the state's legislative reapportionment system, accused his opponents of trying to keep him off the ballot. Local black leaders throughout the state actively campaigned against him and neutralized any hopes that he could command the attention Charles Evers did in 1971.[22]

Finch's more serious threat in the campaign for black votes came from his Republican opponent, Gil Carmichael. Carmichael, as he did against Eastland in 1972, ran as a moderate Republican who championed economic development and an end to the cheap export of the state's natural resources. Harry Dent, as part of his strategy for building a viable southern GOP, encouraged Carmichael to run for governor, citing the gubernatorial victory of Republican Jim Edwards in South Carolina in 1974. Carmichael also backed a number of progressive issues, including a new constitution, ratification of the Equal Rights Amendment (ERA), compulsory school attendance, reduced punishment for marijuana possession, and handgun licensing. The last issue, which he proposed in the wake of the two attempts to assassinate President Gerald Ford, cost him some support with white voters and alienated more conservative Republicans like state chairman Clarke Reed. Carmichael also said some party conservatives opposed his support for the ERA. Carmichael, whose mother had to work alone to support him after his father died, cited the lower pay she received compared to men as the reason he supported the ERA. His issues-oriented campaign, which he put forth in both personal campaigning and television ads produced by campaign strategist Walter De Vries, contrasted with the vague economic proposals and rhetoric of Finch. Finch ignored Carmichael and refused to hold press conferences, instead issuing muddled statements describing himself as a "progressive, but conservative."[23]

Race remained a significant issue in the election but not in the same manner as past gubernatorial races. With the absence of race-baiting or a major black gubernatorial candidate, both men freely campaigned for the black vote and sought to create black-white coalitions to help them into office. Carmichael countered Finch's black endorsements by employing state representative Robert Clark on his strategy committee. Carmichael had also cultivated goodwill with black residents in Meridian when he hired black salesmen at his car dealership in 1968. He claimed as inspiration Rubel Phillips and his 1967 television ads aimed at black voters. To Carmichael, black political power went hand-in-hand with issues of economics and class, which is why he stressed job creation for the state's impoverished people. To him, the GOP was "the party of emancipation, the party of homeownership, the party of individual responsibility . . . the natural party for the black people to be involved in."[24]

Carmichael's campaign, which marked the peak of the GOP progressives, exacerbated the Republican intraparty schisms and eventually carried over into the national convention the following year. The pragmatists reluctantly supported Carmichael or at least did not oppose him. Thad Cochran stayed neutral, while Clarke Reed swallowed his disdain for Carmichael's positions and said that "for some reason I don't understand, it [the campaign] seems to be working."[25] Some conservative ideologues finally began to break with Carmichael, either publicly or privately. Billy Mounger opposed the proposal for a new state constitution and pressed Carmichael to hire Reagan associate Lyn Nofziger to run his campaign, but he resisted both efforts.[26]

Mounger declined Carmichael's offer to be his campaign finance chairman, but he did raise money for the campaign, including a personal loan of five thousand dollars. He later recalled that he became "progressively disillusioned" with Carmichael's liberal platform, but he did not publicly voice his concerns. When Carmichael, at DeVries's urging, endorsed handgun registration, Mounger quit the campaign. Still convinced that Carmichael was going to win, Mounger wrote a letter on election night renouncing any links to the candidate. Specifically, he cited Carmichael's support of the ERA, handgun registration, and a new constitution as evidence of his "ineptitude" and "Teddy Kennedy appeal to liberals."[27]

Mounger did not voice an opinion on Carmichael's black outreach, instead opting to frame his critiques in ideological terms. Support of the old Constitution of 1890, which had been created specifically to disfranchise black voters, had racial undertones, however. Voting irregularities and intimidation continued to hamstring black voters in 1975, even though the Voting Rights Act had been in existence for ten years. The Justice Department deployed examiners in December 1974 to investigate reports of harassment and other irregularities in thirty-eight counties, more than double the number in Louisiana and Alabama combined.

For the November 1975 election, nineteen counties in the state received federal observers.[28]

Carmichael, on the other hand, recognized the importance of making specific appeals to black voters. He opened a campaign office in Fayette, the stronghold of Finch supporter Charles Evers. An admiring Evers told Carmichael that "he had a lot of nerve coming here" but "there's no hard feelings." Carmichael also highlighted his business record and pointed out that he hired the first black and female salespeople in Mississippi at his Volkswagen dealership. His wife also campaigned for him before black audiences in places such as Alcorn State, which she visited with one of her husband's black staff members. Carmichael himself visited the all-black town of Mound Bayou, a first for any gubernatorial candidate in Mississippi.[29]

State Rep. Robert Clark became one of Carmichael's most prominent supporters and the front man for his outreach to black Mississippians. Clark saw himself not as joining the GOP but as trying to broaden political and economic opportunities for black people. He said that Carmichael's election would "force the [Democratic] party to . . . include all the people." He cited Carmichael's record in Meridian and his pledge to hire blacks and the poor in state agencies. Clark used strong racial imagery, telling black voters that they "can't afford to be a slave to a party." Some black organizations also took Carmichael's efforts seriously. Black cooperatives, which were institutions that promoted community development in the poor areas of the state, were lured to Carmichael by the potential of state funds under his administration.[30]

With the exception of Clark, Carmichael's efforts did not sway most prominent black political and civil rights figures in Mississippi. Aaron Henry publicly endorsed Finch in an open letter to the press but did not even mention Carmichael by name. Henry criticized "the unredeemable posture of the total Republican Party . . . an institution that not only has been against, and vetoed, program after program that would benefit the poor of our state and nation; but an institution that has fostered programs that now has all America teetering on the brink of economic, social, and moral decline." Henry apparently did not consider Carmichael's maverick reputation as sincere or strong enough to break the influence the national GOP would have in the state, and he also dismissed the possible gains in federal funds that the state might get from the Ford administration if the state elected its first Republican governor in the twentieth century.[31]

Henry's disdain for the GOP did not translate into enthusiasm for Finch. He flatly stated that Finch was not his first choice, but that Finch needed black help "to withstand the forces that still exist . . . that would advise him to return to a policy of racism." Charles Evers, while declaring that he admired Carmichael and his platform, said that a vote for a Republican candidate was "a vote of suicide." He echoed Henry's concerns about the national GOP's hostility to social welfare spending and argued that cuts would occur under a Republican administration. The unpredictable Evers refused to endorse all the Democratic statewide candidates. In the lieutenant governor's race he did not support Bill Patrick, the Republican mayor of Laurel, or his Democratic opponent Evelyn Gandy, the state commissioner of insurance. Evers declared, "I'm not for Bill Patrick; I'm just against Evelyn Gandy," and charged that the protégé of racial demagogue Theodore G. Bilbo had a history of racial discrimination in the various state agencies she had headed in the past.[32]

Although most of the state GOP muted their criticism during the 1975 race, some Republican ideologues did not. Conservatives like Mounger avoided racial issues, and Clarke Reed said that race was "not even a Mickey Mouse issue anymore" in Mississippi. Some ideological conservatives linked their critiques of Carmichael's liberalism to race. Prentiss Walker, the archconservative former congressman from the fourth district, ran a column in the *Clarion-Ledger* blasting Carmichael as "a real discredit to all the true Republican principles." Walker referred to Carmichael's call for handgun registration, but he also attacked the Meridian businessman's proposal for a new state constitution. Walker said that Carmichael would rewrite the constitution "under the direction of Senators [Edward] Brooke and [Jacob] Javits," two liberal northern Republicans. He called Javits "a long time communist sympathizer" and Brooke, the only black U.S. senator, "the man who stood on the steps of our nation's capitol and condoned the looting and burning." The last statement referred to Brooke's role on the Kerner Commission, which studied the riots of the 1960s.[33]

Walker made the racial nature of his attack more explicit when he invoked memories of the Lost Cause to criticize Carmichael. He said that Carmichael's criticism of "the last 100 years of Democratic success in Mississippi . . . coincides exactly with the end of Radical Republican control of our state under Reconstruction. This control was gained by the Radical Republicans only by control of the ballot box by Federal troops at the point of the bayonet." Carmichael and his associates, Walker charged, have "reestablished the old school of Radical Republicanism" in Mississippi.[34]

Mississippi Republicans routinely launched attacked on their liberal northern counterparts. When Jacob Javits toured the Mississippi Delta with Robert Kennedy in 1967 to examine the region's poverty, Clarke Reed said that Javits had joined "the destructive revolutionary forces in our nation." Nor was the bugbear of their Radical Reconstruction ancestors off-limits to Mississippi Republicans. Rubel Phillips expropriated the rhetoric of Ross Barnett in 1963 when he accused the Democratic Party of mimicking the Radical program of the 1870s.[35] Yet the vitriol of Walker's attack harkened back to 1960s Mississippi political discourse and was also unique in that it was a public attack by one Mississippi Republican on another. Walker's conjuring the ghost of Radical Republicanism against a colleague openly appealing to black voters indicated that some of the ideological conservatives did not want even the appearance of integration in 1975.

A few days after Walker's advertisement, the *Clarion-Ledger* ran another anti-Carmichael broadside, this one paid for by a Finch supporter. The ad made no specific reference to race but had a very clear pro-segregationist slant in its attack on "Carmichael the cunning." It blasted the national Republican Party and said that Mississippi Democrats "have, since 1948, been in the leadership of all the states in voting independently and for their own rights . . . we voted Strom Thurmond and Fielding Wright, for Eisenhower, Goldwater, and Nixon. We voted unpledged and for George Wallace." The ad painted Carmichael as the thrall of liberal New York Republicans and said that "Republicanism, like the serpent in the Garden of Eden, comes to us in these latter days full of oily words and soothing assurances" and called on voters to "[C]rush the serpent!" Democrats as well as Republicans could invoke Republican racial moderation in an effort to win segregationist votes.[36]

Carmichael ran a strong race but could not win enough of the black vote from Finch to go to the governor's mansion. Black voters ignored Kirksey's campaign and only delivered a few percentage points of the total vote to him. Statewide, Finch won 52.2 percent to Carmichael's 45.1 percent. Finch's populist appeal, along with the traditional identification of black voters to the Democratic Party, gave him eighty percent of the black vote, as opposed to the fifty percent Waller received in 1971. Most of Carmichael's strength came from his home area of east-central

Mississippi and more urbanized areas such as the Gulf Coast and Hinds County. Finch won sixty-six of eighty-two counties, including most of the predominately black counties, while Carmichael only won two black-majority counties. Bill Patrick also lost in a landslide against Evelyn Gandy. According to Carmichael's own estimates, he got sixty percent of the white vote and at best twenty percent of the black vote. He remained optimistic about his campaign and called it "a new approach to politics here in this state" and told President Gerald Ford that he hoped the national Republican leadership would follow his example. Black voters, though, were too firmly entrenched in the state Democratic Party to go to the GOP in 1975. Carmichael made sincere appeals for the black vote, but since the state Republicans had done little substantive groundwork before Carmichael they could not make many inroads. Leslie Burl McLemore, who supported Carmichael, said that the Republicans had needed to "work on people over time" if they wanted a victory in 1975.[37]

Finch recognized the critical role black voters played in his campaign and moved to finally fuse the Loyalist and Regular wings of the Democratic Party. The two sides worked out a compromise after the election but before the 1976 presidential primaries began. Aaron Henry, leader of the Loyalists, and Tom Riddell, leader of the Regulars, became the co-chairs of the new Democratic state party organization. Both factions agreed to a pattern similar to the rules used by the national Democratic Party in 1972. The compromise increased the state executive committee from thirty-five to one hundred members and rotated all party offices among members of different races and genders. The Regulars reentered the national party, and the Loyalists won greater access to state and county politics since the county Democratic executive committees now opened up to black participation. Yet increased access did mean a loss of independence as black Democrats had to surrender the dominant position they had in the Loyalist organization.[38]

Finch held three biracial inaugural balls in January 1976 that heralded both his swearing-in and the healing of the divided Democratic Party. His inauguration dramatically highlighted the fusion when former governor and segregationist Ross Barnett sat a few seats from one of Finch's black aides. Finch also named Charles Evers and Aaron Henry colonels, which were honorary positions on the governor's staff. He enlarged the Minority Affairs Council that William Waller created by broadening black participation on the council and adding Chinese and Choctaw representatives. The new diversity could not obscure continued division in the party. The state's presidential primaries in 1976 illustrated the Janus-faced nature of fusion. In Holmes County, local Democrats elected a slate split between uncommitted delegates and ones pledged for George Wallace and the liberal Sargent Shriver, a situation that repeated itself in other counties across the state. The political marriage of the Loyalists and Regulars held together through the 1976 presidential election, in which Democratic presidential nominee Jimmy Carter carried Mississippi by 49.6 percent over President Gerald Ford's 47.7 percent. As the black Georgia Congressmen Andrew Young said when the Magnolia State decided the Electoral College in favor of Carter, "[T]he hands that picked cotton finally picked the president."[39]

The fusion of the Democratic Party and the integration of black Mississippians into the state's political life also paralleled the decline of the black independent political candidate. Even before fusion, most elected black officials either began their careers as Democrats or started as independents and made the transition to the party later. Robert Clark declared, "[W]e don't have a party in Mississippi," and his career showed the shifting nature of party politics in pre-fusion Mississippi. After winning election in 1967 as a MFDP-backed independent, he chaired both the Regular and Loyalist factions in the Holmes County Democratic Party. After his reelection in 1971, he and other county FDP members moved to the Loyal Democrats to elect delegates for the state Democratic convention, and Clark served as a national convention delegate to the 1972 Democratic convention. In 1975, he ran for reelection in the Democratic primary even as he backed the Republican Carmichael. He switched to the Democratic Party and abandoned his independent status because of the base of white support he had built during his seven years in the legislature. This white base allowed Clark to fend off any potential white challengers. Calvin Moore, the sheriff of Holmes County, explored the idea of a challenge to Clark and visited neighboring Humphreys County to gather support, but the white-dominated board of supervisors refused to back him and Moore abandoned his bid.[40]

Even black Democrats who tied themselves firmly to the Democratic Party sometimes tolerated or understood the shifting boundaries of black officeholders and candidates. Hazel Brannon Smith, the white editor of the *Lexington Advertiser*, demanded that Clark be expelled from the Democratic Party when he backed Carmichael, but Aaron Henry refused to do so. Henry viewed black independent candidacies unfavorably, but he had little interest in punishing a friend and ally who harbored dissatisfaction with the Democratic Party.[41]

Less well-known black politicians also moved across the blurred political boundaries. Bolivar County voters elected Kermit Stanton as an independent supervisor in 1967 and reelected him in 1971. During the 1975 elections he changed and ran as a Democrat. Two other black incumbents in Bolivar County, a constable and a justice of the peace, also made the switch from independent to Democrat in 1975. Some officials waited to make the switch until after Finch officially reunited the parties. Howard Taft Bailey, elected the first black supervisor in Holmes County in 1975, ran as an independent but won reelection in 1979 as a Democrat.[42]

Other black politicians moved in and out of the party as it benefited them. Charles Evers served as a representative of the Loyalists in Chicago in 1968 before his bid for governor as an independent in 1971, but then unsuccessfully sought the Democratic nomination for a state senate seat in 1975. In heavily black counties where black voters exerted influence, such as Holmes and Wilkinson Counties, black politicians sometimes took over the entire local Democratic Party machinery.[43]

The independent candidacy did not completely disappear in the 1970s as an avenue for black office seekers, but few black candidacies outside of the Democratic Party succeeded. In 1975, 126 black independents ran, but only thirty-one won. Independent candidacies continued after fusion but with a similar low rate of success. Occasionally a prominent victory occurred, such as the election of Douglas Anderson. Anderson, a professor at Jackson State University, won a seat in the legislature as an independent from a court-created Hinds County district in 1975. His single-member district had a 91.4 percent black population, a factor that helped override party labels. State election law encouraged the independent candidacies, especially since the federal government had rejected the open primary. Unlike party primaries, independent candidates in the general election only required a plurality to win election, so black candidates often hoped to split the white vote between the Democratic and Republican candidates to win elections.[44]

Black Democrats who won office tended to be "safe" candidates who lacked extensive involvement in civil rights activity, which suggested that conservative blacks and some whites may have been attracted to them because of their lack of activism or "radicalism." In Marshall

County in 1967, Osborne Bell won the Democratic nomination and general election for the office of coroner and ranger. Although a member of the NAACP in the 1960s, he did not appear to be active in the demonstrations of the time. He faced no opposition in the primary or general election in his 1971 reelection bid. Bell actually downplayed his civil rights connections during his successful 1979 sheriff's campaign and described himself as a "supporter" of the NAACP but not an "activist." Unlike the outspoken Skip Robinson or Henry Boyd of the United League, Bell attracted the support of a "certain percent" of whites in Marshall County.[45]

Howard Huggins of Holmes County, who like Bell eventually became one of Mississippi's first black sheriffs since the nineteenth century, also attracted white support and consciously ran as a "safe" black politician. While the election of MFDP-backed Robert Clark gave the county a reputation as an independent third-party stronghold, the rise of the lesser-known Huggins indicated the influence that a black candidate in Mississippi could gain by close association with the existing white power structure. Huggins, according to Robert Clark, had "no direct relations with the Freedom Democrats" and "never rocked the boat." Clark recalled that "there was no reason to not like Howard," who had an easygoing demeanor that whites found nonthreatening. Huggins, who held a seat on the Municipal Democratic Executive Committee, ran for a constable's post in 1971 as a Democrat. Not only did he shun the county FDP, he defeated one of its members, Griffin McLaurin, the black incumbent and independent elected alongside Robert Clark in 1967. McLaurin blamed his loss to Huggins on the redistricting of his beat, which increased the number of voters unfamiliar with him. Huggins won reelection without opposition in 1975 and then in 1979 won a lopsided primary victory for sheriff and ran unopposed in the general election.[46]

Despite the disappointing showing that Carmichael had among black voters, the GOP still made serious attempts to woo them after 1975, perhaps due to the continuing of black independent candidacies. In 1977, with James Eastland's Senate seat up for election the next year, Carmichael and state Republican chairman Charles Pickering both entertained a run. Pickering, a rising star in the party, had first won election in 1971 as the first Republican state senator from Jones County since the nineteenth century. A leader in the Mississippi Baptist Convention, Pickering also established himself as a social conservative by calling for a federal constitutional amendment to outlaw abortion. Although he was more conservative than Carmichael, Pickering showed his pragmatism when he solicited black leaders and their votes, a tactic he would try in later elections. Both men courted black state leaders at the NAACP's annual state conference in 1977. Pickering stressed that "blacks are welcome in the Republican Party" and charged that the Democrats took black votes for granted. The meeting occurred as black leaders in the state began to publicly express their dissatisfaction with the Finch administration over poor minority representation in state offices. Rep. Fred Banks, a black legislator from Hinds County, chaired a biracial advisory committee to develop a statewide affirmative action program, but he complained about a lack of cooperation from the governor's office. At a meeting in Clarksdale in 1977, elected black officials formed a state organization to provide expertise to black candidates and assist currently elected officials. Charles Evers stated that the goal of the newly formed Mississippi Black Elected Officials Association (MBEOA) would be to "have black candidates in every possible election."[47]

While the Republicans tried to lure the black electorate away from the Democrats, prominent black leaders became even more firmly wedded to the Democratic Party. Aaron Henry provided the most striking example of the effects of fusion and black loyalty in 1977 and 1978. James Eastland attended a highly publicized Democratic fundraiser in Biloxi in October 1977 while he entertained another reelection bid to the U.S. Senate. The press came not because Eastland had a history of avoiding such social events but because he attended the first biracial fundraiser held since the marriage of the Loyalists and Regulars. "Big Jim" Eastland, the Citizens' Council supporter who had once boasted that his tailor sewed special pockets in his suits to hold civil rights bills he killed, sat and bowed his head uneasily during a benediction by a black preacher. The highlight came when Henry told the audience, "[T]his is a new experience for some of us, breaking bread with Jim Eastland." Political correspondent Bill Minor observed that Henry's comments "brought down the house."[48]

Fusion showed that Eastland had moved beyond simple advertisements in black newspapers. The unlikely pairing of Henry and Eastland continued in December 1977 at a banquet for the predominantly black Mississippi Industrial College in Holly Springs. Eastland spoke at the banquet and pledged to secure federal funds for the college. Henry spoke as well and endorsed the senator's planned bid for a seventh term

FIGURE 10. Rep. Aaron Henry, Sept. 7, 1987. Unlike Charles
Evers, the longtime president of the state NAACP stayed
loyal to the state Democratic Party and opposed independent and Republican attempts to win black voters. By 1979
he won election to the state House and became one of the
most powerful black Democrats in the state, yet his own
public support of segregationist Democrats for the sake of
party unity, such as his highly publicized fundraiser with
James Eastland in 1977, rankled some civil rights activists. Willie J. Miller Papers, 501–591, Special Collections
Department, Mitchell Memorial Library, Mississippi State
University.

and even said he would campaign for him. The following month, Henry explained his views further in a mailing to NAACP members. Henry said that as a result of two years of contact with Eastland since fusion, he felt that the Doddsville planter had a change of heart on racial issues and now deserved a second chance. In Henry's words, black votes could "make a Javits of an Eastland."[49]

Not everyone in the black community lined up behind Henry. Henry Kirksey, who sought Eastland's seat, complained to NAACP Executive Secretary Benjamin Hooks about Henry's activities for a Democratic candidate and his position as co-chair of the state Democratic Party while at the same time heading the nonpartisan state NAACP. Owen Brooks, director of the Delta Ministry, gave a blunter critique. He said,"[T]o ask black people in this state or anywhere in this country to support James Eastland's candidacy for re-election is the same as to ask the masses of black South Africans to support Vorster and his regime or Ian Smith in Rhodesia." He then called Henry's endorsement of the senator the "foremost" of "a long list of betrayals of black people by black leaders." Henry, in the words of one political observer, had been "a consummate politician from day one" and his endorsement of Eastland proved that.[50]

Henry's actions were a reflection of his own brand of top-down, boss politics. While he never utilized the controversial and authoritarian tactics of Evers, Henry, like the pragmatists in the GOP, was not prepared to let ideology get in the way of political access. With fusion, Henry had allied himself to the state Democratic Party and did not let criticism from other black Mississippians deter him. To Henry, political power required compromise, just as he compromised in 1964 at Atlantic City and alienated the MFDP. To committed civil rights activists in Mississippi, it reeked of ideological betrayal.

The question of whether black Mississippians would support Eastland became moot when the elderly senator declined to run for reelection in 1978. The sudden vacancy triggered a rush of candidates. Nine Democratic candidates, including Gov. Finch and former Gov. William Waller, filed to run. Helen M. Williams, a black Jackson housewife, ran a long-shot campaign for the nomination. Charles Evers and Henry Kirksey filed as independents, while Charles Pickering and Rep. Thad Cochran faced off for the Republican nomination. At a state NAACP meeting in May 1978, Evers lashed out at black leaders who campaigned for the white Democrats and appealed for blacks to vote for him because he was a black man, "somebody who talks like you, has suffered like you." He charged that the Democrats took black voters for granted, a comment echoed by Pickering at the same meeting. Evers's rhetoric highlighted growing fissures in the biracial Democratic Party organization and among black leaders and voters themselves. Aaron Henry refused to endorse any candidate before the primaries. That same May, he addressed the state AFL-CIO, which had endorsed Columbia attorney Maurice Dantin for the Democratic nomination. Henry refused to support Dantin and predicted that most black voters would go with Finch since Dantin had made no attempts to win NAACP support. Despite Henry's claim, Dantin led the first primary and defeated Finch in a runoff to win the Democratic nomination.[51]

The Republicans, much like Finch in 1975, played both sides of the racial divide in Mississippi. The GOP reached out to both black voters and white segregationists. An Evers victory seemed possible with a black plurality and a divided white electorate. Frank Montague, a Hattiesburg attorney, urged Pickering and Cochran to campaign for black votes to deny Evers a unified black vote. At the same time, he suggested they play to racial fears by reminding white voters that their low turnout could mean a black senator.[52]

Cochran easily defeated Pickering in the Republican primary and moved to attract black voters in the general election. Cochran's conservative record in the House was not very different from his fellow Republican Trent Lott, or his three Democratic colleagues, David Bowen, Sonny Montgomery, and Jamie Whitten. All five representatives voted against busing, Medicaid funding of abortions, and mandatory coed physical education. The delegation also voted to restrict lawyers for the Legal Services Corporation from filing suits against government agencies, which would have hampered the suits of civil rights lawyers in Mississippi. On issues of foreign policy and race, the delegation also voted against a ban on chrome imported from Ian Smith's white-minority government in Rhodesia, even though the country was under international sanctions. The vote for closer relations with Rhodesia meant that the Mississippi representatives backed a position not very different from that of the Citizens' Councils, which saw Rhodesia and South Africa as the last bulwarks of white civilization. Yet perhaps the most telling votes concerned suffrage. Despite the increase in black voter registration since 1965, all five representatives opposed the renewal of the

Voting Rights Act in 1975. They also voted against the establishment of a nationwide voter registration system to increase voter registration. Outreach to black voters, regardless of the party, had its limits.[53]

Cochran had a conservative voting record that reflected both the social conservatism of the state and the emerging political influence of the New Right. He never once exceeded a twenty percent rating from the liberal Americans for Democratic Action, which made him slightly more conservative than Bowen and Whitten but barely more liberal than Lott and Montgomery. Yet unlike Lott, Cochran was rather low-key during his House tenure, avoiding many public remarks in the Congressional Record. Lott spoke out in particular against the 1978 IRS guidelines that denied tax-exempt status to segregated private academies and was the only Mississippi representative to do so.[54]

Cochran's limited black support, built during his House campaigns, gave him a veneer of moderation and pragmatism by 1978 that Lott, Mounger, and other conservatives did not possess. Cochran could also look to the recent candidacy of Doug Shanks. Shanks ran as a Republican for the mayor of Jackson in the 1977 municipal elections. He lost the election but won forty-six percent of the city's black votes because of a well-organized campaign in the black community. The "Cochran Black Operation," as the congressman's campaign dubbed its outreach, was a similarly structured campaign to get the black vote. The organization spent over $300,000 to field a network of black county coordinators, canvassers, and speakers to reach black voters. Nehemiah Flowers, a black Cochran congressional staffer, also assisted the program. The campaign also conducted speaking engagements on black college campuses and churches and funded an advertising blitz in the media aimed at black listeners. The Cochran campaign believed that well-educated blacks would be more likely to vote Republican, so it aimed in particular at blacks with high school diplomas and college educations.[55]

Evers's independent bid largely reflected his desire to be the political boss and kingmaker of black Mississippi. Yet his campaign showed the weaknesses in the biracial arrangement the state Democratic Party used to win the governor's race in 1975 and deliver the state to Jimmy Carter in 1976. A strong black candidate running as an independent in the general election could disrupt the coalition by siphoning off black voters, which led white liberals and black Democrats to plead with Evers to drop out of the race. Aaron Henry told former MFDP attorney Joseph Rauh that he had been trying to talk Evers out of the race, but he feared publicly upbraiding him because "the outcome of no political race is worth the splitting of the black community down the middle."[56]

Henry eventually criticized Evers publicly but in thinly veiled terms. During the campaign the Memphis *Commercial Appeal* printed a letter he wrote to Henry Kirksey that condemned Evers's call for black Mississippians to unite behind a single black candidate. Although he never mentioned Evers by name, he responded directly to Evers's proposals, which Kirksey had communicated to Henry. Henry, mindful of his reply to the independent Kirksey, said "[L]et black independents be independents, let black Republicans be Republicans, and let black Democrats be Democrats. Let's not try to mix them to accomplish any selfish, sinister aims." Yet in the same letter Henry said, "[B]lacks say to me that they have worked too hard toward becoming an integral part of the Democratic Party to throw it away on one that has no interest nor identity with the Democratic Party." Henry, ever the Democratic insider, did not address concerns Evers or other black Mississippians had, such as the failure of a single Democratic congressman to vote for the Voting Rights Act extension in 1975.[57]

Such compromises by Henry showed his own brand of boss politics as he continued to vouch for white Democrats with segregationist histories. In a letter to Bernard Coleman, the Secretary of the National Black Republican Council, Henry defended first district congressman Jamie Whitten and cited his support for the Humphrey-Hawkins Full Employment Act, a liberal-backed bill opposed by Thad Cochran and Trent Lott. Henry was not afraid to criticize white Democrats, but he preferred to keep such criticism sparse. He chastised Maurice Dantin in the summer of 1978 for criticizing United Nations Ambassador Andrew Young. Henry reminded Dantin that Young "is an idol to most black citizens of Mississippi" and warned Dantin to not "join the band of racism, regardless to how politically expedient it seems at the moment."[58]

Evers's generally conservative political and social views also motivated him to run and put him on an increasingly separate path from the Democratic Party, especially the national one. In 1976, Evers was the only member of the state Democratic delegation who refused to vote for Jimmy Carter. Although he had eagerly solicited HEW funds as mayor of Fayette, he had become increasingly critical of programs like Aid to Families with Dependent Children (AFDC) and charged that they created welfare dependency. He also criticized President Carter for backing the Panama Canal Treaty. His views on busing drew the ire of Henry and Joseph Rauh, the former legal counsel for the MFDP during the 1964 Atlantic challenge. Evers condemned the busing of black children to white schools, endorsed the concept of neighborhood schools, and even brought in some white segregationists who worked for politicians such as James Eastland to assist with his campaign. Rauh lambasted Evers for his anti-busing stance and told him in a letter that "I have spent my whole life working for integration and am too old to be tolerant of those who give up on integrated schooling." Evers insisted that he was still an integrationist and opposed the busing of black children away from their homes as "stealing their identity," but his stance and his alliance with segregationists shocked liberals like Rauh.

The erosion of Evers's own influence also motivated him to break with the state Democrats. He had been an ally of Gov. Cliff Finch since the 1975 elections. In return for his support, Finch made Evers the first black member of the Mississippi Agricultural and Industrial Board and also gave Evers's daughter and son-in-law jobs in the state government. Evers became dissatisfied when Finch began to appoint white segregationists, another part of Finch's base, to state jobs in larger numbers than he did African Americans. The anger became an open break when Finch rebuffed Evers and a delegation of the state's black mayors when they protested the beating of a fellow mayor by a state patrolman. The early fragility of fusion began to show with the Finch-Evers split.[59]

Rauh and Henry were not the only Democrats to oppose Evers. Labor, a critical part of the biracial Democratic Party, also resisted the Evers candidacy. State labor leader Claude Ramsey, who had refused to back Evers's congressional run in 1968, reacted angrily to Evers's charge that the union never supported black people for public office. He cited labor's support for voter registration drives for Evers in the 1960s and said, "[H]ad it not been for our work, I don't believe he [Evers] would have been elected mayor of Fayette," a claim that ignored the role of the NAACP in registering voters in Jefferson County. Ramsey also pointed to labor's role in the 1960s civil rights movement and the aid his organization gave to Robert Clark.[60]

The three-way race of Evers, Dantin, and Cochran drew considerable national attention.[61] Gov. Finch and President Jimmy Carter threw their support to Dantin, as did both of Mississippi's U.S. Senators. Eastland, in another departure from his old segregationist ways, warned, "[T]he Democratic Party is a big tent. Not to be in that big tent means you're going to be cold outside—you'll just get what's left and that's not very much." Dantin campaigned as "a conservative Mississippi Democrat" who opposed federal programs. Evers, by contrast, called for more funding for public projects in small towns. He also attacked Cochran's conservative voting record and called Dantin indecisive and "afraid to take a stand on anything."[62]

Evers brought in celebrities to help his campaign since much of his liberal support from his 1971 race had evaporated. B. B. King served as the entertainment chairman of the Evers campaign, and Muhammad Ali and Kris Kristofferson took a leave from filming a movie in Natchez to tour with Evers through the Delta just days before the general election.[63] Evers also downplayed his combative past and cultivated an image as a negotiator who could bring both blacks and white together. In October, he helped encourage talks between the United League and the city of Tupelo during a consumer boycott the League had been waging to force the city to adopt an affirmative action program. Evers also won the endorsement of the state's Conference of Black Mayors and the Baptist Ministers' Union along with the endorsement of individual black politicians like Rep. Horace Buckley from Hinds County.[64]

Evers showed his own pragmatism—or Machiavellianism—acting even more blatantly than Henry, attracting unreconstructed white segregationists through his criticism of busing. D. A. Biglane, a Natchez oil millionaire and former fundraiser for Jim Eastland, served as Evers's treasurer. Another supporter was H. R. Morgan, a Hattiesburg contractor who had previously been a campaign manager for gubernatorial candidate Jimmy Swan. When Evers spoke before a Kiwanis Club meeting in Meridian, one white observer said, "[I]f you close your eyes, it could be Ross Barnett up there." Most white segregationists, while perhaps grudgingly respecting Evers, saw his bid as a means to get a white conservative like Thad Cochran into office instead of an unpredictable black maverick. The Evers campaign also lagged in fundraising. Cochran and Dantin raised hundreds of thousands of dollars, while Evers raised only forty thousand by mid-October, and some of that was from his own savings. Cochran himself acknowledged the help Evers was giving him by splitting the Democratic vote and said, "[I]f I had to write a script, I couldn't have done a better job."[65]

On Election Day, the script Cochran desired played itself out. Dantin received 31.8 percent of the vote while Evers took 22.9 percent. Cochran won with a forty-five percent plurality. Evers drew a large number of black votes and won pluralities or majorities in eleven counties, all but one majority-black. In other heavily black areas, Evers polled enough votes to deny Dantin a majority. The Fayette mayor drew over 133,000 votes, more then enough to cost Dantin the election. Dantin clearly had a significant number of black votes since he ran competitively or led in the Delta counties, but the pull Evers had with black voters proved too much for the Columbia attorney.[66]

Evers's spoiler role angered white and black Democrats. Jack Harper, the chancery clerk of Sunflower County and head of the state party's campaign committee, declared, "Evers led them [blacks] right on down the road and out of the party and now he's got them on a limb." Aaron Henry warned Evers that any future independent candidacies could have "a devastating effect" on the black community and declared that "when you lay down with Independents, you wake up with Republicans," a statement at odds with his earlier message to Kirksey defending political diversity in the black community. Owen Brooks of the Delta Ministry, who had savaged Henry for his endorsement of Eastland the previous year, showed no more enthusiasm for Evers's political race and asked the Fayette mayor to "stop ripping off black folk who think you are Jesus." Some black Democrats, while refusing to back Evers, did not break relations with him. Fred Banks said that he "never had a public break with Charles Evers or even a private break with him for that matter. He did what he wanted to do."[67]

The 1978 Senate race overshadowed the race in Cochran's fourth district that same year. When Cochran had declined reelection to his House seat, his administrative assistant, Jon Hinson, ran in his place. John H. Stennis, the son of U.S. Senator John Stennis, won the Democratic nomination. Evan Doss, the black tax-assessor collector of Claiborne County, ran as an independent. Doss received Evers's endorsement, which boosted his standing in the black counties in the district. Hinson wrote off Claiborne, Wilkinson, and Jefferson Counties to Doss and focused on reaching specific target groups, such as black voters in the other counties in the district, to achieve victory. Using the groundwork laid by Cochran, his strategy paid off, and the election results in the fourth district did not repeat the pattern of the senate race. Hinson won a clear majority of 51.6 percent, while Stennis received 26.4 percent and Doss got only 19 percent. Doss took the three aforementioned river counties but did not fare well elsewhere.[68]

The Republican victories in 1978 underscored the fragility of fusion and showed that a strong black independent could disrupt the carefully constructed biracial coalition of the state Democratic Party. Segregationists like James Eastland reluctantly accepted the mostly black Loyalists, but some of the rank-and-file white Regulars were not as willing. Despite their mutual cooperation with white segregationists and their top-down political styles, Evers's insistence on playing the spoiler hastened his split from Aaron Henry and insured the election of the first Republican senator since Reconstruction. The rise of the Republicans also highlighted the progressive Gil Carmichael's very public but largely futile efforts to woo black voters during the 1975 gubernatorial race and turn the GOP into a biracial party as well. Thad Cochran's victories also utilized Carmichael's approach, but his success ultimately rested more on the support of conservative whites than on disaffected blacks. As the state prepared for the 1979 elections, the Republicans clearly had more success using black voters and candidates to divide the Democrats rather than resurrecting the biracial party of the nineteenth century.

Reapportionment

Giving Clark Some Company

THE ELECTIONS IN 1979 created the first significant core of black political power on the state level since the passage of the Voting Rights Act. While the growth of black politics on the county and municipal levels continued to produce most of the state's elected black officials, the publicity around the black legislators elected in 1979 overshadowed these gains. Even before the onset of black voting in 1965, the issue of race influenced the reapportionment of the state's legislative districts, especially after the Supreme Court ruled against malapportionment in the landmark cases of *Baker v. Carr* and *Reynolds v. Sims*. The fourteen-year legal battle by civil rights activists to elect significant numbers of black legislators centered on issues of racial dilution and gerrymandering, specifically Mississippi's use of multimember districts to offset centers of black voting strength. Henry Kirksey and the MFDP, joined later by civil rights attorney Frank Parker, brought suits against the state legislature and resisted the efforts by white incumbents to make the black vote as meaningless as possible. The court challenges led to single-member districts with significant black majorities and the creation of the second generation of elected black officials to replace the old civil rights activist-politicians of the 1960s and early 1970s. Indeed, the legal suits brought by civil rights attorneys marked a return to the legalistic focus of the pre-*Brown* era, with the decline but not disappearance of mass demonstrations and other organizing in the 1970s. With civil rights laws now on the books, activists turned to the courts to make sure they were enforced.

Mississippi's early history included a fairly regular rate of reapportionment. From its admission as a state in 1817 to the enactment of the Constitution of 1890, the legislature reapportioned itself sixteen times, an average of one reapportionment every 4.5 years. Apportionment did not become a volatile issue until the 1890 constitutional convention. While the Constitution of 1890 is best remembered for the disfranchisement of black voters, the convention debates also featured conflict between the white delegates over apportionment. Predominantly black counties that were dominated by white oligarchies clashed with white-majority counties about representation in the state legislature. Despite their political infighting, both sides agreed on the importance of white supremacy, which the Committee on Elective Franchisement, Apportionment and Elections clearly stated when it said its job was to establish "permanent white intelligent rule" in the state government.[1]

The Constitution of 1890 empowered but did not require the legislature to reapportion itself every ten years. The lack of compulsory reapportionment meant that the legislature did not correct malapportioned legislative districts during the decades after 1890. The first significant legal challenge to malapportionment was against Mississippi's congressional, not state, legislative districts. In 1932, a Mississippian named Stewart Broom challenged the unequal distribution of inhabitants in the state's seven congressional districts. The seventh district, for example, had 414,000 residents to the fourth district's 184,000. The seventh district's high population resulted from the legislature folding the eighth district into the seventh district to meet congressional redistricting requirements. The U.S. Supreme Court unanimously upheld the unequal distribution in October 1932. The suit dealt with congressional districts, but a favorable ruling for Broom could have also opened up challenges to the state reapportionment system.[2] The *Daily Clarion-Ledger* praised the Court's decision, calling it "a victory for Mississippi and state rights," and called on white Mississippians to "join hands in the name of a common democracy—a democracy under which white men have lived and labored and voted in the protection of white supremacy for the past 60 years."[3]

Malapportionment received further judicial protection in 1946 when the Court ruled against the plaintiffs in *Colegrove v. Green*, an Illinois case that challenged congressional districts with population imbalances. *Colegrove* stymied reapportionment suits nationwide for another thirteen years. By the end of the 1950s a new apportionment challenge

FIGURE 11. Mississippi State Capitol, Jackson. Continued use of multimember districts and county lines in redistricting kept the Mississippi House of Representatives almost all-white in the 1970s, with only one black representative from 1968 to 1975. Not until the adoption of single-member districts by court order in 1979 did a significant number of black candidates win state House and Senate elections. William F. "Bill" Minor Papers, 80–597a, Special Collections Department, Mitchell Memorial Library, Mississippi State University.

had emerged from Mississippi's northern neighbor. In 1959, a coalition of plaintiffs from Tennessee's four major cities filed a lawsuit against the overrepresentation of rural areas in the state legislature, which had not reapportioned since 1901. The case, *Baker v. Carr*, made its way to the Supreme Court in April 1961.[4]

Mississippians dissatisfied with unequal representation soon seized on the opportunities that *Baker* offered. The 1960 census showed the inequalities of the state legislative districts under the old apportionment system. Urban growth and the population shift towards the coast and Hinds County meant 1,120,000 people lived in thirty-six counties, which had 53½ seats in the House. Less than half the population had 86½ seats representing them. Harrison County on the Mississippi Gulf Coast had one-and-one-half representatives for 119,033 people (one per 80,000 residents), while rural Carroll County had two representatives for 11,150 people (one per 5,575 residents). After the census, the state government still took no action on reapportionment.[5]

Six businessmen from the state's Gulf Coast filed suit in state court in 1961 to challenge the overrepresented rural areas in the state's legislature. The plaintiffs successfully petitioned for their case, *Fortner v. Barnett*, to be added as *animus curiae* to the appeal of *Baker v. Carr*.[6] In a reference to Mississippi's racial climate and resistance to school desegregation, Upton Sisson, the attorney for the men, told a lawyer for the appellants in *Baker* the following:

> [T]here is perhaps no great admiration for . . . the State of Mississippi by the U.S. Supreme Court for obvious reasons unnecessary to discuss. If then it could be appropriately pointed out to the court that Mississippi may not be as bad a state as is generally considered, if its control were placed in the hands of the majority, rather than a small minority which has controlled it for many years . . . this would carry favorable weight with the court, all of which would enure to the benefit of the Tennessee case.[7]

Walter Chandler, another *Baker* attorney, made the racial reference more explicit when he concurred with the Mississippi plaintiffs, declaring that "[I]t should be very beneficial to us to have as many petitions as possible to intervene as *animus curiae*, and I would favor the intervention of Mississippi where apportionment has been very disadvantageous to Negroes, for instance."[8] Both the Tennesseans and the Mississippians then saw the *Baker* appeal as dealing at least indirectly with race and hoped to use the Warren Court's hostility to racial discrimination to benefit the cause of reapportionment. By playing on the Court's sympathies to the plight of black Mississippians, the white urban plaintiffs hoped to break the rural lock on the state government.

While self-interest clearly influenced the white plaintiffs' views on matters of racial equality, their willingness to challenge the white oligarchy that ruled Mississippi showed the varying dimensions of white thought in the era of "massive resistance." Rural black-belt neobourbons who benefited from legislative malapportionment led the opposition to school desegregation in the 1950s. The South's business conservatives, mostly composed of the urban middle class, did not favor Jim Crow if it threatened their own economic status or advancement. The most extreme forms of white supremacy, such as the closing of public schools to prevent integration, could drive them to join with black voters and abandon the neobourbons. Labor also showed a willingness to challenge malapportionment. The Mississippi Labor Council filed a lawsuit that challenged Mississippi's right-to-work law on the grounds of unequal representation from apportionment.[9] Although massive resistance referred to school desegregation, the comments from Sisson and Chandler show that the business conservatives also held the same views regarding apportionment. The "common democracy" of white supremacy that newspapers praised in 1932 did not mean that urban whites of 1960 would settle for less political influence.

On March 26, 1962, the U.S. Supreme Court ruled 6–2 in favor of the metropolitan plaintiffs of Tennessee in *Baker v. Carr* and opened the door to federal challenges to state apportionment systems nationwide. Urban legislators in Mississippi quickly voiced approval for the decision, while rural politicians expressed unhappiness with the ruling. U.S. Sen. John Stennis from rural Kemper County said the decision "sweeps away" the balance of powers in the U.S. Constitution.[10]

The Mississippi Legislature took up reapportionment again, but waited until after the fall elections and the desegregation crisis at the University of Mississippi had subsided to pass an apportionment plan that increased the representation of the more heavily populated counties. The plan kept the provision in the state constitution that each county have at least one representative and the remaining representatives of the House be divided on a population basis amongst the counties. While this plan did not equitably apportion the new seats, it did reduce some of the most egregious disparities in population, and the plan satisfied enough legislators to win passage. Voters approved the plan in February 1963.[11]

Reapportionment resurfaced once again when the Warren Court handed down its ruling in *Reynolds v. Sims*, an Alabama case that extended the reach of the federal government even further into apportionment by enunciating the "one man, one vote" principle. Chief Justice Earl Warren cited population as the main standard for representation and apportionment and invalidated severe population inequities that allowed a minority to elect a majority of a state legislature. Apportionment systems that gave each county automatic representation or state constitutions that made population secondary or balanced it with other factors no longer enjoyed the immunity that *Colegrove* had provided.[12]

Attorney General Joe Patterson predicted incorrectly that the *Reynolds* ruling would have no effect on Mississippi.[13] Although many white Mississippians favored the reapportionment plan passed as a result of *Baker*, the state's black residents did not. After the Voting Rights Act of 1965 took effect, the Freedom Democrats challenged discrimination in the apportionment of the state legislature. The Lawyers' Constitutional Defense Committee (LCDC) filed a lawsuit on behalf of the MFDP in the U.S. District Court in Jackson in October 1965. Civil rights attorney William Kunstler and other lawyers represented eight MFDP plaintiffs, including cartographer Henry Kirksey and party secretary Peggy Conner, who would lend her name to the MFDP reapportionment suits then and in the coming years. The suit challenged both congressional districting and state legislative apportionment and alleged that the unequal districts violated black rights under the Equal Protection Clause of the Fourteenth Amendment.[14]

The three-judge panel that the MFDP plaintiffs faced could scarcely have been more hostile to their cause. Fifth Circuit Judge J. P. Coleman, a recent appointee to the bench, had served as governor of the state from 1956 to 1960. Coleman had previously called for the closing of all public schools in the state to prevent "education by federal bayonet." Despite his record, President Lyndon Johnson appointed him over NAACP objections. District Judge Harold Cox, the second member of the panel and a Kennedy appointee, also vigorously defended white supremacy. The Sunflower County native and close friend of U.S. Senator James Eastland once referred to black voting applicants in Canton as "a bunch of niggers" who acted like "chimpanzees." Cox's legal harassment of black plaintiffs became so infamous that *The New Republic* ran an editorial calling for his impeachment. District Judge Dan Russell, a Gulf Coast lawyer and the third justice, also had a record of hostility to school desegregation cases, and both Russell and Cox in particular experienced high reversal rates on their decisions.[15]

The MFDP plaintiffs also had few local allies outside of the black community to count on in their fight. The state AFL-CIO seemed a natural partner in the fight, given its involvement in earlier reapportionment suits and the national organization's support for civil rights, but labor leader Claude Ramsey, a supporter of the Loyalists, rejected any association with the MFDP.[16]

As the case went to trial in 1966, Lieutenant Governor Carroll Gartin signed into law a new congressional redistricting plan that divided the black-majority Delta among three congressional districts. The legislature fragmented the potential black voting strength of the region by creating four majority-white districts in the state and another with a tiny black majority to head off any racial gerrymandering claims. The black district contained a 1,819-member black majority, but when broken down by age to reflect people over twenty-one, the white residents held a 32,581 majority.[17]

The MFDP plaintiffs and their two main attorneys, Alvin J. Bronstein of the LCDC and Peter Marcuse of the American Civil Liberties Union (ACLU), added the new redistricting plan to their apportionment suit of *Conner v. Johnson* and challenged both it and legislative malapportionment as dilutions of voting strength under the *Reynolds* "one-man, one-vote" standard. The court, citing *Reynolds*, agreed with the plaintiffs that the legislature needed to reapportion. The court ordered reapportionment since forty percent of the state's population could "conceivably" elect a majority in the House, and thirty-seven percent could do so in the Senate. Failure to reapportion on a population basis, the court ruled, violated the Equal Protection Clause of the Fourteenth Amendment. Instead of creating an apportionment plan itself, the court ordered the legislature to pass a new one by December 1.[18]

The court delayed ruling on the MFDP-challenged congressional districting plan until October and, unlike the apportionment plan, upheld it. The verdict that ordered state legislative reapportionment did not yield significant gains for the MFDP either. The judges dismissed claims by the MFDP and Charles Evers that the state legislative plan diluted black voting strength through its use of multimember districts. Attorney General Patterson in turn charged that the MFDP wanted reverse gerrymandering and an end to the election of white legislators. The judges' ruling and their refusal to mandate a new specific plan for reapportionment showed the limited scope of the decision. They dismissed race as a factor and instead stuck to narrow legal precedent that allowed the legislature to interpret *Reynolds* in a racially discriminatory fashion. The court and legislature stuck to the letter of the Voting Rights Act and interpreted it as narrowly as possible.[19]

Gov. Paul Johnson called the legislature into a special session in November 1966 and the legislators approved a plan at the end of the month, which Johnson signed into law on December 1, the court-ordered deadline. Disparities between urban and rural areas still irritated some urban senators. Sen. Hayden Campbell of Jackson said he opposed the bill because "of the many inequities that still remain." Sen. Ellis Bodron of Vicksburg expressed "serious doubts" about the bill. Six of the Senate districts and ten of the House districts varied from the norm of 41,877 people per senator and 17,854 per representative by twenty percent or more.[20]

Bodron was right. On March 3, 1967, the court agreed with the MFDP's challenge to the new apportionment plan and invalidated it, ordering its own apportionment plan that reduced the variance in population. The judges rejected the MFDP request to consider race in the plan and instead opted for a color-blind approach. At the end of March, MFDP counsel Alvin Bronstein proposed a realignment of eight counties to make the population more equitable, but the judges rejected it. The civil rights forces suffered a further blow when the U.S. Supreme Court upheld the legislature's congressional redistricting plan of 1966, which split the Delta's black electorate.[21]

Baker and *Reynolds*, however, meant the state could no longer ignore regular reapportionment. The 1970 census showed an increase in Mississippi's population, the first such rise in thirty years, which meant a new plan of apportionment. Gov. John Bell Williams urged the legislature in January 1971 to create a plan that would pass federal scrutiny, and the legislature reduced the population variance between districts to under ten percent, with the exception of Simpson County, which had a population of 10.67 percent over the mean. The bill passed with eighty-five representatives voting yes and thirty-three voting no. Williams signed it into law in March 1971.[22]

Half of the nay votes came from Harrison and Hinds Counties, urban areas that historically suffered malapportionment. Rep. John Stennis of

Hinds County charged that the bill violated the Equal Protection Clause by underrepresenting the Hinds County electorate. Rep. Charles Bullock of Harrison County predicted that "the judiciary must again assume the legislative duties which the Legislature declines to perform."[23] Bullock's statement underscores the lack of a unified white resistance, even with the growth of the black electorate after 1965. Unlike Mississippi's governors, he did not see judicial intervention as a bad thing if it meant increasing his own constituents' representation in the legislature. While he made reference to the "one-man, one-vote" doctrine of *Reynolds* and not to the *Conner* case and its racial issues, he and many other urban legislators clearly did not find the status quo satisfactory.

Attorney General A. F. Summer began a vigorous defense of the plan. Summer, a longtime critic of civil rights legislation, said at the Neshoba County Fair in 1969 that the Voting Rights Act "says that Mississippi must register and vote every illiterate human being over the age of twenty-one." He had pledged to "fight this type of punitive legislation with all the power" of the Attorney General's office. Summer submitted the reapportionment plan to the three-man court for approval, but the unsatisfied justices struck it down in May. As in 1967, the court enacted its own plan for the elections. MFDP attorney George Taylor, a member of the Lawyers' Committee for Civil Rights Under Law (LCCRUL), asked for districts with black majorities, but Judge Coleman said that would put the court "back to the very thing we were told not to do—consider race." Coleman stressed the court only looked at population, as mandated by *Reynolds*. Summer objected to Taylor's proposal to end the use of county lines as boundaries for legislative districts as an attempt to subdivide Hinds County "based solely on race" and end multimember districts. Summer used the "one man, one vote" principle as a defense against racial gerrymandering and argued that the court could only consider population as a factor.[24]

The court agreed with Summer and rejected the black plaintiffs' attempts to divide the counties but delayed a ruling on the Hinds County question until after the 1971 elections. Summer praised the court's ruling as being "without any racism" at all. The court still deferred to the legislature on reapportionment and did not require that the plan be submitted for section five preclearance under the Voting Rights Act. Taylor and his associates with the LCCRUL appealed the ruling and challenged the court's order to fill all twelve seats in Hinds County by countywide voting, which diluted the black vote in the white-majority county. John

Maxey of the Jackson-Hinds County Community Legal Services, an arm of the Office of Economic Opportunity (OEO), joined in the appeal, as did Rep. Robert Clark.[25]

The U.S. Supreme Court quickly overturned the lower court's ruling and ordered the three judges to split Hinds County into single-member districts. The Court said that such districts were "preferable" to large multimember districts. The 6–3 ruling produced a strong dissent from Justice Hugo Black, joined by Justice John Harlan and Chief Justice Warren Burger. Black objected to "throwing a monkey wrench into the county election procedure at this late date." Summer still saw the ruling favorably because the Court denied the plaintiffs' request to submit the plan for approval under section five and for upholding apportionment in the other eighty-one counties of Mississippi. Taylor also interpreted the ruling positively and expressed the hope that the Burger Court's opinion would spread single-member districts to the entire state.[26]

The lower court held hearings in June and heard arguments from both sides on how to redistrict Hinds County in time for the primary elections. The hearings came amid the Supreme Court's ruling in *Whitcomb v. Chavis*, an Indiana reapportionment case where the justices upheld multimember districts even though they recognized that they diluted black voting strength. Summer, who had joined the attorney generals of eleven other states in an *amicus curiae* urging the Supreme Court to side with Indiana, cited *Whitcomb* and asked the Supreme Court to "bring the Hinds County decision in line with the rest of the nation." Justice Byron White's opinion in *Whitcomb* upheld the Indiana multimember districts because they had not been decided with discriminatory intent, a defense that a southern state with a history of disfranchisement would have difficulty making.[27]

The Hinds case lingered further as Special Master William Neal, a former state auditor appointed by the federal panel to redistrict the county, declared the task impossible and cited a lack of population data as the reason. Neal recommended holding the elections on an at-large basis, which the civil rights attorneys opposed and Summer favored. The federal court sided with Summer and Neal on June 16, refusing to create single-member districts. Both sides flew to Washington as MFDP lawyers appealed the ruling to the Supreme Court, but the justices, in a unanimous decision, backed away from their earlier ruling and declined to get involved. Summer crowed that the ruling was "a significant victory for fair play."[28] The civil rights forces filed an appeal, *Conner v.*

Williams, to try to force a new reapportionment and election, but the Supreme Court rejected the case in January 1972 and allowed the legislature to devise a new plan before the 1975 elections.[29] While *Conner v. Johnson* led to the creation of single-member districts outside of Mississippi, it had no immediate impact in the state.[30]

The legislature reapportioned again in April 1973 by copying the 1971 court-ordered plan, and the federal panel delayed hearings on the subsequent legal challenge by the civil rights attorneys until February 1975. Between 1971 and 1975, litigation and section five objections had eliminated multimember districts in Alabama, Georgia, South Carolina, Louisiana, and Texas. The resulting single-member districts greatly increased minority representation in the affected states. These developments left Mississippi as the only state that used multimember districts in both houses of the state legislature.[31] During the regular session of the legislature in 1975, the legislators rejected proposals from both Charles Evers and the *Conner* plaintiffs and passed an apportionment plan with a variance in population of less than ten percent. The legislators fell back on the old defense of the sanctity of county lines for legislative districting, while the *Conner* plaintiffs wanted to subdivide the counties. The legislators hoped that the court's lack of an explicit demand for single-member districts would allow them to win approval for a multimember plan. Gov. William Waller signed the bill into law in April 1975.[32]

During the legislative debates on reapportionment that year, the black plaintiffs mobilized again. By that time a thirty-four-year-old lawyer named Frank Parker took over representation of the MFDP plaintiffs. The red-bearded attorney had worked since 1968 for the LCCRUL in Jackson and became assistant chief counsel in 1972. Parker pushed the creation of single-member districts, which the judges still opposed. Parker squared off against Attorney General Summer over issues other than reapportionment. During hearings in Washington to extend the Voting Rights Act in 1975, Summer complained of federal review of state voting changes, while Parker defended the Act. Parker also charged that the state purposely fragmented black areas of Hinds County into districts to prevent black candidates from being elected in county elections. Summer called the charges "a bunch of bull" and said that the election of black candidates could be assured "only by taking the ballot away from the whites."[33]

In April, the federal court dismissed the plaintiffs' case and made them refile an amended complaint directed at the 1975 reapportionment plan. In May, the court ruled in *Conner v. Waller* that the plan did not violate the one-man, one-vote principle and dismissed Parker's calls for creating majority-black districts. The judges concluded that since overt legal barriers to black voting had been removed no discrimination occurred now. Parker immediately appealed and asked for a delay in the 1975 elections or for the immediate creation of single-member districts. Gov. Waller confidently predicted a state victory, and Summer dismissed the appeal as the actions of "the usual crowd" and condemned the Justice Department's "knee-jerk action" when Solicitor General Robert Bork suggested in a brief that the elections be delayed until an interim plan could be crafted.[34]

The Supreme Court sided with the "usual crowd" and reversed the lower court's ruling on June 5 and ordered the reapportionment plan submitted to the Justice Department for approval under section five. Justice Thurgood Marshall backed a delay in the elections, but the Court did not take that action. Parker praised the decision as "a substantial victory for the black voters of Mississippi" and predicted the impending creation of single-member districts in Hinds, Harrison, and Jackson Counties, the state's three most populous counties. U.S. Assistant Attorney General J. Stanley Pottinger backed the civil rights forces and told Summer that the reapportionment plan did not meet the criteria of the Voting Rights Act. Single-member districts now seemed more likely, and the *Jackson Daily News* predicted their enactment by the end of 1975.[35]

Both sides returned to the three-man court and reargued their cases for and against single-member districts. Summer continued to push for the old plan despite the Justice Department's objections. Judge Coleman still clung to the use of county lines and declared that he did not want to "butcher" them in a reapportionment plan. The Supreme Court's failure to void single-member districts in *Whitcomb* bolstered Coleman's view, and he said the panel did "not feel compelled" to mandate such changes. Russell Davis, the mayor of Jackson, also expressed his hostility to single-member districts and threatened a lawsuit to block any such action. Yet in a surprise statement in Hattiesburg, Gov. Waller publicly suggested that single-member districts might be desirable to reduce voter apathy. He also indicated that he had some disagreements with Summer over his defense of the state in the *Conner* case.[36]

The court, citing the lack of time to create a permanent plan, ignored the Justice Department and ordered the legislature's plan into effect for the 1975 elections. In July, the court ordered Hinds, Madison, and Rankin Counties split into single-member House districts but did not order them for the entire state or change Senate districts in the counties, which Parker wanted. Parker still called the decision "precedent setting" for drawing districts across county lines.[37]

The legal action of the apportionment case took place amid the backdrop of the 1975 primary elections. Although the courts ordered a new desegregation plan for Jackson's public schools that April, the *Jackson Daily News* commented that racial tension had "been fairly well neutralized by registration of black voters and [the] changing attitudes of whites." Of the eight gubernatorial candidates that year, Henry Kirksey, one of the *Conner* plaintiffs, ran as the only black candidate and as an independent. The single-member districts did surface briefly as an issue. Tom Minniece, a Democrat who unsuccessfully tried to defeat Summer, criticized him for not pushing redistricting two or three years ago. Three of the white candidates in the race, including future governor William Winter, endorsed single-member districts. The NAACP entered the fray and assailed the three-judge panel for being "steeped in Mississippi tradition." Kirksey also brought up single-member districts and accused Charles Evers and state Rep. Robert Clark of not really wanting to do away with multimember districts. He delivered a sharp attack on Clark and said he did not want "any more blacks up there (in the House) anyway, because he would lose his importance."[38]

Parker later called the Supreme Court's intervention a "meaningful court victory" that led to the election of three additional black legislators from Hinds County in 1975. That August, Congress and President Gerald Ford extended the Voting Rights Act for another seven years, but the existence of white-majority multimember districts still obstructed black officeholding.[39] When the three-judge court tried to delay its self-appointed February 1976 deadline for a permanent reapportionment plan, Parker and his clients filed a petition for a writ of mandamus to the Supreme Court. The Court sided with the plaintiffs and ordered the lower court to draw up a permanent plan of reapportionment.[40]

Judge Coleman, humbled by the Court's 8–1 decision, announced that "there will be no reluctance, no foot-dragging and no hanging back" in complying with the order and the court reluctantly agreed to implement single-member districts for the entire state legislature. The judges abandoned the one-representative-per-county standard but at the same time tried to preserve "as much as possible the spirit of the rule against breaking counties apart" and decreed the districts to be in effect for the 1979 elections. The court recognized that the Supreme Court would likely not tolerate any future unequal reapportionment plans and that adhering to population equity and the one-man, one-vote rule meant breaking county lines and using precincts and beats. Parker called the court's plan "a substantial advance over all prior court plans" but still unacceptable to his clients because the new district boundaries continued to dilute black votes. Summer opposed Parker and the Justice Department's call for special elections in some of the new court-created districts. The following month the court extended the single-member district order to the House.[41]

Summer reacted bitterly to the end of county boundaries in reapportionment and declared that "the Constitution, the laws, and state policy of 159 years' standing have again had to bow and tip their hat to the Department of Justice in Washington." House Speaker C. B. "Buddy" Newman, whose own Delta district was redrawn, accused single-member districts of creating "divisiveness." The judges ordered elections in only two House districts, rejecting a midterm redrawing of the legislature. Citing black turnout in the just-completed presidential race in which Mississippi went for Jimmy Carter, the court declared that interference with the black vote in Mississippi had ended.[42]

The Supreme Court heard Parker's appeal, and he and Summer faced off once more in February. Summer continued to cling to the hope of multimember districts because the court had not explicitly banned them. When attorney Jarris Leonard charged that "things have changed in Mississippi" and black people had representation in the state's politics, Justice Thurgood Marshall asked him how many blacks held seats in the legislature.[43]

The Supreme Court delayed ruling until the end of May. On May 31, the justices, in a 7–1 decision with only Justice Lewis Powell dissenting, rejected the state's apportionment plan yet again. The court said the most recent plan yet again violated the Equal Protection Clause due to population deviations that occurred when the state used county lines as boundaries for districts. Five of the eight justices said that county lines should be disregarded in favor of population balance because strict adherence to county lines "must inevitably collide with . . . one person, one vote." Parker hailed the decision and said he hoped that the district court would "see the handwriting on the wall" and quickly approve a new plan. Summer considered the ruling a draw, partly because the court did not order special elections.[44]

Gov. Cliff Finch, resigned to the Burger Court's decision, said that the legislature should "bite the bullet" and draft an acceptable plan of reapportionment. Finch, the uniter of the Loyalists and Regulars, no doubt wanted the racially divisive issue of the *Conner* cases to go away. In October 1977, he convened a special session of the legislature to approve a plan by the end of October, but the debates dragged past this date. Some legislators still fought the fragmenting of county lines, such as Sen. Jim Walters of Hinds County who called a proposal to divide south Jackson among three different senate districts an "outrageous action." The Legislature recognized that the Supreme Court would not approve a plan that did not have population equity and passed a single-member district reapportionment plan for the 1979 elections, which finally ended multimember districts in Mississippi.[45]

The enactment of single-member districts did not mean that racial issues disappeared from future legislative reapportioning, but their arrival meant an end to an important mechanism of minority vote dilution. Race had influenced legislative reapportionment in Mississippi since the era of Jim Crow, just as it had shaped everything else in the state's political life. With the rise of the civil rights movement and the Supreme Court's decisions against malapportionment, race became the predominant issue as the state legislature used multimember districts to dilute newly enfranchised black voters. The long but eventually successful legal challenges of the MFDP and its civil rights attorneys led to a plan that expanded the number of black legislators in 1975 and showed real promise for the elections of 1979. As white and black Mississippians readied themselves for the 1979 elections, the question that lingered was not if any black candidates would win legislative office but how many.

6 The Class of 1979 and the Second Generation of Black Political Power

THE USE OF single-member state legislative districts for the 1979 elections led to the first significant number of black legislators in the twentieth century. The "class of 1979" represented the Democratic Party establishment and formed a caucus of college-educated black men who represented the pinnacle of the new black politics in Mississippi. Black officeholders on the local level joined this second generation of black political power by securing control of county governments and even sheriffs' offices in some black-majority areas. The growth of black politics contributed directly to white voters' dissatisfaction with the Democrats and their subsequent attraction to the Republican Party. The racial problems that fusion had not completely solved still erupted into public view, most dramatically in 1980 when William Winter appointed a white Democratic Party chairman. The Republicans themselves continued with their own internal clashes as the conservative and progressive wings of the party feuded over whether the party should try to become truly biracial or instead bring segregationist whites into the fold.

With a Republican senator representing Mississippi in Washington, the question that loomed for the 1979 elections was whether the GOP would take the governor's mansion as well. Gil Carmichael prepared another run for the governor's office, but he now faced opposition from the ideological wing of his party over his moderate views. Conservatives in the Mississippi GOP had opposed Carmichael in 1975 but kept quiet

FIGURE 12. Lt. Gov. William Winter. Like virtually all white Democrats in Mississippi, Winter began as a segregationist politician but shifted his support to fusion as the realities of the Voting Rights Act changed Mississippi politics. The benefits of fusion paid dividends in 1979, when he defeated progressive Republican Gil Carmichael for the governor's office and then pushed through a major reform of the state's public education system with the help of the Black Legislative Caucus. Yet his own attempts to keep the top-party leadership white to keep white voters in the party angered many of his black allies. William F. "Bill" Minor Papers, 80–534–1, Special Collections Department, Mitchell Memorial Library, Mississippi State University.

for the sake of party unity. After Carmichael's loss to Cliff Finch, all of that changed.[1]

The conservative and moderate factions in the state party erupted into a nasty public squabble at the Republican National Convention in Kansas City in 1976. Carmichael backed the nomination of Gerald Ford, while Billy Mounger became the state chairman for Ronald Reagan who challenged the incumbent president. Within the Mississippi GOP, the moderates backed Ford while the conservative ideologues supported Reagan. The state delegation was officially uncommitted, but the Ford campaign diverted its resources elsewhere after Reagan's string of victories in the southern primaries. Yet Harry Dent, the architect of Nixon's "Southern Strategy" and now a Ford advisor, saw a chance for Ford to win the state's winner-take-all primary.[2]

Clarke Reed had reason to be dissatisfied with Gerald Ford, in particular over civil rights issues. As chairman of the Southern Association of Republican State Chairmen, Reed continued to try to exert influence on Ford, just as he had done with Nixon on school desegregation. However, Ford waffled over extending the Voting Rights Act extension in 1975 to all fifty states, a position Reed supported and was also sponsored by Sen. John Stennis (D-Miss). Ford's clumsy endorsement of Reed's position and his subsequent retraction in the wake of liberal Republican concerns angered Reed and led some observers to brand Ford incompetent. Reed in particular had a long history of conflict with J. Stanley Pottinger, head of the Justice Department's Civil Rights Division. Pottinger, a moderate Republican from the Ripon Society, worked closely with civil rights advocacy groups in Mississippi. He and Reed had feuded as far back as 1970 when Pottinger worked as Director of the Office of Civil Rights in President Nixon's HEW department.[3]

Ford backers Carmichael and Doug Shanks, a Jackson city commissioner, were state delegates at the convention, a pairing that one political observer likened to "boarding a couple of vampires at a blood bank." Dent, who had no respect for the ideological "purist conservatives," reached out to the pragmatists, including his longtime friend and ally Reed. Carmichael provided intelligence to Dent, giving him information on the delegates so that he could contact and pressure them. Dent said that Reed, despite his conservatism, understood the importance of winning, while one conservative less kindly described Reed as weak "because he wanted to please everybody."[4]

The Dent strategy of working on the pragmatists showed how fluid and circumstantial some of these ideological categories were in the Mississippi Republican Party. Reed wanted to maintain influence by supporting the winner, even if it meant a less conservative nominee. Dent played to Reed's ambition by telling him that he would be the "kingmaker" at the convention and earn Ford's gratitude. Yet Dent also worked on state senator and party chairman Charles Pickering, even arranging a personal audience with Ford. Pickering was the leader of the Mississippi Baptist Convention and an anti-abortion conservative. Pickering, whom Mounger liked and supported, eventually backed Reagan even though he did consider switching his support to Ford.[5]

Billy Mounger used his clout as the party's chief fundraiser to keep the delegates aligned with Reagan. Mounger had already broken privately with Carmichael, but the Meridian businessman's maneuvering for both Ford and himself led to a public rupture. Incensed when Carmichael unsuccessfully challenged him for the delegation's vice-chairmanship, Mounger called him "a man of all-consuming ego with no vestige of humility." Carmichael tried to mend fences by publicly urging Reagan at a press conference to accept a vice-presidential slot on the Ford ticket, but the effort failed.[6]

Reed's vacillation between Ford and Reagan particularly infuriated Mounger. The party fundraiser put a high value on loyalty, and any perceived betrayal earned his lasting enmity. In 1975, Reed had encouraged Reagan to run for president, so Mounger interpreted Reed's wavering as a personal betrayal of both Reagan and the ideologues of the party. Mounger saw Reed's failure to squelch the moderates as "spinelessness." Reed finally abandoned Reagan when he picked liberal Sen. Richard Schweiker (R-Penn.) to be his running mate, declaring Schweiker unpalatable to Mississippi conservatives, but in reality Reed was looking for an excuse to back Ford. Yet Mounger, despite his distaste for Schweiker, stayed loyal to Reagan, reasoning that a liberal vice-president was tolerable as long as the conservative Reagan headed the ticket. The ideological splits carried over to other prominent state GOP figures as well. Ideologues such as Wirt Yerger and Trent Lott backed Reagan, while the pragmatist Cochran favored Ford. Lott, as an elected official, showed more willingness to compromise than an ideologue such as Mounger. At Ford's urging, Lott reluctantly endorsed the president prior to the convention. His support was lukewarm, however, and he did not campaign against Reagan and skipped the Kansas City convention, but he did support Ford during his campaign stops in Mississippi that fall.[7]

In the end, the delegates voted 31–28 to give the delegation's thirty votes to Ford. The drawn-out affair created lasting political enemies. Mounger felt betrayed by pro-Reagan delegates who "apostatized" by voting for Ford, and he never spoke to Reed again after the convention. While Pickering worked to keep the peace at the convention, fallout from the Ford-Reagan feud would also have implications for the state GOP and the direction it would take with black voters.[8]

With the party divisions now publicly laid open after Kansas City, the GOP struggle over black voters became more visible as a key component of the ideological clashes. Carmichael said that his goal was to make sure the Republican Party did not become "lily white and hard right." The conservative faction in the party, by implication, wanted to do the opposite of Carmichael. The Mounger faction of conservative ideologues did not make open appeals to segregationists or use other forms of overt race-baiting as Prentiss Walker and Rubel Phillips did in the first half of the 1960s. Sensitive to charges of racism, they adopted the nonracist discourse of the New Right discussed by scholars like Joseph Crespino, Matthew Lassiter, and Kevin Kruse. While more astute than Walker had been in his 1975 attack on Carmichael, the ideologues' actions betrayed little interest in party integration. Mounger generally did not support other Republicans who made interracial appeals. When Doug Shanks, who helped engineer Ford's nomination, ran for mayor of Jackson in 1977 and openly sought black voters, Mounger took no active part in the election and privately worked to cut off Shanks's funds. Mounger admitted that the GOP needed "to try to make an appeal to a certain portion of the black vote," but he did not seem willing to support those who tried to do so.[9]

Even more pragmatic Republicans drew the wrath of Mounger if they received his support but did not reciprocate with conservative votes. Mounger's displeasure with the pragmatist Cochran surfaced quickly after the new senator assumed his duties in 1979. Cochran himself was irritated at Mounger's decision to stay neutral in the Senate Republican primary, so he excluded Mounger from his steering committee. Mounger had raised money for Cochran and had given him a personal donation in the primary, and one to Pickering as well. This financial support, Mounger felt, would be reciprocated with close adherence to conservative doctrine. Mounger wrote a letter to Cochran urging him to support Sen. Orrin Hatch (R-Utah) over the more liberal Sen. H. J. Heinz II (R-Penn.) for the chairmanship of the Senatorial Campaign Committee, but Cochran voted for Heinz who won by one vote. A furious Mounger wrote Cochran to castigate him for this vote and then circulated the letter in Republican circles, creating a rift between the two men for several years. What Cochran apparently saw as political dealmaking and compromise the ideological Mounger saw as personal betrayal.[10]

Mounger defended conservative doctrine against another campaign by Gil Carmichael. Carmichael prepared another run for the governor's office in 1979, but Mounger and Wirt Yerger rallied Leon Bramlett, a wealthy Clarksdale cotton planter, to oppose him. Bramlett, a former chairman of the Regular Democrats, had opposed fusion with the mostly black Loyalists and switched to the GOP shortly after Cliff Finch's election in 1975. Bramlett's break with the Democrats had clear racial overtones. When Finch brought the opposing wings of the party together in early 1976, Bramlett said, "[I]t became painfully obvious that the party had left me," citing "quotas and preferential treatment" as a source of his discontent. He raised the old Reconstruction bugbear of a black-controlled party manipulated by radical white outsiders when he declared that the party "is no longer the party we know; there is no place for us in it, except on the terms of the Aaron Henrys and the George McGoverns."[11]

Bramlett directly attacked Carmichael's platform of handgun registration and a new state constitution. Carmichael responded by criticizing Bramlett's borrowing of thousands of dollars under a low-interest federal farm program. The primary vote was a close victory for Carmichael who won by a margin of about two thousand votes out of over thirty-two thousand.[12]

Charles Evers entertained another political race while the Republicans debated the future of their party. With his showing in the previous year's Senate race, the Fayette mayor appeared to be a political boss who could deliver a bloc of black votes to a candidate in the statewide elections. In January 1979, he formed the Independent Coalition of Mississippi, an umbrella organization of political groups and leaders created to endorse candidates for office.[13] Evers's presence guaranteed that race would remain a prominent political issue. Racial demagoguery may have faded from Mississippi politics, but race as an issue remained, especially with white candidates reaching out to black voters.

Even without Evers, local civil rights activists kept racial issues in the headlines. The United League of Marshall County continued its tradition of direct action when it spread throughout north Mississippi in 1978 and 1979. The League sponsored demonstrations or opened new chapters in Lexington, Okolona, Corinth, Canton, Tupelo, and Indianola in 1978 and 1979. Alfred "Skip" Robinson and his followers organized boycotts and demonstrations against job discrimination and police brutality. The League, with the support of Aaron Henry and the state NAACP, protested white violence and Klan activity in Okolona and demanded in the fall of 1978 that Tupelo's city government and merchants hire more African Americans. The protests in Tupelo led to arrests and a counter-demonstration by the Klan, but eventually the city government adopted an affirmative action program.[14]

Evers's growing anger at his former ally Gov. Finch fueled his 1979 ambitions. The 1979 session of the legislature revived open primary legislation, which Evers saw as a measure to eliminate black candidates like him from statewide office. If the law had been in effect in 1978, Evers would have been eliminated and Maurice Dantin, the Democratic candidate, would likely have defeated Cochran in the runoff. Finch signed the bill into law over black objections. Democrats such as Rep. Stone Barefield of Hattiesburg pushed the bill as a way to prevent Republicans from winning with pluralities as Cochran did the previous year. The bill also won the endorsement of Charles Pickering despite Cochran's success in 1978. The white bipartisan backing and the vocal opposition of prominent African Americans like Evers and Rep. Fred Banks suggested that the real motivation was to curb black independent candidacies. Banks said that nonracial reasons motivated the Republicans to back the open primary as well, namely their belief that the lack of party designation would make them more viable.[15]

Although the Justice Department rejected the open primary in June, Finch's support for the law led Evers to leave the Democrats and accuse them of disfranchisement. Calling Finch "the worst ever" Mississippi governor, Evers decided to play the kingmaker by offering his endorsement. Evers refused to endorse Carmichael and declared that he did not "know much" about the Meridian businessman, a comment at odds with his past dealings with him.[16]

Evers, despite his pledge to oppose the Democratic Party, continued his closeness with segregationists by backing former Hinds County state representative John Arthur Eaves in the Democratic primary. Eaves, an attorney who ran as a segregationist in the 1975 Democratic gubernatorial primary, had backed Evers during his Senate race the previous year. Evers attempted to swing the endorsement of the Independent Coalition of Mississippi behind Eaves, but the organization could not agree on a candidate. The dissatisfaction that many black leaders had with Evers publicly surfaced at the meeting. The Conference of Black Mayors, headed by Shaw Mayor Gregory Flippins, ignored Evers and backed another primary candidate, Jim Herring of Canton. Evers also angered the conference members when he refused to back Bolton mayor Bennie Thompson in a race to fill a Hinds County supervisor's position.[17]

Evers's habit of backing recently reformed segregationists did not play well with many black voters. Aaron Henry's rapport with James Eastland closely resembled Evers's backing of old segregationists and indicated their evolution from civil rights activists to political bosses. The key difference between Henry and Evers was that Henry's position within the Democratic Party organization gave him the institutional support that the independent Evers lacked. Two of the most prominent gubernatorial candidates in 1979, William Winter and Evelyn Gandy, had considerable black support. Although Evers castigated him as a "pseudo-liberal," Winter still enjoyed black support for his long-standing racial moderation that had hurt him with white voters in the 1967 election. Gandy solicited black voters and had built black patronage through her service as the state's Commissioner of Public Welfare, but her early association with Theodore Bilbo cost her some black support. The legislative races, not the governor's race, attracted the most African-American interest. Black candidates looked to make impressive gains in 1979 since the courts ordered the legislature to end the use of multimember districts that hindered the election of black politicians.[18]

Like the Independent Coalition of Mississippi, other black political groups split into public feuding over endorsements. A generational gap opened in Bolivar County where older, more conservative groups such as the Bolivar County Voters League clashed with Gregory Flippins and the Mississippi Conference of Black Mayors. The Voters League followed Evers's advice and backed Eaves. Flippins backed Herring and declared Evers to be "finished." Several black religious groups also split over endorsements. The Bolivar County General Baptist Association (GBA) endorsed Herring, while the Bolivar County Educational Baptist Association (EBA) and the Ministerial Alliance went with Eaves. The groups also split on local races, such as the reelection of longtime black supervisor Kermit Stanton, who was running for his fourth term. The Voters League backed the veteran black politician, while Flippins and his organization backed his black challenger.[19]

Evelyn Gandy led the field of gubernatorial candidates but did not get a majority. William Winter placed second, while Eaves finished third and Herring fourth. Evers's failure to deliver the black vote to Eaves revealed that the fallout from the 1978 election had crippled his political might. Southwest Mississippi, including Evers's base in Jefferson County, did not support Eaves. As one black voter stated, Eaves "came across as just another 'cracker' in the black community." The four top candidates won roughly equal shares of the overall black vote.[20]

Evers, apparently unperturbed by his decline, announced his candidacy as an independent for the state senate in a four-county southwestern district.[21] In the primary runoff, Winter soundly defeated Gandy to win the Democratic nomination and face Gil Carmichael. Carmichael repeated his earlier theme of economic development, declaring that he would attract high-paying industrial jobs to the state. In speeches before black audiences, he echoed Evers's theme of replacing social programs with jobs. He played to anti-welfare sentiment but at the same time declared that he would not cut existing programs and took pains to deflect the charge that as a Republican he was an enemy of federal entitlement programs.[22]

Although the campaign pitted two racial moderates against each other, some lingering racial issues created tensions. Busing, with its emotional appeal to white voters, emerged, and Carmichael irritated some black voters by waffling. He cited Charles Evers's opposition to busing as indication that the black community did not support the practice and instead predicted that the energy crisis would curtail it. He continued to stress the economic integration of blacks into Mississippi's economy and avoided issues of social integration, calling it "a private matter between people." He emphasized his own record, namely his employment of African Americans at his Volkswagen dealership, and called attention to the lack of black employees at Winter's law firm. Yet Carmichael admitted his own shortcomings when he apologized before an NAACP meeting for his membership in an all-white country club and confessed he was "not perfect."[23]

Carmichael continued his black outreach, especially to ministers, businessmen, and elected black officials to run operations in black precincts. He won the support of the Pike County Voters League, a black organization which backed Jim Herring in the Democratic primary. Winter in turn reminded black voters that his moderation likely cost him the governor's race in 1967. Like Carmichael, he spoke before the NAACP audiences. Charles Evers accused Winter of opposing the current redistricting plan that benefited black legislators and of being allied with "white bigots" in the state Senate. The outspoken mayor refused to endorse Carmichael and only said that he was not supporting Winter.[24]

Carmichael's biggest handicap, as in 1975, remained his Republican Party label. As one black voter put it, the Republicans "don't really want blacks and poor people to join their club, just vote for them." Although black voters favored Winter because they saw him as "decent and fairminded," many voted against Carmichael because of the actions of others in his party. Carmichael solicited help from national conservatives such as Ronald Reagan, who did not enjoy wide popularity among black people. Mississippi Republican Jon Hinson also stirred anger from black voters and Evers when the congressman first opposed a national holiday for Martin Luther King Jr. then later called for it to be established on a Sunday to minimize the economic loss to the country. His opposition to the extension of the Voting Rights Act also did not win him or the Republican Party in his district many black friends.[25]

Racial matters also surfaced late in the campaign in another statewide race. In the attorney general's race, political observers favored Republican nominee Charles Pickering over assistant attorney general and Democratic nominee Bill Allain. Pickering ran commercials on several black radio stations the weekend before Election Day that accused Allain of previous membership in the White Citizens' Councils. The ads made a direct reference to Allain's tenure as assistant attorney general from 1962 to 1975 when he represented the state in the *Conner* cases. One of the radio spots said that "in the reapportionment cases, Bill Allain fought equal representation for blacks." The ads misfired, especially when the Citizens' Council allegation proved to be untrue. Pickering backed off from the ads, but the fallout over them created a last-minute backlash giving Allain a narrow victory.[26]

Billy Mounger, who was unaware of the development of the ad campaign, called it "disastrous" and said he would have opposed it. To Mounger, ever-attuned to the racial feelings of conservative whites, the ads had the opposite effect and made Allain more palatable to them by linking him to the Councils. He made clear the importance of white racial conservatism to the expanding state GOP when he said after the election, "[T]he greatest errors Mississippi Republican candidates commit are those concerning appeals for liberal or black votes." Mounger recognized, as Dan Carter has pointed out about the GOP generally, that the George Wallace Democrats were the GOP's "natural constituency" and in order to win "never alienate these groups." He blamed the fiasco on influence from the national Republican National Committee, which had dispatched two black staffers with thousands of dollars in funds for black voter outreach.[27]

Although avoiding racist commentary, Mounger laid out his party's direction regarding which voters to pursue in clear racial terms. Black voters were welcome but only if they shared the totality of Mounger's conservatism. Compromise, so abhorrent to him, would not be tolerated for the sake of party biracialism. Regarding the memory of the civil rights movement, Mounger saw even a rhetorical condemnation of the state's past as undesirable. The wooing of Wallace voters rested squarely on race, as Mounger and other ideologues were opposed to the populist economic agenda of Wallace and instead backed the pro-corporate orientation of the national New Right.

Mounger no doubt felt his views vindicated when Carmichael lost again, with dire consequences for the GOP moderates. On Election Day, William Winter easily won with 413,000 votes to Carmichael's 263,000. Carmichael failed to carry a single majority-black county. His standing with white voters declined as well, and he even lost his home county of Lauderdale. Carmichael did not even get the support of some Bramlett Republicans who voted for Winter or not at all because of their dislike for the Republican nominee.[28]

The defeat of Carmichael, along with Doug Shanks's failed Jackson race in 1977, marked the permanent decline of the moderate wing of the state Republican Party. Carmichael blamed party conservatives like Billy Mounger and Wirt Yerger for his loss, claiming that the bloody Republican primary challenge they bankrolled forced him to spend funds he could have used against Winter. With the exception of Cochran, GOP pragmatists largely drifted away from interracial outreach. Political commentator Wayne Weidie, who had chaired Carmichael's 1972 Senate campaign, took a swipe at Mounger when he bluntly declared, "[T]he Mississippi Republican Party has a majority which has never heard of the twentieth century."[29]

Evers's condemnation of Winter, like his failed backing of Eaves in the primary, did not turn away appreciable numbers of black voters from the Democrats. Even southwestern Mississippi where Evers had the most influence went solidly for Winter. Evers won Claiborne and Jefferson Counties in his state senate race, but his white opponent edged him out elsewhere. Evers claimed voting irregularities cost him the race, but the defeat only hastened the civil rights leader's political irrelevancy.[30]

The state legislative races yielded significant gains for black candidates. Black voters elected fifteen black House members and two Senate members, including Henry Kirksey, one of the plaintiffs in the reapportionment suits. Kirksey and the other black senate candidate, Doug Anderson, won election from Hinds County. Aaron Henry won a House seat in an unopposed election in Coahoma County. All of the elected African Americans also won nominations in the Democratic primaries, which showed the continuing decline in successful independent candidacies. Several black Republican candidates also failed in their election bids, including Nehemiah Flowers, a former aide to U.S. Senator Thad Cochran. Civil rights attorney Frank Parker, who represented Kirksey and the other plaintiffs in the reapportionment suits, called the gains by black Mississippians in the elections "just tremendous." Henry Kirksey defeated redistricting foe Sen. Jim Walters by campaigning on his fourteen-year struggle for reapportionment and single-member districts with the slogan "He made it happen." Kirksey said simply that Election Day had been "a pretty good day."[31]

While the governor and legislative races attracted the most attention, black candidates also made significant gains on the county level. Hinds County voters put two black men on the board of supervisors for the first time since Reconstruction. One of the new supervisors, Bolton mayor Bennie Thompson, swept aside his black independent opponent and a white Republican to win his race. In all, Hinds County voters elected four black state representatives, two black state senators, and two black supervisors.[32]

The most notable county victories came in the sheriff's races. In the counties of Holmes, Claiborne, and Marshall, voters elected the state's first black sheriffs in the twentieth century.[33] In Holmes County, Howard Huggins, the "safe" black constable, won the Democratic primary by an overwhelming margin and faced no opposition in the general election. He had the full backing of outgoing sheriff Calvin Moore, which helped neutralize any serious opposition. Huggins admitted that when he first started as a deputy in the 1960s, "[P]eople didn't accept me as well as they do now." He emphasized his even-handedness, declaring that he arrested "black people and white people—it's all the same."[34]

In Claiborne County, Frank Davis, a thirty-one year old Port Gibson policeman and civil defense director, challenged Democratic incumbent sheriff Dan McKay as an independent. The three-to-one black majority, building on the earlier gains by black officeholders and civil rights activists in the county, allowed Davis to win outside the Democratic Party system. Davis, a former deputy sheriff, unseated McKay. Black officeholders further increased the majority of county offices they gained in the 1975 elections with Davis's election and the addition of another African American to the board of supervisors to create a four-to-one black majority.[35]

In Marshall County, the activities of the United League almost overshadowed the election of Osborne Bell as sheriff. The League, fresh from its highly publicized activities throughout northern Mississippi in 1978 and early 1979, flexed its muscle during the 1979 county elections. The presence of the United League worried members of the Marshall County Democratic Executive Committee enough for them to request federal observers for the primary election. Robinson himself was ousted from the committee by the state party. According to party authorities, Robinson had added himself and five of his black allies to the committee to further increase the black majority.[36]

As the primary drew near, the League endorsed several black candidates running for office, including Osborne Bell for sheriff and League secretary Henry Boyd for state representative. In a repeat of 1975, Boyd challenged state Rep. Ralph Doxey. The League also endorsed one white candidate, Chancery Court Clerk J. M. "Flick" Ash, who ran against two white opponents in his reelection bid. Ash, who as a deputy sheriff had harassed SNCC workers during Freedom Summer, now worked for the Head Start program in the county and ran ads picturing him with black residents. The Marshall County elections stayed tense as more than one hundred federal observers heeded the white members' request and arrived in the county.[37]

Although most of the black candidates lost the primary, Bell won the Democratic nomination for sheriff and Bernice Totten won renomination for her supervisor's position. The racial tensions deepened after the state party ousted him and his allies from the county's Democratic committee, leading Robinson to declare himself an independent candidate for county supervisor. Robinson's personal life also spilled into the headlines when police arrested him for threatening to kill his ex-wife.[38]

The primary runoff went quietly but had barely ended when the ballot swelled with independents who filed to run in the general election. African Americans affiliated with the League made up most of the candidates, but some white independents also qualified to challenge the Democratic candidates. Two white independents opposed Bell in the sheriff's election. The wife of Kenneth Smith, the incumbent sheriff whom Bell defeated in the primary, ran as an independent candidate against Bell. The other white candidate, W. O. Fitch, told the media that he or Smith would drop out to leave only one opponent to challenge Bell.[39]

Like Huggins in Holmes County, Bell played up his image as a "safe" black candidate before the white and black voters of Marshall County. The publicity surrounding Robinson and the United League could have hurt Bell because he had the League's endorsement in the primary, but he distanced himself from the civil rights organization. He made a concerted effort to deracialize his politics, even his association with more moderate groups like the NAACP. He described himself as a "supporter" but not an "activist" in the NAACP and used the slogan "Fairness to All" in his campaign. He later claimed that race "was never an issue" in the election, but the comments of Fitch, who dropped out of the race, suggested that some whites in the county sought to limit the number of white candidates to prevent a split in the white vote.[40]

Bell easily defeated Smith in November, and the other independent candidates also lost, but the voters did elect a black superintendent of education. While black officeholders did not dominate county offices to the extent that African Americans did in Claiborne County, they now held two countywide offices, a board of supervisor's seat, a majority on the election commission, and a scattering of other minor offices.[41]

Robinson and others claimed fraud in some of the elections, but like the 1975 challenge by Henry Boyd against Ralph Doxey nothing came of the allegations. While Robinson and Boyd had once again lost bids for public office, the black mobilization and voter registration helped elect Bell and other black candidates. Bobby Joe Adkins, who later became the second black sheriff of Marshall County, said Robinson and the United League's work in the 1970s "paved the way" for his and Bell's elections.[42]

With the increase in black political strength in the legislature and the inauguration of a longtime racial moderate as governor, black voters and politicians appeared to be poised to reach ever-higher levels of political power and access in Mississippi. Despite the advances, racial troubles plagued the early days of the Winter administration. Winter made two black appointments to the all-white Health Care Commission but only after complaints by the mostly black Mississippi Medical and Surgical Association. Part of Winter's problems came from the professional organizations that by law had the right to make nominations to boards that regulated their professions. The mostly white and male boards generally neglected minority and female appointments. For example, Winter appointed three white male lawyers to the Board of Corrections in the first four months of his administration. He did break some racial barriers by naming the first black warden of Parchman State Prison and by placing Constance Slaughter-Harvey, a classmate of Bennie Thompson and the first black woman to graduate from the University of Mississippi's School of Law, in the Office of Human Development.[43]

Some of the harshest criticism of Winter came from the black press. The *Jackson Advocate* steadily criticized Winter and other white Democrats, from President Jimmy Carter down to the city commissioners of Jackson. The *Advocate* had come a long way from the 1960s, when Percy Greene, the original publisher of the paper and a paid informant for the Mississippi State Sovereignty Commission, frequently ran anti-civil rights editorials. Greene died in 1978, and the following year Charles W. Tisdale, a Memphis journalist, purchased the paper from Greene's widow. He changed the paper radically by introducing investigative journalism and more coverage of local events. One scholar of the paper calls this period the "age of awareness" since Tisdale ran editorials strongly emphasizing black pride and criticizing black leaders he thought were overly self-serving. His bluntness won him many enemies, especially from whites who regarded him as a racist.[44]

A much greater racial brouhaha erupted when Winter moved to abolish the biracial co-chairmanship of the Democratic Party, a key part of Finch's 1976 fusion agreement. In the spring of 1980 he announced the nomination of Danny Cupit, a white Jackson lawyer, as a single party head to replace co-chairs Tom Riddell and Aaron Henry. The issue drew immediate opposition from black Democrats. A special committee of state Democrats tried to solve the problem in May 1980, but they split along racial lines. Aaron Henry lobbied for preserving the co-chairmanship, but Winter and his supporters stressed that party administration would be improved by a single chair. Winter inflamed racial tensions at the committee meetings when he announced that "at this time the chairman of the party should be white." The black members of the committee abstained or voted against Cupit, who was elected by a 56–34 vote. Angry at the outcome, the black members present refused to accept nominations to party treasurer and vice chairman, posts they were entitled to under the constitution.[45]

Aaron Henry, who probably more than any other African American in the state had publicly urged black Mississippians to stay with the party, put on a public face of party unity and embraced Cupit after his election but left the meeting "visibly upset." Keeping with his desire to be the power broker, Henry tried to mollify the black committee members immediately after the meeting, but with limited success. White Democrats still held all the statewide offices, and a white governor served as the titular head of the state party. Rep. Fred Banks angrily pointed out the white overrepresentation in the state leadership when he argued that the party did not need a white chairman, and Banks speculated that "maybe the Democratic Party isn't worth identifying with." Bennie Thompson harkened back to his militant days with SNCC and said that he and Banks were "fed up with all this shit" and that "maybe this will teach us that you can't go around hugging the enemy and trying to create harmony when there is none." Although the *Jackson Advocate* invoked the Constitution of 1890 when it said that Henry's actions contained "shades of Isaiah T. Montgomery," the black delegate who had voted for disfranchisement, Henry carried his displeasure over the election of Cupit to Washington in talks with national Democratic Party officials. Rep. Robert Clark also voiced his preference for a co-chair and, like Henry, worked in the party to heal the wounds caused by the incident.[46]

Winter and his conservative allies, such as Rep. Stone Barefield of Hattiesburg, pushed the election of a white party chair as a way to prevent the defection of white Mississippians to the Republican Party. White interest in the GOP had already helped Thad Cochran's election to the U.S. Senate and threatened to deliver the state to Republican presidential nominee Ronald Reagan that fall. Winter and his allies wanted a biracial party but a party that did not look so "black" that the old Wallace Democrats and segregationists would leave. A couple of weeks after the election of Cupit, Winter refused to apologize for his statements and said that he was concerned about white defections. Already Jan

Little, the former Democratic National Committeewoman from Mississippi, had been expelled from the party for publicly supporting Gil Carmichael in 1979. Other Democrats also flirted with the GOP, such as State Senate President Pro Tempore W.B Alexander of Cleveland, who won reelection in 1980 as a Democrat but had publicly backed Ronald Reagan in 1976. Many black Democrats, however, saw the abolition of a black co-chairman as a demotion to a subordinate role in the state party. The *Jackson Advocate* warned that black voters might stay away from the polls in November.[47] For Aaron Henry, who had faced the ire of SNCC and the MFDP for backing the Atlantic City compromise in 1964, the Cupit affair must have seemed like déjà vu but was not surprising given his previous support for Eastland.

Ironically, Cupit was a product of the old Loyalist wing of the party and had a long reputation as a racial moderate. He had been a Young Democrat at Mississippi State University and then went on to the University of Mississippi Law School. In 1968, he successfully sued the university's board of trustees when they tried to block Charles Evers from speaking on campus and in 1970 criticized the university's expulsion of eight black students involved in a campus disturbance.[48]

In a compromise that June, Henry and Winter negotiated a new set of rules for sharing power and ended the co-chair but created the new position of executive vice chairperson, which went to Ed Cole, Sen. Eastland's first black staff member. Henry and other African Americans in the state party formed the Coalition of Determined Democrats (CDD) to lobby for the position of black Democrats in the party, and Henry stayed with the party in an unofficial emeritus position. Henry asked black party members to support the compromise, and the party then delivered a unified slate of delegates for President Jimmy Carter at the national Democratic Convention in New York City. Years later, Winter defended the abolition of the biracial co-chair as "the right thing to do even though it caused a little heartburn at the time," but he admitted that expressing support for a white party chair was "perhaps an unwise statement." For many black Democrats, Winter's long history of racial moderation made the pain of the incident especially acute.[49]

Black anger over the Cupit affair lingered throughout 1980. The Black Legislative Caucus, comprising all the black members in the legislature, tried to increase its influence by endorsing Henry Kirksey for the Democratic nomination in the fourth district to challenge Republican U.S. Rep. Jon Hinson. Kirksey lost the primary runoff to Britt Singletary, a thirty-year-old former staffer of James Eastland. Another black candidate then emerged to challenge Hinson and Singletary in the general election. Leslie Burl McLemore, a Jackson State political science professor and member of the 1964 MFDP delegation to Atlantic City, declared his candidacy as an independent in the race. McLemore, like Robert Clark, had a political background marked less by party loyalty and more by ideology. He worked with the Loyalist Democrats in the 1970s, but in 1975 he joined Clark to work for Gil Carmichael and later helped with Bennie Thompson's county supervisor campaign. McLemore ran to protest the abolition of the co-chair. He announced his "people's crusade" after meeting with a number of black leaders, who nominated him at a "counterconvention." McLemore won the backing of several members of the Black Legislative Caucus.[50]

The *Jackson Advocate*, which had earlier denounced "black sell-outs and Uncle Toms" among elected black officials, greeted McLemore's announcement with some caution and speculated that the black community in the district would vote for McLemore out of anger. McLemore hoped to win with a plurality, relying on the over-forty-percent black population of the district, with the white candidates splitting the white vote. Ivory Phillips, a columnist in the *Advocate*, called the candidacy a "golden opportunity" to prove the viability of black independent politics. Charles Tisdale, the publisher of the *Advocate*, endorsed McLemore as the election drew closer and called him "the best qualified of the candidates." Even Winter, who did not endorse the independent McLemore, called him a "very attractive candidate."[51]

McLemore campaigned in Hinds, Warren, Adams, and Pike Counties, the four most populous counties in the fourth district. The counties, while majority-white, had large black populations and were critical to victory. He ignored the more sparsely populated white counties and counted on heavy support from Claiborne, Jefferson, and Wilkinson Counties, a tactic also dictated by lack of funds.[52]

McLemore's candidacy and the anger over the Cupit affair also pointed to the problem of rising black expectations that had not been fulfilled by fusion. The uniting of the party, according to McLemore, led to inflated hopes of just how high black Mississippians could rise politically, but by 1980 a sense of disillusionment had set it in. White Democrats expected black Mississippians to forgive old segregationists like James Eastland and accept a supporting role in the state party. The same white Democrats did not reciprocate by offering or supporting black candidates for any statewide offices, which angered some black Democrats.[53] After Evers's showing in the 1978 Senate race, many white state party leaders likely felt a black candidate could not win a statewide election and would only push white voters to the Republicans.

Black state Democratic leaders understood that many black voters felt angry over the end of the co-chair and would support McLemore and siphon critical black votes from Singletary. Ed Cole, recently appointed to the position of executive vice chairman of the party, refused to condemn McLemore and said that "any black man is torn by having to make a choice between two equally qualified candidates." He openly sympathized with angry black voters and their "legitimate concerns about how they may not have been served by the Democratic Party."[54]

Although the Republican Party and top ideologues like Billy Mounger and Wirt Yerger backed incumbent Jon Hinson, he realized he needed every vote he could muster. Hinson's 1980 campaign was hamstrung by revelations of his homosexuality, including a prior arrest at a gay cruising area in Washington, D.C. Hinson denied he was gay, but the allegations weakened his support. Hinson tried to win black votes by announcing his support in September for the proposed Urban Jobs and Enterprise Zone Act, a tax-cutting bill that had been introduced more than three months earlier. He cited statistics on black unemployment and said that the nation needed a new urban policy to help the urban underclass. The bill would have designated five "enterprise zones" in Jackson and Hinds County for various tax cuts to stimulate investment and employment.[55]

Despite overtures such as the tax bill, Hinson and Singletary both made more appeals to white segregationists than to black voters. Both men opposed re-extending the Voting Rights Act, just as Mississippi's bipartisan congressional delegation had done in 1975. Singletary was about as conservative as Hinson on almost every social issue exception abortion, which Hinson wanted to outlaw by constitutional amendment and Singletary did not. McLemore ran as a liberal and was the only candidate to support the Equal Rights Amendment (ERA), sex education in public schools, and federal funding of abortions for poor women. He defended the ERA and the Voting Rights Act as necessary providers of equality for women and minorities.[56]

On Election Day, Hinson won thirty-nine percent of the vote, a sharp erosion of support since his freshman election in 1978. McLemore, with thirty-one percent, did much better than Doss's showing two years earlier. He showed that he had made a serious and viable effort at winning, but he still could not overcome the problems of the lack of a Democratic Party label and a white majority in the district. Singletary emerged as the biggest loser, trailing in third place with less than thirty percent.[57]

The Republican Party, which had done well by exploiting divisions in the state Democratic Party, saw potential with the Democratic schism over the co-chair. Pragmatists such as Clarke Reed still held power, but he had to beat back an attempt by the ideologues to oust him at the state party's convention. Billy Mounger and Wirt Yerger, angry at Reed for backing Gerald Ford over Ronald Reagan in 1976, still had little interest in an interracial party, and one journalist observing the battles frankly stated that the ideologues sought "to return the party to its 1960s complexion." Mississippi's Republican members of Congress urged the party to unify to win the state for Reagan that fall, which led to Reed keeping his position as national committeeman.[58]

The Cupit affair and the possibility of black votes for the GOP played into the hands of black Republicans. African Americans in the Mississippi Republican Party successfully pushed for the election of three black alternate delegates to the national convention by calling attention to the racial divides in the Democratic Party over the Cupit affair. Mike Retzer, the GOP party chairman and a pragmatist who resisted the challenge by Wirt and Mounger, tried to reap political gain from the Democratic problems by calling for black Mississippians to join the party, but *Clarion-Ledger* reporter Jo Ann Klein dubbed this the GOP's "annual request for blacks." The state GOP sent an all-white delegation to the national convention in 1980, and only three of the twenty-two alternates were black, while the Democratic delegation that year was thirty-four percent black. Although Retzer accused the Democrats of taking black voters for granted, he refused to endorse a biracial chairmanship for his party even though it had no black members on its executive committee.[59] Party ideologues would likely interpret such an approach as racial quotas, which had prompted whites such as Leon Bramlett to leave the Democratic Party.

The nomination of Ronald Reagan satisfied Republican conservatives in Mississippi, who knew the former California governor could attract white southern support. Although black voters were not completely written off in heavily black districts, the Mississippi GOP's limitations on race did not make the party attractive enough for black voters to bolt the Democratic Party, and most stayed with Jimmy Carter. Reagan did not help his standing with black Mississippians when in August 1980 he campaigned at the Neshoba County Fair in Philadelphia, site of the Freedom Summer murders in 1964. Reagan had come at the urging of Rep. Trent Lott and other Republicans who felt an appearance could carry the state for Reagan. The Neshoba visit highlighted the lingering ideological differences in the state GOP, as Sen. Thad Cochran, ever the pragmatist, opposed the inclusion of any mention of "states' rights" in the speech, fearful of the connotation at Neshoba and a possible linkage of the campaign to white supremacy. While Cochran supported the visit to the fair, some of Reagan's aides and even Nancy Reagan opposed the governor appearing at the fair because of the memory of the murders. The ideological Lott pushed hard for the inclusion of the phrase and won out in the end. Reagan spoke before a nearly all-white crowd about how he "believed in states' rights" and would return power to state and local governments. Lott also made similar comments during the campaign at another pro-Reagan rally. Although a variety of issues factored in the election and hamstrung Carter—from the Iranian hostage situation to the energy crisis—the rallying of white voters also reaped dividends for Reagan in Mississippi. Carter also had problems nationally with black voters, many of whom were angry at him for his lack of support for social welfare programs and his dismissal of Andrew Young as the U.S. ambassador to the United Nations. Carter lost the state by a narrow margin that fall.[60]

A few black Mississippians did make a home in the Republican Party by 1980. The state's Black Republican Council had twelve county chapters by 1980 but only a few hundred members. Like some of the black candidates in the 1960s and 1970s, its members saw themselves less as ideological party loyalists than as activists for their race who believed that an overwhelming black vote for the Democratic Party would lead white politicians to take them for granted. The Lowdnes County chapter of the Black Republican Council accused the Democratic Party of that very thing and urged black voters to move to the GOP. Wilbur Colom, a Columbus attorney and spokesman for the Council, criticized "blind loyalty" to the Democratic Party but refrained from attacking black Democrats and called for "structured participation by blacks in both parties." Nehemiah Flowers, a black staffer for Thad Cochran, also pushed the idea of blacks not aligning with a single party and instead voting en masse for specific candidates. While Colom embraced the economic

FIGURE 13. Wilbur Colom, July 11, 1987. A Columbus attorney and member of the Black Republican Council, Colom broke with the main trend of black political sentiment in Mississippi, fearing that if black voters did not remain independent politically their interests would be ignored or taken for granted. He also voiced opposition to party conservatives who favored pursuing racially conservative whites as the base of party strength. Willie J. Miller Papers, 501–580, Special Collections Department, Mitchell Memorial Library, Mississippi State University.

conservatism of the Republicans, he saw a viable effort by the GOP to win black votes as a way to create meaningful competition for the black vote and thus improve the political status of the African-American community. He and other black Republicans reasoned that an independent black vote would only benefit the black community and increase its political influence, the same thing McLemore tried to do.[61]

Later attempts at party integration still met the fierce resistance of Mounger. He opposed the renewal of the Voting Rights Act in 1982, telling Reagan it was an "inequitable, invidious, and iniquitous" law. He again dismissed black votes for Republicans, insisting that "they are only for sale through government handouts." In another sign of the rift between him and Thad Cochran over ideology and black outreach, Mounger blasted a proposal from Cochran to add five black Republican delegates to the state party's Executive Committee, calling it "incestuous proliferation" and "worse than any quota." He admitted the party needed to attract black voters, but he felt the integration of the Executive Committee violated conservative principles. Mounger's rhetoric, while ostensibly nonracist, was laden with the racial anxieties of white segregationists and certainly not the colorblind discourse or ideology that scholars such as Matthew Lassiter say emerged in the southern suburbs of the 1970s. The overt hostility of conservatives such as Mounger to the institutionalization of racial progress cannot be deemed nonracial in tone or rhetoric despite what some scholars have argued.[62]

The failure of the moderates in 1979 and the victory of Reagan in 1980 was the death knell of major black outreach by the Mississippi GOP. Although individual candidates continued the efforts, the party preferred the ever-increasing numbers of defecting white Democrats. The second "Great White Switch" of white southern Democrats by the 1980s to a partisan identification with the Republican Party, combined with a comparable black identification with the Democratic Party, ended the efforts of the moderates.[63]

As Mississippi's moderate Republicans disappeared into the political wilderness, the state's black Democrats were now firmly out of it. The events of 1980 showed the importance of the second generation of black political power that had won election to the state legislature in 1979. Single-member districts led directly to the establishment of the Black Legislative Caucus and its power within the Democratic Party. Early elected officials such as Charles Evers and Robert Clark and civil rights veterans such as Aaron Henry and Henry Kirksey made up the first generation. While most of these men held continuing influence in the state, some did not. Evers, whose stature declined sharply after the 1979 election, eroded it further when he endorsed Ronald Reagan in 1980, and in 1981 he lost his bid for a fourth term as mayor of Fayette.[64]

The legislators who made up the second generation of black political power won election from majority-black, single member districts created by the 1979 apportionment plan. The black legislators were all college-educated men and hailed from the black bourgeoisie, with most of them either businessmen or professionals such as lawyers or educators. Most of them represented urban areas, unlike the early post-1965 black politics of small towns and rural areas.[65] The counties that had strong civil rights organizing traditions and a body of black elected officials yielded the majority of the rural legislators. Many of them were younger than the average middle-aged elected black official. Eleven were in their twenties or thirties, and Sen. Doug Anderson won election at age forty.[66]

There was some overlap with the first generation of civil rights activists. Henry Kirksey and Aaron Henry were members of the class of 1979, and Robert Clark and the three other black legislators elected in 1975 won reelection as well. The older veterans had long records in the civil rights movement, such as Aaron Henry in the NAACP and Progressive Voters League and Henry Kirksey as an MFDP activist and litigator. Most of the new generation had only childhood memories of the civil rights activism of the 1960s. Some, such as Fred Banks, had credentials going back to the late 1960s and early 1970s. A few of the legislators had other government experience, such as Rep. Barney Schoby, a former Adams County supervisor, but for most the legislature was their first political office. Others had gained government experience by working for white moderates, such as Rep. Hillman Frazier, a former staffer of William Winter.[67]

The new urban legislators represented a change from the rural and small-town politics of Charles Evers and Robert Clark. Just as the new members likely ignored the advice of Charles Evers, some of them clashed with Clark over issues such as the specifics of education reform and Clark's close relationship with conservative House Speaker C. B. "Buddy" Newman. According to Clark, one of the legislators called him "that damn 'Buddy' Newman lovin' nigger" who betrayed black Mississippians by backing a sales tax increase to fund public education. The feeling was mutual, and Clark did not view the addition of more black legislators as necessarily a good thing. He said that "the most progressive time in the legislature for black folks" was from 1975 to 1979, when there were only four black men in the House who won more concessions from the white leadership than they did with more black state legislators later. Clark complained that some of the legislators from the class of 1979 would not consult him on issues and decided instead to arbitrarily vote against an issue "to intimidate the white folks," a behavior he held in low esteem. Some younger and more radical blacks thought Clark a sellout because of his dealings with conservative whites, but he said he had the ability to go behind closed doors and work with whites and insisted that he did "not give up my identity."[68] Just as the black electorate did not always vote in concert, the new generation of black political power did not always work in harmony.

Many black political leaders did not abandon the racial advocacy of the civil rights era. In his first year in office, Fred Banks publicly criticized the low number of African Americans working in state government and their absence from administrative positions. He and the other three black legislators introduced three bills in 1975 that urged state agencies to adopt nondiscrimination clauses. Despite the frictions that developed among the new black legislators and the older veterans, an experienced legislator like Banks described his relations with the newer legislators as "good." The real threat, he said, was the attempts by the white Democrats to draw him into the House leadership and effectively co-opt him. He said it was difficult "to fight against the establishment and at the same time be a part of the establishment."[69]

The gender of the legislators also revealed another characteristic of the newer, younger strain of black politics. Men composed the bulk of elected black officials in Mississippi and made up the entire 1979 class of black legislators. Black men, not women, dominated the new black politics. The South had a higher number of black women in elected office than any other region of the country, but most of the elected women served in local offices.[70] In July 1979, fifty-two elected black women held office in Mississippi out of a total of 327 elected black officials. Only eight held county offices, and only one, Bernice Totten of Marshall County, occupied a supervisor's seat. Two women, one of them MFDP veteran Unita Blackwell of Mayersville, served as mayors out of a total of seventeen black mayors, and like many of their male counterparts they represented small, rural towns of fewer than one thousand people.

The rest of the women served as city alderwomen, members of boards of education, and judicial offices. Voters did not send black women to the Mississippi House until 1985 and the Senate until 1987.[71]

The less-visible participation of black women in politics was an extension of their historic invisibility to both historians and general observers. Black women served as the backbone of the churches and other grassroots organizations in the civil rights movement while male ministers occupied prominent leadership positions.[72] During Freedom Summer and the 1960s Mississippi civil rights movement, the gender division in movement work foreshadowed the future divisions in black politics. Male civil rights workers gravitated towards the more dangerous work of voter registration, partly as a way to express masculine bravery in a nonviolent movement. Women, by contrast, took a lead in running the Freedom Schools that provided civic and academic education to black Mississippians. Male movement activists held the vital citizenship education of the Freedom Schools in low regard compared to voter registration. The male disdain for teaching extended to clerical work and other forms of feminized labor, which male recruiters in civil rights organizations frequently channeled towards white and black women. Despite these constraints, black women took an active part in civil rights demonstrations, such as Constance Slaughter (later Slaughter-Harvey), who served as the Tougaloo College student body president and organized a protest with Jackson State University students in 1967.[73]

The divisions reinforced already existing stereotypes of education as feminine and political activity as masculine and carried over into the new black politics. Black power radicals in the mid- and late-1960s made frequent appeals to manhood and identified power with masculinity. The development of black politics as black radicalism declined then became an extension of that masculine power, albeit without the rhetoric. Women would serve at the bottom, not the top. They performed low-level but vital voter outreach work, or "grunt work," for both white and black candidates, much as they had done during civil rights campaigns.[74]

The disproportionately low representation of black women was not unique to black politics. White women in politics, like black Mississippians, held office in fewer numbers than white men and in lesser positions. The numbers reflected the status of women in politics nationwide and in Mississippi in particular. In white Mississippi, politics remained a man's game. The first woman to hold a prominent public office in Mississippi was Mary Moraney, elected to post of state librarian by the legislature in 1876. After women won the right to vote with the ratification of the Nineteenth Amendment in 1920, women began to win office to both houses of the state legislature, but the number of women in office at one time peaked at a high of only five in 1949. A woman did not win state-wide elective office until 1947 when Mrs. Thomas L. Bailey won election to tax collector. Even the female-owned *Lexington Advertiser*, edited by unsuccessful state senate candidate Hazel Brannon Smith, reinforced the notion of politics as a masculine space in an article on a reception for outgoing U.S. Senator James Eastland by asking elected officials "to invite their wives to come."[75] The legislature elected in 1979, with its increased numbers of black male legislators, had only one white woman in the House and none in the Senate. No women ran for the Senate that year, which led a female journalist to comment that 1979 was "a bad year for women." When Alyce Clark entered the House as the first black woman in 1985, her white female colleagues greeted her warmly—all three of them.[76]

Women's rights in general had little support in the state. While women had served as state judges and U.S. attorneys since the 1950s, a court did not call a woman as a juror until 1962. Women held some elective law enforcement positions, including county sheriffs, but most elected women in Mississippi occupied clerical positions. The state's representatives and senators consistently opposed legislation promoting gender equity or reproductive rights. Mississippi and fourteen other states, mostly in the South, also did not ratify the Equal Rights Amendment (ERA) during the 1970s and early 1980s, and at the International Women's Year Conference in Houston, Texas, in 1977, antifeminists controlled the state's delegation. Gil Carmichael backed the ERA in his unsuccessful 1975 gubernatorial campaign, and he claimed that it was one of the reasons for his lack of support from some of the state's conservative Republicans.[77]

Even the political language of black politics suggested that keeping black men from being elected robbed them of their manhood. Henry Kirksey, who ran for governor in 1975, declared that black Mississippians were "politically and economically raped and castrated" by the white power structure. The Fifth Circuit Court of Appeals, in a ruling against racially discriminatory gerrymandering in Hinds County, declared that the districts would "emasculate the efforts of racial minorities to break out of patterns of racial discrimination."[78]

The case of Evelyn Gandy shows the perils of women in state politics. Gandy, lieutenant governor during the Finch administration, held the mantle of the state's most prominent woman politician. She served as a state legislator in the 1950s, and her election as state treasurer in 1960 made her the first woman ever to win a statewide constitutional office in Mississippi (The state tax collector office won by Bailey was not constitutionally prescribed.). She held various state offices in the 1960s and 1970s until her election as lieutenant governor in 1975. Despite her experience, she failed in her two bids for the governor's mansion in 1979 in 1983.[79] In 1979, Gandy, despite attracting top leadership from the defeated Democrats in the first primary, could not convince the voters who supported her rivals to aid her in the runoff with William Winter. One political observer bluntly blamed sexism. Gandy received many male votes but not enough to win. Her ads showed her walking through fields of flowers and portrayed her as the stereotype of the ideal, properly feminine (white) lady. The scholarly Winter, by contrast, exaggerated his masculinity by firing pistols and appearing with military hardware in his ads, a bit of machismo that Winter's media consultant admitted was designed specifically to defeat a woman candidate.[80]

When Gandy made her final political race in 1983, she made it to the runoff against Attorney General Bill Allain. She learned from 1979 and addressed the gender issue directly and argued that the voters were too "sophisticated" to judge a candidate by their sex. She downplayed her own gender, updated her hairstyle and wardrobe, and hired a Washington media consultant who ran ads that described her as "tough." She appealed to black voters on the basis of her sex, telling them she too knew the pain of discrimination. She also addressed her segregationist past head-on and apologized for her former views. The *Jackson Advocate* reported that some black voters did not warm to Gandy since they preferred to see a black man (but not a black woman, apparently) as governor before a white woman. Such views illustrated both a masculine bias in the black community and an unwillingness to consider sexism on par with racism. The new "tough" Gandy did not do any better with whites or blacks, and she lost the runoff to Allain.[81]

The new generation of black political leadership also included some prominent people in offices below the legislature. One of them, Bennie Thompson, deviated from the norm with his extensive civil rights activity as a member of SNCC in the 1960s. He entered politics in his early twenties and was a Hinds County supervisor by thirty-one. By 1983, when Bill Allain won the governor's race, Thompson counted the former attorney general as an ally because of his early support for Allain's campaign and for delivering black votes to him. Political columnist Bill Minor called Thompson "the rising star of a new breed of black leadership in Mississippi."[82]

Throughout his early career, whites often branded Thompson as a "militant." Thompson did become involved in SNCC during the post-1965 period when the civil rights organization became more radical and embraced black power. Thompson pursued black power but through electoral means. His militant label came from his assertiveness and outspokenness in his pursuit of his goals of bringing social programs and welfare assistance to his largely impoverished constituents. One observer described this strategy as "neo-populist," echoing the class-based economic programs of the Populists in the late nineteenth century.[83] Thompson's assertiveness or "militancy" owes as much to the setting of Bolton as it does to his 1960s civil rights record. Unlike Robert Clark or other black politicians, Thompson was able to operate in Bolton with an all-black government. While he dealt with white officials on the county, state, and federal level, they were not as present in his day-to-day business as they would have been if he were in the legislature or a town with a larger white population. He did not have to be as diplomatic as Clark or other black politicians in a white-majority institution, and this made him "militant." An all-black government in a majority-black town was the application of black power that Stokely Carmichael had outlined in the 1960s. In this sense he was like Charles Evers who also had an all black-government, but Thompson did not cut deals with white segregationists. Thompson moved up in the Democratic Party after fusion, unlike Evers.

Bill Minor described the second generation of black political leadership as less unified. The strong personality of Charles Evers overshadowed many other black officeholders and centered white attention on him. Black politics became more diverse and fractured with his decline and the absence of a central charismatic figure. Minor referred to the efforts of black Mississippians to define a "younger, more broadly based" kind of leadership. While the Legislative Black Caucus and ascending politicians such as Thompson captured the attention of white political observers, others in the second generation wielded power at the local level. Two notable black mayors who came to power in the latter half of the 1970s were Eddie James Carthan of Tchula and Gregory Flippins of Shaw. Like Thompson, they both represented small, majority-black towns. Carthan, educated at state universities, won election to the Holmes County Board of Education in 1972. He followed in the footsteps of his father who had made an unsuccessful run for the board of supervisors in 1971. In 1977, he scored an upset victory over the white incumbent mayor with a platform that called for improved city services. Flippins, a twenty-six-year-old former IRS worker, took the Shaw town hall in 1977 in his second attempt at the office. He rose to head the Mississippi Conference of Black Mayors.[84]

Carthan and Flippins illustrated the problems that some members of the second generation of black political power still faced in Mississippi. As had Robert Clark, who had argued against bills he supported to get white legislators to vote for them, black politicians still ran into white, or even interracial, resistance. In Shaw, white residents formed the Citizens for Good Government (CGG) in 1979 to pressure the Flippins administration on city services and tougher law enforcement. While the mayor addressed the CGG's concerns, some of his supporters criticized the timing of the group's founding, since the same problems existed under previous white mayors. Flippins also held a seat on the Rosedale-Bolivar County Port Commission as part of an agreement with the federal government to secure funds, but he was ousted when he questioned the way white members ran the commission. In neighboring Shelby, black mayor Robert Gray faced similar problems from white citizens when they formed a watchdog group to monitor the town's financial affairs. Sometimes resistance could be self-inflicted or the result of poor communication. In Tchula, Carthan embarked on a controversial term and alienated the majority-black board when he refused to make financial records available to the public. The board responded to a growing fiscal crisis in the town by cutting Carthan's salary from six hundred to sixty dollars per month. The *Lexington Advertiser* reported that the aldermen meetings erupted into acrimonious affairs of shouting and yelling.[85] Carthan's troubled tenure as mayor would not end with squabbling over the town coffers.[86]

The real strength of the second generation of black political power emerged during the Winter administration. The Black Legislative Caucus, despite members' anger over the Cupit affair, stayed with the governor and provided a unified vote for the centerpiece of his administration, the 1982 Education Reform Act. The act re-established compulsory education, which had been abolished in the 1950s during massive resistance, and set up public kindergartens for the state's schoolchildren. Robert Clark, the chairman of the House Education Committee, played a central role in negotiating the bill's passage. Originally, the backers of education reform wanted to pay for it with an increase in the oil and gas severance tax, which had not been increased since 1944. The state's powerful energy industry waged a lobbying campaign, including full-page newspaper advertisements, to successfully kill the proposed increase. The bill's authors then inserted language that increased state sales taxes, which some black legislators opposed since it would disproportionately affect poor and black Mississippians, but the entire caucus eventually backed the bill because most black children in Mississippi attended public schools and would benefit from improvements. Black politicians on the local level also mobilized to support the education bill. Unita Blackwell, the mayor of Mayersville, worked on behalf of Winter to convince black constituents to pressure their representatives to support the bill. She used her skills acquired from organizing voter registration drives for SNCC in the 1960s to mobilize Delta residents to now use their political influence for a major change in public education. The bill passed in December 1982. Many of the black legislators would later look back with pride on the role they played in passing the Act. Winter described his relations with the black legislators as "almost ideal" once the Cupit affair played out.[87]

As the 1980s opened and a second generation of black politicians clearly emerged to replace aging civil-rights-era activists, black politics reached a level of influence not seen since Reconstruction. The coalition that Finch helped forge in 1975 held together and put the moderate William Winter into the governor's mansion. Yet fusion had its limits, for white defections to the Republican Party and the Cupit affair showed the continuing weaknesses of the new biracial politics. Although by the 1980s black representation in Mississippi had increased markedly since the late 1960s, many counties continued to utilize vote dilution schemes to limit the number of black county supervisors. Just as they had in the struggle against discriminatory legislative reapportionment, black plaintiffs and civil rights activists used the judiciary to increase black political opportunities on the county level.

7 Lead into Gold?

The Alchemy of County Redistricting

WHILE KIRKSEY AND the *Conner* plaintiffs waged their battle to reapportion the legislature, similar fights occurred at the county level. Civil rights lawyers and black plaintiffs fought against discriminatory gerrymandering with as much ardor as they had against multimember legislative districts, but they experienced limited success since they could not prove discriminatory intent. The strengthened Voting Rights Act in 1982 changed that, and Mississippi's black voters found an unlikely ally in the Reagan administration. The federal government's intervention in 1983 greatly increased black representation on the county boards of supervisors and removed yet another mechanism of vote dilution in Mississippi.

The 410 elected county supervisors were among the most powerful local offices in the state's eighty-two counties, controlling road and bridge construction and other public works. Like the legislative districts, severe malapportionment from demographic changes affected many supervisors' districts. The legislature, as part of its efforts to limit the impact of the Voting Rights Act, allowed boards of supervisors to adopt at-large elections instead of mandating redistricting. The new countywide voting amendment, which passed in the first legislative session after President Johnson signed the Voting Rights Act into law, undercut the ability of voters in black-majority districts to elect black supervisors. Countywide voting also complied with the letter of the *Reynolds* "one-man, one-vote" principle by treating all voters in the county the same. Several counties adopted at-large voting after the amendment passed in 1966.[1]

In 1969, the Supreme Court in *Allen v. State Board of Elections* held that section five of the Voting Rights Act covered not just obstacles to voting but also dilution of black voting strength, such as at-large systems and stricter qualifications for candidates. Shifts from single-district to at-large voting, while complying with the letter of the law by appearing racially neutral, could potentially be declared void for their *effect* on black voters. Although two years later the Court ruled in *Whitcomb v. Chavis* that plans passed by state and local governments without racist *intent* passed constitutional muster, the long history of racial discrimination in Mississippi made any voting shift suspect. Rather than face lawsuits that would likely overturn the at-large systems, many Mississippi counties shifted instead to gerrymandering their single-member districts to prevent or limit the election of black supervisors. Boards of supervisors devised plans that "cracked" black voting strength among several districts to prevent a black majority, or "stacked" white population areas onto black-majority districts to dilute black votes.[2]

Black county residents, with the aid of civil rights attorneys, challenged the new gerrymandering in the courts. In Adams County, a black minister named Leon Howard and another black man, Barney Schoby, filed a lawsuit against the single-member districts the board of supervisors had created in 1970 with the aid of Comprehensive Planners, Inc. (CPI), a West Point mapping firm. The board created one black-majority district of sixty-seven percent and four other white-majority districts. CPI utilized a plan that equalized road and bridge mileage in each supervisor's beat. While ostensibly a color-blind plan, the presence of most county roads in rural areas meant that the CPI method of equalization involved dividing up the urban areas that lacked county-maintained roads. Such a plan, which CPI used in numerous other Mississippi counties, resulted in the "cracking" of heavily black Natchez into subdivisions to be added to white-majority rural areas. Each district converged, in the words of the court, in a "spoke-like fashion" into Natchez. Howard and Schoby, with the aid of attorneys Frank Parker and George Taylor, asked the U.S. Fifth Circuit Court of Appeals in 1972 for two black-majority districts, but a three-member panel cited *Whitcomb* and upheld the CPI plan, saying that their requests amounted to proportional representation or a racial quota.[3]

Parker and black residents in Leflore County had more success securing a favorable redistricting plan than the *Howard* plaintiffs. In 1971,
seven black residents of the Delta county sued county authorities for
holding at-large elections, and the courts ordered equally apportioned
districts for the next election. The board created a plan in 1972 that established five black-majority districts of equal population, and all but
one of the districts had their black majorities reduced from their old
pre-1965 malapportioned numbers. The black plaintiffs found some
unlikely allies when two of the white board members objected to the
board's plan on the grounds of unequal road and bridge mileage in the
districts. Judge William Keady of the Northern District Court rejected
the supervisors' plan on racial gerrymandering grounds alone and also
cited the lack of equalization of road and bridge mileage. Keady, a native
of Greenville and former state senator, was a Johnson appointee who
had been sworn in 1968. He had notably more moderate views on civil
rights than many of his Mississippi colleagues, and his rulings in this
case and future ones would reflect that.[4]

Keady appointed a special master, Hoyt Holland Jr., to craft a new
plan. Holland, a CPI vice president, created four districts with black
voting-age population majorities in a similar geographic pattern as the
one his firm drew up for Adams County. Keady approved the plan in
1973 and ordered that future elections be held from the CPI-drawn districts. Ironically, both sides in the case appealed the Holland Plan to
the Fifth Circuit on grounds of racial discrimination. Since the number
of black registered voters exceeded fifty percent in only three of the
four districts, the plaintiffs called the plan a dilution of black voting
strength and cited past discrimination as the cause of lower voter registration. The defendants argued that the plan gerrymandered white
residents into a majority-white district, although the district included
all-white neighborhoods concentrated in north Greenwood. In 1974, the
three-judge panel rejected both claims and declared that blacks had "full
access to the reigns of government" in the county and should be able to
increase their registration.[5]

The most prominent county redistricting case came in Hinds County,
the state's most populous and urbanized county. Prior to 1969, the
county had a forty percent black population and two supervisor districts
with black majorities of seventy-six and sixty-seven percent. That year
the board of supervisors, under a court order to equalize population,

created five white-majority districts. The CPI-drawn plan successfully kept the board all white, and the black candidates in the 1971 elections lost. The same year, Henry Kirksey and the LCCRUL led a group of black residents of Hinds County in a suit that challenged the districts under section five. The following year, the district court ordered a new redistricting because of demographic malapportionment but did not invalidate the plan on racial grounds. In 1973, the board submitted a new CPI plan that equalized population and road and bridge mileage but cracked the black neighborhoods in Jackson. Like Adams County, the CPI plan attached large rural areas of the county to fragments of the urban areas.[6]

Judge Walter Nixon heard arguments in the case of *Kirksey v. Board of Supervisors of Hinds County, Mississippi* in August 1974. Nixon, a former damage suit lawyer and protégé of Sen. James Eastland, had already ruled against the black plaintiffs in the *Howard* case. Kirksey pushed for two black-majority districts, like the pre-1969 plan. The 1973 plan had two black-majority districts but not in black voting-age population (VAP). James Loewen, a sociology professor at Tougaloo College, testified that adult black outmigration caused the age imbalance in districts two and five, the black-majority districts. Up until 1970, black Mississippians had outmigrated to escape poverty and Jim Crow. Most of the migrants were adults, which led to a preponderance of children and the elderly left behind. By the time the Voting Rights Act became law, the effects of adult migration meant a lower black VAP than white. Gordon Henderson, a Tougaloo political science professor, supported Loewen's testimony with census data. The plaintiffs also cited the long history of racial discrimination in the county as a factor that depressed black voter registration. Hoyt Holland Jr. testified for the defense and supported the firm's plan. Holland stated that the county authorities instructed him to ignore race and he did not compile racial data until ordered to by the court.[7]

Judge Nixon upheld the CPI plan on April 25, 1975. He rejected any precedent from the Leflore Moore case and cited Leflore County's majority-black population as a fundamental difference from Hinds County. He blamed low black voter registration on "lack of interest or complete apathy" since the Voting Rights Act and the end of the poll tax had removed barriers to registration. He called the proposed plaintiffs' redistricting plan, which created districts with black majorities in excess of sixty-five percent, an "intentional racial gerrymander" and thus unconstitutional.

He commented on the unusual shape of the CPI-created districts, which had long corridors of land running from Jackson out into the county. Nixon said that one of the districts resembled a "turkey" and another a "baby elephant," but he held that the CPI plan satisfied the population equity principles of *Reynolds*. Nixon, like the appellate court in *Howard*, rejected the idea of proportional representation. Black Hinds Countians "are not precluded from effective participation in the election system," Nixon wrote in his opinion, and the CPI plan offers them "a realistic opportunity to elect officials of their choice, whether they be white or black."[8]

The plaintiffs appealed their case to the Fifth Circuit and received aid from the Ford administration. Although Ford had angered some civil rights activists with his clumsy handling of the Voting Rights Act extension of 1975 and opposition to busing, his administration did move on behalf of the black plaintiffs. Jessica Dunsay Silver, a Justice Department attorney, filed an *amicus curiae* brief arguing that section five applied since the court *formulated* but did not *order* redistricting. Under precedents laid out in *Conner v. Johnson* and *Zimmer v. McKeithen*, a Louisiana at-large voting case, section five applied only to political subdivisions that reapportioned themselves, not court-ordered plans. The brief said that since CPI, an outside entity, had prepared the redistricting, section five review applied.[9]

The three-judge panel of the Court of Appeals said the *amicus* "misses the point of *Conner* and *Zimmer*," and also took a similarly unsympathetic stance regarding the merits of the plaintiffs' appeal. Judge Thomas Gibbs Gee, a conservative Texas jurist appointed by President Nixon, rejected the plaintiffs' desire for two "safe" black districts inside Jackson as "plainly drawn across racial lines alone" and warned drafters of redistricting plans to resist considering race. Gee demanded plans that "deny to no group an equal access to the political process or a fair chance to realize its full voting potential—even one based on the irrelevant criterion of race." Gee did not consider that white and black Hinds Countians, and Mississippians in general, did not consider race "irrelevant," given the inability of black candidates to win in districts where whites had majorities and the only notable black political gains were in black-majority areas.[10]

The Supreme Court soon intervened in a separate case that inadvertently aided the *Kirksey* plaintiffs. The plaintiffs won an *en banc* rehearing[11] in May 1976 and the Court of Appeals met in September to hear the case. Although the Supreme Court had not upheld racial gerrymandering or proportional representation, a case winding through the federal docket would soon change that. The Fifth Circuit, apparently sensing that the Court might make a ruling that would affect the outcome of the *Kirksey* case, decided to grant the full hearing. The Supreme Court case began in October 1976 and involved a suit in Kings County, New York. A community of Hasidic Jews protested the division of their community in 1974 to increase nonwhite majorities in the state senate and assembly districts. The Jewish plaintiffs claimed a violation of their rights under the Fourteenth and Fifteenth Amendments since the racially motivated divisions diluted their own voting strength. On March 1, 1977, the Supreme Court in *United Jewish Organizations v. Carey* denied the right of the Hasidic Jews to separate community recognition and instead recognized only white and nonwhite divisions. The Court ruled that the political fragmenting of the Hasidic community did not disfranchise them. More notably, the Court cited its precedent in *Allen* and said that race could be considered in redistricting to correct past discrimination.[12]

Almost three months after the *Carey* decision, the full Fifth Circuit, by a 10–3 vote, reversed the three-judge panel that originally upheld the CPI plan. The "unrefuted" evidence of past racial discrimination that Judge Gee had dismissed swayed a majority of the judges. Judge John Godbold, a pro-civil rights Alabama jurist appointed to the bench by President Johnson in 1966, said "the pattern [in the CPI plan] is clear and stark, and is unexplainable on any grounds other than race." The court also rejected Nixon's contention that the plan lacked racial bias because of its ostensible color-blindness. Such a plan would be unbiased, Godbold said, only if no past discrimination existed. He had little respect for the CPI bridge-and-road plans and declared that the equalization came at the expense of minority participation and could not be placed on equal footing with constitutional issues like voting rights. Godbold also declared that court-ordered plans had *higher* standards than legislatively enacted plans, and the CPI plan violated the Fourteenth and Fifteenth Amendments.[13]

Judge Gee joined the majority but expressed his displeasure in a concurring opinion and explained his legal grounds for why he initially ruled in favor of the CPI plan. He reversed himself due to the *Carey* ruling but went on to criticize the decision, saying that it created gerrymanders that "dictate the outcomes of elections and insure proportionate representation." He accused the Supreme Court of allowing judges to select local legislators and said that the decision sanctions a "tribal" form of government, a curious word given the racial implications of the *Kirksey* case. The three dissenting judges each wrote sharply critical separate opinions of the full court's decision. One of them, Judge James C. Hill, an Atlanta lawyer only recently appointed to the court by President Ford, scathingly declared that "surely, no one believes that all that this court must do is insure that a few blacks are elected in Hinds County and nirvana shall be reached."[14]

Parker exulted in the ruling and called it a "great victory," which came shortly before the U.S. Supreme Court overturned the state's legislative reapportionment plan in *Conner v. Finch*. After losing an appeal to the Supreme Court, the supervisors adopted a new plan that created two "safe" districts with black majorities of over sixty-five percent. The plan went into effect for the 1979 elections and led to the election of the first black county supervisors since Reconstruction.[15]

County redistricting challenges did not end with *Kirksey*. After redistricting from the 1980 census, more lawsuits that aimed to redraw county supervisor districts emerged. Despite earlier victories, black supervisors remained scarce in 1980s Mississippi. In 1982, the state had only twenty-seven black supervisors, most in black-majority counties. Only in Claiborne and Jefferson Counties did African Americans have majority control of the boards. Both counties had large numbers of black officeholders that resulted from the strong political organizing traditions that went back to Charles Evers and the efforts of the NAACP and local activists in the 1960s and early 1970s. In counties where black representation lagged, elected black officials, with the backing of black communities, pressured the federal government to intervene.[16]

They received a boost in 1982 when Congress debated strengthened vote dilution standards in the extension of the Voting Rights Act. A bipartisan group of voting supporters introduced an amendment to section two of the act to prohibit any practice "which results in a denial or abridgement" of the right to vote. The change, known as "the results test," represented a throwback to the old *Allen* decision of 1969. Future suits would be able to focus less on proving racist intent in local governments and election systems and more on effect, regardless of the original circumstances of the examined law or system. Although the proposed change clearly rejected proportional representation, it did utilize the "totality of circumstances" that the courts had established in voting bias cases instead of narrow remedies like bridge-and-road equalization.[17]

Prominent conservatives opposed the strengthened section two. William Bradford Reynolds, the head of Reagan's Civil Rights Division, called the revised section "a proportional representations scheme . . . inconsistent with the democratic traditions of our pluralist society." The results test stayed intact, however, when Senator Robert Dole (R-Kan.) fashioned a compromise that preserved it while publicly disavowing any move towards proportional representation. On June 29, 1982, President Ronald Reagan signed the renewal into law, extending the Voting Rights Act by twenty-five years and with provisions even stronger than the original 1965 act.[18]

In the spring of 1983, black residents in Bolivar County lobbied the Justice Department to reject the county's redistricting plan. Former Shaw mayor Gregory Flippins charged that the plan fragmented black voting power, and he and other black officials traveled to Washington to plead their case. Local activists received a boost when the Rev. Jesse Jackson arrived in the Mississippi Delta in early June 1983 as part of a voter registration campaign targeting seven southern states. Jackson coordinated the campaign as a precursor to his formal announcement of candidacy for the Democratic presidential nomination in 1984. He criticized lingering barriers in Mississippi such as dual registration, where a voter had to register separately for municipal and county elections. This system, he charged, handicapped poor, black, and rural voters by requiring them to travel to separate locations to register. Jackson won editorial support from the *Delta Democrat-Times* for the end of dual registration, and Gov. William Winter echoed these views when he met Jackson at the state capital.[19]

When Jackson returned to Mississippi in mid-June, he returned with a powerful and unlikely companion. William Bradford Reynolds, whom President Ronald Reagan had appointed to head the Justice Department's Civil Rights Division, seemed to be the last person that would appear publicly with the liberal black preacher. Reynolds, dubbed by one critic "the iceman," was a patrician in the wealthy du Pont family and a former corporate lawyer who had alienated the nation's civil rights lobby through his enforcement of Reagan's conservative civil rights policies. Since arriving in the Justice Department in 1981, he defended Bob Jones University against the Internal Revenue Service, which had tried to deny tax-exempt status to the racially segregated school. He opposed all busing programs, even voluntary ones. Probably his most controversial stance was his fervent opposition to affirmative action programs, which he said "bestowed benefits on people who are not victims of discrimination at the expense of those who have done no wrong at all." He favored limiting antidiscrimination cases to relief for individuals who actually could prove discrimination versus class-action remedies that aided groups. He also lacked strong voting rights credentials. In 1982, he urged the Reagan administration to side with an all-white county government in Georgia in a voting discrimination suit. Many Carter-era Justice Department attorneys, including many of the black lawyers in civil rights enforcement, left the administration rather than continue working under Reynolds.[20]

Reynolds's visit may have been motivated by political factors. He came at the invitation of Jackson, Rep. John Conyers (D-Mich.), and other prominent black leaders. Reynolds also came the week before President Reagan's visit to Mississippi to speak at a dinner honoring Rep. Trent Lott. The timing of the visit drew criticism from state Democratic Party chairman Danny Cupit, who called the trip an attempt to interfere in the August Democratic primary. Jackson accompanied Reynolds in Jackson's Winnebago on a two-day trip across the Delta. Reynolds arrived in Greenville and toured several Delta towns over the next two days before going to Jackson. At each stop, Reynolds heard local African Americans give testimony about the problems they encountered trying to register and vote, including stories of economic intimidation of black workers by plantation owners and factory managers. White employers used methods such as required overtime and no lunch breaks on Election Day to prevent voting, and one woman reported an eviction of a black family from a plantation for voting.[21]

Throughout the two days Reynolds and his staff listened to the complaints, but he remained noncommittal on what course he would take. Still, Reynolds appeared to be moved by what he heard. At a diner in Belzoni, he expressed amazement at the charges of voter intimidation and declared that he "never heard anything like that before." As he sang "We Shall Overcome" with Jackson (which he said Jackson insisted on doing at the end of each meeting), he commented that "the ability to register is not as open and accessible as it might be." He recalled numerous and blatant voting irregularities in the Delta and said that some of the "subtle gerrymandering [was] not so subtle." After his return to

FIGURE 14. Myrlie Evers (*left*) and Jesse Jackson (*right*), July 31, 1982. Jackson, as part of his groundwork for his presidential run in 1984, helped convince officials in President Reagan's Justice Department to overturn racial gerrymandering plans in county elections in Mississippi. The new redistricting plans doubled the number of black county supervisors in the state. Willie J. Miller Papers, 501–155, Special Collections Department, Mitchell Memorial Library, Mississippi State University.

Washington, Reynolds ordered federal voting registrars into five majority-black counties. He also declared that the Voting Rights Act "is the most precious civil rights legislation ever passed," a marked change from his criticism of portions of the Act during the debates over extension the previous year.[22]

Reynolds's actions drew quick condemnation from Rep. Webb Franklin of the second congressional district, which encompassed the majority-black Delta. Franklin, a white Republican who had won his seat in a racially charged election against black state representative Robert Clark the previous year,[23] had little sympathy for any effort to increase black voter registration in his majority-black district. Franklin said that Reynolds "has caused Mississippi to be tried and convicted in the national press without a fair hearing" and also claimed that he did not talk to city or county officials in any of the areas he visited. Reynolds denied the charge that he ignored local white officials who, he claimed, were "adamant" in defending themselves against charges of voter exclusion. State Democrats were also sensitive to Reynolds' investigation. Tommy McWilliams, attorney for the Sunflower County board of supervisors, called Reynolds's visit one-sided and "extremely unfair," and Gov. Winter said that Mississippi "has done a good job of opening the process up for all our people."[24]

Reynolds took criticism from the national civil rights establishment as well. Lani Guinier, a former Justice Department lawyer now with the NAACP Legal Defense and Educational Fund, said that the trip was not "an indication that [Reynolds] has seen the light." Reynolds's actions did force local officials to move. Hours before registrars arrived in Leflore County, the circuit clerk announced she was conducting mobile registration in rural areas of the county, something black leaders told Reynolds that she had been reluctant to do. With the exception of a brief story in *Newsweek* and some coverage in major newspapers such as the *Washington Post*, the trip garnered relatively little national attention. When President Reagan came to Jackson the Monday following Reynolds's trip, he made no public mention of Reynolds's visit.[25]

Reynolds also moved quickly on the county supervisor cases and the August elections. He struck down an Oktibbeha County redistricting plan that divided the Mississippi State University campus to minimize student voting strength. Although the supervisors' plan lacked racially discriminatory intent, Reynolds invoked the precedent laid in *Allen* and said that since the plan divided Starkville, as a byproduct it had the effect of diluting black voting strength in the county. Like many Mississippi counties, most of the black population in Oktibbeha County resided in the urban county seat. In August, Reynolds sent 322 observers to eight Mississippi counties to monitor the primary elections, but some saw the effort as mere tokenism. Robert Walker, the field director for the Mississippi NAACP, criticized Reynolds for sending observers to only eight counties. Jesse Jackson, however, sought to take advantage of the situation. To build support for his presidential campaign, he returned to stump in the Delta the weekend before the primary with former U.S. Sen. George McGovern (D-S.D.) and another Democratic presidential hopeful, Sen. Alan Cranston (D-Calif.).[26]

Reynolds objected to thirty-six Mississippi redistricting plans in all, most of them after his June trip. Much of the push for Reynolds to act came from the twenty-eight county redistricting lawsuits that black voters and civil rights lawyers filed. Lawsuits delayed many of the elections and led to federal court orders that halted the August supervisors' elections in fourteen counties on the grounds of unconstitutional district lines, an action that Webb Franklin sharply criticized. After the counties held the delayed elections in 1984, the number of black supervisors in the state almost doubled from twenty-seven to forty-seven. Most of the growth came in counties without black majorities, which marked the first black representation that many African Americans enjoyed in their home counties. Black-majority Madison County and white-majority Pike County made the most dramatic gains, going from zero black supervisors to two apiece. Humphreys County also increased its black supervisors from one to three to give them control of the board, and Holmes County added a black supervisor to gain a majority.[27]

Despite the obvious and tangible gains in black representation from Justice Department and court intervention, a survey of all eighty-two counties showed the limits of legal reform in advancing black electoral power. Many counties that gained black supervisors still had low levels of black representation. Tunica County, which Jesse Jackson visited in 1985 and said contained "America's Ethiopia,"[28] had a black-majority population but only one supervisor. Many of the Delta counties with black majorities did not increase their black supervisors over their numbers before the lawsuits. Coahoma, Leflore, Quitman, Issaquena, Bolivar, and Yazoo Counties still had only one black supervisor apiece. Even though twenty years had passed since the Voting Rights Act became law, seven counties with black populations of forty-five percent or higher still had no black representation at all on their boards of supervisors. Not surprisingly, the most heavily black-counties usually had the highest numbers of black supervisors, with Holmes, Humphreys, Claiborne, and Jefferson having the heaviest black representation. Claiborne and Jefferson had the same number of supervisors prior to the suits and owed their representation to their strong civil rights organization from the 1960s and 1970s.[29]

Poverty, much like it had in the 1960s, contributed to the lagging black representation and limited electoral and legal reform in the era of civil rights enforcement. In 1983 in Quitman County, Judge William Keady rejected the white supervisors' desire to use old 1970s lines that diluted black voting strength. Local black residents negotiated a redistricting deal with the four whites on the board of supervisors to create three black-majority districts, each with an excess of sixty-five percent black population. Judge Keady approved the deal, and black candidates ran in the county elections in August 1983. All but one of the black candidates for the board either lost outright or in the runoffs, leaving the four-to-one racial ratio unchanged. Sheriff Jack Harrison, who had won an acquittal from an all-white federal jury in 1980 for allegedly beating a black inmate, received one out of four black votes in his re-election. James Figgs, chairman of the county Democratic Executive Committee and president of the county NAACP, blamed poor voter turnout. "The revolution just didn't happen," he lamented. The white sheriff and supervisors, much like what white officeholders had done in the 1960s in response to black voting, used their economic clout to exert a major influence on the black vote. Harrison extended liberal credit from his furniture store to the hundreds of black customers who flocked to his store to take advantage of the half-price sale he held in July, a tactic also used by another white supervisor. Black voters repaid the favors with votes on Election Day.[30]

The county's white elite condescendingly praised blacks who voted for them. "Black folks can't give 'em anything," said Harrison's father, who managed his son's store. "Only white folks can help 'em." White politicians effectively used the extension of credit to build a support base of poor rural African Americans who lacked access to capital from alternative sources like banks. Such economic paternalism served to reinforce hierarchies of race and class, undermine legal reform, and preserve the white power structure well after the 1960s movement. The white politician-merchants, like their predecessors in the era of tenancy under Jim Crow, extended their influence over poor blacks well after the election by creating patterns of debt and dependency. Jackson State professor and former congressional candidate Leslie McLemore echoed Figgs when he declared that "white people own everything" and "that's why black people can't have no damn revolution."[31]

As Manning Marable has noted, the primary beneficiaries of the civil rights movement were the black elite. He challenges the notion that race would cease to be an issue as black people became more thoroughly integrated into the American economic system. He argues that "for the unemployed, the poor, and those without marketable skills or re-sources, for those whose lives were circumscribed by illiteracy, disease, and desperation, 'race' continued to be a central factor in their marginal existence." In Quitman County and elsewhere in Mississippi where poor black voters were susceptible to the economic power of a white elite this analysis held true.[32]

Despite the limited outcomes, the redrawing of the county supervi-sors' districts in the early 1980s and William Bradford Reynolds's 1983 trip raise some curious if unanswered questions. Reynolds's actual mo-tives for the trip and his swift action to redistrict the counties remain unclear. One theory is that he wanted to exacerbate the racial split in the fragile biracial state Democratic Party. The redistricting affected a statewide Democratic primary and pitted white incumbent Democrats against black Democrats, so any fissure could only help the Republicans who would profit from further white defections from the Democratic Party, a charge made by political scientist Abigail Thernstrom about GOP redistricting plans. She charged that Republicans favored redistricting that drew up majority-black districts since such plans also created heav-ily white districts that favored white conservative candidates.[33]

Reynolds could also have been trying to boost Jesse Jackson's can-didacy by building a stronger black base and viable candidacy for him so that the national Democratic Party would face a racially divisive presidential nomination process in 1984 and help President Reagan's reelection. That is exactly what Jackson's candidacy did to former Vice President Walter Mondale in 1984. Many southern whites, inflamed or frightened by Jackson's campaign and his eventual support for Mondale, turned out in large numbers to defeat the Democratic ticket. The three million new southern white voters that voted in 1984 overwhelmed the 1.3 million new southern black voters that Jackson's campaign had helped to register.[34]

Perhaps Reynolds had other intentions. The man whom critics said saw the law as an abstraction rather than an instrument that affected people might have been truly moved by what he saw and heard from black workers in the economically depressed Delta towns. Reynolds's actions may also have been what Frank Parker called "the national consensus on voting rights." Parker argued that in the years after the enactment of Voting Rights Act, a broad-based consensus that crossed partisan lines developed to protect minority voting rights. The act won extensions from bipartisan coalitions in Congress despite the attempts of Republican presidents to weaken it. In the case of all four extensions, a Republican president signed them into law. Their Justice Departments often lent aid as well, such as Silver's brief in the Hinds County case and Reynolds's own intervention. The Supreme Court contributed to the consensus by expanding interpretations of what constituted vote dilution and discrimination. Voting rights protections, Parker argued, do not raise the same emotional white opposition as affirmative action and busing. While white officials on the state and local levels continued to obstruct political access in various ways, national pressure from Congress and the Justice Department remedied the situation. Reynolds, as a national figure in the Reagan administration, had come to share the same views of the voting rights consensus. His job as an enforcer of the law and legal precedent likely pushed him in this direction despite his earlier objections to the 1982 amendments.[35]

Reynolds denied any ulterior motives, insisting he "didn't have a hidden agenda" for his redistricting rulings, and pointed out that conservatives criticized him for his appearances with Jesse Jackson. He said that the trip had been an "eye opener" that revealed the continuing problems of racial voting discrimination.[36] According to him, local officials' actions proved their intent to discriminate on race, a clear violation of the original intent of the Voting Rights Act. Reynolds could then enforce the law but still legitimately criticize the broadened provisions of the 1982 extension as an overreaching of the Act's 1965 boundaries.

Whatever the reason for his actions, Reynolds profited little from his redistricting orders. His nomination by Reagan to be Associate Attorney General in the summer of 1985 failed to make out of committee. A coalition of Democratic and liberal Republican senators, troubled by his apparent untruthfulness during earlier congressional testimony on voting rights cases, blocked his nomination. The national press made almost no mention of his actions in Mississippi two years earlier, and even his defenders in conservative publications such as National Review did not point to the change he wrought in numerous Mississippi counties, instead praising his opposition to racial quotas. Reynolds stayed on as head of the Civil Rights Division for the rest of the Reagan administration and continued to serve as a lightning rod for criticism from the civil rights lobby. Despite his controversial handling of other civil rights measures, his intervention on behalf of black voters greatly increased black representation in the county governments of Mississippi.[37]

The struggles by Henry Kirksey and other black plaintiffs and their white allies to increase black officeholding on the county level eventually yielded tangible increases in black political power. Legal reform could still only do so much, for poverty and the existing white power structure in some majority-black Mississippi counties still inhibited black officeholding. As Judge Godbold said in his legal opinion on the Hinds County redistricting case, "[N]o mechanistic solution is an alchemistic philosopher's stone that will turn all the problems of past and present to future gold."[38] The fight against racial gerrymandering in Mississippi's counties also occurred alongside efforts to eliminate racially discriminatory at-large elections in Jackson and other municipalities. This fight, which involved many of the same figures from the county redistricting cases, also lasted well into the 1980s and ultimately depended on the extended Voting Rights Act.

8 City Wards and Jacksonian Democracy

THE STRUGGLE AGAINST vote dilution in Mississippi's municipalities resembled the fight against discrimination in legislative and county supervisors' districts. Many of the same actors played major roles, and initial legal reverses could not overcome ultimate success for the civil rights forces. The challenges on the municipal level also differed from other battles, with a focus on at-large elections in Jackson, the state's largest city, while litigants waged numerous other battles in smaller towns across the state. The effort to create a ward system in Jackson and put black representation in a city with an almost fifty percent black population developed slowly, with the extension of the Voting Rights Act in 1982 finally changing Jackson's city government and breaking its racial and gender barriers twenty years after the Act's initial passage.

In the nineteenth century, Mississippi towns, like most other U.S. municipalities, operated under a ward system where the voters of each ward elected an alderman to represent them. During the progressive era in early twentieth century, a new plan came to the state. Business elites and urban progressives throughout the United States pushed the commission form of municipal government, a system first used in Galveston, Texas, in which voters elected commissioners citywide.[1]

While the commission system effectively diluted the black vote, the Constitution of 1890 had already disfranchised black Mississippians and thus minimized the role of race in the adoption of the commissions in Mississippi. Clarksdale first adopted the plan in 1910, and other urban areas followed. Mississippi's municipal code allowed but did not require ward voting for towns with fewer than 10,000 residents, so the practice of ward voting continued in many other Mississippi towns even while the larger cities created commissions.[2]

The next push for at-large voting had clearer racial overtones. In 1962 the Mississippi legislature, in the midst of the civil rights movement, amended the municipal code to require all municipalities with mayor-alderman forms of government to elect their council members at-large, effectively nullifying any future black voting.[3]

Since the legislature amended the code prior to the Voting Rights Act, at-large elections initially escaped the scrutiny of the Justice Department. The Supreme Court's 1969 decision in *Allen v. State Board of Elections* opened the way for more voting rights lawsuits by expanding the interpretation of section five to include vote dilution schemes such as at-large voting. The state's first federal ruling against at-large municipal voting came in *Perkins v. Matthews*, a suit challenging Canton's 1969 switch to at-large elections. The Supreme Court said that section five preclearance did apply to municipal changes in government, but most Mississippi cities adopted their at-large systems earlier than 1965 and thus were not affected by the ruling. The court limited its ruling to Canton and left the legality of the 1962 law unresolved.[4]

The 1962 law did not last much longer than Canton's at-large elections. In 1973, eight black plaintiffs from the Mississippi cities of Moss Point, Macon, Starkville, and West Point, with the aid of civil rights attorneys, filed a lawsuit against the statute. The U.S. District Court for the Northern District of Mississippi heard the case of *Stewart v. Waller*, so named for a Starkville woman in the case, Rosa Stewart.[5]

On July 14, 1975, the judges declared the 1962 statute unconstitutional. They recognized that according to the Fifth Circuit's ruling in *Zimmer v. McKeithen*, a Louisiana case from 1972, at-large voting measures were not inherently unconstitutional, but the judges clearly believed that the 1962 law discriminated on the basis of race, which *Whitcomb v. Chavis* prohibited.[6]

The court cited a number of factors, in particular the difficulties black candidates had in winning at-large elections. Statewide, the number of black aldermen elected since 1962 in cities with a less than a two-to-one population ratio of blacks to whites had never exceeded one percent of the total number of elected aldermen. With this evidence in mind, the court ruled that the 1962 statute *purposefully* violated the Fourteenth and Fifteenth Amendments.[7]

The limited ruling did not represent a total victory for the black plaintiffs. The court's injunction forced forty-seven municipalities to revert to the method of election they used prior to 1962. That meant a return to ward voting in thirty of the affected cities. The court did not void the at-large systems for all of Mississippi's 265 cities with aldermanic forms of government, instead declaring that each city represented a "separate and distinct factual situation," guaranteeing years of individual lawsuits by black plaintiffs to rewrite the election systems of almost every city and town in Mississippi.[8]

Over the next decade, more and more Mississippi cities adopted ward voting under court order or lawsuit. The number of black city council members also increased, from sixty-one in 1974 to 143 in 1979. Twenty-four of the eighty-two council members elected after 1975 came from cities that adopted ward voting plans as a result of *Stewart*.[9] The main resistance to ward elections occurred in Jackson, the state's capital and largest city. The legal challenges here commanded the most public attention and exerted an influence on other municipalities in the state.

Jackson first adopted the commission form of government in 1912, well after official disfranchisement. The racial effects of the commission system did not become clear until after the Voting Rights Act restored black voting and some black candidates sought commission seats in the majority-white city. In the 1969 and 1973 elections, black candidates lost bids for seats on the city commission.[10]

Stewart v. Waller did not affect Jackson or ten other Mississippi cities because of their pre-1962 adoption of the commission.[11] The commission form of government had by the 1970s largely been replaced by mayor-city council forms of government in most major U.S. cities. In 1976, only three cities in the United States with populations of over 250,000, including Jackson, still operated commission forms of government.[12]

A push to change the government of Jackson came from Kathryn Hester, a white law student and member of the Urban League. In 1971, she and Kane Ditto, a white Jackson attorney, co-chaired the Chimneyville Society, a predominately white organization dedicated to reforming Jackson's government. Hester's lobbying led the legislature in 1976 to pass a bill that allowed all Mississippi cities to hold referenda on adopting mayor-council systems. On August 9, 1976, the pro-council forces announced a formal campaign to pass a referendum and change the city's government. They proposed the city abandon its three-man, at-large commission in which the voters elected a mayor and two commissioners, in favor of a system with a mayor and nine council members, elected from separate wards.[13]

Three days later, Henry Kirksey called a press conference and denounced Hester and Ditto's organization because it did not include black members on its committee. When confronted with evidence that twenty of the sixty-six members on the steering committee were black, including Hinds County's three black legislators, the mercurial Kirksey called them "hand picked blacks." During a televised debate with Hester, he called the referendum a "northeast Jackson scheme." Jackson's northeastern neighborhoods contained many of Jackson's wealthier residents and political leaders, and many poorer Jacksonians viewed the northeast with suspicion.[14]

Kirksey's comments highlighted the dissatisfaction many black Jacksonians had over the city's neglect of their community. In 1976, Jackson television station WLBT-TV aired a story on the Grove Park Community Center, one of the two full-size parks in Jackson's black neighborhoods. Many of the facilities in the park lacked proper maintenance. Rep. Fred Banks had complained to Commissioner Tom Kelly as far back as 1971 about the park's disrepair. Banks drew an explicit link between the lack of improvements and the all-white city government, charging that it made white politicians unresponsive to the black community. City officials claimed a scarcity of resources when confronted by the WBLT-TV reporter.[15]

Proponents of the mayor-council form said that city government would be more efficient, while opponents, headed by a group called United Groups for Better City Government, feared that the mayor would dominate the city council and become too powerful. The specter of race, raised by Kirksey, remained present during the election. Leslie McLemore, NAACP director Emmett Burns, and Fred Banks all supported the ward plan because of its potential to elect black aldermen. The mostly white groups on the pro-council side dodged the issue of race when reporters asked their leaders about the possible increase in minority participation under the plan, but few had any illusions that race played a role. Political observers noted that with cases such as Mobile, Alabama's commission system facing a federal court battle over racial discrimination, a legal challenge would likely come if voters did not approve the ward system. Mayor Russell Davis later recalled a number of white organizations and individuals on the anti-referendum side opposed any measure that would increase black representation.[16]

The White Citizens' Councils introduced the most blatantly racist measure into the campaign. *The Citizen*, its official journal, ran an editorial in October 1976 that opposed drives for mayor-council forms of government in Jackson and Shreveport, Louisiana, citing potential black representation. Gery A. Cummings, a coordinator of the petition effort for the referendum, said that whites who refused to sign the petitions asked either if he worked for the NAACP or if he was trying to "get niggers elected to the government."[17]

On February 22, 1977, the voters of Jackson rejected the proposed change and kept the commission form of government. With less than 27,000 votes cast, fifty-six percent of the voters favored the commission system. The voting split largely along racial lines, with seventy percent of the white voters favoring the commission system while ninety-two percent of black voters opposed. Kane Ditto expressed disappointment and blamed voter confusion over the plan for the loss, while others cited voter apathy.[18]

The day after the referendum, Frank Parker of the LCCRUL launched a challenge to the city's at-large system in court. Parker filed his suit on behalf of Henry Kirksey, who also served as a plaintiff in the Hinds County redistricting case and the *Conner* reapportionment suits. Fifteen other black voters joined the suit, including Hinds County's three black legislators. Mayor Russell Davis indicated that the city would defend itself despite his support for the change to a ward system.[19]

Judge Walter Nixon rejected Parker's attempt to postpone city elections that year. With the elections on as scheduled, Russell Davis sought his third term as mayor and faced three opponents in the Democratic primary, including Dale Danks, the Hinds County prosecutor. Davis also faced Helen Williams, a black candidate who had run unsuccessfully in 1973, but Davis and Danks were the clear frontrunners. Danks scored an upset over Davis to win the Democratic nomination for mayor, a victory fueled by low black voter turnout, and an anti-Davis backlash by white voters in a neighborhood that the city had recently annexed.[20]

The Republican Party made sure that Danks did not have the election already won. The GOP fielded strong candidates that year in several mayors' races in Mississippi, and in Jackson Danks faced fellow city commissioner Doug Shanks. Shanks, who had been Davis's public relations director, became the first elected Republican in modern Jackson in 1973 at the age of twenty-six, almost half the age of Mayor Davis at the time. Shanks represented the progressive wing of the GOP and had helped secure Gerald Ford's nomination in 1976. He campaigned on a platform of reorganizing city government and consolidating city departments and services.[21]

Both candidates competed vigorously for black votes. Black Jacksonians could not elect one of their own race to the council, but they represented a voting population that could spell victory or defeat for a candidate. The city's black leadership split during the race. Shanks won support from state NAACP field director Emmett Burns and eighteen members of the Jackson Ministers' Union. Danks enjoyed the backing of the small but growing black Democratic Party establishment, such as Rep. Fred Banks. One notable white Republican who refused to back Shanks was the conservative financier Billy Mounger who backed a Republican running for a commission seat but stayed silent during the mayor's race, refusing to support the progressive Shanks out of anger over his backing of Gerald Ford in 1976.[22]

In the June election, Danks won. Shanks won forty-six percent of the black vote, doing far better than Gil Carmichael in the 1975 governor's race, but he still fell short. The endorsement of prominent black politicians like Banks and Danks's Democratic affiliation helped sway many black voters to him. The defeat of Shanks in 1977 and of Carmichael two years later in the governor's race, along with the lack of support of key Republican bosses such as Mounger, marked the decline of GOP progressives and serious outreach to black voters by the GOP in Mississippi.[23]

In July, the trial began in the case of *Kirksey v. City of Jackson*, the lawsuit Frank Parker filed against the city's at-large voting system. On July 6, Fred Banks testified and blamed white "bloc voting" against black candidates for their demise in the polls. Banks stated that the lack of black representation created a city hall unresponsive to black needs, and he believed a nine-member council elected from wards would help remedy the problem.[24]

Other witnesses included Rueben Anderson, a black municipal judge who had previously run for the commission and lost. Gordon G. Henderson, the political science professor at Tougaloo College who had testified in the county redistricting cases, provided analysis of election returns for the plaintiffs. He argued that race had a strong correlation to the vote received by a candidate, which created patterns of racially polarized voting. He cited the 1973 municipal elections, when white candidates

FIGURE 15. Jackson City Hall. By the 1980s, Jackson, the state's largest city, was over forty percent black but had an all-white city commission due to at-large voting. The city's antiquated at-large commission system remained until the renewed and strengthened Voting Rights Act of 1982 forced the adoption of district representation in the city and thus the election of blacks and women to the city government. William F. "Bill" Minor Papers, 80–630, Special Collections Department, Mitchell Memorial Library, Mississippi State University.

carried every white precinct and black candidates won only the black precincts.[25]

James P. Dahlberg also testified as an expert witness for the plaintiffs. Dahlberg, a twenty-seven year old employee of LCCRUL, worked as the organization's municipal services consultant. He had previously worked fourteen months in the Government Services Equalization Center in Washington, D.C., but had no formal training in engineering or urban planning. Using data from city departments, Dahlberg argued that black residents received a lesser share of city services. He provided a list of services underrepresented in black communities, from street paving to city lighting to park acreage. Former Tougaloo professor James Loewen, who had testified in the county redistricting trials, also spoke on the deficiencies in municipal services. City officials countered that Dahlberg's statistics distorted actual progress in black neighborhoods in recent years, and the city's attorney explained that deficiencies existed because many black residents used city facilities in white neighborhoods. The head of the city's planning department also defended the presence of only two black members on the fifteen-member planning board, calling the two members "very active, very vocal and represent[ing] well the community they represent."[26]

On August 28, 1978, Judge Nixon ruled for the city of Jackson. He cited *Zimmer*, which had established that an aggregate of factors determined vote dilution. The factors considered included the access candidates had to filing for office, the responsiveness of representatives to the minority community, state policy on at-large redistricting, and evidence of past racial discrimination. Nixon agreed with Gordon Henderson's analysis that racially polarized voting existed in Jackson, but he said no evidence existed that black candidates or voters faced any obstruction to their right to vote or run for office. Nixon dismissed any claim to a right to black representation, citing *White v. Register*. Although *White* struck down at-large state legislative elections in Dallas and Bexar Counties in Texas for discrimination against blacks and Latinos, the Supreme Court ruled that minorities did not have the right to representation in proportion to their voting potential. They only had the *opportunity*, not an *entitlement*, to representation.[27]

Nixon recognized that no blacks served on city boards prior to 1969, but he still praised the city's "affirmative steps" to increase black participation. Although over half of the city's thirty-five appointive boards still had all-white memberships, and black members made up only fourteen percent of the 320 seats on the various city agencies and commissions, Nixon again cited a bias against proportionality. Regarding city employment, he pointed to court-ordered affirmative action programs in the city's police and fire departments as evidence that hiring bias no longer existed, even though most of the new hires worked in unskilled laboring positions.[28]

Nixon singled out James Dahlberg for criticism, specifically his youth, lack of credentials and inexperience. In each case that Dahlberg raised, Nixon cited other factors or pointed to recent city efforts to up-grade services as proof of a lack of discrimination. All in all, he said that the city of Jackson had become "representative of all its constituency." He did not give much attention to the fact that the city adopted many of the remedies only because of legal action by black Jacksonians. He closed by upholding the city's at-large system and dismissing the case.[29]

Parker and Barbara Phillips, another LCCRUL attorney, quickly filed an appeal to the Fifth Circuit. In their appeal, the plaintiffs admitted that the Jackson city commission "is not totally unresponsive to the needs and interests of black citizens" but argued that past racial dis-crimination and present patterns of racially polarized voting met the vote dilution standards of precedents like *Zimmer* and *White*. They reminded the court that ward voting produced five black aldermen in Jackson from 1872 to 1899. The plaintiffs made the key argument that the backers of the 1912 referendum had the goal of eliminating black men from Jackson City Hall and cited E. C. Foster, a Jackson State his-tory professor, to bolster their claim. They also mentioned the decline of multimember districts, which meant that black Jacksonians had rep-resentation in the state legislature but not the city commission. Parker and Phillips highlighted present inequalities between blacks and whites in education, voter registration, socio-economic rankings, and the per-sistence of housing segregation, all factors which they said impacted the political process. Finally, they cited *Kirksey v. Board of Supervisors of Hinds County*, arguing that if Hinds County had racial discrimination then the county seat of Jackson did as well.[30]

In their lengthy response to the appeal, the city's lawyers sounded similar to the state in its ultimately unsuccessful battle with Kirksey and Parker over legislative reapportionment. The city attorneys re-minded the court that the Supreme Court had not ruled all at-large vot-ing systems inherently unconstitutional and insisted Russell Davis's ad-ministration had greatly reduced racial discrimination, again citing the city's affirmative action plan. They also argued that the 1912 commission plan had no racial motivations since black Mississippians had been ef-fectively disenfranchised by the Constitution of 1890.[31] The city lawyers did not address the notion that there could be something inherently racist about a government passing laws that affected minority residents who could not vote at all.

The city attorneys painted a picture of a racially progressive Jackson to counter the gloomy synopsis of the LCCRUL. Point by point, they rebutted the allegations of discrimination in municipal employment and services. They conceded the lawsuits that black applicants had filed against city departments but insisted that the city had admitted no wrongdoing as part of the consent decrees. The city in effect turned on its head the voting rights consensus that Frank Parker had described. Parker argued that a bipartisan consensus had developed during the extensions of the Voting Rights Act that viewed voting rights and measures against vote dilution as different from and less controversial than more divisive issues such as affirmative action. The lawyers for the city of Jackson boosted their affirmative action programs to forestall charges of vote dilution and thus defended what should have been the more controversial program. The city attorneys asked if the division of the city into wards might be "a permanent division into political ghettos or tribes," an interesting choice of words in an African-American redistricting case.[32]

History itself, or historiography, also shaped the legal arguments in the case. In their reply brief to the defense, the plaintiffs argued that "there is no evidence that there ever was a progressive movement in Mississippi" and that the defense just "assumed" one existed since Jackson had adopted a commission form of government. The defense's historian, Mississippi College professor Billy Hicks, could not identify any leaders of the progressive movement in Mississippi. E. C. Foster, Jackson State history professor for the plaintiffs, argued that the "corruption" politicians cited represented coded language for black officeholding, but the plaintiffs also lacked solid historical evidence for their own argument. The textbook selections they cited as proof covered the Reconstruction period, not the early twentieth century.[33]

The Supreme Court soon intervened in the case. With the appeal pending in the Fifth Circuit, the Burger Court ruled on *City of Mobile v. Bolden*, another at-large municipal case. No black candidates had ever won a seat on the city's three-man commission, even though the city had a thirty-five percent black population by 1970. When Wiley Bolden, a black resident of Mobile, filed a suit on April 22, 1980, the Supreme Court sided with the city, sending it back to the lower courts. The justices ruled that racial intent was required for proof of discrimination and to act otherwise would be endorsing proportional representation.[34]

Because of the similarities between *Bolden* and *Kirksey*, the Fifth Circuit remanded the case back to Mississippi. By now, some whites in the city also questioned the commission form of government, especially since thirty percent of the white voters in 1977 also voted to abolish the system. As the Fifth Circuit held oral arguments on *Kirksey* in the wake of *Bolden* in May 1980, the League of Women Voters sponsored a panel to discuss proposed changes in the city government. The panel of six included Frank Parker, Kane Ditto, and Kathryn Hester.[35]

By the end of 1980, Jackson City Hall remained the last bastion of all-white government in Hinds County. Black citizens, with the aid of the LCCRUL, now had representation in the county government and the state legislature but not in the city government. The black residents of tiny towns like Bolton and Edwards in rural Hinds County had more municipal representation than an African American living in Jackson. Henry Kirksey had benefited from these changes, having been elected a state senator from Hinds County in 1979. To many white Jacksoni-ans, the at-large commission system represented a last line of defense against the new black politics and symbolized the last holdover of local Jim Crow politics.

Since the *Bolden* standard now required proof of discriminatory in-tent in the adoption of the commission system, Parker and the LCCRUL shifted their focus away from the argument that the city shortchanged black Jacksonians in municipal services. The plaintiffs instead aimed to prove that city fathers adopted the plan in 1912 to specifically exclude black officeholding. Judge Nixon also had to address the issue of racial intent, which he ignored in his first opinion and decided the case on the grounds of the effect on black residents.[36]

In October the case resumed and the plaintiffs called two other ex-perts. James Loewen, now at the University of Vermont, returned to testify on racially polarized voting in the 1977 referendum and cited a precinct-by-precinct statistical analysis of voting patterns. He claimed that racial factors accounted for eighty-eight percent of the votes cast. The second witness, Charles Sallis, provided historical testimony that the commission form of government had racist intent. Sallis, a history professor at Millsaps College, claimed that white reformers adopted commission forms of government in the South to exclude black vot-ers. On cross-examination, however, he admitted that he could not prove his contention with historical evidence on the Jackson commis-sion plan and could do so only for the plan Greenville adopted in 1906. His testimony took a further blow when he also conceded that Jackson's all-white electorate defeated an earlier referendum to change to a commission form of government in 1908.[37]

The next day, Henry Kirksey took the stand. A cartographer by trade, he provided maps he had drawn on the results of the referendum in Jackson's ninety-two voting precincts. He said that sixty-one of the sixty-six predominantly white precincts voted to keep the commission system, while all twenty-six black precincts opted to change to a mayor-council form of government. The outspoken Kirksey engaged in what a reporter described as a "heated" exchange with Jackson attorney Thomas Lily.[38]

Kane Ditto, the white lawyer who had gathered petitions for the change in government, backed the claims of Loewen and Kirksey that race played a major issue in the campaign. He said some of the whites leading the opposition to the referendum used the charge that the proposed plan made the mayor too powerful as a cover for their racist feelings.[39]

Gordon Henderson, who had provided expert testimony and statistical analysis in the first trial, also returned. The former Tougaloo College professor now taught political science and directed the computer center at Earlham College in Richmond, Indiana. He said that the commission form of government had lost popularity since 1917 because of inherent flaws in the system. He said that a "unanimous consensus" of political scientists and their literature scored the at-large commission system as "the worst in terms of responsiveness and efficiency." The system promoted secrecy in government decision-making and a resulted in a lack of responsiveness and openness.[40]

The defense countered by putting referendum organizer Kathryn Hester on the stand. She criticized Henry Kirksey for his comments in August 1976 that her organization, Jacksonians for a Mayor-Council Form of Government, pushed the referendum as part of a "northeast Jackson scheme." She also took issue with Ditto's testimony and said that race had little to do with white voter motivations. Instead, she said that opponents invoked Chicago mayor Richard Daley as a cautionary tale about what a strong-mayor system could produce in Jackson. She countered that race had a positive effect on the campaign since referendum organizers worked with black residents on the issue.[41]

Another defense witness, Larry Powell, told the court that voter confusion, not race, led to the defeat of the referendum. Powell, a communications professor at Mississippi State University, outlined the city's defense. Based on a study of campaign materials from 1977, Powell argued that generational factors played a significant role in the defeat. Specifically, older voters feared the potential increase of centralized power under a mayor-council system and that "confusion, uncertainty, and doubt" influenced the electorate. Under what a reporter described as a "strenuous" cross examination, Parker forced Powell to admit that anti-ward opponents made coded racial appeals, including a newspaper advertisement that warned of section five preclearance under the Voting Rights Act.[42]

On January 21, 1981, Nixon delivered his ruling on the second hearing of *Kirksey v. City of Jackson*. The plaintiffs and defendants made different arguments the second time around, but the judge again ruled for the city. He found the historical evidence the plaintiffs had presented to prove racist intent in the 1912 commission vote to be lacking, since the last black alderman elected won his seat in 1899. Charles Sallis had even conceded that former governor and senator James K. Vardaman, in his opinion "the foremost racist of his time," supported the 1908 commission system plan that the white voters in Jackson defeated. Nixon also cited Sallis and Loewen's 1974 Mississippi history textbook, *Mississippi: Conflict and Change*, which did not mention the commission system as a disfranchising measure.[43]

Nixon then dismissed the plaintiffs' contentions that the commission system violated the Voting Rights Act and the Fifteenth Amendment, again because the plaintiffs had not proven racial intent, as required under *Bolden*. He also cited the "totality of circumstances" standard for discrimination laid down in *Zimmer* and found that wanting as well. In fact, he blamed the plaintiffs and referendum backers for raising race as an issue.[44]

Nixon's opinion meant that the Constitution of 1890 acted as a shield for the city's all-white commission, as the city used an earlier mechanism of white supremacy to argue that its form of government had no racist motivations. The absence of overtly racist appeals also hurt the plaintiffs. By the time of the 1977 referendum, the old white supremacist cries of the civil rights era had given way to the subtle racial appeals of post–civil rights politics. Such changes had been underway since the late 1960s with Richard Nixon who as part of his "southern strategy" to win white votes had used veiled code words that appealed to working-class

FIGURE 16. Sen. Henry Kirksey (*right*) receives an honorary doctor of laws degree from President George Owens of Tougaloo College, May 29, 1982. Kirksey, a cartographer and longtime civil rights activist, was a plaintiff in numerous redistricting cases, as well as a frequent candidate for political office. In 1979, with the adoption of single-member districts in state House and Senate elections, he became one of the first two black state senators since Reconstruction. Willie J. Miller Papers, 501–119, Special Collections Department, Mitchell Memorial Library, Mississippi State University.

whites. State and local politicians quickly adopted such phrases, which included "forced busing," "law and order," "neighborhood schools," and, in particular, attacks on welfare and urban crime.[45]

Frank Parker quickly filed another appeal to the Fifth Circuit and threatened to file a suit to halt the city's 1981 elections. The threat had some validity because Mobile had not held municipal elections since 1973 because of the *Bolden* litigation. Kirksey used his legislative influence, introducing a bill to allow cities with commission systems to expand their councils from three to five members and elect them from wards. By 1981, Greenville, Greenwood, and Hattiesburg all faced federal lawsuits over their commission governments as well, so Kirksey's legislation could have ended the legal challenges in those cities too.[46]

Despite the suits in other Mississippi cities, Jackson's legal troubles remained the focus of the vote dilution struggle, in part because the other cases had not yet come to trial. Parker tried to secure federal intervention to delay the Jackson municipal elections, but the Justice Department refused to delay the elections.[47]

The federal government may not have halted the elections like Parker wanted, but it gave the civil rights lawyer a different form of relief. In May 1981 the Civil Rights Division filed a brief on behalf of the plaintiffs' appeal to the Fifth Circuit. It argued that the city adopted and maintained the commission system as a tool of racial disfranchisement and said that the referendum, which determined *how*, not *which* candidates would be elected, represented an exercise of legislative power and thus had to meet constitutional standards. The Justice Department decided to come down firmly against at-large commission forms of government because it also filed a brief supporting the plaintiffs in the rehearing of *Bolden*.[48]

As the lawyers for both sides took their appeals to New Orleans, Jackson readied for another round of elections. The election resembled 1977 because Doug Shanks won the Republican primary and faced Dale Danks again. One key factor made the race different. Henry Kirksey, although a sitting state senator, filed and ran as an independent candidate for mayor. Kirksey made his push for ward voting the centerpiece of his campaign. He also played to the greatest fears of whites who opposed the ward system for racial reasons. African Americans, after the 1980 census, now composed forty-seven percent of the city's population. Kirksey warned that without single-member wards the black population would eventually assume majority status and win control of the entire government. Wards could then preserve a white presence in the city government.[49]

Another black Democrat, Shirley Watson, made a serious bid for the commission. A native of Yazoo County, she grew up in Jackson and became involved with politics in 1980 while working for independent Republican John Anderson during his presidential bid. The thirty-year-old's previous work experience included employment with various federal agencies. If Watson won, her victory would not only break racial but also gender barriers. Although municipal and other local offices tended to be where both black and white women in Mississippi had the greatest chance of holding office, Jackson's city commission remained a bastion of white male privilege as no woman had ever won a seat on the commission or boards of aldermen in the city's history.[50]

During the May municipal primary, Watson, however, made history when she won one of the two Democratic nominations for the commission posts. She won on a shoestring budget run out of her dining room and using unpaid volunteers. Watson and Kirksey both received a boost in May when the Rev. Jesse Jackson, as part of his nationwide campaign to renew the Voting Rights Act in 1982, arrived in Jackson to stump for them. One white city official warned that the tactic could backfire because black voter registration lagged behind white numbers and Jackson's presence could boost a white backlash. Kirksey, since he ran as an independent, did not enjoy the backing of prominent black Democrats who supported Danks.[51]

When the voters went to the polls on June 2, Kirksey hoped that a fifty-fifty split in white votes between Danks and Shanks would allow him to win with a plurality. Yet Danks, who had the backing of the Democratic establishment, received enough of the black vote to deny either Shanks or Kirksey a victory. Shirley Watson placed fourth out of the five candidates, a loss that greatly disappointed the black community. The persistence of all-white government in Jackson in 1981 stood in sharp contrast to cities like Columbus where voters elected two black aldermen after the city adopted a court-ordered ward system.[52]

Frank Parker hoped to use Kirksey's and Watson's defeats to show the effects the commission system had on racially polarized voting. Like the brief the Justice Department filed to aid him, he mainly focused on proving the racist intent of the creation and maintenance of the commission system.[53]

However, in December 1981, the three-judge panel ruled that voters' motivations could not be used as evidence against the city. Judge Henry Politz, a Carter appointee from Louisiana, declared that no evidence existed of racially discriminatory intent in the creation of the commission form of government. With racist intent not proven, questions of effect had little relevance because of the tighter standards the Supreme Court laid out in *Bolden*. When the full Court of Appeals rejected Parker's request for an *en banc* hearing in March 1982, *Kirksey v. City of Jackson* finally came to a close.[54]

All seemed lost for the plaintiffs, but in 1982 Congress intervened by renewing the Voting Rights Act with strengthened vote dilution standards. The Supreme Court's decision in *Bolden* had a significant effect on the debate over renewal. Fearing the long-term effects of the Court's ruling in the Mobile case, national civil rights leaders, including Frank Parker, lobbied members of Congress to undo the *Bolden* standards. The

FIGURE 17. Election signs for the Jackson mayor's race, 1981. Kirksey, a plaintiff in a suit to adopt ward voting in the city, ran as an independent and could not garner any significant black support, most of which went for the Democratic incumbent, Dale Danks. Doug Shanks, a progressive Republican who had faced Danks in 1977, lost again and also failed to win many black votes. William F. "Bill" Minor Papers, 80–712, Special Collections Department, Mitchell Memorial Library, Mississippi State University.

strengthened section two of the act meant that plaintiffs now only had to prove that an election scheme had discriminatory *effect* instead of producing evidence that the plan had been enacted with racist *intent*. Under the new standards, the lack of racial discrimination in the adoption of Jackson's commission system in 1912 was now irrelevant and could no longer be used as a defense against ward voting. Parker and his clients now had the power they needed to renew the lawsuit.[55]

They wasted little time in returning to the courts. In February 1983, the LCCRUL filed a new suit against the city. The city commissioners knew that with the strengthened section two of the Voting Rights Act the days of at-large elections were numbered, but despite $150,000 in legal bills from fighting the suits, none of the commissioners wanted to give in to the plaintiffs. Commissioner Luther Roan complained that the Voting Rights Act meant that "the South, or a few states, are still the whipping boy for the rest of the nation." The plaintiffs' case gained momentum when Judge William Barbour of the District Court for the

Southern District ruled in January 1984 that the plaintiffs could use evidence of voter intent in the 1977 referendum, testimony opposed by Barbour's predecessor Walter Nixon.[56]

Meanwhile, a special election helped draw attention to the continuing racial polarization of the Jackson electorate. Commissioner Nielson Cochran resigned his seat in December 1983 after he won election to a seat on the state Public Service Commission. On Valentine's Day 1984, Jacksonians voted in a special election to replace Cochran. Shirley Watson made another bid to be the first African American and woman on the commission, and she faced George Porter, a white Republican and mechanical engineer with no political experience. Porter raised significant sums from his Republican base and from Democrats who opposed Watson. He easily defeated Watson with almost sixty percent of the votes cast. Watson's race clearly cost her the election, and she received single-digit percentages of the vote in many of the predominantly white precincts of the city. She said that the lawsuit "has been vindicated by this race."[57]

Watson's loss disturbed Mayor Danks. Less than a week after the election, he called Jackson "a divided city" and appointed an eighty-seven member biracial advisory committee to study the feasibility of changing the city's form of government. In March 1984, a subcommittee on the newly formed Mayor's Form of Government Committee endorsed a plan with a mayor with strong administrative powers and a seven-member council elected from wards.[58]

Danks pushed ahead with another referendum to change the city government, and the city clerk set an election for September 4. The referendum called for a seven-member council, not a nine-member, which Kirksey opposed, saying it would give Danks "fewer arms to twist to get what he wants." Yet by September Kirksey capitulated and endorsed the seven-member council. Many of the old opponents of the commission system, such as Kane Ditto, also stumped for it. The city's main newspaper, The Clarion-Ledger, also endorsed the change, focusing on the improved efficiency a strong mayor could bring. The prognosis for at-large elections in Jackson did not look good since the federal courts, using the results standard under the 1982 Voting Rights Act extension, had voided elections in Greenwood, Hattiesburg, and Laurel.[59]

The city and the plaintiffs went to trial for the latest round of the Kirksey case on September 4, the same day as the referendum. In a reverse of 1977, the mayor-council form passed overwhelmingly, with a sixty-five percent majority. The media campaign that council proponents used, along with the backing of the mayor and the press, secured the needed votes. Some white voters also likely voted for the system in hopes of settling the lawsuit before the federal courts secured a less favorable judgment for the city, while others cited complaints over inefficient government prompted them to vote for change.[60]

After the vote, Kirksey declared that "the lawsuit is over," and for once the city attorney agreed with him. The real legacy of the case came the next year when Jackson voters went to the polls to elect a council under the new system. Four other cities, Greenwood, Gulfport, Hattiesburg, and Laurel, also joined the state capital and elected candidates under ward systems for the first time. In the primaries and resulting runoffs, three black Democrats in Jackson won nominations in the three majority-black wards created under the new system.[61]

During the June elections, Dale Danks won a third term as mayor, this time to a much more powerful office then he had in the past. He easily defeated Henry Kirksey in a rematch of their 1981 race. The new council broke racial and gender barriers, with voters electing two white women, a black woman, and two black men. These victories represented the first time women had ever held seats on the Jackson city council and the first time in almost a century for black men. Only Danks and Luther Roan survived the change from the old commission system. Voters in ward two put Louis Armstrong of the North Mississippi Legal Services Coalition on the council. Armstrong, a lawyer, helped black voters in other Mississippi cites and towns challenge at-large voting systems, and he had helped redraw districts in thirty-five Mississippi counties over the past two years. Black voters also elected E. C. Foster, the Jackson State professor who had testified during the earlier trial. Black candidates running under the ward systems in other cities also fared well. Three black office seekers each won seats on the boards of aldermen in Greenwood and Laurel, and two to Hattiesburg's board.[62]

The challenges to the at-large system did not cease in Mississippi with the resolution of the *Kirksey* cases. In 1985 alone, over twenty municipalities faced lawsuits over their at-large systems.[63] The victories in Jackson and other cities increased black representation on the municipal level and brought the cities in line with developments in county redistricting and state legislative districts. By the mid-1980s, black

Mississippians had won representation in the city halls, county court-houses, and state legislature, but one final obstacle of vote dilution still remained glaringly obvious. Mississippi still had not integrated its congressional delegation. The strengthening of the Voting Rights Act broke down vote dilution in municipalities and counties but also restored a black-majority district in the state. Despite the power of the act, the elections of the 1980s would show that electing a black congressman would prove more difficult than simply drawing lines on a map.

9 The Delta District and the Continuing Politics of Race

BY THE 1980s, many of the legal barriers that diluted the black vote had fallen or would fall soon. Although the total percentage of elected black officials did not equal the percentage of African Americans in the Mississippi population, civil rights activists had made major strides in the state legislature and on the local level. During the 1980s the Delta became the major campaign of black political activists, where they pushed for the restoration of a majority-black congressional district that would lead to the first black representative since the nineteenth century. While eventually successful in electing a black congressman, black Democrats faced a number of hurdles in their quest, from whites in their own party as well Republicans. The successful election of Mike Espy in 1986 showed that not only did race remain a salient issue in Mississippi politics in the post–civil rights era, but it also influenced what kind of black candidate could win an election in a biracial district.

The Mississippi Delta is a geographically and culturally distinct area, a rich diamond-shaped alluvial basin hemmed in by bluffs and the Yazoo River on the east and the Mississippi River on the west. Stretching two hundred miles south of Memphis to Vicksburg, the humid subtropical Delta remained largely a wilderness until after the Civil War, with only a small portion settled. Since antebellum times, the Delta has also possessed a majority-black population as white southerners used slaves to grow cotton for export, and this white domination continued after emancipation. With the exception of a brief moment during

Reconstruction, the Delta and its rural black proletariat remained wholly under the thrall of a white elite, who combined the twin features of white supremacist paternalism and economic development.[1]

While the racial paternalism of the planters contrasted somewhat with the rabidly racist populism of the hills, white Deltans hardly treated their black neighbors with goodwill. Lynching, while less common per capita in the Delta than in other parts of the state, still enjoyed significant white support as a means of racial subjugation. White landlords in the Jim Crow era, despite their imagined benevolence, regularly cheated and exploited their tenants. Even the New Deal strengthened the planters' hold over the lives of their workers. Only a few programs, such as the Farm Security Administration's loans to allow black farmers in Holmes County to buy land, provided relief to black Deltans.[2]

The state legislature in 1882 created a separate congressional district encompassing the Delta's geographic borders and maintained it for decades afterwards. By the 1950s, eleven black-majority Delta counties made up the third congressional district, represented by Frank Smith, a moderate Democrat who won his seat in 1950 by advocating economic development and promised "to support the traditional viewpoint" of white voters on race. Despite his personal opposition to segregation and lack of demagoguery, he publicly supported it and signed the Southern Manifesto.[3]

Smith openly backed John F. Kennedy for president in 1960, which led Gov. Ross Barnett and state Speaker of the House Walter Sillers to redraw the state's congressional districts and reflect loss of a seat due to the 1960 census. In 1962, they absorbed Smith's third district into archconservative Rep. Jamie Whitten's second district, creating a new second district with a black majority of 113,000. The district remained culturally and geographically the Delta, especially since some of the new counties lay partly in the Delta. Whitten, a native of Tallahatchie County and an eleven-term incumbent, defeated Smith in the 1962 elections.[4]

Whitten did not represent the Delta in its entirety for long. The Voting Rights Act soon prompted the legislature to take action on congressional redistricting mid-decade. In October 1965, Henry Kirksey and the MFDP filed the first of the *Conner* lawsuits against redistricting and legislative malapportionment under the "one man, one vote" standard of *Reynolds v. Sims*. The legislature had not redrawn the other districts, so the new second district had a population of 608,411, over twice the population of the least-populous fourth district. The legislature knew that such a plan would not be upheld in the wake of *Reynolds*, so it moved to redraw the districts before the court hearing in 1966.[5]

The legislature adopted a plan in April that would nullify the potential black voting strength of the Delta and save Whitten's seat. The plan, sponsored by Sen. W. B. Alexander of majority-black Bolivar County, preserved a small black-population majority in one district. His version created a black-majority district with a 51.36 percent black population but with a majority-white voting age population, or a "phantom" black majority.[6]

Although the district court had earlier struck down the state's legislative reapportionment plan for violating *Reynolds*, the judges upheld the congressional redistricting plan at an October hearing, and the Supreme Court upheld the lower court's ruling. The new plan divided Mississippi into five districts with most of the Delta split into the newly redrawn first, second, and fourth districts. Only the fifth district, which contained the Gulf Coast and piney woods region of south Mississippi, remained unchanged from the old 1962 plan.[7]

With the case dismissed, the Delta district ceased to exist for the next fifteen years. After the 1970 census the Justice Department approved Mississippi's congressional districts under section five preclearance.[8] Civil rights attorneys and black voting rights plaintiffs shifted their energies to vote dilution in the 1970s. The emphasis on increasing state- and local-level black political power pushed any new challenges to congressional gerrymandering to the background for the entire decade.

In 1980, questions again arose about congressional gerrymandering now that the state legislature had its first significant numbers of black legislators since the nineteenth century. Mississippi now had 327 elected black officials, trailing Louisiana by only seven. Black officeholders held seats from the state Senate to the school boards, and this made the lack of a black congressman even more noticeable. Mississippi in 1980 had a black population of thirty-five percent, the highest in the country, but states with lesser black populations had already elected black representatives. The black representatives in the House in 1980 came from northern or western states with significantly lower black populations than Mississippi but with more urbanized and concentrated black populations than rural Mississippi.[9]

Most southern states still lacked black representation in their congressional delegations. Only two southern states, Tennessee and Texas, had black House members in 1980, and they represented the urban areas of Memphis and Houston.[10] While Mississippi lacked a major urban area outside of Jackson, the Delta with its natural geographic boundaries and black majority raised the possibility of a black congressman who represented rural black interests.

Redistricting remained the main obstacle to a black House member. Leslie Burl McLemore's loss in the fourth district in 1980 triggered a debate on the lack of black congressional representation. Sen. Henry Kirksey and other black leaders, as well as some moderate whites, backed the re-creation of the Delta district and held public hearings on the matter.[11] Sen. Tommy Campbell, a Democrat from Yazoo City, chaired a special joint congressional redistricting panel. He did not rule out a Delta district but called Kirksey's proposal, which created a north-to-south district along the entire state line on the Mississippi River, racial gerrymandering. He said a Delta district would have to be in "a concentrated area" and would likely have a fifty-one to fifty-five percent black population majority, not the higher numbers of the other plans.[12]

Campbell had another concern as well. He and many other Democrats wanted to avoid redrawing the districts to prevent two incumbents, Jamie Whitten of the first district and David Bowen of the second district from running against each other. Bowen, a resident of Cleveland, had graduated from Harvard and Oxford and taught political science at Millsaps and Mississippi Colleges before entering politics in 1972. Although he did not approach the perceived liberalism of the national Democratic Party, he did have a more moderate reputation than his fellow Mississippi congressmen. In a black-majority District, Bowen would likely have an advantage over the archconservative Whitten. Although both men had voted against the extension of the Voting Rights Act in 1975, Whitten had a longer history of racial bias. He had opposed food stamps and the civil rights legislation of the 1960s and called *Brown* "the downhill road to integration, amalgamation, and ruin." The desire to avoid a Bowen-Whitten contest overrode efforts to create a black-majority district, and in July 1981, the committee voted to maintain the present configurations of the districts. The plan, known as the "least change" option, only adjusted lines to correct population inequities to satisfy *Reynolds*.[13]

The committee's plan drew the ire of some black citizens since testimony at the public hearings favored a Delta district. The committee rebuffed attempts by Kirksey and other black legislators to introduce plans to change the state's east-west district lines. Kirksey asked for a Delta district like the one that existed in the past and received help from Rep. Jim Simpson, a white legislator from Harrison County. He proposed a Delta district with a 53.7 percent black population, but the motion also failed.[14]

The full legislature passed the least change plan in August 1981, which Gov. Winter then signed into law. The plan then went to the Justice Department for section five preclearance review, but in April 1982 it rejected the least change plan. It dodged the issue of racial intent and instead claimed that two of the earlier redistricting plans had never been reviewed properly under the Voting Rights Act.[15]

After Justice's objections became official, Frank Parker filed a motion on behalf of thirteen black plaintiffs in the U.S. District Court for the District of Colombia to join the Justice Department's efforts to block the plan. Gov. Winter, anticipating electoral problems from the cases, asked the court to postpone all of the state's primary elections. The court met Winter halfway and ordered the House primaries delayed until September 14, which gave the NAACP time to register more black voters.[16]

The debate over the Delta district again exposed the weaknesses of the state Democratic Party's fusion. With the state's black Democrats still angry over the Cupit affair of the previous year, the 1981–82 intra-party squabble over congressional redistricting exacerbated tensions. Sen. Campbell did not want to "rob," in his words, other districts of black voters and thus enhance the viability of Republicans against incumbent Democratic congressmen. He termed a black district an "affirmative action" plan that would not pass the state legislature, which had already killed a public kindergarten bill that year because of the opposition of some white legislators to a "baby-sitting service for Negroes." Claude Ramsey of the state AFL-CIO also opposed a sixty-five percent district like Kirksey proposed, arguing that it could lead to "one black congressman and four damn Republicans." He instead backed Simpson's proposed black district, which had a smaller black majority. The Republicans no doubt fueled Ramsey's fears when state GOP chairman Mike Retzer lobbied the Justice Department to scrap the legislature's plan. Retzer argued that a Delta district would benefit the GOP, since David Bowen and Jamie Whitten would likely have to run against each other.[17]

On June 8, 1982, the District Court ordered a compromise plan that restored the Delta district. The judges rejected the Kirksey plan, which they said violated a state practice to create "high impact" districts.

High-impact districts had black majorities of forty percent or higher, with the idea that black voters had a significant amount of influence in the district even if they could not elect one of their own to office. The court adopted the Simpson plan, which recreated the Delta district as the second congressional district but added six non-Delta counties, which all had white voting-age populations of fifty-nine percent or higher. This inclusion created a district with a 53.77 percent black population but only a forty-eight percent black voting age population.[18]

The Simpson plan seemed peculiar as a Delta district. None of the other earlier Delta configurations, even as far back as 1882, included the six non-Delta counties, with the exception of the 1962 combination of the second and third districts.[19] The judges condemned racial gerrymandering but then deliberately added non-Delta counties to the Delta district, while they kept all but three precincts of the mostly Delta Tallahatchie County in the first district. Such a move itself smacked of political considerations since Jamie Whitten lived in Tallahatchie County. Frank Parker appealed for a district more akin to the Kirksey plan, but the Justice Department sided with the Simpson plan. Many in the white Democratic establishment, including Gov. Winter, came out for the Simpson plan.[20]

Against the backdrop of the legislative debates and lawsuits of 1981 and 1982, a special election in the fourth district showed the continuing importance of the black vote to the Democratic Party and drove home how party leaders could not take black voters for granted. GOP Rep. Jon Hinson resigned his seat in early 1981 after an arrest for oral sodomy, confirming the earlier reports about his homosexuality. The Democrats backed Wayne Dowdy, the mayor of McComb, for the seat, which the Republicans had held since 1972. He faced Republican Liles Williams, an electrical company vice president from Jackson, in the July special election which became a referendum on the extension of the Voting Rights Act, which Williams opposed and Dowdy favored. Black voters and politicians rallied to Dowdy, but labor issues also played a key role. Dowdy supported continuing food stamps for striking workers, a position that brought him the support of the state AFL-CIO.[21]

Dowdy broke new ground for a white Mississippi politician because he became the first white congressional Democrat to openly endorse a civil rights bill. Even a racial moderate like William Winter opposed extending the Voting Rights Act because he believed it singled out the southern states for "undue scrutiny." Dowdy's open labor endorsement

FIGURE 18. Rep. Wayne Dowdy, with history students of Jackson State University, August 21, 1982. Dowdy, the mayor of McComb, became the first white Democrat to openly endorse a civil rights bill when he supported extension of the Voting Rights Act in a special election in 1981. His narrow victory over his Republican opponent resulted from a coalition of African Americans and labor and prompted President Reagan to not oppose renewal of the Act in 1982. Willie J. Miller Papers, 501–170, Special Collections Department, Mitchell Memorial Library, Mississippi State University.

also broke taboos because conventional Mississippi political wisdom dictated that Democrats solicited labor support clandestinely. The Mc-Comb mayor's gamble paid off, and his blue-black coalition beat Williams by a narrow margin of 50.5 to 49.5 percent, or 1200 votes. The high black-voter turnout due to the debate over the act showed that civil rights issues still had saliency in Mississippi almost twenty years later after the initial legislation.[22]

Williams's loss sent a clear message to the Reagan White House, which concluded that it could not weaken the act to any significant degree. While the Republican Party recognized that it would have difficulty gaining any significant percentage of the black vote, the Dowdy victory showed that they could not afford to anger black constituents either. President Reagan resisted conservative pressure to kill or significantly weaken extension of the bill that passed the House in 1981.[23]

Mississippi politicians got the message as well. For the first time, a majority of Mississippi's representatives voted for the act. David Bowen and Jamie Whitten joined Dowdy in voting for the act, an especially notable feat given Whitten's long segregationist history. Sonny Montgomery and Trent Lott continued to vote against renewal, but they risked little by doing so. With black populations of thirty-one percent in Montgomery's third district and twenty percent in Lott's fifth district, the two candidates owed far more to their conservative white supporters than to their black constituents.[24]

Sen. Thad Cochran, who more than any other Republican officeholder had successfully solicited black votes, also faced a dilemma over the Voting Rights Act. His original base of support included many conservative whites opposed to the act or any other perceived special preferences for black Mississippians, which led him to oppose renewal when he was a representative in 1975. Cochran now faced reelection to the U.S. Senate in 1984, and he needed to not anger black voters.

Cochran tried to compromise with an approach that included lip service against the act and attempts to broaden its geographic coverage. He criticized the act for making local officials "go to Washington, get on their knees, kiss the ring and tug their forelock to all these third-rate bureaucrats" and also introduced into the *Congressional Record* editorials from the *Clarion-Ledger* that opposed re-extension of the act in its present form. He avoided outright opposition to renewal and tried but failed to extend section five preclearance nationwide to take its focus off of the South. Cochran in the end voted for extension, and his grudging acceptance of the act reflected the pragmatist views of Clarke Reed, the GOP national committeeman from Mississippi, who said that "the Voting Rights Act wasn't all that bad . . . and a lot of good came out of it."[25]

For a freshman senator like Cochran who entered public service after the 1960s and without the baggage of segregationist lawmakers like Whitten, supporting extension surprised few people. The same could not be said about the senior senator from Mississippi, John Stennis, who had a long history as a civil rights opponent. Although he kept a low profile and avoided the race-baiting of James Eastland, Stennis had never supported a civil rights bill and as late as the 1970s did not answer letters from his black constituents. Stennis initially shared the view of Gov. Winter that the Act should expire in 1982, but Winter himself changed his viewpoint after discussions with black leaders in the state.[26]

In 1982, the eighty-one-year-old senator ran for his sixth term. His well-funded Republican opponent was Haley Barbour, a thirty-five-year-old Yazoo County attorney. Both men held conservative viewpoints, so Barbour decided to make the senator's age a campaign issue. Winter traveled to Washington in the summer of 1982 and told Stennis that he should support extension, which would convince black voters to support him. Stennis had already appointed Ed Cole, a former Eastland staffer who became the black vice-chairman of the state Democratic Party in 1980, to a staff post earlier in the year, providing him with a line of communication on black issues. For the first time, Stennis had also hired a professional campaign consultant to coordinate an advertising and polling campaign, which included mobilizing a high black-voter turnout. In May, Stennis publicly endorsed extension of the Voting Rights Act. His incumbency and vigorous campaign paid off, and he won in the fall of 1982 with 63.9 percent of the vote to Barbour's 36.1 percent.[27]

While Stennis waged his last election battle and the appeals in the redistricting case made their way to the Supreme Court, the state's Republicans and Democrats prepared for the 1982 congressional elections under the court-ordered Simpson plan. In the second district, incumbent Rep. David Bowen became the first casualty when he decided not to seek another term because of the addition of Republican-leaning counties to his district. The addition of more black counties also raised the specter of a black independent spoiler. Bowen already faced a strong challenge from Greenwood attorney Webb Franklin. Franklin had served as a circuit judge in Leflore County, but in 1982 he resigned and became a

Republican. A self-described fiscal conservative, he voiced familiar Republican themes of smaller government as his reason for leaving the Democratic Party in the early Reagan era.[28]

A number of Democrats entered the fray over who would be the successor to Bowen. Not surprisingly, race immediately became a political issue in the majority-black district. Three white Democrats entered the primary, and of the three, Clarksdale banker Pete Johnson had the greatest name recognition. Johnson's uncle, the former governor Paul Johnson Jr., had gained fame in 1962 when as lieutenant governor he tried to block the admission of James Meredith to the University of Mississippi, and Pete Johnson's grandfather, Paul Johnson Sr., had been governor in the 1940s. The restoration of a majority-black district created a feeling among black Democrats that the Mississippi Democratic Party needed to do the historic thing and get behind a black nominee for Congress, a view shared by some white Democrats as well.[29]

Black Democrats met on their own to push a black nominee, with over two hundred black delegates and political leaders caucusing in Greenwood to nominate a candidate. They chose Rep. Robert Clark of Holmes County, who as the state's first modern black legislator had the name recognition few other black candidates had. Clark accepted and said he planned to run "not as a spoiler, but . . . to win." That August, Clark easily won the primary with a majority of over 34,000 votes, mostly from the black Delta counties that gave him strong returns.[30]

Clark needed to win some white votes from Franklin because of the forty-eight percent black voting age population in the district. White Democrats like U.S. Reps. Wayne Dowdy and David Bowen and state House Speaker C. B. "Buddie" Newman publicly endorsed Clark. The two biggest public endorsements came from Gov. Winter and Sen. Stennis. Claude Ramsey of the AFL-CIO also endorsed Clark for his pro-labor record, but Clark did shy away from some endorsements. He welcomed the endorsements of white state Democrats like Winter and Stennis but declined aid from prominent national Democrats like Sen. Edward Kennedy and former Vice President Walter Mondale out of fear of linking himself too closely to the national Democratic Party.[31]

Franklin received some impressive endorsements as well. One of his biggest came from former President Gerald Ford, who spoke on behalf of Franklin at a stop in Greenwood. Trent Lott and Thad Cochran also gave their support in public appearances. The national publicity of the race also gave Franklin financial support from the Republican Congressional

Campaign Committee, the National Rifle Association, the U.S. Chamber of Commerce, and the Cattlemen's Association. Some of Franklin's support also came from white supremacist groups such as the Citizens' Councils.[32]

The Citizens' Councils endorsement only highlighted an issue that became the focal point in the election. Franklin said that he realized that race, not his background or ideological differences, played the most important factor in the election. Franklin recalled the 1982 campaign as a difficult but largely civil affair. He focused his attacks on party labels and called Clark a "closet liberal" connected with the national Democratic Party. One Franklin campaign ad caused a racial stir when it ran on television. The commercial used the slogan, "Elect Webb Franklin. He's one of us." Franklin chose the line when he thought David Bowen would be his opponent, and he planned to make Bowen's frequent foreign travels and Oxford education an issue. When Clark became the nominee, Democrats accused the line of having racial overtones, and Franklin's campaign changed the slogan to "A Congressman for us." Another ad opened and closed with images of the Leflore County Courthouse and its Confederate monument. In the ad, Franklin said that Mississippians "cannot forget a heritage that has been sacred" through multiple generations. Although the ad included a shot of black factory workers, the inclusion of the Confederate monument with words such as "heritage," "traditions," and "what has gone before" created a stir. Danny Cupit, the Democratic state chairman, called the ad an effort "to inflame racial passion."[33]

Franklin denied that the ad had any racist intent, and both in 1982 and years later he insisted the Confederate monument appeared because of the courthouse behind it, where he had served for four years as a circuit judge. Franklin admitted that he deliberately appealed to white voters during his campaign but insisted that his campaign did not use the ad "in a sleazy or illicit way." Clarke Reed echoed Franklin's view and complained of a double standard that penalized Franklin appealing directly for white votes but not Clark if he asked blacks to vote for him because of his race. Franklin did admit that some of his supporters circulated posters that featured pictures of him and Clark that had been doctored to make Clark look darker and Franklin look whiter. He said his campaign had nothing to do with the circulars, but the *New York Times* quoted an anonymous Franklin campaign advisor who said the campaign had approved the ads. Franklin also used appeals that critics said injected race in coded terms into the campaign, such as accusing Clark of wanting a seat on the House Agriculture Committee to exploit federal welfare programs such as food stamps.[34]

Whatever Franklin's appeals to white voters, he recognized that he had to make inroads with black voters, especially since Clark might win some white votes due to his heavy endorsements from key state Democrats. Franklin employed paid black campaign staffers as part of his outreach to the black community. He considered each black vote he won a "twofer," since it represented a vote he did not expect to get and also a vote he took from Clark's base.[35]

When it came to outreach, Clark had more problems. In addition to being a black man trying to win white votes in Mississippi, he also had problems with his political base in the black community. The media came to the Delta in 1982 for more than just the House race. In Holmes County, the state put Eddie Carthan, the former mayor of Tchula, on trial for murder. Carthan had been elected mayor of Tchula in 1977, and during his first term, two of his black allies on city council lost their seats to two black men not affiliated with Carthan. The two men allied with the only white on the council and fought with the mayor over budgetary matters. In June 1981, armed robbers shot and killed one of the black councilmen, Roosevelt Granderson, at a convenience store. One of the men arrested pleaded guilty to a lesser charge and accused Carthan of hiring him to murder Granderson. Carthan received significant support during his trial because many civil rights groups saw the trial as a frame-up. The National Council of Churches, the national organization of the United Methodist Church all lent him aid, and black celebrities like Dick Gregory and Ossie Davis came to rally support as well.[36]

As the trial in Lexington went on, the publicity began to overlap with Clark's race and hurt him. The Conference of Black Mayors supported Carthan and put pressure on Clark to make a statement about the trial. Clark privately distrusted Carthan and made no public comment. His refusal to come out for Carthan led the Conference of Black Mayors to demand that individual members withdraw their support for Clark, and some local ones refused to accompany Clark when he campaigned in their neighborhoods. Carthan's supporters began to urge black voters to stay away from the polls on Election Day and even circulated an anti-Clark flier. Although the effectiveness of the anti-Clark tactics cannot be fully known, they likely helped keep black voter turnout low.[37]

Clark's own image did not help his campaign. Clark held a master's degree in education from Michigan State University and a teaching fellowship at the John F. Kennedy School of Government at Harvard. Despite his educational background, he could not shake the image of a country farmer from Holmes County. His opponent described him as "a good man" who may not have been "as articulate as I think maybe many of the voters would like to have had." Clark's press secretary, Melany Neilson, confirmed the problems with Clark's image, including poor grammar and a heavy dialect. One friend told Neilson that she did not know if Clark could win because "he just don't act white enough." Clark's lack of polish may have helped remind voters that he came from the Delta, but it contrasted with a white lawyer from Greenwood.[38]

Clark went to Election Day hamstrung by his image and the Carthan trial, but race remained the primary issue. He lost to Franklin by less than three thousand votes. Although the election attracted the best-ever black turnout for a non-presidential year, he could not overcome the high white-voter turnout. Although he received between ten to twelve percent of white votes, most the white voters who supported Stennis split their tickets and gave their votes in the House race to Franklin.[39]

Although Clark conceded on a positive note, other black observers gave less positive assessments of the election. Charles Tisdale, the editor of the *Jackson Advocate*, said that Clark "ran a campaign too black for whites and too white for blacks." Tisdale accused white Democrats like Winter of giving only lip service to Clark, and Aaron Henry blamed the failure of white Democrats to vote for Clark.[40]

As the election passed, the federal courts heard the legal suits against the racial composition of the second district, and now the plaintiffs used the election results as evidence for the need for a higher black voting age population. Once again, the strengthened Voting Rights Act came into play. In May 1983, the Supreme Court, citing the modified section two and the results test, vacated and remanded the lower court's ruling upholding the Simpson plan. Later in December, the case of *Brooks v. Winter* went to trial in Greenville. Gordon Henderson, the political scientist who had testified in the vote dilution cases for Hinds County and Jackson, testified for the black plaintiffs on the prevalence of racially polarized voting in the 1982 election. Some of the key evidence included Franklin's television advertising, in particular the ad with the Confederate monument.[41]

In January 1984, Judge William Keady ordered a redrawing of the district that increased the black population to 58.3 percent, almost five percent higher than the Simpson plan. The newly drawn district had a black voting age population of 52.83 percent. The court added new heavily black areas and removed most of the east-central hill counties that voted for Franklin. Wayne Dowdy's fourth district suffered as a result, since the overwhelmingly Democratic counties of Claiborne and Jefferson went to the second district.[42]

As the litigation over the district continued, the 1983 statewide races reinforced how institutionalized the black vote had become in the state Democratic Party. The elections showed once and for all that the black independent political route had finally reached irrelevancy. Never viable as a way to win, the black independent candidacy had frightened white Democrats and black party loyalists and led to some Republican victories. In 1983, Charles Evers made his final statewide political race when he ran as an independent for governor, but his political influence had evaporated. The maverick civil rights veteran had lost the support of many black and white Democrats over his 1978 Senate race, and he even lost his seat as mayor of Fayette after he backed Ronald Reagan for president in 1980. Attorney General Bill Allain of Natchez won the Democratic nomination in 1983 and faced Republican Leon Bramlett of Clarksdale, who had almost wrested the Republican nomination away from Gil Carmichael in 1979. The race quickly became one of the most sordid in modern Mississippi history when Billy Mounger, the conservative GOP financier, made allegations that Allain had patronized black transvestite prostitutes in the Jackson area. Allain denied the charges but they became a central issue in the campaign and raised questions about his personal life, such as his earlier divorce and lack of children.[43]

The scandal failed to shake black voters from Allain, and they turned out to elect him and other Democrats and swept the party into all the statewide offices that year. Although black voters would not likely defect to the conservative Bramlett, they could have backed Evers, but they gave him only slightly over 30,000 votes. Allain recognized that black Democrats had stayed with the party, and after the election he thanked NAACP members at their convention in Clarksdale.[44]

Although the state's biracial coalition held together in 1983, state Democratic leaders had reason to worry in 1984. White Democrats were increasingly abandoning the party for the Republicans. State Rep. Ed Buelow of Vicksburg faced party sanctions for openly backing Ronald

Reagan, so he switched parties. His defection highlighted the fragile nature of the racial coalition because Buelow said he left out of anger at party leaders who negotiated with a group of disgruntled black Democrats. The black Democrats threatened to run an independent in the Senate reelection bid of Thad Cochran. Other elected Democrats, such as state Sen. Bill Minor of Holly Springs, remained in the party but backed Cochran. Danny Cupit, who stepped down as party chair the same year, complained about "an almost constant, inevitable tension between groups" in the party that led to taking "one step forward and two steps back." Some pointed the finger at the younger generation of black political leadership who were replacing the old civil rights veterans of the 1960s. These leaders included people such as Bennie Thompson, who moved up the party ranks that year at the state convention, as well as unelected officials, such as Jonnie Walls and Victor McTeer, two Greenville attorneys active in vote dilution cases, who held seats on the party's executive committee.[45]

The 1984 election featured two high-profile races besides the national presidential election. Thad Cochran sought a second term as senator, and the Democrats solicited outgoing Gov. William Winter, who enjoyed a populist appeal for pushing through the 1982 education reform bill that provided for publicly funded kindergartens beginning in 1986. Winter accepted the Democratic nomination but stumbled badly from the beginning against the genial Cochran. Much of Winter's support rested on the black vote, but Cochran's careful years of outreach combined with a feeling among black voters that white Democrats took them for granted meant that Winter could not count on unconditional black support.[46]

Race again played a major role in the second district House campaign when Robert Clark announced that he planned to challenge Franklin again. Clark's role in passing the education reforms under Gov. Winter represented a new height of influence that a black legislator had reached in Mississippi. Despite his accomplishments, he faced his first black opponents in primary opposition for the House seat. Some black voters felt that Clark had spent too much time soliciting white votes in the 1982 race, and his opponents exploited that theme. Robert Gray, the black mayor of Shelby, announced as a candidate almost a year before the primary. Evan Doss, the black tax-assessor collector of Claiborne County, also challenged Clark. Gray and Doss, emboldened by the newly redrawn district with a fifty-three percent black voting-age population, accused Clark of not being "black" enough. Clark, in a private comment to his press secretary, highlighted the generational conflict between an old veteran like him and younger black politicians like Doss and Gray, complaining that he "was on the front getting death threats and catching all kinds of hell when Gray and Doss . . . was just babies."[47]

Despite Clark's comments, Gray did have civil rights credentials of his own. He helped elect Kermit Stanton as the first modern black supervisor in Bolivar County in 1967, an action for which Gray lost his job. Doss, who had held office in Claiborne County since 1972, also had numerous clashes with white residents and officials in the county before black officeholders attained majority status. Clark easily swept aside his opponents during the primary, but voter turnout remained low, especially since many whites did not bother to vote.[48]

The primary created other problems as well. Clark left the primary victorious but with his campaign funds exhausted. He accused Franklin of engineering Doss and Gray's challenges to force him to spend critical funds and run in the general election with a deficit. Franklin had also built up his black base in the district during his term through his constituent services, which included a "rolling office" that traveled the district to reach areas distant from his main offices. He also had the added bonus of a presidential election year and could expect to benefit from Ronald Reagan's coattails in Mississippi. Some white Democrats, most notably Sen. John Stennis, refused to endorse Clark.[49]

Clark also had reason to be optimistic. The black voting-age population of the district had increased to a majority, and the courts had eliminated much of Franklin's hill-country base. Many black residents of the state had turned out in force in March for Democratic Party caucuses and gave Jesse Jackson forty-five percent of the vote, beating Walter Mondale, the eventual nominee, by almost two-to-one. Poor economic conditions raised the hopes of black political activists that a strong black voter turnout could elect Clark. The statewide school dropout rate was forty-two percent and black male unemployment was twenty percent, and the black per-capita income was below $7,000 in thirty-two of the state's eighty-two counties. The rematch attracted less media attention than 1982, but Clark received favorable coverage in national black publications such as Jet. Franklin made a Republican list as one of the eight most vulnerable GOP House members.[50]

Clark brought in famous outsiders, such as Coretta Scott King, to campaign for him, a sharp contrast from his style in 1982. Clark made poverty and Reaganomics the major themes of his campaign. He also counted on some white support from farmers angered over the White House's farm policies. Franklin, in turn, downplayed any perceived racial rhetoric and highlighted his constituent services to court black voters. Still, the flyer with his picture next to Clark's made a return appearance. Race also flared up rather sharply when both candidates appeared at an NAACP meeting in Raymond. Clark said that when Franklin "runs my picture and he says 'I'm one of you,' I believe he's saying, 'I'm one of those who sold my [Clark's] great-grandmother'" into slavery. Franklin responded that he had tired of hearing Clark "whining" that he had not been responsive to black issues."[51]

Reagan's landslide victory over Mondale that November crushed the Democrats in Mississippi, and Reagan nationally won the support of two-thirds of all white voters and over eighty percent of southern white voters. Thad Cochran soundly defeated William Winter, who lost by almost 200,000 votes and outpolled the Mondale-Ferraro ticket by only about 20,000 votes. Bitter results for black Democrats came in the second district, where Clark lost by a wider margin than he had in 1982. He lost by about three thousand votes and fared more poorly in counties he did well in 1982. Franklin credited Reagan's coattails for the win, and one of his managers readily acknowledged that they had siphoned off some of Clark's black base.[52]

Leslie McLemore, who worked for Clark and analyzed the two campaigns, concluded in an academic paper that Clark lacked the necessary political organization outside of his base in Holmes County, a charge Clark angrily called "a damnable lie." Clark said that McLemore's comments served as an example of how some in the black community ignored the work he and his volunteers had done.[53]

Clark had barely conceded the election when the Supreme Court ruled on the redistricting case. On November 13, in a one-line opinion, the justices affirmed the district's court decision, refusing to approve a sixty-five percent district. Frank Parker lamented the court's refusal and that a new district would have to wait until after redistricting from the 1990 census. Webb Franklin welcomed the ruling and said that he intended to be the second district representative for many years to come.[54]

Although he spoke with the benefit of hindsight, Franklin later indicated that his statements contained more wishful thinking then reality. He built up what organization he could in his two terms to keep him in office, but he said that due to the court's redistricting, he knew he "was not going to be a thirty-year retiree from Congress." Franklin also had problems besides redistricting during his second term in Congress. In 1985, the Federal Election Commission revealed that he had accepted $60,000 in illegal contributions composed of bank overdrafts from the Bank of Greenwood and loans from his campaign manager and other supporters. The money partly funded a series of donations to black churches in the 1982 election. His campaign made the donations the day after the polls closed.[55]

Farming issues, not illegal contributions, would prove to be the undoing of Franklin and the catalyst for the election of a black congressman. Across the country, farmers in the middle of the 1980s experienced one of the worst agricultural depressions in U.S. history. Low prices from overabundant harvests plagued the Midwest while a crippling drought devastated the rural South. Georgia, which had 50,000 farmers in 1986, saw 22,250 delinquent loans by September. Rising foreclosures increased homelessness and forced migrants into the cities to look for work. In the Southeast, the drought and heat wave cost farmers $2 billion in crops and livestock. President Reagan signed into law the Farm Security Act of 1985, but the bill only ballooned farm subsidies and government funding of agriculture exports. The farm crisis dropped Reagan's approval rating among farmers to a low of thirty-nine percent by April 1985.[56]

While most of the media coverage focused on the Midwest's farm problems and the threat to that region's Republican legislators in the midterm elections, the agrarian slump put rural-district southern congressmen like Franklin at risk. Agriculture Secretary Richard Lyng came to the Delta at the end of May 1986 to sell local farmers on the administration's trade policies, and Reagan ordered the creation of the Federal Drought Assistance Task Force to help southeastern farmers, but he squandered much of his support in the textile industry when he vetoed a bill limiting textile and shoe imports.[57]

The southern drought and extreme heat killed both crops and people during the summer months of 1986, in particular the three Delta staples of catfish, cotton, and soybeans. In response, the state committee of the Agricultural Stabilization and Conservation Service asked that thirty-eight Mississippi counties be declared disaster areas, and Gov. Bill Allain applied for federal disaster relief for forty-one counties, fourteen of them counties in the second district. Eventually the Agriculture Department allowed emergency federal loans in every county in the second district, except Claiborne and Jefferson.[58]

While the sun ruined acre after acre of Delta cropland along with Franklin's reelection chances, a new black candidate emerged. Michael Espy, a native of Yazoo City, came from an affluent family that owned a chain of funeral parlors and burial insurance companies in the Delta. He graduated from Howard University and received his law degree from the University of Santa Clara then served on the staff of Central Mississippi Legal Services for two years before being named director of the public lands division in 1980. He then became the assistant attorney general for consumer protection, the first African American to hold that office.[59]

Espy did not enter the Democratic primary uncontested, or even with the unified support of black political leaders in the Delta. After Clark's defeats in 1982 and 1984, some black leaders felt that a progressive white Democrat remained the best hope to unseat Franklin. When two white Democrats announced themselves as candidates for the 1986 Democratic primary, they received some black support. One of the candidates, former 1982 candidate Pete Johnson, had campaigned for Robert Clark in 1982 and 1984, which helped him to pull some prominent black Deltans into his campaign. Espy did secure some impressive backing of his own, including an endorsement by Jesse Jackson. During the primary, the candidates focused their attacks more on Franklin and Reaganomics than on each other.[60]

Espy, as the only black candidate in the majority-black district, had an undeniable advantage over his opponents. The Democratic state executive committee declared Espy the winner, but Johnson charged voter fraud in the close election. Johnson filed challenges in several counties but to no avail, and he withdrew them and then backed Espy.[61]

Throughout the fall campaign, Espy hammered away at Franklin's record on agricultural issues. Just as Franklin had previously linked Robert Clark to an unpopular national Democratic Party, Espy sought to forge a similar link between the Greenwood lawyer and Reagan's farm polices. Pledging to be "the best congressman a Mississippi farmer ever had," Espy sponsored a farm hearing in Washington County with Sen. Tom Harkin (D-Iowa). Although some observers thought that Espy could not campaign well in the black community since he "hasn't toiled in the vineyards," he showed an affinity for canvassing black and white voters. He employed his skills as a lawyer and veteran of state government and cultivated important contacts with the county Democratic organizations in the district. Espy won an important coup when he received the endorsement of the *Clarion-Ledger* and the *Jackson Daily News*, the state's largest daily newspapers. Both papers had endorsed Franklin in 1982 and 1984.[62]

During the debates between Franklin and Espy, the Yazoo city lawyer proved to be a formidable opponent. At the first debate the two men held, Franklin tried to paint Espy as a liberal by accusing of him of having the endorsement of the *Village Voice*, a liberal New York newspaper. Harriet DeCell, the program host, told Franklin that "ninety percent of the people listening to this program don't know what the *Village Voice* is." Espy denied he had the endorsement and also disputed Franklin's charge that he had spoken with Bella Abzug, the liberal and former New York congresswoman. At another debate, Espy hit Franklin for voting against a spending bill that included funding for agriculture and flood control and for missing votes on Social Security. Espy also supported a moratorium on farm foreclosures, which Franklin opposed. Franklin recalled Espy as a very skilled debater during the 1986 campaign. He "was a hell of a candidate," Franklin said, "twenty times the candidate Robert Clark was."[63]

Franklin continued his overtures to the black community. In addition to employing a black congressional aide, he hired Estelle Pryor, a black woman who ran unsuccessfully as a Democrat in 1984 for the Washington County circuit clerk's position. He also received the endorsement of Charles Evers, who had won reelection as mayor of Fayette the previous year. Espy had more success with the white community then Franklin had with African Americans. His outreach to influential whites, which he began even before he announced his candidacy, paid off. Franklin slightly outdid Espy in fundraising totals, but donations to the Espy campaign exceeded Franklin's in the months before the election, a situation that Robert Clark never came close to achieving. Both men raised most of their money from individual contributions and political action committees. Espy raised almost $70,000 from labor unions, abortion rights groups, and other traditionally Democratic sources, while Franklin drew much of his money from business and medical lobbyists.[64]

The white endorsement that may have done the most for Espy came from Grenada County. Espy asked Grenada County sheriff Jesse Strider to film a television ad for him to win over white voters who might be reluctant to vote for a black man. "Big Daddy" Strider, as the locals called him, obliged, and the endorsement carried particular weight given his family's history. His late uncle, Clarence Strider of Leflore County, had received national infamy for his racist behavior during the Emmett Till trial in 1955.[65]

On Election Day, Espy broke the racial barrier in the second district and defeated Franklin with fifty-two percent of the vote, which Owen Brooks of the Delta Ministry said "signals a new day for the Mississippi Delta and for Democratic Party politics." Clarke Reed of the state Republican Party said that "the Espy people ran a good campaign" and that second district Republicans may have become overconfident. Espy said that the state had "matured" because he received some of the white vote.[66]

The Espy win raised the question of why—specifically, why Espy and not Clark. The low voter turnout of 1986, compared with the presidential election year of 1984, played a part. Espy won with fewer votes than Clark received in 1984. Clark received 89,000 votes in 1984 and lost, while Espy won with only 73,000 in 1986. The low turnout apparently came mostly from white voters, especially farmers angry at Franklin and Reagan and who then voted by *not* voting. Frank Parker called Espy's victory an aberration and cited the fifty-one percent white turnout, and gave credit to white farmers who did not vote out of anger at the farm foreclosures and Reagan's farm policies. Political columnist Bill Minor also echoed the theme of a white boycott coupled with high black-voter turnout, stating that many "voted with their rumps" and stayed home.[67]

Espy also won because he was *not* Robert Clark. He was a black candidate but a very different one from Clark. Unlike Clark, he could win some of the white vote, which Minor admitted. A later study by the Voter Education Project concluded that Espy won five percent more of the white vote than Clark did. His opponent confirmed much of this and pointed to Espy's skill as a negotiator who could soothe white anxieties about a black Democrat. Espy met with white agricultural interests, such as the Delta Council, and promised to work with them if elected by seeking a seat on the House Agriculture Committee, and he did so after his election. His actions, Franklin said, broke into the Republican's core constituency, and Espy also "never presented any threat to anybody." Espy's training as a lawyer also helped. Numerous commentators and participants in the election described him as "articulate," "sophisticated," and a "more appealing candidate." Clark, a "country man" from Holmes County, by implication lacked polish, despite his advanced education. A writer for a Clarksdale newspaper said that although Clark had name recognition in the black community, Espy was "a more articulate and intellectual candidate who mingles with ease in the white community."[68]

The issues of class and color also likely influenced white voters. Espy clearly did not take the black vote for granted and made an organized effort in black precincts that yielded a high black turnout. His upper-middle class background from his family's funeral home and burial insurance business did set him apart from the mass of black residents in the second district, so much so that some thought his wealth could hurt him with black voters. A background of such privilege would not have hurt him with the white elite of the Delta. Espy also likely benefited from his skin color. He had a light skin tone, although no news commentators publicly raised such an impolitic issue, instead commenting on subtler racial issues like his "articulate" speech. Clark, by contrast, had dark skin, which made ads by Franklin supporters highlighting the differences between the two candidates all the more effective. Leslie McLemore, who studied politics in the second district, agreed that Espy's skin color played a factor even though such an issue would not have been openly discussed.[69]

Espy's youth also helped. Only thirty-two at the time of his victory, Espy had come of age after the civil rights movement and had none of the scars of the Loyalist-Regular schism. He, perhaps more than any other black Mississippi politician, symbolized the second generation of black political power. His brief stint with Central Mississippi Legal Services represented his only connection to any kind of social activism, with most of his career consisting of service in the unelected state bureaucracy, which meant he had less exposure than an old civil rights veteran like Clark. That anonymity helped Espy with white voters. Older white voters looked at Clark and remembered his record, which McLemore called a liability.[70] That record included involvement with the MFDP, which most Mississippi whites viewed as a radical organization, and a precedent-setting win in 1967 as the first black state legislator since the nineteenth century. Whites saw Clark as a product of the civil rights movement, which did not sit well with them, especially older ones. Espy, by contrast, resisted any identification with black civil rights activism and even refused to bring Jesse Jackson to the district to campaign for him out of a fear of a pro-Franklin white backlash.[71] For all of the afore-

FIGURE 19. Rep. Mike Espy (*right*) and Rep. Jack Kemp, January 4, 1987. The first black U.S. representative in Mississippi since the 19th century, Espy won in the reconstituted Second District (the so-called "Delta District") in 1986 where earlier black Democrats had failed. He won through a combination of court redistricting and coalition building with powerful Delta whites, benefiting as well from his youth and lack of association with the Mississippi civil rights movement. Mike Espy Collection, Congressional and Political Research Center, Mitchell Memorial Library, Mississippi State University.

mentioned reasons, Espy won the election, and he won because he was the anti-Clark.

The rebirth of the Delta congressional district in the 1980s was the last major vote dilution and voting rights campaign of the post–civil rights era of Mississippi. While other issues, namely the expansion of black-majority districts for the legislature, continued after the 1990 Census, the election of a black congressman forced the integration of the state's congressional delegation.[72] The district, which had historically encompassed the Delta for most of it history until its fragmentation in the 1960s, provided the best opportunity for electing a black congressman in the late twentieth century. The Democratic Party, still not healed from the damage over the end of the biracial co-chair in 1980, had again divided along racial lines over a majority-black district. The intervention of the federal courts settled the issue of a Delta district, but a lack of white enthusiasm for black candidate Robert Clark led to the election of white Republican Webb Franklin. Only with the arrival of Mike Espy, a very different black candidate, did voters finally integrate the state's congressional delegation.

To an observer familiar with Mississippi's racial history, the 1987 state congressional delegation must have seemed a strange lot indeed. The two U.S. senators showed the transition that marked the white South in the post–civil rights era. The elderly John Stennis, the Old Guard Democrat and segregationist who had slowly liberalized by the 1980s, finally voted for a civil rights bill and eventually opposed Robert Bork's nomination to the Supreme Court.[73] The younger Thad Cochran, the first Republican senator since Reconstruction, represented the resurgent southern GOP and the New Right's support base of conservative whites, yet his own career showed the effects of racial moderation and change brought by the civil rights movement.

An even more diverse lot occupied the House. Sonny Montgomery represented the old southern Democrats. The development of black voting strength and political power had done little to change his voting record, even as he gained black votes because of his party label. Wayne Dowdy, who won his seat with the help of blacks and labor, the twin enemies of the Jim Crow South, pointedly refused to join the Boll Weevils, a congressional coalition of conservative southern Democrats that included Montgomery. Dowdy's populist leanings marked a break from Mississippi's conservative Democrats. Somewhere in between them lay Jamie Whitten, the once outspoken white supremacist who by the late 1970s had reconciled himself to racial liberalism and reversed his previous opposition to issues such as civil rights and food stamps.[74] Trent Lott, the Gulf Coast Republican, seemed more of a throwback to the old days. His later tenure as Mississippi's junior senator gave the Magnolia State two conservative Republicans, but his impolitic yearning for the pre-civil rights South showed him to be far removed from the carefully cultivated black base that Cochran had built.

The newest member, Mike Espy, perhaps best represented the post–civil rights South. The first African American in the state since Reconstruction to hold a congressional office, he simultaneously embodied the legacy and passing of the civil rights era. Although a beneficiary of the struggles of the movement, his youth and background meant he had little connection with the period that to many southerners, both black and white, was increasingly a distant memory. The delegation, for all its odd mix of old and new, represented in many ways the transition in racial attitudes the South had undergone since the 1960s.

It would be misleading to read this integration as sign of complete satisfaction on the part of black Mississippians, or even a closing of the struggle for power on their part. The same year that Espy won his election, one of the towns in his district experienced a new wave of civil rights activism. In Indianola, black residents came together and launched a successful boycott of white businesses in the town when the school board refused to select a highly qualified black man to be the county superintendent. The black middle class led this throwback to the 1960s activism of Port Gibson and other selective buying campaigns, heading a cross-class movement of racial solidarity. Yet this new movement showed, similar to Quitman County in 1983, the problem of poverty and how the issues of class increasingly divided the black community in the era of growing black political access. Later that year, when the low-paid employees of the Delta Pride catfish processing plant began a unionization drive, the same middle-class leaders that organized the boycott refused to support this drive for economic rights for impoverished black workers. The unionization of the Delta Pride workforce succeeded but exposed the divide between the black middle class, which narrowly saw civil rights as black officeholders and political access, and the black working class, which continued the spirit of Fannie Lou Hamer's efforts and did not artificially separate political and economic rights. As Manning Marable pointed out, the class division in the African American community by the 1980s often weakened black middle-class support for the black working class, who had not reaped the benefits of the civil rights movement. This dichotomy meant that the overall gains in black political power, however impressive in the number of offices held, would continue to be limited by those same politicians' timidity regarding the economic deprivation of many black Mississippians.[75]

Espy himself reflected this trend as a black officeholder, moving to appease his conservative white constituents and avoid any labeling as a civil rights-era liberal. While he had a relatively liberal voting record, with an 85% rating from Americans for Democratic Action and a 77% rating from the American Civil Liberties Union, he voted against gun control measures and for expanding the death penalty. He won the endorsement of the National Rifle Association, appearing in one of their advertisements, and aided catfish companies like Delta Pride by securing a 65% increase in catfish purchases by the Army. His close relationship with powerful Delta interests paid off, and Espy defeated his white Republican opponent in 1988 with 65% of the vote, winning more than one in three white votes. Espy followed what Marable later called the "Wilder Model," after Douglas Wilder, who became the first black governor of Virginia in 1989 largely by embracing conservative positions to win white voters. Espy's election then yielded a symbolic victory, but one that did little to remedy the problems of his impoverished black constituents.[76]

Epilogue

Javitses into Eastlands, Eastlands into Barbours

WHILE MIKE ESPY was taking his House oath in 1987, the Mississippi Republican Party experienced its last serious attempt at wooing black voters. That year, Jack Reed, a department store owner in Tupelo, won the Republican nomination for governor. Reed, like Gil Carmichael and William Winter, had a long history as a racial moderate. During the integration riot at the University of Mississippi in 1962, Reed, as head of the Mississippi Economic Council, publicly criticized anti-integration violence and the efforts to close the state's public schools. Later, during the United League boycott and protest against police brutality in Tupelo in the late 1970s, he worked behind the scenes to settle the crisis.[1]

In the 1980s, Reed served as chairman of the state board of education and supported Winter's education reform initiatives. Like Gil Carmichael and Rubel Phillips before him, Reed saw segregation and racial prejudice as barriers to Mississippi's economy. While such a stance was radical in the 1960s and progressive in the 1970s, it was mainstream for a gubernatorial candidate in the 1980s. Reed's Democratic opponent, state auditor Ray Mabus, had a similar pro-education record. Reed tried to revive Carmichael's efforts to bring black voters into the Republican Party and described himself as an independent with few party loyalties. A few black businessmen and politicians backed Reed, but no significant black support materialized for the Republican. He balanced his efforts at black outreach by supporting school prayer and restrictions on abortion, efforts to win conservative white Democrats and Republicans.[2]

Reed lost to Mabus and scored few black votes since African Americans in the 1980s were even more firmly wedded to the Democratic Party than in the 1970s. Like the moderate Carmichael and the conservative Bramlett, Reed did better with conservative white voters. His association with the party of Ronald Reagan helped him with white voters, but not with black ones, who turned out in high numbers for Mabus. Mabus carried all of the state's black majority counties and won with fifty-three percent of the vote even though Reed's showing was the best a Republican candidate had done that century.[3]

Reed's moderation, at least on racial issues, represented only a brief detour of the Republican Party in the 1980s and not a resurgence of moderate strength in the state organization. The 1988 presidential election, meanwhile, marked the further decline of the Democratic Party in Mississippi. Democratic presidential nominee Michael Dukakis stumbled badly at the Neshoba County Fair. Dukakis, who spoke on the twenty-four-year anniversary of the discovery of the bodies of the slain Freedom Summer workers, avoided any direct mention of civil rights or the 1964 murders. He did so at the request of Mississippi Secretary of State Dick Molpus and other state Democrats, who once again tried to preserve a fragile balance between white and black voters and hoped to avoid a white backlash. It failed as the national media highlighted Dukakis's omission and the liberal governor proved unpalatable for conservative white voters in Mississippi. Vice President George Herbert Walker Bush easily won the state in November.[4]

The 1991 governor's race showed the continuing conservative domination of the party and a preference for building a base of conservative whites who opposed a significantly black political party. Kirk Fordice, a construction executive from Vicksburg, carried the standard for the GOP. Fordice had become a Republican during the 1964 Goldwater campaign, and he was able to pick up the support of moderates like Gil Carmichael since he had worked as Carmichael's Warren County chairman during his 1970s gubernatorial races.[5]

Race entered the 1991 campaign, at least obliquely, in the form of coded racial appeals, such as Fordice's call for welfare reform, an issue that led Democratic National Chairman Ron Brown to criticize Fordice. The Republican also won the unsolicited support of the Nationalist Movement, a white supremacist organization headed by Richard Barrett, an unsuccessful gubernatorial and congressional candidate. Fordice had responded to a questionnaire from Barrett's organization, in which he responded favorably to Barrett's call for repealing the Voting Rights Act and affirmative action. Fordice later said that the act should be repealed "if it is not going to apply nationwide," a position not very different from William Winter's when he was governor. He also criticized the creation of the second congressional district, declaring that he was "dumbfounded" when he was told that he "would have to have a congressman of a certain color."[6]

Fordice won with a narrow 50.8 percent of the vote, while Mabus suffered from low black-voter turnout in the Delta, in part from the closure of charity hospitals under his budget cuts and his unsuccessful attempt to replace Ed Cole, the black state Democratic chairman, with a white woman.[7]

Fordice ran for re-election in 1995 and faced Dick Molpus, a former Secretary of State who had worked with Ray Mabus and William Winter to pass the Education Reform Act of 1982. At the Neshoba County Fair, Fordice took a direct swipe at the memory of the civil rights movement by criticizing the movie *Mississippi Burning* for its depiction of the 1964 Freedom Summer murders. He called for the need to "speak positive Mississippi" and also indirectly took Molpus to task for his 1989 public apology for those events. Fordice won again with fifty-five percent and took all but seven of the state's white-majority counties, while Molpus took nearly all of the black-majority counties. Such a division showed how strong the Republican Party had become among white voters, both rural and suburban.[8]

White voters for Fordice did not give their support for Bill Jordan, a black Jackson attorney who won the Republican nomination for attorney general. Jordan won 23.6 percent of the vote against white Democrat Mike Moore, which was still the highest vote ever earned by a black candidate in a general election at the time, even surpassing Charles Evers' 1971 vote. Still, many white voters who backed Fordice, as well as many black voters, gave their votes to Moore. To black voters in Mississippi, black Republicans apparently fell under suspicion for their ideological viewpoints, while many conservative whites still preferred a white Democrat to a black Republican.[9]

By the end of the twentieth century, those who looked back on Mississippi could see that profound changes had taken place because of the Voting Rights Act and the resultant black voting and officeholding. Such changes had not come easily or quickly. Although the Voting Rights Act enfranchised large numbers of black voters in the 1960s, it did not immediately integrate the state's Democratic Party structure. White Democrats continued to resist meaningful integration, and their resistance created a dual party system of black Democrats and white liberals with national party recognition but little officeholding, and a white state party that controlled state and local government. Some black politicians had made small inroads, such as Robert Clark in the state legislature and Charles Evers as mayor of Fayette and gubernatorial candidate in 1971. Black officeholding in some majority black towns and counties, especially those that had active civil rights organizations in the 1960s, continued to expand in the 1970s.

The threat of a rising Republican Party and its efforts to solicit both black voters and conservative whites helped push the opposing factions of the Democratic Party to reunite under Cliff Finch in 1975. The increased access of black Democrats to the party did not stop the efforts of white Democrats to restrict black access to leadership positions in the hopes of keeping whites from defecting to the Republicans. White defenses of vote-dilution schemes also lingered, and black plaintiffs and civil rights lawyers continued to expand the scope of the Voting Rights Act beyond just giving African Americans the vote and instead guaranteeing black political access and officeholding as well. The challenges to vote dilution on the state, county, and municipal level all succeeded but only after years of struggle and setbacks. The strengthened Voting Rights Act amendments in 1982 finally allowed the courts to shatter some of the remaining obstacles to black political power. The peak of these efforts was the re-creation of the Delta congressional district and the election of a black congressman in 1986.

The defection of white voters to the GOP continued unabated as many disaffected Democrats felt that their old party had become too "black" and had made too many concessions to African Americans. The second "Great White Switch" had occurred in the eighties with Ronald Reagan's victories. The switch continued into the nineties, leading to the first Republican governor since the nineteenth century, a governor far different in his racial outreach than Gil Carmichael had been. More and more Mississippi whites, along with white southerners in general, had come to identify themselves as Republicans, and whites in the state became less aligned with the Democratic Party and more likely to vote Republican or split their tickets.[10]

As the twenty-first century opened, black political power had unquestionably grown as black men and women held prominent posts in the state Democratic Party and occupied the state legislature, county governments, and city halls. The trade-off appeared to be the ascendancy of a white Republican Party that could afford to ignore black voters and benefit from the continuance of racially polarized voting. The fragile fusion that had led to Jimmy Carter's narrow victory in Mississippi in 1976 had by 2001 largely slipped away. On April 17, 2001, Mississippi voters rejected a proposal to change the state flag from the old 1894 design, which incorporated the Confederate battle flag. Sixty-four percent of voters favored the old flag, and voting largely split along racial lines as most majority-black counties favored the new flag while majority-white counties overwhelmingly voted for the 1894 version.[11]

The flag issue, rather than just an election over a state symbol, powerfully resonated to the continuance of racial divisions in Mississippi voting in the new century. This was clear in the 2003 statewide elections when the 2001 flag referendum combined with the Democratic Party's increasingly black presence to deliver a strong white backlash for the Republicans. During the August primaries, the state Democratic Party nominated black candidates for statewide office for the first time in its history. Barbara Blackmon, a lawyer and state senator from Canton, won the nomination for lieutenant governor. Her nomination was historic not only for her race but also her gender, for she faced incumbent lieutenant governor Amy Tuck, a white Republican, making it the first time two women faced each other for the lieutenant governor's office. The other black candidate, Gary Anderson, won the Democratic nomination for state treasurer.[12]

The presence of two black statewide candidates guaranteed that race would be an issue in the November election, but the Republican gubernatorial nominee, Haley Barbour, took further steps to use race to stimulate a high-white turnout for him. Barbour faced incumbent Democratic governor Ronnie Musgrove, so the Republican began to publically refer to the "Musgrove-Blackmon ticket" even though governors and lieutenant governors do not run on affiliated tickets in Mississippi elections. Editorialists and political observers called the language an attempt by Barbour to link Blackmon to Musgrove and undermine his white support. Barbour went further in October and brought up the flag referendum, declaring that he was "not in favor of changing it," even though voters had decided just that in 2001.[13]

The rather unsubtle racial references paid off as Barbour easily defeated Musgrove with fifty-three percent of the vote. The black

Democrats fared no better. Blackmon showed political ineptness during her campaign, wounding herself by suggesting that Tuck had once had an abortion, a misstep that led the *Clarion-Ledger* to endorse Tuck over her, breaking from its endorsement of most of the Democratic candidates. Blackmon lost to Tuck, who won sixty-one percent of the vote.[14]

Blackmon's loss can be blamed in part on herself, but the same cannot be said for the treasurer's race. Anderson, who at age forty-seven had fifteen years' state government experience, faced a twenty-nine-year old white Republican, Tate Reeves, who had only private sector experience. Editorialists frequently cited this experience when endorsing Anderson. Reeves did not inject race into the campaign the way Barbour did, but he did not need to, as he won with fifty-two percent of the vote. The indication that many white voters split their tickets became apparent when Jim Hood, the white Democratic nominee for attorney general, defeated his Republican opponent by a two-to-one margin. The *Clarion-Ledger* criticized the use of race in the campaign by Barbour and Tuck through the flag issue and in particular the outcome of the treasurer's race. The paper flatly declared that "the better candidate lost."[15] Although the Mississippi Democrats had made history in 2003 by nominating black candidates for statewide office, the use of thinly veiled racial symbols and rhetoric, as well as the defection of white voters to the GOP, reduced such nominations to mere symbolism.

Despite these setbacks, the civil rights movement had become firmly mainstreamed into the life of the United States, and even Mississippi to some degree, by the opening of the twentieth century. The voting rights consensus that Frank Parker described finally led to a unified vote for the renewal of the Voting Rights Act in 2006. The U.S. Senate voted 98–0 to renew the Act for another twenty-five years, and GOP senators Thad Cochran and Trent Lott voted for the final bill, known as H.R. 9, the Fannie Lou Hamer, Rosa Parks, and Coretta Scott King Voting Rights Act Reauthorization and Amendments Act. Although some southern congressmen objected to the continuation of section five preclearance regarding southern voting changes, much of the controversy concerned the renewal of the 1975 amendments covering foreign-language minorities and the printing of multilingual ballots. In the end, all of Mississippi's congressional delegation voted for renewal of the Act.[16]

Although scholars in recent years have declared the prevalence of class over race in partisan realignment or the end of southern exceptionalism, the South's distinctiveness as a white Republican bulwark continued in the 2008 presidential election. With the precedent-setting nomination of a black man by the Democrats, pundits debated the possibility of a nationwide "Bradley Effect" on Barack Obama's candidacy, either narrowing his victory to a razor-thin margin or triggering a white backlash that would give victory to Republican nominee John McCain. The fears proved false, as many whites joined African-American and Hispanic voters to elect Obama, with key states that voted for Bush in 2004 going to the Democratic column. Within the states of the old Confederacy, only Virginia, North Carolina, and Florida, all with significant influxes of non-southern whites, went for Obama. Many of Obama's inroads into traditionally Republican suburbs aided him in those states but not in the more rural South. The Deep South, including Upper and Rim South states, such as Texas, Tennessee, and Kentucky, went firmly for McCain. In Mississippi, heavily black counties in the Delta voted for Obama while the rest of the state went by large margins for McCain. In the words of Bill Minor, Mississippi did "its best to fight the tide in presidential voting." The results of the elections of the twentieth-first century showed the continuance of a racially divided electorate in Mississippi and indicated that Aaron Henry's hope that the Voting Rights Act and black voters would "make a Javits of an Eastland" indicated that for every Eastland that became a Javits, many more instead became Barbours.[17]

Notes

Introduction

1. Nash and Taggart, *Mississippi Politics*, 85; Lee, *For Freedom's Sake*, 177–78; Mills, *This Little Light of Mine*, 308.

2. Nash and Taggart, *Mississippi Politics*, 85, 146; Bass and DeVries, *The Transformation of Southern Politics*, 213; Lee, *For Freedom's Sake*, 176.

3. Bayard Rustin quoted in Hall, "The Long Civil Rights Movement and the Political Uses of the Past," 1234.

4. Hall, "The Long Civil Rights Movement and the Political Uses of the Past," 1233–63.

5. Minchin, "Making Best Use of the New Laws: The NAACP and the Fight for Civil Rights in the South, 1965–1975," 669–702.

6. Crespino, *In Search of Another Country*, 4.

7. Lassiter, *The Silent Majority*; Kruse, *White Flight*.

8. Marable, *Race, Reform, and Rebellion*, 146–47.

9. Lawson, *In Pursuit of Power*, xii; Andrews, *Freedom is a Constant Struggle*, 9–10; Shelia Byrd, "Mississippi Looks to Iran for Rural Health Care Model," http://news.yahoo.com/s/ap/20100602/ap_on_re_us/us_mississippi_s_iranian_model (accessed 6 June 2010).

10. Black and Black, *The Rise of Southern Republicans*; Lassiter, *The Silent Majority*; Schafer and Johnston, *The End of Southern Exceptionalism*; Kruse, *White Flight*; Nash and Taggart, *Mississippi Politics*, 7; Sokol, *There Goes My Everything*, 274–75.

11. Woodward, *Thinking Back*, 140.

12. Marsh, *God's Long Summer*, 4.

13. Andrews, *Freedom is a Constant Struggle*.

14. Parker, *Black Votes Count*.

15. Crosby, *A Little Taste of Freedom: The Black Freedom Struggle in Claiborne County, Mississippi*; Moye, *Let the People Decide*.

Chapter 1. Black Politics in Mississippi to 1965

1. McMillen, *Dark Journey*, 37.

2. Foner, *Reconstruction*, 352–56, 362. For an overview of black officeholding during Reconstruction and the subsequent decline of black political participation after 1875, see chapters 12–14 of Wharton, *The Negro in Mississippi*.

3. McMillen, *Dark Journey*, 38; Foner, *Reconstruction*, 558–62. The best and most exhaustive overview of Reconstruction in Mississippi is Harris, *Day of the Carpetbagger*. Harris focuses on the overall political picture of Reconstruction on blacks and whites; see Wharton, *The Negro in Mississippi* for a study emphasizing the black experience in Reconstruction Mississippi.

4. McMillen, *Dark Journey*, 39–43, 46–51, 58–64.

5. Ibid., 60–61, 64; Key, *Southern Politics in State and Nation*, 233; Fortenberry and Abney, "Mississippi: Unreconstructed and Unredeemed," in Havard, ed., *The Changing Politics of the South*; Dyer, *Theodore Roosevelt and the Idea of Race*, 102–3; Love, "A Community in Transition: A Study of Mound Bayou, Mississippi," 14. Roosevelt sought to steer a middle course in his federal appointments in the South by making a limited number of black appointments while reassuring southern whites with a far greater share of federal patronage. Dyer, 102–3. For a survey of white and black southerners' reactions to Roosevelt's southern policies, see Woodward, *The Origins of the New South*, 463–67.

6. Bass and DeVries, *The Transformation of Southern Politics*, 193. For a more detailed study of the Vardaman and Bilbo administrations, see Key, *Southern Politics in State and Nation*, Ch. 11. The main biography of Vardaman is Holmes, *The White Chief*. Morgan, *Redneck Liberal* provides a balanced study of Bilbo's economic liberalism and his white supremacist views, much like Holmes does for Vardaman. A study that focuses on Bilbo's racial demagoguery is Giroux, "Theodore G. Bilbo: Progressive to Public Racist." For studies of the oratory of Vardaman and Bilbo, see chapters by Strickland and Hendrix in Logue and Dorgan, *The Oratory of Southern Demagogues*.

7. Cobb, *The Most Southern Place on Earth*, 196. For a study of the Farm Security Administration and congressional opposition to it, see Conkin, *Tomorrow a New World*, 220–231. The main study of the FSA is Baldwin, *Poverty and Politics*. See also chapter four of Alston, *Southern Paternalism and the American Welfare State* for a study of the FSA and its threat to the South's economic status quo.

8. Dittmer, *Local People*, 25–29. Sitikoff, "African American Militancy in the World War II South," and McMillen, "Fighting For What We Didn't Have," in McMillen, ed., *Remaking Dixie*. Sitikoff argues that World War II was not a watershed event in American race relations since black Americans and the Left muted dissent and criticism of Jim Crow during the war. The direct action of the 1950s and 1960s civil rights movement, he says, was not an extension of the moderate reform efforts that civil rights organizations pushed during the war. Neil McMillen agrees with Sitikoff on the lack of wartime and immediate postwar challenges to the South's Jim Crow system, but insists that the war shaped "an emerging racial consciousness" that influenced the civil rights movement.

9. Lawson, *Black Ballots*, 133–36; Dittmer, *Local People*, 52–53, 70–72.

10. McMillen, *Dark Journey*, 60–64, 69.

11. Payne, *I've Got the Light of Freedom*, 47–56; Dittmer, *Local People*, 32, 49. Also see M. Evers and Peters, *For Us, the Living*.

12. Dittmer, *Local People*, 79, 85–87; Lawson, *Black Ballots*, 260–62. For an analysis of Kennedy's political concerns and how they shaped and limited his civil rights policies, see Brauer, *John F. Kennedy and the Second Reconstruction*, especially chapter four for voting rights.

13. Payne, *I've Got the Light of Freedom*, 56–60; Dittmer, *Local People*, 118–19.

14. Carson, *In Struggle*, 48–51, 104–6.

15. Lawson, *Black Ballots*, 264–65; Bass and DeVries, *The Transformation of Southern Politics*, 203; Dittmer, *Local People*, 121–23.

16. Lee, *For Freedom's Sake*, 25; Dittmer, *Local People*, 125–26.

17. "2 Negroes On State Ballot," *Mississippi Free Press* (Jackson), 21 April 1962, 1; Charles M. Hills, "Affairs of State," *Clarion-Ledger*, 20 April 1962; Mills, *Changing Channels*, 76–78; Undated and untitled campaign handbill by Robert L.T. Smith, Robert L. T. Smith Papers, Folder 1, Box 1, Mississippi Department of Archives and History.

18. Mills, *Changing Channels*, 32–33; Undated and untitled campaign handbill by Robert L.T. Smith, Robert L. T. Smith Papers, Folder 1, Box 1, Mississippi Department of Archives and History.

19. "Rev. Merrill W. Lindsey Candidate For Congress Hit Campaign Trail," *Jackson Advocate*, 5 May 1962; "9 Negroes face Trial here Today," undated newspaper clipping in State Sovereignty Commission Files, SCR ID # 2-72-1-102-1-1-1; Untitled State Sovereignty Commission report on Robert L. T. Smith, Sr., SCR ID # 2-55-2-48-1-1-1; Dittmer, 30; "Collins is Candidate For Justice of the Peace In Laurel, Miss," *Mississippi Free Press*, 20 July 1963; A.L. Hopkins to J. Clifford Watson, 30 August 1960, SCR ID # 2-49-0-3-1-1-1; "Collins Rally Crowd Hears 3 Speakers," *Laurel Leader-Call*, 1 August 1963.

20. Marsh, *God's Long Summer*, 116–27.

21. Dittmer, *Local People*, 165–66.

22. Dittmer, *Local People*, 200–207; Bass and DeVries, *The Transformation of Southern Politics*, 204; Lamis, *The Two-Party South*, 45–46; "500 Unsigned Negroes Try To Cast Statewide Ballots," *Laurel Leader-Call*, 7 August 1963.

23. Carson, *In Struggle*, 111–21. For more on the Freedom Schools, see McAdam, *Freedom Summer*, 83–86.

24. Lawson, *Black Ballots*, 300–301. For coverage of Atlantic City, see Carson, *In Struggle*, 123–29, and Lawson, 300–307. For more detailed narratives and analyses, see Dittmer, *Local People*, 272–302, and Sistrom, "Authors of the Liberation." For accounts of Freedom Summer and the 1964 murders, see Cagin and Dray, *We are not Afraid* and McAdam, *Freedom Summer*.

25. Dittmer, *Local People*, 333–34; Untitled election handbill for Clifton Whitley and Ed King, MFDP Records 1963–1971, reel 2.

26. Dittmer, *Local People*, 338–340; "City Voters To Go To Polls Tuesday," *Clarksdale Press Register*, 10 May 1965; Unsigned Sovereignty Commission Report, 16 April

1965, SCR ID # 2-166-3-36-1-1-1; Freedom Democratic Party Expense Report, SCR ID # 2-165-6-1-12-1-1; Report of Credentials Committee of Leflore County Convention, 23 June 1964, SCR ID # 2-165-3-5-6-1-1 and 2-165-3-5-11-1-1; "Democrats Smash First GOP Drive In State Elections," *Greenwood Commonwealth*, 12 May 1965.

27. Dittmer, *Local People*, 191–92; Lawson, *Black Ballots*, 285.

28. Lawson, *Black Ballots*, 284.

29. Dittmer, *Local People*, 341–43, Lawson, *In Pursuit of Power*, 96.

Chapter 2. Plates of Silver, Plates of Mud

1. Lawson, *Black Ballots*, 312, 321–22, 333–36; Bass and DeVries, *The Transformation of Southern Politics*, 206.

2. Lawson, *In Pursuit of Power*, 97.

3. Evers and Szanton, *Have No Fear*, 55, 58–59, 94, 100–104; "Report from Mississippi," 29 October 1965, MFDP Records, 1963–1971, reel 2; Lawson, *In Pursuit of Power*, 94, 96–98; Dittmer, *Local People*, 177–78, 341–43; Parker, *Black Votes Count*, 69–71; Gloster Current to Charles Evers, 5 August 1966, Papers of the NAACP, Part 29, Series D; Gloster Current to Henry Lee Moon, 18 May 1966; Gloster Current to Roy Wilkins and John Morsell, 21 June 1966, Papers of the NAACP, Part 29, Series D.

4. Parker, *Black Votes Count*, 36–37, 40–41.

5. "FDP Candidates Are Qualified," *Commercial Appeal* (Memphis), 5 April 1966; "5 Negroes, 1 White FDP Congressional Entrants," *Clarion-Ledger* (Jackson), 5 April 1966; "Quiet Prevails Here After Tense Situation," *Holmes County Herald*, 11 April 1963. While Hayes was the chair of the Holmes County FDP, he had a history of activism prior to SNCC's arrival. In 1954, he lost his job when he tried to register to vote. "Biographies of the Candidates," MFDP Records, 1963–1971, reel 2.

6. *Mississippi Official and Statistical Register 1968–1972*, 439–440; Marsh, *God's Long Summer*, 195.

7. Dittmer, *Local People*, 408–9; *Whitley v. Johnson* 260 F. Supp. 630 (1966).

8. Sistrom, "Authors of the Liberation," 364.

9. Rowland Evans and Robert Novak, "Ford's Natchez Boycott Symbolic," *Clarion Ledger*, 20 November 1965; "GOP's Walker Says He Fears Rusk," unknown newspaper clipping from State Sovereignty Commission Online, November 15, 1965, SCR # 10-11-0-25-1-1-1, 15 November 1965; "Negroes Eye State Republican Party," *Jackson Advocate*, 14 May 1966.

10. Lamis, *The Two-Party South*, 45–46; *Mississippi Official and Statistical Register, 1968–1972*, 442.

11. Crespino, *In Search of Another Country*, 84–85, 87; Schulman, *From Cotton Belt to Sunbelt*, 215; Resume of Wirt A. Yerger, Jr., Mississippi Republican Party Papers, Biographies Folder, Box H-1, Special Collections, Mississippi State University. Hathorn, "Challenging the Status Quo" *Journal of Mississippi History*; Robert Webb, "Kennedy 'Absolved' of Link to Riders," unknown newspaper clipping from State Sovereignty Commission Online, SCR ID# 2-140-1-49-1-1-1. For a detailed narrative of the

transition from the Black and Tans to the Lily Whites in Mississippi, see Crespino, "Strategic Accommodation," 121–29. Crespino's dissertation has been revised into his book *In Search of Another Country*, but the quotes are only in the dissertation, and the account of the Black and Tan overthrow is longer. In Mississippi, urban areas are defined as municipalities 10,000 or more in population. Parker, *Black Votes Count*, 143.

12. Crespino, *In Search of Another Country*, 89; Black and Black, *The Rise of Southern Republicans*, 4.

13. James Saggus, "Incumbent Office Holders To Face Heated Opposition," *Clarion Ledger*, 5 June 1966; "Eastland Gains Smash Win Over Republicans," *Clarion-Ledger*, 9 November 1966; "Whitley Will Seek Jobs, He Declares," *Clarion-Ledger*, 28 October 1966; "Negro Candidates Cloud Mississippi Election Scene," *Commercial Appeal*, 27 October 1966. The *Delta Democrat-Times* gave some attention to the stationing of poll watchers in the state to help the MFDP, but generally limited its commentary to black voter turnout during the election. "Poll Watchers To Be Stationed For June 7 Elections," 1 June 1966; John Childs, "Voting Here Is Extremely Light," 7 June 1966.

14. "FDP Candidates Are Qualified," *Commercial Appeal*, 5 April 1966; Dittmer, *Local People*, 409–10; Untitled election handbill for Clifton Whitley and Ed King, MFDP Records 1963–1971, reel 2; McLemore, "The Mississippi Freedom Democratic Party," 334; Curtis Wilkie, "Negro Voters Lack Candidate" and "County, State Give Demos Wide Support," *Clarksdale Press Register*, 8 and 9 November 1966; Frank Parker, 50, 93; *Mississippi Official and Statistical Register, 1968–1972*, 442–43.

15. "General Election Set November 8," and "Montgomery And Eastland Win Here," *Lexington Advertiser*, 3 and 10 November 1966; "Eastland, Williams, Collins Win; Amendments Pass in Tuesday's Election"; Gloster Current to Charles Evers, 21 June 1966, Papers of the NAACP, Part 29 Series C, reel 2 of 10. Some historians, such as John Dittmer and Steven Lawson, use MFDP and FDP (Freedom Democratic Party) interchangeably. In this manuscript, MFDP will be used unless the reference is to a county chapter of the state party, in which FDP will be used: for example, "the Hinds County FDP" or "the local FDP."

16. *Fayette Chronicle*, 10 November 1966; Sistrom, "Authors of the Liberation," 364; "Negroes Seek School Board Posts Nearby," *Natchez Democrat*, 3 November 1966; "School Board Race Set in Jefferson," *Natchez Democrat*, 5 November 1966.

17. Dittmer, *Local People*, 411–13; McLemore, "The Mississippi Freedom Democratic Party," 349–54; *Hamer v. Campbell*, 358 F.2d 215 (1966).

18. Dittmer, *Local People*, 410.

19. "Are Negroes Qualified?" *Hinds County FDP News*, 25 February 1967; Sue-Henry Lorenzi, "How Our Machine Can Win The Elections!! A Campaign Manual for Precinct Leaders," May 1967, MFDP Records, 1963–1971, reel 2.

20. Coahoma County Branch NAACP Cryer, 21 August 1966, Papers of the NAACP, Part 29: Branch Department Series C: Branch Newsletters and Regional Office Files, 1966–71, reel 2 of 10; Coahoma County Branch NAACP to Gloster Current, 1 June 1967, Papers of the NAACP, Part 29, Branch Department Series D: General Subject Files 1966–70, reel 13 of 13.

21. Lawson, *In Pursuit of Power*, 99; Sistrom, "Authors of the Liberation," 394–95.

22. William Chapman, "Negroes Learning Tammany-Style Politics in Miss.," *Washington Post*, 17 July 1967.

23. "Beat 2 Race Quickens," *Hinds County FDP News*, 4 March 1967; "Warren Seeks F.D.P. Support" and "Just More Indian Promises," *Hinds County FDP News*, 18 March 1967.

24. Dittmer, *Local People*, 411–13; Moye, *Let the People Decide*, 162, 164; McLemore, "The Mississippi Freedom Democratic Party," 349–54; Pic Firmin and Jane Stafford, "Negroes Turn Out In Sunflower Vote; Legal Action Eyed," *Delta Democrat-Times*, 2 May 1967; Jane Stafford, "Tension Not Evident As Moorhead Balloted," *Delta Democrat-Times*, 3 May 1967; "Sunflower, Moorhead Return White Officials," *Clarion-Ledger*, 3 May 1967.

25. Dittmer, *Local People*, 412; McLemore, "The Mississippi Freedom Democratic Party," 353–70, 373–77.

26. Dittmer, *Local People*, 416; *Mississippi Newsletter* (Tougaloo College), 4 August 1967; Parker, *Black Votes Count*, 36–37.

27. Dittmer, *Local People*, 417; "John Bell Williams; Sullivan Win Top Posts In Democratic Election; Pritchard; Smith Win In County," *Fayette Chronicle*, 31 August 1967; "Record Turnout At Polls Tuesday; Four Negro Candidates Win," *Port Gibson Reveille*, 10 August 1967; Advertisement for Mrs. Dan S. McCay for Sheriff, *Port Gibson Reveille*, 24 August 1967; *Mississippi Official and Statistical Register, 1972–1976*, 26. *Mississippi Official and Statistical Register, 1968–1972*, 458.

28. The actual percentages of black residents in the counties, as of 1960, was as follows: Bolivar, 67 percent; Claiborne, 76 percent; Coahoma, 68 percent; Holmes, 72 percent; Jefferson, 75 percent; Marshall, 70 percent; Wilkinson, 71 percent. *Census of Population: 1960, Vol. 1 Characteristics of the Population, Part 26 Mississippi*, United States Department of Commerce, Bureau of the Census (Washington, D.C.: U.S. Government Printing Office, 1963). In the 1970s, the courts in redistricting cases established the so-called "sixty-five percent rule," a standard that said that a black population of that number or higher was needed for black voters to elect candidates of their choice. Parker, *Black Votes Count*, 138–39.

29. Robert G. Clark, interview by author, tape recording, Ebenezer, Miss., 23 July 2005; Campbell, *Robert G. Clark's Journey to the House*, 29; Walter Rugaber, "Negro Elected to All-White Mississippi Legislature," *New York Times*, 9 November 1967; McLemore, "The Mississippi Freedom Democratic Party," 382–83.

30. "Holmes May Lose State Programs," *Lexington Advertiser*, 19 January 1967; Parker, *Black Votes Count*, 74–75; Cobb, *The Most Southern Place on Earth*, 116; "First Negro Page For Mississippi," *Lexington Advertiser*, 1 February 1968; "Spotlight On Holmes In General Election," Lexington Advertiser, 2 November 1967.

31. "Rep. Clark Assumes Office," *Lexington Advertiser*, 4 January 1968; McLemore, "The Mississippi Freedom Democratic Party," 382–83; Clark interview, 23 July 2005.

32. McLemore, "The Mississippi Freedom Democratic Party," 378–79; Cobb, *The Most Southern Place on Earth*, 196, 241–42; "Rep. Clark Assumes Office," *Lexington Advertiser*, 4 January 1968; "Miss. Negro Takes His Lonely Seat, Oath," *Newsday*,

undated, William F. "Bill" Minor Papers, Box 2, Folder 80. Mississippi State University; Griffin McLaurin, interview by Harriet Tanzman, University of Southern Mississippi Oral History Collection, 6 March 2000.

33. "Primary Officials Named; Voters' League Asks For Negro Officials," *Lexington Advertiser*, 27 July 1967; "Record 7,111 Voter Turnout in Holmes," *Lexington Advertiser*, 31 August 1971; Dittmer, *Local People*, 417.

34. "J.W. Moses Wins Mayor's Office," Lexington Advertiser, 15 May 1969; "State Elects First Three Black Sheriffs," *Northeast Mississippi Daily Journal*, 8 November 1979; McLemore, 387–88.

35. "Spotlight On Holmes In General Election," *Lexington Advertiser*, 2 November 1967; "General Election Vote Equals Primary Tally," *Lexington Advertiser*, 9 November 1967; Parker, 63–64, 74–75.

36. "General Election Vote Equals Primary Tally," *Lexington Advertiser*, 9 November 1967; "Circuit Clerk Named in Voter Registration Suit," *Lexington Advertiser*, 6 August 1964; Cobb, 246; "Selective Buying Continued," *Lexington Advertiser*, 6 June 1968; "J.W. Moses Wins Mayor's Office," *Lexington Advertiser*, 15 May 1969; "State Elects First Three Black Sheriffs," *Northeast Mississippi Daily Journal*, 8 November 1979; Lamis, *The Two-Party South*, 47.

37. Sistrom, "Authors of the Liberation," 396; Lawson, *In Pursuit of Power*, 99; "John Bell Williams; Sullivan Win Top Posts In Democratic Election; Pritchard; Smith Win In County," *Fayette Chronicle*, 31 August 1967; "Southwide Conference of Black Elected Officials," Atlanta: Southern Regional Council, 11–14 December 1968, 61; "Record Turnout At Polls Tuesday; Four Negro Candidates Win," *Port Gibson Reveille*, 10 August 1967; Advertisement for Mrs. Dan S. McKay for Sheriff, *Port Gibson Reveille*, 24 August 1967; Crosby, "Common Courtesy," 361, 366. Coverage of this election also appears in Crosby, *A Little Taste of Freedom*, 228–29, but the actual quote appears in the dissertation.

38. John M. Pearce, "Woodville Negro Charges Irregularities In Draft," *Jackson Daily News*, 17 February 1967.

39. Andrews, *Freedom Is a Constant Struggle*, 100–104; "Election Committee Rules Against Nash," *Bolivar Commercial*, 5 October 1967; "Alexander Elected, Negro Wins Office In Tuesday Election," *Bolivar Commercial*, 9 November 1967; Ted Weiss, "Campaigning in the Black Belt," *Westside News and Free Press* (New York), 16 November 1967.

40. "Injunction Ordered; Picketing Stops Here," *South Reporter*, 11 August 1966; "Congressman, senator to be elected Nov.," *South Reporter*, 27 October 1966; "Eastland and Whitten defeat GOP opponents," *South Reporter*, 10 November 1966. For a firsthand account of civil rights activities at Rust College and Holly Springs, see Sellers and Terrell, *The River of No Return*.

41. Biographies of the Candidates for the 1966 Elections, undated, MFDP Records, 1963–1971, reel 2; Key List Mailing # 5, p. 6, 7 January 1966, MFDP Records, 1963–1971, reel 2; "Osborne Bell candidate for County Coroner," *South Reporter*, 20 July 1967; "Charles Owen candidate for Coroner," *South Reporter*, 13 July 1967; "Second primary election expected to draw a record number of voters," August 24 1967; "Unofficial

Election returns show Ash, DeBerry and Moore elected," *South Reporter*, 10 August 1967; "Official county returns by precinct," *South Reporter*, 17 August 1967.

42. Dittmer, *Local People*, 416–17; Lawson, *In Pursuit of Power*, 99.

43. Payne, *I've Got the Light of Freedom*, 67.

44. Dittmer, 280; Crosby, *A Little Taste of Freedom*, 217; Payne, 342.

45. Marable, *Race, Reform, and Rebellion*, 112; Dittmer, 72–73.

46. Dittmer, 360–61, 364–65; Payne, 310.

47. Dittmer, 368–70; Payne, 342–47.

48. Bartley, *The Rise of Massive Resistance*.

49. Crespino, *In Search of Another Country*, 4.

50. Lassiter, *The Silent Majority*.

51. Sokol, *There Goes My Everything*, 17.

52. *Hinds County FDP News*, 3 November 1967; Crespino, *In Search of Another Country*, 217–18.

53. Hathorn, "Challenging the Status Quo," *Journal of Mississippi History*, 244; Lamis, *The Two-Party South*, 47; Crespino, *In Search of Another Country*, 217–18; "General Election Vote Equals Primary Tally," *Lexington Advertiser*, 9 November 1967.

54. Frank Parker interpreted the results as a victory for the obstructionist legislature whose actions had "ensured that the new black vote would have little impact on the politics or operations of the state and local government in Mississippi." Steven Lawson deemed the election results "mixed" and an insufficient antidote to the loss in Sunflower County. John Dittmer called the election of twenty-two black candidates "an achievement of no small historical significance," but he echoed Lawson and termed the results "disappointing." James Cobb, in his history of the Mississippi Delta, emphasized the positive by focusing on the election of Clark. Dittmer, *Local People*, 416–17, 297, 311–80; Lawson, *In Pursuit of Power*, 99; Mississippi Newsletter, 4 August 1967; Parker, *Black Votes Count*, 36–37, 76; Cobb, *The Most Southern Place on Earth*, 246.

55. "Charles Evers State NAACP Secy Is Candidate For Congress," *Jackson Advocate*, 3 February 1968; "Hinds County F.D.P. Supports Evers!" *Hinds County FDP News*, 27 January 1968; "The Negro and the End of Another Mississippi Election Campaign," *Jackson Advocate*, 24 February 1968; Dittmer, *Local People*, 74.

56. "Evers Tours Hinds County," *Clarion-Ledger*, 25 February 1968; "Bodron Sets War's Blame," *Clarion-Ledger*, 25 February 1968; "Candidates Plotting Final Moves Today," *Clarion-Ledger*, 26 February 1968; "Evers and Griffin In Congress Runoff," *Clarion-Ledger*, 28 February 1968; James Saggus, "Evers Confirms Appeal In Runoff Election," *Clarion-Ledger*, 1 March 1968; "Evers Urges Quitting War; Gets Support," *Clarion-Ledger*, 6 March 1968.

57. "Labor Still Uncommitted For Tuesday," *Clarion-Ledger*, 9 March 1968; "Congressional Vote Tuesday 'Important,'" *Clarion-Ledger*, 10 March 1968; "Race For Congress Hits Climax Today," *Clarion-Ledger*, 12 March 1968; Evers and Szanton, *Have No Fear*, 233–36; *Mississippi Official and Statistical Register 1968–1972*, 465; Dittmer, *Local People*, 420; Lawson, *In Pursuit of Power*, 103. Claude Ramsey generally preferred to maintain ties with the Regular Democrats and was not a consistent supporter of

the Loyalists. He did not back Aaron Henry's challenge to the seating of the Regular Democrats at the national convention in 1968, citing efforts the state AFL-CIO had made to increase black participation with the Regulars on the county level. Claude Ramsey to Aaron Henry, 24 June 1968, Patricia Derian Papers, Box 3, Folder 72, Special Collections, Mitchell Memorial Library, Mississippi State University.

58. MFDP Newsletter, Sunflower, Miss., 5 April 1968; "Jolliff Guilty, Relieved Of Office, Wells Named," *Woodville Republican*, 29 March 1968.

59. Landon, *The Honor and Dignity of the Profession*, 158–60; Landon, *The Challenge of Service*, 68; Williamson, *Radicalizing the Ebony Tower*, 124, 144. Mississippi was not even the main focus of the national LCCRUL. Two-thirds of the organization's national budget went to activities and offices in fourteen cities, with only one (Atlanta) in the South. Landon, *The Honor and Dignity of the Profession*, 160.

60. MFDP Newsletter, Sunflower, Miss., 5 April 1968; "Court Cancels May 28 Vote For Supervisor," *Woodville Republican*, 3 May 1968; "Court Orders Jolliff Reinstated On County Board," *Woodville Republican*, 1 November 1968; Emilye Crosby, *A Little Taste of Freedom*, 251; Salamon, "Leadership and Modernization," *The Journal of Politics*, 639.

61. "Executive Committee's Procedures Protested," *Lexington Advertiser*, 16 May 1968; "Demos Deny Negro Delegates," *Lexington Advertiser*, 23 May 1968; "Selective Buying Campaign Begins," *Lexington Advertiser*, 30 May 1968; "Holmes Delegation Challenged At State Convention," *Lexington Advertiser*, 11 July 1968; "Democrat Loyalists Plan Own Convention," *Lexington Advertiser*, 18 July 1968.

62. Lamis, *The Two-Party South*, 45; Dittmer, *Local People*, 420–22; *Mississippi Newsletter*, 16 August 1968; Clark interview, 23 July 2005.

63. *Mississippi Freedom Democratic Party News*, 5 November 1968; *Mississippi Newsletter*, 8 November 1968; "Holmes Citizens Vote Tuesday," *Lexington Advertiser*, 29 October 1970; 8 November 1968; "Defeated candidates ask for recount of Nov. 5 election results," *South Reporter*, 21 November 1968; "Marshall Jones files suit in Circuit Court," *South Reporter*, 28 November 1968; "Board Declares Marshall Jones election winner," *South Reporter*, 5 December 1968; Lawson, *In Pursuit of Power*, 122.

64. Dittmer, *Local People*, 420.

65. Parker, Colby, and Morrison, "Mississippi," in *Quiet Revolution in the South*, eds. Davidson and Grofman.

66. "Shelby Chamber of Commerce Reorganizes," *Bolivar Commercial*, 8 August 1968; Clifton Langford, "The Shelby Boycott," *Bolivar Commercial*, 5 September 1968; "Shelby Calls Election To Fill Vacated Post," *Bolivar Commercial*, 22 January 1970; "Griffin Wins In Alderman Race At Shelby," *Bolivar Commercial*, 19 February 1970.

67. *National Roster of Black Elected Officials* (1970); "148 Negroes On Ballots As State Votes Today," *Clarksdale Press Register*, 13 May 1969; "Whites Win All Primary Races Here," *Woodville Republican*, 16 May 1969; "Friars Point Voters Reject Insurgent Ticket," *Clarksdale Press Register*, 4 June 1969.

68. "J.W. Moses Wins Mayor's Office," *Lexington Advertiser*, 15 May 1969; "State Elects First Three Black Sheriffs," *Northeast Mississippi Daily Journal*, 8 November 1979.

69. "State Voting Results," *Clarksdale Press Register*, 14 May 1969; Advertisement

for Charles Evers for Mayor, *Fayette Chronicle*, 1 May 1969; Evers and Szanton, *Have No Fear*, 242–44.

70. "Charles Evers Elected Mayor; Five Negro Aldermen Win Also," *Fayette Chronicle*, 15 May 1969; "Charles Evers Become Fayette's Mayor In Day Long Inaugural Ceremonies Monday," *Fayette Chronicle*, 10 July 1969.

71. Lawson, "From Boycotts to Ballots," in *New Directions in Civil Rights Studies*, eds. Robinson and Sullivan, 197; Dittmer, *Local People*, 361. For a narrative and analysis of the Natchez movement, see Dittmer, 353–62.

72. Ownby, *American Dreams in Mississippi*, 154; "Selective Buying Campaign Begins," *Lexington Advertiser*, 30 May 1968; "'Freedom and Justice' Asked of Whites by Local Negroes," *Lexington Advertiser*, 20 June 1968; "'Dollars and Ballot are Weapons Negroes Must Use to Win Rights,' Says Evers," *Lexington Advertiser*, 27 June 1968.

73. James Bonney, "Negro Bloc Vote Is Over-Rated," *Jackson Daily News*, 19 June 1967; McLemore, "The Mississippi Freedom Democratic Party," 387–88.

74. Coahoma County Branch NAACP Cryer, 5 September 1967, Papers of the NAACP, Part 29: Branch Department Series C: Branch Newsletters and Regional Field Office Files, 1966–1971, reel 2 of 10; Bond, *Black Candidates*, 13–14.

75. Dittmer, *Local People*, 341–43; Lawson, *In Pursuit of Power*, 94; Sistrom, "Authors of the Liberation," 392; Williamson, *Radicalizing the Ebony Tower*, 34, 57.

76. "Black Power is Fire Power!" *Utica FDP News*, 4 February 1967; "The United States Armed Forces = The Ku Klux Klan of Vietnam," cartoon, MFDP newsletter, 13 October 1967; "Don't buy California grapes," MFDP newsletter, 5 November 1968 (Sunflower, Miss.); "MFDP Supports Dr. King's March," MFDP newsletter, 5 April 1968.

77. "Battle of the Republic," *Newsweek*, 30 August 1971, 27; "Mississippi . . . old and new," Southern Conference Educational Fund letter (Jackson, Miss.); Berry, *Amazing Grace*, 136, 139–40, 189.

78. "Candidates Visit President" and "RNA Calls for Unity in Mississippi Races," *The New African*, 17 August 1971, Charles Ramberg Papers, Folder 5, Box 16, Mississippi Department of Archives and History.

79. "Meeting Set to Form New Black Nation," *Jackson Daily News*, 30 July 1970; John F. Nichols to Kenneth W. Fairly, 20 May 1969, Sovereignty Commission Files, SCR ID# 1–95–0–38–1–1–1; "Clark Says Not RNA Member," *Clarion-Ledger*, 10 February 1973; Negro Is Hopeful On Mississippi Bid," *New York Times*, 30 April 1967; Clark interview, 23 July 2005.

80. "NAACP Sets Freedom Drive For Sunday," *Clarion-Ledger*, 20 March 1971; Joe Bonney, "11 RNA Members Held For Grand Jury," *Clarion-Ledger*, date unknown; A.B. Albritton, "Evers' Lawyer Given Little Hope In Challenging Waller's Spending," *Commercial Appeal*, 1 October 1971; Judge Fred L. Banks, Jr., interview by Charles Bolton, 5 March 1998, Center for Oral History and Cultural Heritage, University of Southern Mississippi.

81. Hill, *The Deacons for Defense*, 211. The Woodville Deacons were involved in at least one incident of using a display of weaponry to protect a nonviolent activist from an armed white man. Wendt, *The Spirit and the Shotgun*, 149–50.

82. Lee, *For Freedom's Sake*, 130; Dittmer, *Local People*, 354, 408; Wendt, *The Spirit and the Shotgun*, 126–28; Crosby, *A Little Taste of Freedom*, 178–88; Hill, ch. 11. See that chapter for information on the Mississippi Deacons and their activities and chapters.

83. "Blacks Boycott White Stores," *Chicago Tribune*, 21 December 1968; *NAACP v. Claiborne Hardware Co.*, Miss. 393 So. 2d 1290, 102 S. Ct. 3409 (1982); Wendt, *The Spirit and the Shotgun*, 148–49.

84. *NAACP v. Claiborne Hardware Co*; Evers, *Evers*, ed. Grace Halsell, 9.

85. *NAACP v. Claiborne Hardware Co.*; King, *Stride Towards Freedom*, 54–55.

86. Sistrom, "Authors of the Liberation," 504–8.

87. *National Roster of Black Elected Officials* (1970); Dittmer, *Local People*, 425; *Conference Proceedings of Southwide Conference of Black Elected Officials*.

Chapter 3. Gubernatorial Fantasies and Gradual Gains

1. For Nixon's "Southern Strategy" and the extension of the Voting Rights Act, see Kotlowski, *Nixon's Civil Rights*.

2. Lawson, *In Pursuit of Power*, 135–36, 155–56.

3. Ibid, 163–64, 170–71; Parker, *Black Votes Count*, 62–63, 185–87.

4. "Negro Coach Apparent Winner," *Clarion-Ledger*, 10 April 1970. In 1969, eleven major stories appeared in national newsmagazines about Evers and his election, and eight stories followed over the next two years on his administration of Fayette and the changes he and his followers implemented. *Readers' Guide to Periodical Literature*, Vols. 29–31.

5. Robert L. Levey, "Black Mayor in Mississippi," *Boston Globe*, 26 October 1969; Evers and Szanton, *Have No Fear*, 253; John T. Wheeler, "Negro Political," *Greensboro Daily News*, 9 November 1969; William Thomas, "Black City Hall, White Courthouse," *Commercial Appeal Mid-South Magazine*, 9 November 1969; "Gun Control Ord. Adopted By Mayor Evers," *Fayette Chronicle*, 30 July 1970.

6. The state legislature and Gov. J.P. Coleman repealed the state's compulsory attendance laws in 1956 as part of resistance to *Brown*. Dittmer, *Local People*, 59.

7. John T. Wheeler, "Negro Political," *Greensboro Daily News*, 9 November 1969; "The Evers Administration: Two Years of Progress in Fayette," *Christian Century*, 28 July 1971, 909–10.

8. *1970 Census of the Population, Vol. 1 Characteristics of the Population, Part 26, Mississippi*, 144; "The Evers Administration," 908–9; "Fayette's Mayor One Year Later," *Business Week*, 4 July 1970, 79; John T. Wheeler, "Negro Political," *Greensboro Daily News*, 9 November 1969.

9. Evers and Szanton, *Have No Fear*, 253; "Town Officials Issue Statement," *Fayette Chronicle*, 4 December 1969; Flyer for the Tony Lawrence Music Festival, Charles Ramberg Papers, Printed Material, Box 16, Folder 13, Mississippi Department of Archives and History.

10. "Fayette's Finances Prompts Mayor To Seek Aid Of Nation For Help," *Fayette Chronicle*, 17 July 1969; Berry, *Amazing Grace*, 23; Untitled memo by Charles Ram-

berg, December 1969, Charles Ramberg Papers, Printed Material, Box 16, Folder 11; Untitled and undated memo by Charles Ramberg, Printed Material, Box 16, Folder 11.

11. "Fayette's Finances Prompts Mayor To Seek Aid of Nation For Help," *Fayette Chronicle*, 17 July 1969; "The Evers Administration," 909–10; "Fayette's Mayor One Year Later," 79; William Thomas, "Black City Hall, White Courthouse," *Commercial Appeal Mid-South Magazine*, 9 November 1969.

12. Ron Harrist, "Evers Will Remain Active In Civil Rights Activities," *Clarion-Ledger*, 15 May 1969; Marie Farr Walker, "Just Whittling," *Fayette Chronicle*, 11 September 1969; William Thomas, "Black City Hall, White Courthouse," *Commercial Appeal Mid-South Magazine*, 9 November 1969; "Threats Against Charles Evers Lead To Arrest Of Tupelo Man," *Fayette Chronicle*, 11 September 1969; Evers and Szanton, *Have No Fear*, 264; "Highway Department Removes Fayette Road Signs," *Clarion-Ledger*, 11 June 1970.

13. Evers and Szanton, *Have No Fear*, 255, emphasis in original; "Row Existing Between Mayor and Aldermen On Policeman's Suspension," *Fayette Chronicle*, 17 September 1970; "Negroes March On Evers," *Fayette Chronicle*, 24 September 1970.

14. Evers and Szanton, *Have No Fear*, 255; Undated and untitled memo by Charles Ramberg, Subject Files, Box 1, Folder 4; Crosby, *A Little Taste of Freedom*, 191.

15. Marie Farr Walker, "Just Whittling," *Fayette Chronicle*, 4 November 1970; Evers and Szanton, *Have No Fear*, 257–58. For information on the *Loving* case, see Moran, *Interracial Intimacy* and Wallenstein, *Tell The Court I Love My Wife*.

16. "Fayette's Mayor One Year Later," *Business Week*, 4 July 1970, 79.

17. Marie Farr Walker, "Just Whittling," *Fayette Chronicle*, 23 July and 31 July 1969; "Mississippi State Flag Trampled By Marchers," *Fayette Chronicle*, 23 July 1970.

18. "Civil Rights Complaint Filed With Justice Dept. By White Citizens," *Fayette Chronicle*, 30 July 1970; "Judge Willie Thompson Fines Claudie Lott For Trespassing," *Fayette Chronicle*, 6 August 1970; "Editor Demands Retraction Of Businessweek," *Fayette Chronicle*, 30 July 1970; "Attempt at Intimidation," *Fayette Chronicle*, 13 August 1970.

19. Evers and Szanton, *Have No Fear*, 259–60; Berry, *Amazing Grace*, 16.

20. Evers and Szanton, *Have No Fear*, 259–60; Undated and untitled memorandum by Charles Ramberg, Box 1, Folder 17.

21. "'You Gotta Love Me'" *Newsweek*, 2 August 1971, 22; Bass and DeVries, *The Transformation of Southern Politics*, 208; "Friday Deadline For Candidates In Primary Races," *Woodville Republican*, 4 June 1971.

22. Berry, *Amazing Grace*, 43–45, 50–52, 114–15.

23. *Ibid*, 119–21, 123.

24. Bass and De Vries, *The Transformation of Southern Politics*, 209; Berry, *Amazing Grace*, 148; *Mississippi Official and Statistical Register, 1972–1976*, 448.

25. Berry, *Amazing Grace*, 50–51; Walter R. Gordon, "White Politicians Woo Mississippi Negroes," *Baltimore Sun*, 29 July 1971; "Charles Sullivan, Bill Waller In Run-Off Race August 24," *Fayette Chronicle*, 5 August 1971; "'You Gotta Love Me,'" *Newsweek*, 2 August 1971.

26. Bass and De Vries, *The Transformation of Southern Politics*, 209; "Friday Deadline For Candidates In Primary Races," *Woodville Republican*, 4 June 1971; "Official county returns by precinct," *South Reporter*, 12 August 1971.

27. Berry, *Amazing Grace*, 167–68.

28. Rodgers and Bullock, *Law and Social Change*, 27, 30–31.

29. Berry, *Amazing Grace*, 152–53, 157–58, 201–2, 271; James Saggus, "Evers Rout Will Provoke Much Political Ruminating," *Clarksdale Press Register*, 4 November 1971.

30. "'You Gotta Love Me,'" *Newsweek*, 2 August 1971, 22; Bass and De Vries, *The Transformation of Southern Politics*, 208–9; Berry, *Amazing Grace*, 263.

31. Clark interview, 23 July 2005.

32. "Candidates Visit President" and "RNA Calls for Unity in Mississippi Races," *The New African*, 17 August 1971, Charles Ramberg Papers, Folder 5, Box 16, Mississippi Department of Archives and History; Howard-Pitney, *Martin Luther King Jr., Malcolm X, and the Civil Rights Struggle of the 1950s and 1960s*, 165–76.

33. "Candidates Visit President" and "RNA Calls for Unity in Mississippi Races," *The New African*, 17 August 1971, Charles Ramberg Papers, Folder 5, Box 16.

34. Berry, *Amazing Grace*, 263, 269–70, 327, 331, 333; *Mississippi Official and Statistical Register 1972–1976*, 455; "Black Setback in Mississippi," *Time*, 15 November 1971, 17–18.

35. "Black Setback in Mississippi," 17–18; "Cleve McDowell enters Rep. race," *The Enterprise-Tocsin* (Indianola), 16 September 1971; "Waller wins handily in record turnout," *Enterprise-Tocsin*, 4 November 1971.

36. "Black Candidates Elected in 1971 Elections," Charles Ramberg Papers, Folder 2, Box 1; "All County and Supervisor Incumbents Win, Waller 4–1," *Woodville Republican*, 5 November 1971; "Meredith Faults Evers On Campaign 'To Lose,'" *Clarksdale Press Register*, 5 November 1971.

37. "Williams, Alexander, Criss Pearson, Crook, Re-Elected," *Bolivar Commercial*, 4 November 1971.

38. "Two New Supervisors To Join Board In January As Result Of 1971 Election Held Recently," *Clarksdale Press Register*, 3 November 1971; "Old Familiar Faces To Linger Around Courthouse," *Clarksdale Press Register*, 3 November 1971; "Tunica, Quitman Positions All Go To White Candidates," *Clarksdale Press Register*, 3 November 1971.

39. "Runoff Alderman's Race Set For Tuesday, May 15th," *Fayette Chronicle*, 10 May 1973; "Bolivar towns elect officials," *Bolivar Commercial*, 6 June 1973; "Pace elects all-black slate," *Bolivar Commercial*, 6 June 1973; "Winstonville election results finally given," *Bolivar Commercial*, 8 June 1973; *National Roster of Black Elected Officials*, Vol. 4.

40. "Runoff in Shaw," *Bolivar Commercial*, 9 May 1973; "Shaw runoff date set," *Bolivar Commercial*, 10 May 1973; "Burns defeats Flippins," *Bolivar Commercial*, 10 May 1973; Clark Rumfelt, "Shaw Race Studied," *Bolivar Commercial*, 15 May 1973; "Shaw to rerun primary," *Bolivar Commercial*, 17 May 1973; "Same slate wins in Shaw rerun," *Bolivar Commercial*, 23 May 1973; "Curry wins Shaw city clerk post," *Bolivar Commercial*, 4 January 1974.

41. "Hearing Friday on shootout in Shaw," *Bolivar Commercial*, 19 June 1975; "Self defense ruled," *Bolivar Commercial*, 20 June 1975; "Boycott apparently underway in Shaw," *Bolivar Commercial*, 26 June 1975; "Shaw board okays committee," *Bolivar Commercial*, 2 July 1975; "Boycott Continuing," *Bolivar Commercial*, 3 July 1975; "Shaw to vote on street program," *Bolivar Commercial*, 6 August 1975.

42. Pam Bullard, "Bond issue defeated," *Bolivar Commercial*, 25 September 1975; "Flippins wins in Shaw; Gray re-elected in Shelby," *Bolivar Commercial*, 8 June 1977; Rob Cosgrove, "Gray wins in Shelby," *Bolivar Commercial*, 22 December 1976.

43. For 1970 population figures for the counties and municipalities, see the *Mississippi Official and Statistical Register, 1968–1972*, 237–38, 403.

44. Curtis Wilkie, "Farris Wins, Will Become Clarksdale's Next Mayor," *Clarksdale Press Register*, 14 May 1969; Curtis Wilkie, "Ayles, Garmon, Garrett, Weiss Winners In Municipal Races," *Clarksdale Press Register*, 21 May 1969; John M. Mayo, "NAACP Holds Annual Event Here Thursday," *Clarksdale Press Register*, 5 May 1973; "City Voters Poised For First Primary," *Clarksdale Press Register*, 7 May 1973.

45. "City Voters Balloting Today," *Clarksdale Press Register*, 8 May 1973; "City's Run-off Primary Includes Two Races," Clarksdale Press Register, 9 May 1973; "Mayo Wilson Appointed School Board Trustee," *Clarksdale Press Register*, 22 May 1973.

46. "Elijah Wilson Files Protest On Election," *Clarksdale Press Register*, 25 May 1973; Pam McPhail, "Local Political Rally Held In City Tuesday," *Clarksdale Press Register*, 30 May 1973.

47. "Jonestown Vote Probed," *Clarksdale Press Register*, 9 May 1973; "Area Towns Pick Slates For 1973–77," *Clarksdale Press Register*, 6 June 1973; "Area municipal election results," *Clarksdale Press Register*, 8 June 1977.

48. *National Roster of Black Elected Officials*, Vol. 7 and 11; Susan Linnee, "Mississippi Tops The Nation With Black Mayors," *Commercial Appeal*, 4 July 1977.

49. Morrison, *Black Political Mobilization*, 62, 65; Bennie G. Thompson, interview by Chester Morgan, 13 February 1974, Center for Oral History and Cultural Heritage, University of Southern Mississippi; Williamson, *Radicalizing the Ebony Tower*, 138; Susan Linnee, "Mississippi Tops The Nation With Black Mayors," *Commercial Appeal*, 4 July 1977; "Charles Griffin Wins in Landslide Vote," Hinds County Gazette, 15 March 1968; Jan Hillegas, "Black Activists Charge Draft Conspiracy," *The New African*, March 1970.

50. Jan Hillegas, "Black Activists Charge Draft Conspiracy," *The New African*, March 1970; Bennie Thompson, interview by Chester Morgan.

51. Jan Hillegas, "Black Activists Charge Draft Conspiracy," *The New African*, March 1970; Davis Smith, "Bolton Black Says Beatings Occurred" and "No Massive Patrol Probe; Declares FBI," *Jackson Daily News*, 11 June 1971; Charles M. Hills, Jr., "Collegians To Huddle With ACLU," *Clarion-Ledger*, 18 November 1971; Newsletter of the American Civil Liberties Union of Mississippi, Inc., September 1971, State Sovereignty Commission, SCR ID # 6–71–0–40–2–1–1; Salamon, "Leadership and Modernization," 642.

52. Bennie Thompson, interview by Chester Morgan; Nancy Stevens, "Blacks In Election Sweep At Bolton," *Jackson Daily News*, 9 May 1973.

53. Morrison, *Black Political Mobilization*, 84, 88–92; Bass and De Vries, *The Transformation of Southern Politics*, 191; Parker, *Black Votes Count*, 166; Susan Linnee, "Mississippi Tops The Nation With Black Mayors," *Commercial Appeal*, 4 July 1977; Blackwell and Morris, *Barefootin',* 212–13.

54. "All County and Supervisor Incumbents Win, Waller 4–1," *Woodville Republican*, 5 November 1971; "Waller Wins Over Evers," *Fayette Chronicle*, 4 November 1971.

55. "Gordon, 2 Aldermen Are Reelected," *Port Gibson Reveille*, 10 December 1970; Crosby, "Common Courtesy," 451–52.

56. Crosby, "Common Courtesy," 367, 375, 397, 450–52; "No Official Count on Today's Election, But Many New Faces to be in Courthouse," *Port Gibson Reveille*, 4 November 1971; Advertisement for Shelton Segrest, *Port Gibson Reveille*, 28 October 1971. The election details are in Crosby's dissertation, but not in her book *A Little Taste of Freedom*.

57. "Blacks Take Over Democratic Party In Wilkinson Co.," *Woodville Republican*, 18 February 1972; "Grand Jury Returns 12 Bills; Jolliff Indicted On 2 Counts," *Woodville Republican*, 17 March 1972; "Jolliff Pleads Guilty; Ordered Removed From Office Wed.," *Woodville Republican*, 6 October 1972; "Gaulden Winner Supervisor Race," *Woodville Republican*, 1 December 1972.

58. Sewell and Dwight, *Mississippi Black History Makers*, 73–75; "2nd Mandamus on Car Tag Sales," *Port Gibson Reveille*, 8 November 1973; Crosby, *A Little Taste of Freedom*, 248–49.

59. Crosby, "Common Courtesy," 456–57; "District 5 supervisor's race still undecided; recount probable," *Port Gibson Reveille*, 7 August 1975; "Claiborne native is elected chancellor," *Port Gibson Reveille*, 7 November 1974; "Two more black supervisors elected in record voter turnout," *Port Gibson Reveille*, 8 November 1975; "Numerous independents on ballot," *Port Gibson Reveille*, 6 October 1975. Emilye Crosby covers the 1975 elections in *A Little Taste of Freedom*, 249, but in far less detail than her dissertation.

60. "Unofficial Returns, Democratic Primary, Jefferson County," *Fayette Chronicle*, 8 August 1975; "Winter, Finch-Dye, Gandy In Run-off; Evers Loses," *Fayette Chronicle*, 7 August 1975; "Finch Wins For Governor," *Fayette Chronicle*, 6 November 1975; "Waller Wins Over Evers," *Fayette Chronicle*, 4 November 1971; "Finch Leads Gov. Race; Waites Only County Incumbent To Suffer Defeat," *Woodville Republican*, 7 November 1975; *National Roster of Black Elected Officials*, vol. 6.

61. Henry Boyd, Jr., interview by author, tape recording, Oxford, Miss., 28 April 2004; Untitled memo from State Sovereignty Commission Investigator Fulton Tutor, 24 January 1968, Sovereignty Commission Online, SCR ID # 2-20-2-61-1-1-1; Lincoln Warren, "Freedom Demos Widen Breach With Loyalists," *Clarion-Ledger*, 6 January 1969; Landon, *The Honor and Dignity of the Profession*, 161. The indigent had few legal options besides the federally funded NMRLS in the 1960s. The state bar administered a legal aid program to help victims of Hurricane Camille in 1969, but that program was OEO-funded as well. The legislature did not pass the Public Defender Act, which gave state funding to indigent legal aid, until 1971. The OEO continued to fund NMRLS, as well as a similar program for Hinds County, after 1971 despite objections from the state bar over the organizations' civil rights activities. Landon, 161–62.

62. Memorandum from Fulton Tutor to W. Webb Burke, 30 September 1969, SCR ID # 2-20-2-65-1-1-1; Tutor to Burke, 20 October 1969, SCR ID # 8-19-1-67-1-1-1; Tutor to Burke, 3 November 1969, SCR ID # 8-19-1-77-1-1-1; Refunding Application for NMRLS, 12 August 1970, Mississippi Republican Party Papers, Box G-5, Office of Economic Opportunity Folder–North Mississippi Rural Legal Service, Mississippi State University.

63. "'Food First' Fund Drive Gaining Backers In City," unknown and undated newspaper clipping, SCR ID # 10-57-0-9-1-1-1; Margaret Banman, "Students Cheer Visiting Athletes," *Daily Camera* (Boulder), date unknown; Untitled advertisement for food and clothing drive in Boulder, SCR ID # 10-57-0-19-1-1-1; "Delegation Tries To Patch Torn Holly Springs Image," *Commercial Appeal*, 5 May 1970; George M. Yarborough to W. Webb Burke, 7 May 1970, SCR ID # 2-20-2-82-1-1-1; Weekly Report of Fulton Tutor, June 22 to June 27 1970, SCR ID # 2-20-2-87-2-1-1; "Food Stamps program approved for county," *South Reporter*, 24 June 1971.

64. "Eddie L. Smith announces for superintendent," *South Reporter*, 10 June 1971; S.V. Mullikin for Superintendent ad, *South Reporter*, 22 July 1971.

65. "United League receives load of food, clothes," *South Reporter*, 18 June 1970; "'Skip' Robinson announces for Sheriff," *South Reporter*, 2 September 1971; "George Caldwell announces for JP, District 1," *South Reporter*, 28 October 1971; "Henry Boyd, Jr. candidate for Chancery Clerk," *South Reporter*, 2 September 1971.

66. "United League receives load of food, clothes," *South Reporter*, 18 June 1970; "Democrats poll large majority in General Election; bond issue ok'd," *South Reporter*, 4 November 1971; "Coopwood wins; Autry and Bryant to run off," *South Reporter*, 10 May 1973.

67. George Yarborough, "Why can't we have peace and harmony in Byhalia?" *South Reporter*, 25 July 1974; "Byhalia boycotters under injunction; two buildings burned, arson suspected," *South Reporter*, 8 August 1974; "Grand Jury refutes charges, claims made by United League," *South Reporter*, 15 August 1974; "Byhalia boycotters under injunction; two buildings burned, arson suspected," *South Reporter*, 8 August 1974.

68. "Bernice Totten candidate for supervisor," *South Reporter*, 5 September 1974; "Totten and Wilson to run-off," *South Reporter*, 13 March 1974; Boyd interview, 28 April 2004; George Yarborough, "SOUTH REPORTER position stated," *South Reporter*, 13 March 1975; "Supervisor sworn in," *South Reporter*, 10 October 1974.

69. "Demands Made To The City Of Holly Springs, Town of Byhalia and Marshall County by United League, October 15, 1974," *South Reporter*, 21 November 1974; "County officers report three shootings, beating," *South Reporter*, 6 February 1975.

70. "Byhalia citizens meet to discuss future of city," *South Reporter*, 27 February 1975; "Committees appointed by group at Byhalia meeting," *South Reporter*, 27 March 1975; "Members of Byhalia human relations group selected," *South Reporter*, 10 April 1975.

71. "Lawsuit filed by United League to halt election," *South Reporter*, date unknown; "Injunction Sought to stop election," *South Reporter*, 31 July 1975.

72. Advertisement for Edwin Callicutt, *South Reporter*, 14 August 1975; Boyd interview, 28 April 2004.

73. Election returns for Marshall County, *South Reporter*, 4 September 1975; "One ballot box exam over; five others underway," *South Reporter*, 11 September 1975; "Jack F. Clements, candidate for Circuit Clerk, Marshall County," *South Reporter*, 16 October 1975; Advertisement for Jack Clements, *South Reporter*, 23 October 1975; "Unofficial Returns from Nov. General Election," *South Reporter*, 6 November 1975. Boyd claimed that the League enjoyed the help of "good white folks" who secretly reported planned efforts of white intimidation to the group. Boyd interview, 28 April 2004.

74. "Unofficial Returns from Nov. 4 General Election," *South Reporter*, 20 November 1975; *Biographical Dictionary of the American Congress 1774–1971*, 879; Norma Fields, "Doxey Conditionally Seated in Marshall Post," *Daily Journal*, January 1976.

75. Lawrence Busher, "Ballot Gets Prober's OK In Marshall," *Commercial Appeal*, 13 January 1976; "Doxey takes seat in House despite challenge by Boyd," *South Reporter*, 15 January 1976; "House To Vote On Seating Doxey," *Commercial Appeal*, 22 January 1976; Norma Fields, "Body Unconditionally Backs Doxey," *Daily Journal*, 22 January 1976; Boyd interview, 28 April 2004; Robert P. Crutcher to Bill Wilkins, 14 May 1970, Mississippi Republican Party Papers, Box G-5, Office of Economic Opportunity Folder–North Mississippi Rural Legal Service, Mississippi State University.

76. *National Roster of Black Elected Officials*, Vol. 6, 112–18.

Chapter 4. Fused but Not Healed

1. Ken Bode, "Mississippi's Two Democratic Parties," *The New Republic*, 25 March 1972.

2. Parker, *Black Votes Count*, 149.

3. Lawson, *In Pursuit of Power*, 193–96, 198–200, 339n12; 17; Bode, "Mississippi's Two Democratic Parties"; Lee, *For Freedom's Sake*, 175.

4. Bass and DeVries, *The Transformation of Southern Politics*, 212–13; Roy Reed, "A New, Biracial Course Found in Mississippi," *New York Times*, 21 January 1976; Edward Blackmon, Jr. to Bill Minor, 3 May 1978, William F. Minor Papers, Box 5, 1978 Senate Election Folder, Special Collections Department, Mississippi State University. Dahmer was killed by Klansmen who firebombed his Hattiesburg home in 1966. Dittmer, *Local People*, 391.

5. Biography of Clarke Thomas Reed, Mississippi Republican Party Papers, Biographies Folder, Box H-1, Special Collections, Mississippi State University; Paul Squires to W.T. Wilkins, 13 May 1970, Mississippi Republican Party Papers, Box G-1, Census Civil Rights Folder.

6. Bruce Galphin, "Miss. GOP Chief Blocked Evers Aid Bill," *Washington Post*, 20 March 1970; Don Oberdorfer, "HEW Approves Grant Requested by Evers," *Washington Post*, 4 May 1970.

7. Crespino, *In Search of Another Country*, 226; Paul Pittman, "Reed is facing trouble on school desegregation," *Delta Democrat-Times*, 20 February 1969; W.T. Wilkins to Harry Dent, 6 January 1968, Mississippi Republican Party Papers, Box G-3, HEW Coahoma County Schools Folder; Wilson F. Minor, "Reed: Chicken-fired Machiavellian or conservative True Believer?" Eyes on Mississippi column, newspaper unknown, 11 July 1976, Minor Papers, Box 10, Eyes on Mississippi Folder.

8. Memorandum from Clarke Reed to Harry Dent, 9 February 1970, Harry Dent Papers, Box 5, Folder 159, Special Collections, Robert Muldrow Cooper Library, Clemson University; Memorandum from Harry Dent to Clarke Reed, 12 November 1969, Harry Dent Papers, Box 18, Folder 456; Harry Dent to Clarke Reed, 11 July 1969, Harry Dent Papers, Box 18, Folder 456; Harry Dent to Clarke Reed, 16 December 1971, Harry Dent Papers, Box 22, Folder 506. For an example of Mississippi Republican complaints about school desegregation under Nixon, see James M. Moye to Harry Dent, 13 August 1970, Harry Dent Papers, Box 5, Folder 159.

9. Mounger and Maxwell, *Amidst the Fray*, 58, 69–71, 75.

10. *Ibid*, 64–65, 88, 125, 145, 350, 371. For coverage of the IRS private school decision, which culminated in the *Bob Jones v. U.S.* case, see Crespino, *In Search of Another Country*, 237–66.

11. Gil Carmichael, interview by author, tape recording, Meridian, Miss., 13 October 2004.

12. *Mississippi Official and Statistical Register, 1972–1976*, 475, 480; Biography of Gilbert Ellzey Carmichael, Mississippi Republican Party Papers, Biographies Folder, Box H-1, Special Collections, Mitchell Memorial Library, Mississippi State University; J.F. Barbour III to Tommy Giordano, Gilbert E. Carmichael Papers (hereafter referred to as GEC Papers), 1972 Campaign Correspondence, Folder 150, Special Collections Department, Mississippi State University; Membership card of Gilbert E. Carmichael for the U.S. Commission on Civil Rights, GEC Papers, Organizations, Folder 16; Bass and De Vries, *The Transformation of Southern Politics*, 214.

13. Mounger and Maxwell, *Amidst the Fray*, 136–39, 141–42, 155.

14. Carmichael interview, 13 October 2004; Advertisement for Sen. Jim Eastland, *Jackson Advocate*, 27 May 1972; Nash and Taggart, *Mississippi Politics*, 51.

15. Lamis, *The Two-Party South*, 49–50; *Mississippi Official and Statistical Register, 1972–1976*, 480. Bass and De Vries describe Carmichael's black support in 1972 as "substantial," and while he did run strong in some black-majority counties, in others he trailed badly, including most of the black Delta counties. Bass and De Vries, *The Transformation of Southern Politics*, 215; *Mississippi Official and Statistical Register, 1972–1976*, 480. As an example of Meredith's ever-changing political nature, he ran as a Democrat in 1974 in the fifth congressional district but then withdrew after leading in the first primary and ran as independent in the general election. "Meredith After Winning Withdraws; Dean, Sturgeon In Runoff," *Fayette Chronicle*, 6 June 1974.

16. Hinds had a 39.3 percent black population in 1970 but was the most populous county in the state. Amite and Copiah actually had slight black majorities in 1970 (50.5 and 50.3 percent, respectively), but they had declined to 47.6 and 48.4 percent by 1980. *1970 and 1980 Census of the Population, Vol. 1, General Characteristics of the Population*; Mounger and Maxwell, *Amidst the Fray*, 139, 143.

17. *Mississippi Official and Statistical Register, 1972–1976*, 149–50; Bass and De Vries, *The Transformation of Southern Politics*, 215; *Mississippi Official and Statistical Register, 1976–80*, 432; Barone, Ujifusa, and Matthews, *The Almanac of American Politics 1978*, 466. Bass and De Vries completely omit mention of Eddie McBride's independent candidacy and lead the reader to believe that Cochran won his election solely by

siphoning black votes away from his Democratic opponent. Lamis gives attention to McBride and credits his 8.2 percent showing with throwing the race to Cochran. Bass and De Vries, *The Transformation of Southern Politics*, 215; Lamis, *The Two-Party South*, 57.

18. Leslie Burl McLemore, interview by author, tape recording, 19 November 2004, Oxford, Mississippi. For continued reports of voting discrimination in Mississippi in the early 1970s, see Lawson, *In Pursuit of Power*, 231–33.

19. "Mayor Evers In Meridian To Welcome Nixon," *Fayette Chronicle*, 3 May 1973; Charles Evers to the Secretary of the Army, *Fayette Chronicle*, 8 January 1975.

20. Bill Pardue, "Senate Approves Delegate Election," *Clarion-Ledger*, 22 January 1975.

21. "The Common Touch," *Newsweek*, 8 September 1975; Bass and De Vries, *The Transformation of Southern Politics*, 216. Winter had also black staffers in his 1975 campaign. R.W. Apple, Jr., "Republican Courts Mississippi Blacks," *New York Times*, 18 August 1975; Fred Banks, interview by author, tape recording, Jackson, Miss., 28 June 2005.

22. Sewell and Dwight, *Mississippi Black History Makers*, 79; Jack Elliot, "Kirksey Charges State, Opponents Trying To Keep Him Off Ballot," *Clarion-Ledger*, 2 August 1975; Linda Buford, "Kirksey Vote: No Counties Won, No Black Support," *Clarion-Ledger*, 6 November 1975. For more on Kirksey and the reapportionment suits, see chapter five.

23. Lamis, *The Two-Party South*, 50–51; Harry Dent to Gil Carmichael, 13 November 1974, Harry Dent Papers, Box 25, Folder 554; Apple, *New York Times*, 18 August 1975; "New Breezes Blowing On the Old Magnolia," *Time*, 3 November 1975; Roland Evans and Robert Novak, "Carmichael's Mississippi Is Viewed," *Clarion-Ledger*, 18 October 2005; Jack Elliot, "Batesville's Backing Its Man, Finch," *Clarion-Ledger*, 1 November 1975; Telephone interview with Gil Carmichael, 31 August 2006.

24. Bass and De Vries, *The Transformation of Southern Politics*, 210; Carmichael interview, 13 October 2004.

25. Lamis, *The Two-Party South*, 51; "Cochran Not Endorsing His Fellow Republican," *Clarion-Ledger*, 16 October 1975.

26. Mounger and Maxwell, *Amidst the Fray*, 157–58.

27. Ibid, 153–55, 160–61.

28. *Exhibits to the Testimony of J. Stanley Pottinger before the Subcommittee on Civil and Constitutional Rights, Committee on the Judiciary, U.S. House of Representatives, March 5, 1975*, J. Stanley Pottinger Papers, Box 94, Folder 270, Gerald R. Ford Presidential Library; J. Stanley Pottinger to Gerry Jones, 30 October 1975, J. Stanley Pottinger Papers, Box 64, Folder 133, Gerald R. Ford Presidential Library. For an example of harassment of black voters in 1975, see Memorandum for the Attorney General from J. Stanley Pottinger, 30 October 1975, J. Stanley Pottinger Papers, Box 64, Folder 133, Gerald R. Ford Presidential Library.

29. "Gil Carmichael Opens Campaign Office Here," *Fayette Chronicle*, 30 October 1975; Gil Carmichael, interview by Jeff Broadwater, transcript, Washington, D.C., 18 July 1991, Congressional and Political Research Center, Mississippi State University;

"Mrs. Gil Carmichael Campaigns Wednesday in Claiborne County," *Port Gibson Reveille*, 18 September 1975; Walter C. Gough to Gil Carmichael, GEC Papers, 1975 Campaign Correspondence, Folder 328.

30. Robert Clark press conference, GEC Papers, 1975 Campaign, Folder 454; John M. Perkins to the Voice of Calvary, GEC Papers, 1975 Campaign, Folder 47.

31. "Finch 'Recommended' For Governor; 'Our Only Viable Choice'; Total GOP Posture 'Unredeemable' For Poor," *Lexington Advertiser*, 23 October 1973.

32. "Evers Raps GOP Candidates; Calls For Support OF Finch," *Fayette Chronicle*, 30 October 1975. Gandy, a Hattiesburg lawyer and former state representative, was elected as state treasurer in 1960 and 1967, served as commissioner of public welfare from 1964 to 1967, and was elected commissioner of insurance in 1971. She served as a legislative assistant to Sen. Theodore Bilbo (D-Miss.) in the 1940s. *Mississippi Official and Statistical Register, 1972–1976*, 30.

33. Advertisement by Prentiss Walker, *Clarion-Ledger*, 18 October 1975.

34. Ibid.

35. Crespino, In Search of Another Country, 217; Hathorn, "Challenging the Status Quo," 240.

36. Advertisement by Elmore Douglass Greaves, *Clarion-Ledger*, 3 November 1975.

37. Mississippi Official and Statistical Register, 497, 500; Gil Carmichael to President Gerald Ford, GEC Papers, General Political, Folder 167; Bass and De Vries, *The Transformation of Southern* Politics, 216; Lamis, *The Two-Party South*, 51; Buford, *Clarion-Ledger*, 6 November 1975; Jack Elliot, "Finch Shows Rural, Black Strength," *Clarion-Ledger*, 6 November 1975; McLemore interview, 19 November 2004.

38. Parker, *Black Votes Count*, 149–50; Lamis, *The Two-Party South*, 52.

39. Roy Reed, "A New, Biracial Course Found in Mississippi," *New York Times*, 21 January 1976; "Mayor Evers Attends Governor's Council in Jackson," *Fayette Chronicle*, 29 January 1976; "Holmes Democrats Elect Delegates And Executive Committee," *Lexington Advertiser*, 19 February 1976; Lamis, *The Two-Party South*, 52; Lawson, *In Pursuit of Power*, 256. For example, in Jefferson County the Wallace-Shriver spilt occurred, in Wilkinson County Wallace polled a majority, and in Claiborne County the entire delegate slate was uncommitted. "Jefferson County Elects Democratic Executive Committee and Delegates," *Fayette Chronicle*, 19 February 1976; "Wallace Polls 55% of County Ballots at Precinct Meetings," *Woodville Republican*, 30 January 1976; " Claiborne Democratic slate uncommitted," *Port Gibson Reveille*, 19 February 1976.

40. "68 Democrats In Contest For 24 Political Offices," *Lexington Advertiser*, 19 June 1975; "Loyalists Elect Delegates For Feb. Convention," *Lexington Advertiser*, 27 January 1972; Bass and De Vries, *The Transformation of Southern Politics*, 210; Dittmer, *Local People*, 421–22; Clark interview, 23 July 2005.

41. Clark interview, 23 July 2005.

42. "Holmes Represented At Both Demo Conventions," 2 March 1975; "Candidates," *Bolivar Commercial*, 9 June 1975; "Howard Taft Bailey Announces For Supervisor, Beat 1," *Lexington Advertiser*, 4 September 1975; "Holmes County Official Returns Democratic Primary, August 7, 1979," *Lexington Advertiser*, 16 August 1979.

43. "The Common Touch," *Newsweek*, 8 September 1975; "Blacks Take Over Democratic Party In Wilkinson County," *Woodville Republican*, 18 February 1972.

44. "Hinds Legislative Ballots Crowded," *Clarion-Ledger*, 3 November 1975; Tim O'Neil, "Democrats Lead In Hinds County Legislative Races," *Clarion-Ledger*, 5 November 1975; Parker, 122–23, 150–51. For more on the creation of single-member districts, see chapter five.

45. "State Elects First Three Black Sheriffs," *Northeast Mississippi Daily Journal*, 8 November 1979; Boyd interview, 28 April 2004; "Marshall County vote light in primary; few results are available," *South Reporter*, 5 August 1971; "Democrats poll large majority in General Election; bond issue ok'd," *South Reporter*, 4 November 1971.

46. "State Elects First Three Black Sheriffs," *Northeast Mississippi Daily Journal*, 8 November 1979; "General Election Set November 2," *Lexington Advertiser*, 28 October 1971; "68 Democrats In Contest For 28 Political Offices," *Lexington Advertiser*, 19 June 1975; "Heavy Voter Turnout In Holmes County Despite Torrential Rains," *Lexington Advertiser*, 6 November 1975; Interview with Griffin McLaurin, 6 March 2000, by Harriet Tanzman, Civil Rights Documentation Project, Tougaloo College Archives; Clark interview, 23 July 2005.

47. "NAACP Object of GOP Wooing," *Clarksdale Press Register*, 4 November 1977; "Finch displeasing black leaders," *Clarksdale Press Register*, 30 May 1977; Ken Faulkner, "State black officials form organization," *Clarksdale Press Register*, 8 November 1977; Biographical Sketch of Charles Pickering, Mississippi Republican Party Papers, Box H-1, Biographies, Special Collections Department, Mitchell Memorial Library, Mississippi State University.

48. Bill Minor, "Breaking bread with blacks," *Capitol Reporter*, 20 October 1977.

49. Norma Fields, "Startling Things Came From Holly Springs," *Northeast Mississippi Daily Journal*, 26 December 1977; Moye, *Let the People Decide*, 19; Aaron Henry to NAACP Leader and Civil and Human Rights Supporter, 1 January 1978, Ed King Papers, Box 1, Folder 9, Department of Archives and Special Collections, J.D. Williams Memorial Library, University of Mississippi; Sewell and Dwight, *Mississippi Black History Makers*, 86.

50. Henry J. Kirksey to Benjamin Hooks, 9 February 1978, Ed King Papers, Box 1, Folder 9; Owen H. Brooks to Friend, 26 January 1978, Ed King Papers, Box 1, Folder 9; McLemore interview, 19 November 2004.

51. "Blacks Are Criticized By Evers For Backing White Candidates," *Commercial Appeal*, 29 May 1978; "Blacks Favoring Finch, NAACP Says," *Commercial Appeal*, 10 May 1978; *Mississippi Official and Statistical Register*, 1980–84, 446–47, 455–56.

52. Frank Montague, Jr. to Charles W. Pickering and Thad Cochran, GEC Papers, General Political, Folder 213.

53. Barone, Ujifsa and Matthews, *The Almanac of American Politics 1976*, xiv–xv, 458–65; *The Almanac of American Politics 1978*, xix, 462–67; Bill Pardue, "Senate Approves Delegate Election," *Clarion-Ledger*, 22 January 1975; Calvin Edward Durden, "All five opposed Voting Rights Act," *Mississippi Press* (Pascagoula), 19 August 1975. For the Citizens' Councils and their support for Rhodesia and South Africa, see McMillen, *The Citizens' Council*, xiii.

54. Barone, Ujifsa, and Matthews, *The Almanac of American Politics 1976*, x, 458–65; *The Almanac of American Politics 1978*, 462–69; Crespino, *In Search of Another Country*, 258.

55. *Mississippi Official and Statistical Register 1980–1984*, 454–55; "The District, County, and Precinct Coordinated Approach to the Recruitment of Black Voters for Thad Cochran in the U.S. Senate Race," GEC Papers, General Political, Folder 215; Jo Ann Klein, "The GOP Sale," *Clarion-Ledger*, 28 August 1978.

56. Aaron Henry to Joseph Rauh, 1 September 1978, Charles Ramberg Papers.

57. Morris Cunningham, "Blacks Split On Candidate Issue," *Commercial Appeal*, undated clipping in Wilson F. Minor Papers, Box Five, 1978 Senate Election Folder.

58. Aaron Henry to Maurice Dantin, 23 July 1978, William F. Minor Papers, Box Five, Senate 1978 Election Folder; Schulman, *The Seventies*, 76.

59. Joseph L. Rauh, Jr. to Charles Evers, 29 August 1978, Charles Ramberg Papers; Henry to Rauh, 1 September 1978, Charles Ramberg Papers; Evers and Szanton, 286–87. Evers had backed George Wallace for president in 1976, declaring that "we [blacks] changed George Wallace's heart." Evers and Szanton, *Have No Fear*, 284.

60. Wilson F. Minor, undated Eyes on Mississippi column, Wilson F. Minor Papers, Box Four, 1978 Congressional Election Folder; "Evers' Remarks Arouse Labor Indignation," *Jackson Advocate*, 8 November 1978; Clark interview, 23 July 2005; Lawson, *In Pursuit of Power*, 103.

61. Henry Kirksey, who lacked the funds and popularity of Evers, dropped out of the race at the last minute and supported Evers. "Reluctant Kirksey throws senate support to Evers," *Bolivar Commercial*, 3 November 1978; Lamis, *The Two-Party South*, 52–53.

62. "Gov. Finch Supports Dantin," *Jackson Advocate*, 8 November 1978; "Dantin Supports Tax Cut," *Fayette Chronicle*, 15 September 1978; "Evers Seeks Help For Small Towns," *Fayette Chronicle*, 15 September 1978.

63. "Cochran–Negative, Dantin–Afraid," *Jackson Advocate*, 1 November 1978; "Evers Gets B.B. King Endorsement," *Fayette Chronicle*, 7 September 1978; "Evers has Ali; Carter boosts Dantin; Cochran in lead," *Bolivar Commercial*, 6 November 1978; Lamis, *The Two-Party South*, 52–53, 349n41; "Ali Steals Evers' Show," *Jackson Advocate*, 15 November 1978. Ali and Kristofferson were filming the made-for-television movie *Freedom Road*, from the Howard Fast novel of same name. The movie, ironically, was about an ex-slave in 1870s Virginia who is elected to the U.S. Senate. http://www.imdb.com/title/tt0079173/plotsummary.

64. Lamis, *The Two-Party South*, 53; David W. Kubissa, "Coalition splits over endorsement," *Clarion-Ledger*, 30 July 1979; Joanna Neuman, "Baptist Ministers' Union Backs Evers for Senate," *Clarion-Ledger*, 17 August 1978; Joanna Neuman, "Evers 'Brings' Both Tupelo Sides Together," *Clarion-Ledger*, 5 October 1978.

65. Vern E. Smith, "A Different Campaign," *Atlanta Journal and Constitution Magazine*, 5 November 1978.

66. *Mississippi Official and Statistical Register, 1980–1984*, 458–59. Jasper was the one county Evers won that was not majority-black.

67. Lamis, *The Two-Party South*, 55; *Mississippi Official and Statistical Register, 1980–1984*, 458–59; "Evers' Senate Bid Hit As 'Tragic Lie' To Blacks," *Commercial Appeal*, date unknown; Fred Banks, interview by author, tape recording, 28 June 2005.

68. *Mississippi Official and Statistical Register, 1980–1984*, 195, 460; GEC Papers, General Political, Folder 218.

Chapter 5. Reapportionment

1. Clark, "Legislative Reapportionment in the 1890 Constitutional Convention," 297–315.

2. *Broom v. Wood*, 1 F. Supp. 134, 53 S. Ct. 1 (1932).

3. "Mississippians Have The Right To Run Their Own Elections," *Daily Clarion-Ledger*, 19 October 1932; "Candidates All Admit Exclusion," *Daily Clarion-Ledger*, 20 October 1932.

4. Cortner, *The Apportionment Cases*, 15–25, 51–132.

5. James Saggus, "Population Figures to Raise New Cries," *Jackson Daily News*, 30 May 1960.

6. Cortner, *The Apportionment Cases*, 124–25, 129–30.

7. Cortner, *The Apportionment Cases*, 124–25; "Mississippi Solons Cheer, Jeer Ruling," *Jackson Daily News*, 27 March 1962.

8. Cortner, *The Apportionment Cases*, 125.

9. Bartley, *The Rise of Massive Resistance*, 18–19, 22; *Barnes v. Barnett*, 129 So. 2d 638 (1961).

10. *Baker v. Carr*, 369 U.S. 186 (1962); "MEC Board Urges Reapportionment," *Jackson Daily News*, 17 November 1960; Cortner, *The Apportionment Cases*, 133–59; "U.S. Courts Will Hear Apportionment Suits," *Jackson Daily News*, 26 March 1962; "Mississippi Solons Cheer, Jeer Ruling," *Jackson Daily News*, 27 March 1962.

11. "Opinions Vary On Court Ruling Reapportionment," *Greenwood Commonwealth*, 27 March 1962; "Reapportionment Fight Scheduled Next Week," *Clarion-Ledger*, 30 March 1962; Ben McCarty, "Apportion Resolution Considered," *Clarion-Ledger*, 5 April 1962; Charles M. Hills, "Reapportioning Study Group Oked In House." *Clarion-Ledger*, 6 April 1962; Mississippi House Journal, 1962 regular session, 986–87; First 1962 Extraordinary Session, 5–7, 37–39; Mississippi House and Senate Journals, Second 1962 Extraordinary Session and First 1963 Extraordinary Session; *Conner v. Johnson* 256 F. Supp. 962 (1966); "Patterson Says Decision Won't Affect State," *Daily Journal*, 16 June 1964.

12. Cortner, *The Apportionment Cases*, 160–251.

13. "Patterson Says Decision Won't Affect State," *Daily Journal*, 16 June 1964; Mississippi Senate Journal, Second 1962 Extraordinary Session.

14. *Conner v. Johnson* 256 F. Supp. 962 (1966); Parker, *Black Votes Count*, 81; W.C. Shoemaker, "Negro Suit Hits State Apportionment," *Jackson Daily News*, 19 October 1965.

15. Dittmer, *Local People*, 223; Parker, *Black Votes Count*, 83–84; Alexander M. Bickel, "Impeach Judge Cox," *New Republic*, 4 September 1965, 13.

16. Lawson, *In Pursuit of Power*, 99, 103.

17. Parker, *Black Votes Count*, 43–47; "State Congressional Redistricting Okayed," *Clarion-Ledger*, 8 April 1966. For more on the congressional gerrymandering of the Mississippi Delta, see chapter eight.

18. *Conner v. Johnson* 256 F. Supp. 962 (1966); Michael Smith, "Suit Attacks Redistricting," *Clarion-Ledger*, 16 July 1966; "Legislature of State Must Be Reapportioned," *Clarion-Ledger*, 24 July 1966; Parker, *Black Votes Count*, 107.

19. Parker, *Black Votes Count*, 107; "Federal Panel Upholds State Congressional Redistricting," *Clarion-Ledger*, 1 October 1966.

20. Charles Hills, "State Solons Open Session Here Today," *Clarion-Ledger*, 9 November 1966; Charles Hills, "Johnson Recommends Speedy Action On Reapportionment," *Clarion-Ledger*, 11 November 1966; Charles Hills and A.B. Albritton, "House, Senate Finally Agree," *Clarion-Ledger*, 1 December 1966; James Saggus, "Gov. Johnson Signs Bill On Reseating," *Clarion-Ledger*, 2 December 1966; A.B. Albritton, "Order Delays Court Ruling," *Clarion-Ledger*, 3 December 1966.

21. *Conner v. Johnson* 265 F. Supp. 492 (1967); James Saggus, "Court Apportionment Plans Given In Detail," *Clarion-Ledger*, 3 March 1967; A.B. Albritton, "Judges Put Into Effect Own Reapportionment Plan," *Clarion-Ledger*, 29 March 1967; "State Districting Plan Is Approved," *Clarion-Ledger*, 27 March 1967; Charles Hills, "Affairs of State," *Clarion-Ledger*, 30 March 1967.

22. "Reapportionment Bill Inked By JBW," *Jackson Daily News*, 24 March 1971.

23. Mississippi House Journal, 1971 Regular Session, 48, 415–16, 432–33, 774, 1149–60; Dittmer, *Local People*, 142, 494.

24. "Reapportionment Bill Inked By JBW," *Jackson Daily News*, 24 March 1971; Charles B. Gordon, "State Reapportion Plan Is Thrown Out," *Jackson Daily News*, 14 May 1971; James Saggus, "Court Rejects State Reshuffle Plan," *Clarion-Ledger*, 15 May 1971; Charles Gordon, "State Files Its Answer To CR Reshuffle Plan," *Jackson Daily News*, 18 May 1971; James Saggus, "CR Forces Offer Court Own Reapportion Plan," *Clarion-Ledger*, 18 May 1971; Speech by A.F. Summer, Neshoba County Fair, 6 August 1969, Minor Papers, Box 80, Folder "Summer, A.F.–1969–1975."

25. *Conner v. Johnson* 330 F. Supp. 506 (1971); Charles Gordon, "Reapportion Plan Okayed By Summer," *Jackson Daily News*, 19 May 1971; James Saggus, "Federal Court Orders Own Reapportionment Plan," *Clarion-Ledger*, 19 May 1971; James Saggus, "Reapportionment Struggle Over In 81 State Counties," *Jackson Daily News*, 22 May 1971; "Election Delay Requested Pending Appeal Decision," *Clarion-Ledger*, 25 May 1971; "Election Delay Request Filed," *Jackson Daily News*, 25 May 1971; "More Southern Vote Rules," *Jackson Daily News*, 28 May 1971; Charles Gordon, "Nobody Knows Fate Of State Election Plan," *Jackson Daily News*, 2 June 1971; Charles Gordon, "Ruling Could Affect Hinds Case–Summer," *Jackson Daily News*, 8 June 1971.

26. *Conner v. Johnson* 91 S. Ct. 1760 (1971); Parker, *Black Votes Count*, 113; "Court Overturns Hinds At-Large Election Plan," *Clarion-Ledger*, 14 June 1971; Charles Gordon, "Candidates Ask Info About Court Ruling," *Jackson Daily News*, 4 June 1971.

27. *Whitcomb v. Chavis*, 403 U.S. 124 (1971); Charles Gordon, "Candidates Ask Info About Court Ruling," *Jackson Daily News*, 4 June 1971.

28. Parker, *Black Votes Count*, 114; "Added Hearings Loom In Hinds Redistricting," *Clarion-Ledger*, 8 June 1971; "Summer Asks Court To Take a New Look At Hinds Case," *Jackson Daily News*, 9 June 1971; "Hinds Reshuffle Impossible Task?" *Clarion-Ledger*, 12 June 1971; Charles Gordon, "Hinds Reshuffle Task Said 'Impossible,'" *Jackson Daily News*, 14 June 1971; Charles Gordon, "New Motions Filed In Hinds Reshuffle," *Jackson Daily News*, 15 June 1971; Charles Hills, "Court Rules Solons In Hinds Should Be Elected At Large," *Clarion-Ledger*, 17 June 1971; Charles Gordon, "Civil Rights Forces Request Stay of Ruling," *Jackson Daily News*, 19 June 1971; "Top Court Declines To Press Hinds Split," *Jackson Daily News*, 21 June 1971; "Court Upholds At-Large Vote," *Clarion-Ledger*, 22 June 1971.

29. *Conner v. Williams* 404 U.S. 549 (1972).

30. Parker, *Black Votes Count*, 115.

31. For a survey of this litigation, see Parker, *Black Votes Count*, 116–19.

32. Mississippi House Journal, 1975 Regular Session, 821, 1426–31, 1476.

33. *Conner v. Waller* 396 F. Supp. 1308 (1975); *Contemporary Authors*, Vol. 136, s.v. "Parker, Frank"; Bonney, Joseph, "Lawyers Argue At Large Districting Is Discriminatory," *Clarion-Ledger*, 8 February 1975; "Court Studies System," *Jackson Daily News*, 8 February 1975; "Official Hits Voting Rights Act," *Jackson Daily News*, 11 April 1975; Frank Van Der Linden, "Gerrymandering Charge Denied," *Jackson Daily News*, 12 April 1975.

34. *Conner v. Waller* 396 F. Supp. 1308 (1975); Charles Gordon, "Waller Urges Cold Shoulder For Ford," *Jackson Daily News*, 28 May 1975; "Mississippi Plans High Court Districting Case," *Jackson Daily News*, 23 May 1975; Will Sentell, Jr., "Court Wants More Reapportion Info," *Jackson Daily News*, 30 May 1975.

35. *Conner v. Waller* 95 S. Ct. 2003 (1975); Jack Elliot, "U.S. Ruling Demands One-Man Districts, Lawyer Says," *Clarion-Ledger*, 6 June 1975; Will Sentell, Jr., "Lawyer Foresees One-Member Plan In State's Future," *Jackson Daily News*, 6 June 1975; Jack Elliot, "U.S. Rejects Redistricting Formula," *Clarion-Ledger*, 11 June 1975; Charles Gordon, "Single Member Districts Appear Certain For 1975," *Jackson Daily News*, 13 June 1975; Charles Gordon, "Waller Takes Aim On Padded Talk," *Jackson Daily News*, 18 June 1975; Ronnie Patriquin, "Waller Attacks Justice Department, Kirksey," *Clarion-Ledger*, 19 June 1975.

36. Will Sentell, Jr., "Reapportionment Issue Narrowed By U.S. Judge," *Jackson Daily News*, 21 June 1975; Jack Elliot, "Judges To Draw Districting Plan," *Clarion-Ledger*, 21 June 1975; Tom Bradley and Will Sentell, "Mayor Gives Warning On Reapportionment Suits," *Jackson Daily News*, 25 June 1975; "Waller Doubts Court Will Interfere With Elections," *Clarion-Ledger*, 25 June 1975.

37. Parker, *Black Votes Count*, 122; Barry Camp, "Federal Panel Will Add House To Hinds Apportionment Plan," *Clarion-Ledger*, 8 July 1975; Ronnie Patriquin, "Single-Member Districts Ruled In Hinds Area," *Clarion-Ledger*, 12 July 1975.

38. Bob Howie, "Here We Go Again," *Jackson Daily News*, 16 April 1975; Joseph Bonney, "Unemotional Campaign Has Another Month To Primary," *Jackson Daily News*, 6 July 1975; Jeffrey Smith, "Minniece Would Have Urged District Changes," *Jackson Daily News*, 8 July 1975; Jack Elliot, "Single Member Districts Asked," *Clarion-Ledger*,

10 July 1975; Jack Elliot, "State-Born Justices Unjust, NAACP Says," *Clarion-Ledger*, 11 June 1975; Otis Sanford, "Kirksey Says Race Issue Important In Campaign," *Clarion-Ledger*, 29 August 1975.

39. Parker, *Black Votes Count*, 122–23; "Voting Rights Act Signed By Ford In Ceremony," Clarion-Ledger, 7 August 1975.

40. Parker, *Black Votes Count*, 123–24; *Conner v. Coleman* 96 S. Ct. 1814 (1976); "Reapportionment Target Date Set," *Jackson Daily News*, 1 August 1975; Jack Elliot, "Reapportion Soon, Court Urges State," 20 May 1976, *Clarion-Ledger*, 20 May 1976.

41. *Conner v. Finch* 419 F. Supp. 1072 (1072), 419 F. Supp. 1089 (1976); Steve Cannizaro, "Panel: Soon Will Draw Own Districting Plan," *Clarion-Ledger*, 16 June 1976; Steve Cannizaro, "Panel Draws 1-Member Senate Lines," *Clarion-Ledger*, 25 August 1976; Steven Cannizaro, "Parker Says New Senate Plan 'Unacceptable,'" *Clarion-Ledger*, 3 September 1976; James Saggus, "Summer Can't See Elections," *Jackson Daily News*, 3 September 1976; James Saggus, "Single-Member Districts Ordered," *Jackson Daily News*, 8 September 1976; "Special Elections Recommended," *Jackson Daily News*, 14 September 1976.

42. *Conner v. Finch*, 422 F. Supp. 1014 (1976); James Saggus, "Summer Dislikes Reapportionment," *Jackson Daily News*, 9 September 1976; "Panel Decrees New Elections In 2 Districts," *Jackson Daily News*, 12 November 1976; Robert Shaw, "Reapportionment Fight May Be Over," *Jackson Daily News*, 13 November 1976.

43. "Supreme Court Sets Reapportion Appeals Feb. 28," *Clarion-Ledger*, 18 January 1977; Steve Cannizaro, "Reapportionment Case Debated Today," *Clarion-Ledger*, 28 February 1977; "Racial Gerrymandering In Mississippi Is Denied," *Jackson Daily News*, 1 March 1977; "Supreme Court Referees State Districting Dispute," *Clarion-Ledger*, 1 March 1977.

44. *Conner v. Finch*, 97 S. Ct. 1828 (1977); "Reapportionment–Try Again!" *Jackson Daily News*, 1 June 1977; "Some See Court's Decision As Victory," *Jackson Daily News*, 1 June 1977; John Hutchinson, "Black Politicians All Smiles," *Jackson Daily News*, 1 June 1977.

45. Mississippi Senate Journal, 1977 Second Extraordinary Session, 27, 30, 63; Mississippi Senate Journal, 1978 Regular Session, 63, 487; Robert Shaw, "Finch: Solons Should Redistrict," *Jackson Daily News*, 2 June 1977.

Chapter 6. The Class of 1979 and the Second Generation of Black Political Power

1. Lamis, *The Two-Party South*.

2. Dent, *The Prodigal South Returns to Power*, 31–32; Witcover, *Marathon*, 446.

3. Rowland Evans and Robert Novak, "The Incompetency Factor," *Washington Post*, 31 July 1975, clipping in the John Stanley Pottinger Papers, Box 95, Folder 270, Gerald R. Ford Presidential Library, University of Michigan; Clarke Reed to J. Stanley Pottinger, 2 October 1970, J. Stanley Pottinger Files, Box 21, file 324N, Gerald R. Ford Presidential Library; Harold Himmelman to Robert Dempsey, 7 September 1973, J. Stanley Pottinger Papers, Box 68, Folder 144, Gerald R. Ford Presidential Library;

Lloyd N. Cutler to J. Stanley Pottinger, 12 June 1973, Box 68, Folder 144, Gerald R. Ford Presidential Library.

4. Witcover, *Marathon*, 446; Dent, *The Prodigal South Returns to Power*, 32; "Mississippi Republican Party 1976 Delegates and Alternate Delegates to the Republican National Convention Elected April 10, 1976," Harry Dent Papers, Box 26, Folder 560.

5. Witcover, Marathon, 449–50; Dent, *The Prodigal South Returns to Power*, 47, 53; James Young, "GOP Looks To Blacks," Undated newspaper clipping, Mississippi Republican Party Papers, Box J-18, Charles Pickering Folder.

6. Mounger and Maxwell, *Amidst the Fray*, 177–81, 218; Bill Minor, "GOP Factional Quarrel Deepens," *Times-Picayune* (New Orleans), 18 April 1976.

7. Mounger and Maxwell, *Amidst the Fray*, 170–71, 197, 199–200; Lott, *Herding Cats*, 68–70.

8. Bill Minor, "GOP Factional Quarrel Deepens," *Times-Picayune*, 18 April 1976; GEC to Richard Cheney, 26 June 1976, GEC Papers, General Political, Folder 201; Charles Pickering to GEC, GEC Papers, General Political, Folder 194; Cannon, *Governor Reagan*, 395, 429; Crespino, *In Search of Another Country*, 236.

9. Telephone interview with Gil Carmichael, 31 August 2006; James Young, "GOP Looks To Blacks," undated newspaper clipping, Mississippi Republican Party Papers, Box J-18, Charles Pickering Folder; Mounger and Maxwell, 223–25; Crespino, *In Search of Another Country*; Lassiter, *The Silent Majority*; Kruse, *White Flight*.

10. Mounger and Maxwell, *Amidst the Fray*, 233–36.

11. GEC to Leon Bramlett, 24 March 1976, GEC Papers, 1975 Campaign Correspondence, Folder 412.

12. "GOP leader blasts Bramlett," *Bolivar Commercial*, undated; Leon Bramlett form letter, GEC Papers, 1979 Campaign Correspondence, Folder 82; *Mississippi Official and Statistical Register, 1980–1984*, 505; Carmichael interview, 13 October 2004; Resume and working draft of Leon Bramlett statement, Mississippi Republican Party Papers, Box H-1, Biographies; Telephone interview with Gil Carmichael, 31 July 2006.

13. David W. Kubissa, "Coalition Splits Over Endorsement," *Clarion-Ledger*, 30 July 1979.

14. Elizabeth Fair, "League Supported By NAACP Group," *Commercial Appeal*, undated, clipping in Minor Papers, 1993 accession, Box 4, NAACP Folder; William Fuller, "United League To Mark Entrance Into Delta With Indianola Chapter," *Commercial Appeal*, 21 March 1979; Elizabeth Fair, "Tension Persists In Okolona As 250 Blacks Renew March," *Commercial Appeal*, 8 October 1978; "Rights Suit Is Sparked By Arrests," *Commercial Appeal*, 8 September 1978; "Pickets in Tupelo Continue Boycott," *Commercial Appeal*, 28 March 1978; Joseph Shapiro, "United League Leader Is Eying Primary Election Endorsements," *Commercial Appeal*, 16 April 1978; Koal Meuchy, "United League Marches In Canton," *Jackson Advocate*, 22 November 1978; Grisham, *Tupelo*, 152–55.

15. "Evers Vows To Run Or Back Carmichael," *Commercial Appeal*, 5 April 1979; Dusty Perkins, "Evers says he hasn't given-up running in this year's election," *Sentinel Star* (Grenada), 21 May 1979; David Bates, "Open primary could be reality for 1979 elections," *Clarion-Ledger*, 21 January 1979; Fred Banks, interview by author, 28 June 2005.

16. "Open Primary Law Rejected; Loss Of Black Advantage Cited," *Commercial Appeal*, 12 June 1979. Aaron Henry and other black leaders were also displeased with Finch. In October 1979, Henry, the Mississippi Conference of Black Mayors, and several black health organizations protested racial discrimination on the all-white Mississippi Health Care Commission, which disbursed federal funds for health care facilities in the state. "Blacks Seeking To Bypass All-White Health Care Commission," *Commercial Appeal*, 23 October 1979.

17. David W. Kubissa, "Coalition Splits Over Endorsement," *Clarion-Ledger*, 30 July 1979; *Mississippi Official and Statistical Register, 1972–76*, 54.

18. Bill Minor, "Charles Evers: Black Machiavelli?" *The Reporter* (Jackson), 22 July 1979; Gov. William Winter, interview by author, tape recording, 28 September 2004, Jackson, Mississippi; Mississippi Senate Journal, 1978 Regular Session, 63, 487. For the story on legislative reapportionment and the *Conner* cases, see chapter five.

19. Louis Hillary Park, "Black Voters May Split," *Bolivar Commercial*, 6 August 1979.

20. "Miss Evelyn Leads in Mississippi," *Newsweek*, 20 August 1979; Bill Minor, "Black voters show Evers not power broker," *Bolivar Commercial*, 17 August 1979; Dunbar Prewitt, Jr. in the *Reporter*, 20 September 1979.

21. "Evers Claims Discrepancies After Loss In Senate Race," *Northeast Mississippi Daily Journal*, 8 November 1979. In his 1997 biography, Evers made no mention of his backing of Eaves or of the 1979 governor's race.

22. *Mississippi Official and Statistical Register, 1980–1984*; GEC Papers, 1979 Campaign, Folder 261; "Carmichael Asks Black Support in Miss. Election," *New Orleans Times-Picayune*, 15 October 1979.

23. Dunbar Prewitt, Jr. in the *Reporter*, 20 September 1979; "Carmichael Says Fuel Crisis May End Busing," *Northeast Mississippi Daily Journal*, 20 July 1979; GEB Papers, 1979 Campaign, Folder 261; "Winter, Carmichael Outline Civil Rights Records To NAACP," *Northeast Mississippi Daily Journal*, 29 October 1979. Winter first hired a black lawyer in the 1980s, after he left public office. Winter interview, 28 September 2004.

24. "Blacks Back Carmichael," *McComb Enterprise Journal*, 3 October 1979; GEC Papers, 1979 campaign, Folder 8; "Winter, Carmichael Outline Civil Rights Records To NAACP," *Northeast Mississippi Daily Journal*, 29 October 1979; Cullen Clark, "Charles Evers opposing Winter," *The Reporter*, 18 October 1979.

25. Dunbar Prewitt, Jr., *The Reporter*, 20 September 1979; Deborah Lesure, "In Commemoration of a King," *Jackson Advocate*, 10–16 January 1980; Howard, *Men Like That*, 270.

26. David Bates, "Pickering ads claim Allain against blacks," *Clarion-Ledger*, 5 November 1979; David Bates, "Allain clings to 2 percent lead in attorney general election," *Clarion-Ledger*, 7 November 1979; *Mississippi Official and Statistical Register, 1980–1984*, 519.

27. Mounger and Maxwell, *Amidst the Fray*, 285–89; Carter, *From George Wallace to New Gingrich* and *The Politics of Rage*.

28. *Mississippi Official and Statistical Register, 1980–1984*, 47, 51, 517, 534

29. Wayne Weidie, "GOP Loses Ground in Municipal Elections," *The Carthaginian* (Carthage, Miss.) 7 July 1977; Winter interview, 28 September 2004; Telephone interview with Gil Carmichael, 31 August 2006; Wayne Weidie, "Don't Pack Your Bags Yet," *Copiah County Courier*, 15 August 1979.

30. "Evers Claims Discrepancies After Loss In Senate Race," *Northeast Mississippi Daily Journal*, 8 November 1979; Don Hoffman, "2 blacks, woman capture runoffs," *Clarion-Ledger*, 28 January 1979; Lynn Watkins, "Incumbent protests," *Clarion-Ledger*, 7 November 1979.

31. Parker, *Black Votes Count*, 126–27; Jo Ann Klein and David Kubissa, *Clarion-Ledger*, 7 November 1979; Peggy Elam, "Kirksey defeats two candidates to win race in Senate District 28," *Clarion-Ledger*, 7 November 1979; *Mississippi Official and Statistical Register, 1980–1984*, 540.

32. Parker, *Black Votes Count*, 156; Judy Putnam, "2 Hinds blacks win seats on Board of Supervisors," *Clarion-Ledger*, 7 November 1979; "Hinds elects black supervisors for the first time since Reconstruction," *Clarion-Ledger*, 7 November 1979; Fred Anklam, Jr., "Blacks Double seats in 1980 Legislature," *Clarion-Ledger*, 7 November 1979.

33. The three black sheriffs were the first elected but not appointed. In May 1979, the board of supervisors in Copiah County appointed Burnell Ramsey, the first and only black deputy in the Copiah County sheriff's department, as interim sheriff after the white sheriff resigned. The board appointed Ramsey when a black delegation requested it, but Ramsey did not run for the office. "Copiah County Appoints First Black Sheriff," *Jackson Advocate*, 6 June 1979; Bill Sumrall, "Guess resigns, Ramsey is sheriff," *The Meteor* (Crystal Springs), 23 May 1979.

34. "Blacks elected sheriffs," *Northeast Mississippi Daily Journal*, 8 November 1979.

35. "Claiborne voters elect first black sheriff," *Port Gibson Reveille*, 8 November 1979.

36. Elizabeth Fair, "Petition Asks Election Guards," *Commercial Appeal*, 27 July 1979; "Panel Status of Robinson Challenged," *Commercial Appeal*, 6 August 1979; Elizabeth Fair, "Note Casts Doubt On Robinson Role," *Commercial Appeal*, 31 July 1979.

37. Elizabeth Fair, 27 July 1979; advertisement for 'Flick' Ash for Chancery Clerk, *Marshall Messenger*, 18 July 1979; "Runoff Goes Quietly For Marshall County," *Commercial Appeal*, 29 August 1979.

38. William Fuller, "Robinson Suit Request Denied," *Commercial Appeal*, 20 August 1979; William Fuller, "Court Stops Robinson, Five Others From Acting As Committee Agents," *Commercial Appeal*, 21 August 1979; "League Chief Is Arrested On Ex-Wife's Complaint," *Commercial Appeal*, 23 August 1979; William Fuller, "Robinson Quits Democrat Post, Intends To Run As Independent," *Commercial Appeal*, 25 August 1979.

39. "Runoff Goes Quietly For Marshall County," *Commercial Appeal*, 29 August 1979.

40. William Fuller, "Surge of Independent Candidates Swells Marshall County Election," *Commercial Appeal*, 8 September 1979. Concerns over Bell's loyalties continued even after the election. In 1980, he refuted a *Commercial Appeal* report that he criticized the hiring of four white deputies in the county, and he denied allegations that he took orders from Robinson. "Bell denies hiring 'mistake,'" *South Reporter*, 8 January 1980.

41. William Fuller, "Blacks Claim Evidence Of Fraud In Uneventful Marshall Elections," *Commercial Appeal*, 7 November 1979; *Mississippi Official and Statistical Register, 1980–1984*, 246.

42. William Fuller, *Commercial Appeal*, 7 November 1979; "State Muslim leader killed in wreck," *Clarion-Ledger*, 19 December 1986; Bobby Harrison, "Civil rights activist dies in car wreck," *Northeast Mississippi Daily Journal*, 19 December 1986. Skip Robinson later became a minister in the Nation of Islam and died in a car wreck in Marshall County in 1986. *Clarion-Ledger*, 19 December 1986.

43. "Winter Accused Of Racism By Black Medical Group," *Commercial Appeal*, 13 March 1980; Tom Bailey, Jr., "Penson's Accepting Posts May Build Racial Bridge," *Commercial Appeal*, 30 April 1980; "Winter defends state appointment plans," *Commercial Appeal*, 3 May 1980; George Alexander Sewell and Margaret L. Dwight, *Mississippi Black History Makers*, 77, 94; Williamson, *Radicalizing the Ebony Tower*, 138.

44. Dittmer, *Local People*, 74; White, "The *Jackson Advocate*," 52–57, 111–12; Winter interview, 28 September 2004.

45. David Kubissa, "Special Dem panel to meet again on chairmanship issue," *Clarion-Ledger*, 4 May 1980; David Kubissa, "Democrats tap one chairman amid party rift," *Clarion-Ledger*, 11 May 1980.

46. David Kubissa, "Democrats tap one chairman amid party rift," *Clarion-Ledger*, 11 May 1980; "White Chairman Causes Rift in Mississippi Democratic Party," *Jackson Advocate*, 21 May 1980; David W. Kubissa, "Dems test reaction to squabble," *Clarion-Ledger*, 13 May 1980.

47. David Bates, "No apology: Winter explains his desire for white party head," *Clarion-Ledger*, 24 May 1980; "Mississippi's Democratic Party taking on a new look," *Clarion-Ledger*, 22 March 1980; "The Republican Victory," *Jackson Advocate*, 4 June 1980.

48. Cohodas, *And the Band Played Dixie*, 131, 153.

49. Politicus Jackson, "Come What May, We Are Here To Stay," *Jackson Advocate*, 23 July 1980; Ed Cole, interview by Betsy Nash, transcript, Jackson, Mississippi, 7 January 1991, Congressional and Political Research Center, Mississippi State University, 22; Winter interview, 28 September 2004; McLemore interview, 19 November 2004.

50. McLemore interview, 19 November 2004; "Black Caucus endorses Kirksey for Congress," *Clarion-Ledger*, 22 May 1980; *Mississippi Official and Statistical Register, 1980–1984*, 554–55; Johanna Neuman, "Singletary seeks funds in Washington," *Clarion-Ledger*, 23 September 1980; Cliff Treyens, "McLemore no newcomer to campaigning for office," *Clarion-Ledger*, 15 October 1980; Verlene Lee, "McLemore Announces 4th District Congressional Bid," *Jackson Advocate*, 9 July 1980; "Evan Doss Declines Race," *Jackson Advocate*, 30 July 1980; "Cleve McDowell, ETC," *Jackson Advocate*, 28 May 1980.

51. "Creating a Black Agenda," *Jackson Advocate*, 9 July 1980; Ivory Phillips, "Black Power Politics?" *Jackson Advocate*, 23 July 1980; Verlene Lee, "McLemore Opens Campaign Office," *Jackson Advocate*, 20 August 1980; "The McLemore Candidacy," *Jackson Advocate*, 1 October 1980; Winter interview, 28 September 2004.

52. Cliff Treyens, "McLemore to concentrate on 4 counties." *Clarion-Ledger*, 4 September 1980.

53. McLemore interview, 19 November 2004.

54. Cliff Treyens, *Clarion-Ledger*, 4 September 1980.

55. Cliff Treyens, "Hinson arrest specifics revealed; Singletary says honesty at issue," *Clarion-Ledger*, 18 October 1980; Cliff Treyens, "Hinson to support jobs bill," *Clarion-Ledger*, 20 September 1980. See Howard, *Men Like That*, chapter seven, for a detailed discussion of Hinson's homosexuality.

56. David W. Kubissa, "Hinson refuses to elaborate on arrest in TV debate," *Clarion-Ledger*, 7 October 1980; Cliff Treyens, "Singletary's compulsion: Unseat Hinson in the 4th," *Clarion-Ledger*, 14 October 1980; Cliff Treyens, "Moral Majority grills 4th District hopefuls, hears Hinson privately," *Clarion-Ledger*, 9 October 1980; Cliff Treyens, *Clarion-Ledger*, 15 October 1980.

57. Lamis, *The Two-Party-South*, 57–58; *Mississippi Official and Statistical Register 1980–1984*, 565.

58. Jo Ann Klein, "State GOP leadership remains intact," *Clarion-Ledger*, 11 May 1980; Jo Ann Klein, "GOP conservatives, moderates, expected to battle," *Clarion-Ledger*, 8 May 1980.

59. Jo Ann Klein, "GOP: Winter building patronage machine," *Clarion-Ledger*, 21 May 1980; Gene Monteith, "Blacks hope to build GOP state strength," *Clarion-Ledger*, 27 September 1980.

60. Cannon, *Governor Reagan*, 477–78; Lott, *Herding Cats*, 253; Bates, "The Reagan Rhetoric," 23–25, 28–30; Marable, *Race, Reform, and Rebellion*, 167–70. Cochran later called his opposition to the Neshoba speech "wrong," given the "great success" of the visit. Bates, 37.

61. David Mould, "Black Group Urges More GOP Support," *Commercial Appeal*, 27 September 1980; Gene Monteith, *Clarion-Ledger*, 27 September 1980; Tom Bailey, Jr., "Black Students Get Double Pitch For Reagan," *Commercial Appeal*, 19 February 1981; "Blacks Back Carmichael," *McComb Enterprise Journal*, 3 October 1979; Jo Ann Klein, "GOP Sale," *Clarion-Ledger*, 28 August 1978.

62. Mounger and Maxwell, *Amidst the Fray*, 262–63, 375; Lassiter, *The Silent Majority*, 14; Crespino, *In Search of Another Country*, 8.

63. Nash and Taggart, *Mississippi Politics*, 198; Black and Black, *The Rise of Southern Republicans*, 4.

64. James Young, "Political Career Of Black 'Symbol of Hope' Folds," *Commercial Appeal*, 14 May 1981.

65. In Mississippi, urban areas are defined as municipalities 10,000 or more in population. Parker, *Black Votes Count*, 143.

66. *Mississippi Official and Statistical Register 1980–1984*, 47, 51, 63–86 *passim*.

67. Ibid.

68. Parker, *Black Votes Count*, 142–43; Clark interview, 53; Winter interview, 28 September 2004; Clark interview, 23 July 2005.

69. Otis L. Sanford, "Rep. Banks: Lack Of State-Hired Blacks Due To Bias," *Clarion-Ledger*, 6 August 1976; Fred Banks, interview by author, 28 June 2005.

70. In the nation, 51.2 percent of elected black women were in the South. *National Roster of Black Elected Officials*, vol. 9, xxii.

71. *Ibid*, xxi, 128–39; *National Roster of Black Elected Officials*, vol. 6, xlix; Parker, *Black Votes Count*, 142–43.

72. See Robinson, *The Montgomery Bus Boycott and the Women Who Started It*; and Robnett, *How Long? How Long?*

73. Payne, *I've Got the Light of Freedom*, 302–6; Rosen, *The World Split Open*, 104–5; Williamson, *Radicalizing the Ebony Tower*, 138.

74. R.W. Apple, Jr., "Republican Courts Mississippi Blacks," *New York Times*, 18 August 1975.

75. "Democrats Sponsor Reception June 16 For Senator Eastland," *Lexington Advertiser*, 7 June 1979. In the late 1970s, women held fewer than ten elected offices in Holmes County, including municipal offices. *Mississippi Official and Statistical Register, 1976–1980*, 198, 256–74 *passim*.

76. "Women Have Increasingly Large Role In Mississippi Government," *Clarion-Ledger*, 4 June 1962; Jo Ann Klein, "Black candidates did well at polls, but women got skunked," *Clarion-Ledger*, 8 November 1979; "First black woman takes seat in House," *Northeast Mississippi Daily Journal*, 21 March 1985.

77. "Women Have Increasingly Large Role In Mississippi Government," *Clarion-Ledger*, 4 June 1962; Rosen, *The World Split Open*, 292–94; http://www.equalrights-amendment.org/era.htm; Telephone interview with Gil Carmichael, 31 August 2006.

78. Otis Sanford, "Kirksey Says Race Issue Important In Campaign," *Clarion-Ledger*, 29 August 1975; *Kirksey v. Board of Supervisors of Hinds County, Mississippi*, 554 F.2d 139 (1977). For more on this case, see chapter eight.

79. Gandy was not the first woman to run for governor. In 1951, Mary Cain, the archconservative editor of the *Summit Sun*, became the first woman in the state's history to try to win the office but placed fifth in a field of eight candidates. Crespino, "Strategic Accommodation," 140; *Mississippi Official and Statistical Register 1952*, 358.

80. Mississippi Official and Statistical Register, 1972–1976, 30; Wayne Weidie, "Being A Woman Lost The Race," *Itawamba County News* (Fulton), 6 September 1979.

81. "Gandy and Allain head into Aug. 23 showdown," *Bolivar Commercial*, 3 August 1983; "Election," *Bolivar Commercial*, 2 August 1983; "Gandy: Is Her Experience Enough?" *Jackson Advocate*, 22 June 1983; Bill Minor, "The new Evelyn Gandy talks tough, could win," undated newspaper clipping, Wilson F. Minor Papers, 1993 Accession, Box Three, Evelyn Gandy Gubernatorial Folder.

82. Bill Minor, "Eyes On Governor-Elect," *Lexington Advertiser*, 17 November 1983.

83. Morrison, *Black Political Mobilization*, 75–77.

84. Bill Minor, "Eyes On Mississippi," *Lexington Advertiser*, 26 January 1984; "Holmes Electors Will Vote For Local Officials On Tuesday, November 7th," *Lexington Advertiser*, 5 October 1972; "McGovern-Eastland Win In Holmes County," *Lexington Advertiser*, 9 November 1972; Eddie James Carthan for Mayor advertisement, *Lexington Advertiser*, 2 June 1977; Danny Davis, "Flippins wins in Shaw; Gray re-elected in Shelby," *Bolivar Commercial*, 8 June 1977.

85. Louis Hillary Park, "Blacks unaware, unconcerned with CGG's political power," *Bolivar Commercial*, 27 July 1979; Louis Hillary Park, "CGG opens membership doors," *Bolivar Commercial*, 27 July 1979; "Flippins Removal Remains in Doubt," *Jackson Advocate*, 6 December 1978; "Black Mayor Ousted From Port Commission Position," *Jackson Advocate*, 6 June 1979; Danny Davis, "Shelby mayor won't support group," *Bolivar Commercial*, 18 November 1979; "Tchula Town Officials Seek Solution For Problems," *Lexington Advertiser*, 12 July 1979; "Tchula Citizens Trying To 'Get Their Town Back,'" *Lexington Advertiser*, 15 November 1979.

86. See chapter nine for Carthan's 1982 murder trial and its effect on the 1982 Delta congressional race.

87. Parker, *Black Votes Count*, 131, 226n2, 134–35; Stephen D. Shaffer, "Public Opinion and Interest Groups," in Krane and Shaffer, eds., *Mississippi Government & Politics*; Robert Clark, interview by Betsy Nash, transcript, Jackson, Mississippi, 18 February 1991, Congressional and Political Research Center, Mississippi State University, 48–55; Winter interview, 28 September 2004; Blackwell and Morris, *Barefootin'*, 233–35.

Chapter 7. Lead into Gold?

1. Parker, "County Studies In Mississippi," 393–94.

2. *Ibid*, 399–400, 402–5; Lawson, *In Pursuit of Power*, 133, 160–61.

3. *Howard v. Adams County Board of Supervisors*, 453 F.2d 455 (1972); Frank Parker, *Black Votes Count*, 153.

4. *Moore v. Leflore County Board of Election Commissioners*, 361 F. Supp. 603 (1972); Landon, *The Honor and Dignity of the Profession*, 123, 172.

5. *Moore v. Leflore County Board of Election Commissioners*, 361 F. Supp. 609 (1973), 502 F.2d 621 (1974).

6. Patrick Larkin, "Hinds Remap Appeal Denied," *Clarion-Ledger*, 29 November 1977; *Kirksey v. Board of Supervisors of Hinds County, Mississippi*, 528 F.2nd 536 (1976); Parker, *Black Votes Count*, 153–54.

7. *Kirksey v. Board of Supervisors of Hinds County, Mississippi*, 402 F. Supp. 658 (1975); McMillen, *Dark Journey*, 270; Keady, *All Rise*, 224.

8. *Kirksey v. Board of Supervisors of Hinds County, Mississippi* (1975); Parker, *Black Votes Count*, 154.

9. *Kirksey v. Hinds County Board of Supervisors*, Mississippi, 528 F.2d 536 (1976); Lawson, *In Pursuit of Power*, 220; Mayer, *Running on Race*, 125. For Ford's handling of the Voting Rights Act extension and the battle over it, see Lawson, *In Pursuit of Power*, 224–53.

10. *Kirksey v. Hinds County Board of Supervisors, Mississippi*, 528 F.2d 536 (1976); Barrow and Walker, *A Court Divided*, 169.

11. A rehearing of the full court, in this case the entire fifteen-member Fifth Circuit Court of Appeals.

12. *United Jewish Organizations v. Carey*, 430 U.S. 144 (1977).

13. *Kirksey v. Hinds County Board of Supervisors*, 554 F.2d 139 (1977); Parker, *Black Votes Count*, 155; Barrow and Walker, *A Court Divided*, 135; Bass, *Unlikely Heroes*, 304.

14. *Kirksey v. Hinds County Board of Supervisors*, 554 F.2d 139 (1977); Barrow and Walker, *A Court Divided*, 182.

15. "State, Hinds Reapportionment Plans Rejected," *Clarion-Ledger*, 1 June 1977; Patrick Larkin, "Hinds Remap Appeal Denied," *Clarion-Ledger*, 28 November 1977; Parker, *Black Votes Count*, 156. See chapter six for details of the 1979 Hinds County elections.

16. Parker, *Black Votes Count*, 157; *National Roster of Black Elected Officials*, Vol. 12, 154–55.

17. Wolters, *Right Turn*, 46–48.

18. *Ibid*, 63–64.

19. Lawson, *In Pursuit of Power*, 290–91; Bob Kyer, "Bolivar Remap Rejected," *Delta Democrat-Times*, 15 June 1983; Jane Egger, "Jackson pushes in Delta," *Delta Democrat-Times*, 5 June 1983; "Dual Registration Should Go," *Delta Democrat-Times*, 7 June 1983; Rachel Brown, "Jackson visits Cleveland, urges blacks to vote," *Bolivar Commercial*, 1 August 1983.

20. "Civil-Rights 'Iceman' or Idealist?" *U.S. News & World Report*, 17 June 1985; "Reynolds's Inquisition," *National Review*, 12 July 1985; Michael S. Serrill, "Uncivil Times at 'Justless,'" *Time*, 13 May 1985; "A Public Disagreement About The Pursuit Of Equality," *Black Enterprise*, January 1982; David M. Alpern, Ann McDaniel and Margaret Garrard Warner, "A Roadblock for Reynolds," *Newsweek*, 8 July 1985.

21. "Civil rights lawyer investigates voting charges," Delta Democrat-Times, 14 June 1983; "Registrars coming to Delta to sign voters," *Delta Democrat-Times*, 16 June 1983; "Reynolds Takes a Ride In the 'Justice Buggy'" *Newsweek*, 27 June 1983; Sandra Camphor, "Blacks' voting rights complaints heard," *Delta Democrat-Times*, 15 June 1983; Sandra Camphor, "Blacks tell justice official of problems," *Delta Democrat-Times*, 15 June 1983.

22. Camphor, "Blacks' voting rights complaints heard," 15 June 1983; *Newsweek*, 27 June 1983; "Registrars coming to Delta to sign voters," *Delta Democrat-Times*, 16 June 1983; Lawson, *In Pursuit of Power*, 288–89; Phone conversation with William Bradford Reynolds, 14 August 2006. The counties were Humphreys, Leflore, Madison, Quitman, and Sunflower. "Franklin says Justice visit unfairly convicts state," *Delta Democrat-Times*, 17 June 1983.

23. For more on the creation of the second district and Franklin's election in 1982, see chapter nine.

24. "Franklin says Justice visit unfairly convicts state," *Delta Democrat-Times*, 17 June 1983; "Blacks hope registrars will help voter turnout," *Delta Democrat-Times*, 19 June 1983; Phone conversation with William Bradford Reynolds, 14 August 2006.

25. *Newsweek*, 27 June 1983; Wolters, *Right Turn*, 70, 90–91; "Remarks at a Mississippi Republican Party Fundraiser Dinner in Jackson, June 20, 1983," Public Papers of the President: Ronald Reagan, 1981–1988, The Ronald Reagan Library, http://www.reagan.utexas.edu/resource/speeches/1983/62083b.htm.

26. "Oktibbeha redistrict plan is turned down," *Delta* Democrat-Times, 22 June 1983. The eight counties were Benton, Grenada, Holmes, Noxubee, Quitman, Tallahatchie, and Tunica. "Feds to watch Bolivar voting," *Delta Democrat-Times*, 1 August

1983; "No serious problems seen by poll watchers," *Delta Democrat-Times*, 4 August 1983; Rachel Brown, "Jackson visits Cleveland, urges blacks to vote," *Bolivar Commercial*, 1 August 1983; "Voter drives pushed," *Clarksdale Press Register*, 1 August 1983.

27. Parker, *Black Votes Count*, 157–58; "No serious problems seen by poll watchers," *Delta Democrat-Times*, 4 August 1983; "Franklin blasts federal agency over confusion," *Delta Democrat-Times*, 2 August 1983; *National Roster of Black Elected Officials*, Vol. 12, 153–54; *National Roster of Black Elected Officials*, 15th ed., 229–31.

28. Cobb, *The Most Southern Place on Earth*, 273.

29. National Roster of Black Elected Officials, 15th ed., 229–31. The seven heavily black counties with no black supervisors were Sunflower, Washington, Carroll, Tallahatchie, Panola, Kemper and Sharkey.

30. Art Harris, "In Mississippi County, Blacks Dissect the Failure of a 'Revolution,'" *Washington Post*, 18 August 1983.

31. *Ibid.*

32. Marable, *Race, Reform, and Rebellion*, 182–84.

33. Mayer, *Running on Race*, 194; Thernstrom, *Whose Votes Count?*, 234.

34. Mayer, *Running on Race*, 194.

35. Parker, *Black Votes Count*, 207–9.

36. Phone conversation with William Bradford Reynolds, 14 August 2006.

37. David M. Alpern, Ann McDaniel and Margaret Garrard Warner, "A Roadblock for Reynolds," *Newsweek*, 8 July 1985; "Reynolds Wrap," *National Review*, 26 July 1985; George F. Will, "Battling the Racial Spoils System," *Newsweek*, 10 June 1985; Colleen O'Conner and Ann McDaniel, "The President's Angry Apostle," *Newsweek*, 6 October 1986. Much of the historical omission of Reynolds's Mississippi visit has carried over to historiography on Reagan's civil rights policies. One exception and defense of Reynolds is by the legal historian Raymond Wolters in his book *Right Turn*.

38. *Kirksey v. Hinds County Board of Supervisors*, 554 F.2d 139 (1977).

Chapter 8. City Wards and Jacksonian Democracy

1. Rice, *Progressive Cities*, 3–18.

2. Kirby, *Darkness at the Dawning*, 49; Rice, *Progressive Cities*, 32, 118; Parker, *Black Votes Count*, 160–61.

3. Parker, *Black Votes Count*, 161. Such disfranchisement measures also existed outside the South in the 1960s and were aimed at curtailing black politics. In 1962, for example, one Michigan municipality adopted at-large elections to eliminate a politically outspoken black city alderman. Patterson, *Black City Politics*, 70–71.

4. Parker, Colby, and Morrison, "Mississippi," in *Quiet Revolution in the South*, 139–140.

5. *Stewart v. Waller*, 404 F. Supp. 206 (1975), 211–12; Parker, *Black Votes Count*, 161.

6. *Stewart v. Waller* (1975), 213–14.

7. *Ibid*, 214–15.

8. *Ibid*, 217–220; Parker, *Black Votes Count*, 161.

9. Parker, *Black Votes Count*, 162; Parker, Colby and Morrison, *Quiet Revolution in the South*, 141.

10. Billy Skelton, "Voters Balloting Today On Bonds, City Officials," *Clarion-Ledger*, 13 May 1969; "A Mississippi First: Black Judge Serves on State Supreme Court," *Ebony*, February 1986, 37, 39; Billy Skelton, "Municipalities Vote For Officials Today," *Clarion-Ledger*, 8 May 1973; "Russell Davis Gets Big In Race For Mayor," *Clarion-Ledger*, 6 June 1973.

11. The other ten cities were Amory, Bay St. Louis, Biloxi, Charleston, Clarksdale, Greenwood, Gulfport, Hattiesburg, Laurel, and Pascagoula. *Stewart v. Waller* (1973), 212.

12. "Group Begins Petition Drive For Mayor-Council In Jackson," *Clarion-Ledger*, 7 August 1976.

13. *Kirksey v. City of Jackson*, 506 F. Supp. 491 (1981), 511–12; "Group Begins Petition Drive For Mayor-Council In Jackson," *Clarion-Ledger*, 7 August 1976; Cliff Treyens, "Panel discusses changing city government," *Clarion-Ledger*, 20 May 1980.

14. *Kirksey v. City of Jackson*, 506 F. Supp. 491 (1981), 512–13.

15. Reply Brief for Appellants, *Kirksey v. City of Jackson* (1978), U.S. Court of Appeals for the Fifth Circuit, No. 78–3294, Appendix A, 1–10.

16. *Ibid*; Robert Paynter, "Jackson Retains Commission Government," *Clarion-Ledger*, 23 February 1977; "Commission Or Council For Jackson?" *Clarion-Ledger*, 22 February 1977; Lawson, *In Pursuit of Power*, 220–22; "Blacks endorse Mayor-Council Plan for Jackson," *Clarion-Ledger*, 15 July 1976; Fred Banks, interview by author, 28 June 2005; Supplemental Brief for Appellant, *Kirksey v. City of Jackson* (1978), U.S. Court of Appeals for the Fifth Circuit, No. 78–3294, 9; *Kirksey v. City of Jackson* (1981), 512. The Mobile case was *City of Mobile v. Bolden*, 446 U.S. 55 (1980), which the Supreme Court decided in Mobile's favor in 1980 and reversed earlier court rulings against the commission system. Lawson, *In Pursuit of Power*, 276–77.

17. Brief for Appellants, *Kirksey v. City of Jackson* (1981), U.S. Court of Appeals for the Fifth Circuit, No. 81–4058, 15–17, 20–21.

18. Robert Paynter, "Jackson Retains Commission Government," *Clarion-Ledger*, 23 February 1977; Cliff Treyens, "Panel discusses changing city government," *Clarion-Ledger*, 20 May 1980.

19. "Parker, Kirksey Plan Reapportionment Challenge," *Clarion-Ledger*, 24 February 1977; *Kirksey v. City of Jackson, Mississippi*, 461 F. Supp. 1282 (1978); Joe Logan, "Resolutions Eye Jackson's Form of Government," *Clarion-Ledger*, 25 February 1977.

20. *Kirksey v. City of Jackson*, 461 F. Supp. 1282 (1978), 1285; 552 F.2d 156 (Fifth Circuit, 1977); Steve Cannizaro, "Suit Says Commission Form Excludes Blacks From Office," *Clarion-Ledger*, 11 March 1977; Lee Ann Taylor, "Voters Choose Mayor Today," *Clarion-Ledger*, 7 June 1977; Steve Cannizaro, "Judge Gives Go-Ahead To Jackson Elections," *Clarion-Ledger*, 1 April 1977; Lee Ann Taylor, "Davis Collects More Money Than Others," *Clarion-Ledger*, 10 May 1977; Lee Ann Taylor, "Danks Upsets Davis In Primary," *Clarion-Ledger*, 11 May 1977.

21. Tim O'Neill, "Major Mayors' Races Appear Close," *Clarion-Ledger*, 5 June 1977; "Russell Davis Gets Big In Race For Mayor," *Clarion-Ledger*, 6 June 1973; "Danks Upsets Davis In Primary," *Clarion-Ledger*, 11 May 1977.

22. Lee Ann Taylor, "Voters Choose Mayor Today," *Clarion-Ledger*, 7 June 1977; Lee Ann Taylor, "City Rule Said To Dilute Black Vote," *Clarion-Ledger*, 7 July 1977; James Young, "GOP Looks To Blacks," Undated newspaper clipping, Mississippi Republican Party Papers, Box J-18, Charles Pickering Folder.

23. "The District, County, and Precinct Coordinated Approach to the Recruitment of Black Voters for Thad Cochran in the U.S. Senate Race," GEC Papers, General Political, Folder 215.

24. Lee Ann Taylor, "City Rule Said To Dilute Black Vote," *Clarion-Ledger*, 7 July 1977.

25. *Ibid*; *Kirksey v. City of Jackson* (1978), 1289–90; Brief for Appellees, *Kirksey v. City of Jackson* (1978), U.S. Court of Appeals for the Fifth Circuit, No. 78–3294, 61.

26. *Kirksey v. City of Jackson* (1978), 1299; Lee Ann Taylor, "Witness: City Short-changes Blacks," *Clarion-Ledger*, 8 July 1977; Brief for Appellants, *Kirksey v. City of Jackson* (1978), U.S. Court of Appeals for the Fifth Circuit, No. 78–3294, 45–46; Lee Ann Taylor, "City Witnesses Testify Blacks Get Services," *Clarion-Ledger*, 9 July 1977.

27. *Kirksey v. City of Jackson* (1978), 1286–90; Parker, *Black Votes Count*, 173.

28. *Kirksey v. City of Jackson*, 1286–87, 1289, 1292–96.

29. *Ibid*, 1296–1313.

30. Brief for Appellants, *Kirksey v. City of Jackson* (1978), U.S. Court of Appeals for the Fifth Circuit, No. 78–3294, 7–9, 15–18, 24–25, 27–28.

31. Brief for Appellees, *Kirksey v. City of Jackson* (1978), U.S. Court of Appeals for the Fifth Circuit, No. 78–3294, 6, 12, 14–16.

32. *Ibid*, 35–36., 38–59, 71; Parker, *Black Votes Count*, 207–9.

33. Reply Brief for Appellants, *Kirksey v. City of Jackson* (1978), U.S. Court of Appeals for the Fifth Circuit, No. 78–3294, 4.

34. Lawson, *In Pursuit of Power*, 276–77.

35. *Ibid*, 277–79; *Kirksey v. City of Jackson*, 625 F.2d 21 (1980); Cliff Treyens, "City's polling to be heard by U.S. panel," *Clarion-Ledger*, 14 August 1980; Cliff Treyens, "City, Parker ask U.S. court to settle suit," *Clarion-Ledger*, 8 May 1980; Cliff Treyens, "Panel discusses changing city government," *Clarion-Ledger*, 20 May 1980; Brian Williams, "City witness: race not an issue," *Clarion-Ledger*, 30 October 1980.

36. Brian Williams, "Blacks ready 2nd challenge to government," *Clarion-Ledger*, 27 October 1980.

37. Brian Williams, "Expert: 'Confusion' swayed form-of-government vote," *Clarion-Ledger*, 31 October 1980; Brian Williams, "2 claim city's form of government is racist," *Clarion-Ledger*, 27 October 1980.

38. Brian Williams, "Race always was an issue, Kirksey says," *Clarion-Ledger*, 29 October 1980.

39. *Ibid*.

40. *Ibid*; Brian Williams, "Expert: 'Confusion' swayed form-of-government vote," *Clarion-Ledger*, 31 October 1980.

41. Brian Williams, "City witness: Race not an issue," *Clarion-Ledger*, 30 October 1980.

42. Brian Williams, "Expert: 'Confusion' swayed form-of-government vote," *Clarion-Ledger*, 31 October 1980.

43. *Kirksey v. City of Jackson* (1981), 497, 501–2.

44. *Ibid*, 504–8, 511–18.

45. Goldfield, *Black, White, and Southern*, 197.

46. Brian Williams, "Black voters may try to stop city elections," *Clarion-Ledger*, 24 January 1981.

47. *Ibid*; Brian Williams, "Justice Department to allow Jackson city elections," *Clarion-Ledger*, 9 May 1981.

48. Brief for the United States as Amicus Curiae, *Kirksey v. City of Jackson* (1981), U.S. Court of Appeals for the Fifth Circuit, No. 81–4058, 9–14, 21; "U.S. joins in challenge by Mobile blacks," *Clarion-Ledger*, 9 May 1981.

49. Brian Williams, "Issue deflates for Tuesday election," *Clarion-Ledger*, 10 May 1981.

50. Brian Williams, "GOP on the center stage for primary Tuesday," *Clarion-Ledger*, 11 May 1981; Eric Stringfellow, "Porter, Watson rally troops for Tuesday's council election," *Clarion-Ledger*, 13 February 1984.

51. Brian Williams, "Shanks gets GOP nod to face Danks," *Clarion-Ledger*, 13 May 1981; Cliff Treyens, "Shirley Watson wins surprisingly," *Clarion-Ledger*, 13 May 1981; Brian Williams, "Poll watchers to be out in force for Jackson election," *Clarion-Ledger*, 1 June 1981; Cliff Treyens, "Jesse Jackson aims to re-enact Voting Rights Act," *Clarion-Ledger*, 1 June 1981; James Anderson and Aaron Shirley to Frank Bluntson, 18 May 1981, William F. Minor Papers, Box 80, 1981 Jackson Mayor Election Folder.

52. Brian Williams, "Danks, Cochran return to seats easily," *Clarion-Ledger*, 3 June 1981; Gene Monteith, "2 blacks elected in Columbus," *Clarion-Ledger*, 3 June 1981.

53. Brian Williams, *Clarion-Ledger*, 4 June 1981; Brief for appellants, *Kirksey v. City of Jackson* (1981), U.S. Court of Appeals for the Fifth Circuit, no. 81–4058.

54. Ted Cilwick, "Ruling jolts Kirksey suit," *Clarion-Ledger*, 12 December 1981; *Kirksey v. City of Jackson*, 663 F.2d 659 (1981); Barrow and Walker, *A Court Divided*, 226.

55. Wolters, *Right Turn*, 46–48.

56. *Kirksey v. Danks*, 608 F. Supp. 1448, 1451 (D.C. Miss. 1985); Martin Zimmerman, "City Council may seek referendum on form of government," *Clarion-Ledger*, 9 February 1983.

57. Eric Stringfellow, "Porter, Watson rally troops for Tuesday's council election," *Clarion-Ledger*, 13 February 1984; Martin Zimmerman, "Clear skies favor election today," *Clarion-Ledger*, 14 February 1984; Martin Zimmerman, "Porter wins council seat in a breeze," *Clarion-Ledger*, 15 February 1984; Martin Zimmerman and Eric Stringfellow, "Watson says election defeat won't curtail black activism," *Clarion-Ledger*, 16 February 1984; Joe Atkins, "Watson's defeat may aid push for new form of city government," *Clarion-Ledger*, 19 February 1984.

58. Joe Atkins, "Watson's defeat may aid push for new form of city government," *Clarion-Ledger*, 19 February 1984; Martin Zimmerman, "Danks names panel to study change in form of government," *Clarion-Ledger*, 21 February 1984; Martin Zimmerman, "City panel endorses strong mayor/council," *Clarion-Ledger*, 23 March 1984.

59. Martin Zimmerman, "Kirksey asks judge to block referendum," *Clarion-Ledger*, 16 August 1984; Eric Stringfellow, "City voters may decide revamp issue," *Clarion-Ledger*, 2 September 1984; "Jackson's future," *Clarion-Ledger*, 30 August 1984.

60. *Kirksey v. Danks* (1981), 1452; Eric Stringfellow, "City approves government change," *Clarion-Ledger*, 5 September 1984.

61. *Kirksey v. Danks* (1981), 1460; "State voters tripped up by ward-system primary," *Clarion-Ledger*, 15 May 1985; Eric Stringfellow, "Commissioner Porter loses Ward 1 runoff," *Clarion-Ledger*, 22 May 1985; John Williams, "Johnson and Watson await word on who faces Armstrong in runoff," *Clarion-Ledger*, 15 May 1985.

62. Eric Stringfellow, "Jackson city races see blacks, women, elected," *Clarion-Ledger*, 5 June 1985; "Blacks plan series of lawsuits challenging at-large elections," *Clarion-Ledger*, 1 May 1985.

63. Eric Stringfellow, "Ward system begins as city goes to polls," *Clarion-Ledger*, 14 May 1985; *Mississippi Official and Statistical Register, 1984–1988*, 267, 278.

Chapter 9. The Delta District and the Continuing Politics of Race

1. Cobb, *The Most Southern Place on Earth*, vii, 3, 5, 30, 96–97.

2. *Ibid*, 154–55; McMillen, *Dark Journey*, 230–32; McLemore, "The Mississippi Freedom Democratic Party," 378–79.

3. Parker, *Black Votes Count*, 41, 43, 45; Cobb, *The Most Southern Place on Earth*, 227; Moye, *Let the People Decide*, 59; Wharton, *The Negro in Mississippi*, 162; Mitchell, *Mississippi Liberal*, 79, 131.

4. Mitchell, *Mississippi Liberal*, 152; Parker, *Black Votes Count*, 43–45; Cobb, *The Most Southern Place on Earth*, 235. For an account of the 1962 Smith-Whitten race, see Mitchell, *Mississippi Liberal*, 154–67.

5. *Conner v. Johnson* 256 F. Supp. 962 (1966); W.C. Shoemaker, "Negro Suit Hits State Apportionment," *Jackson Daily News*, 19 October 1965; Parker, 87.

6. Parker, *Black Votes Count*, 43, 45–48, 51.

7. *Ibid*, 44–46, 49–50, 87, 89, 107; "Federal Panel Upholds State Congressional Redistricting," *Clarion-Ledger*, 1 October 1966.

8. Parker, *Black Votes Count*, 90.

9. *National Roster of Black Elected Officials*, Vol. 10, 50–51, 98–100, 145–46, 158, 193–94.

10. *Ibid*, 27, 84, 123, 233, 244–45, 249–50.

11. "Groups endorse a 'Delta District' at state reapportionment hearing," *Clarion-Ledger*, 4 June 1981; "Black Majority District Proposed," *Jackson Advocate*, 4 June 1981.

12. "State lawmaker sees gerrymandering in black district plan," *Bolivar Commercial*, 7 July 1981.

13. *Ibid*; Cobb, *The Most Southern Place on Earth*, 259–61; "Legislative panel will try to maintain present structure of state's congressional districts," *Bolivar Commercial*, 14 July 1981; Parker, 91; "Remap Plan Spurs Protest From Blacks," *Commercial Appeal*, 13 August 1981; Cliff Treyens, "Panel OKs redistricting with least changes," *Clarion-Ledger*, 14 August 1981.

14. "Remap Plan Spurs Protest From Blacks," *Commercial Appeal*, 13 August 1981; Cliff Treyens, "Panel OKs redistricting with least changes," *Clarion-Ledger*, 14 August 1981; "Black legislators To Fight Remap Plan," *Commercial Appeal*, 23 August 1981.

15. Raymond E. Yancey, "Justice Objects!!!" *Jackson Advocate*, April 1–7, 1982; "Lawyer To Fight 'Discriminatory' Redistricting Plan," *Tupelo Daily Journal*, 14 April 1982.

16. "Lawyer To Fight 'Discriminatory' Redistricting Plan," *Tupelo Daily Journal*, 14 April 1982; *Jordan v. Winter*, 541 F. Supp. 1135 (1982); "State asks for June primary to be delayed," *Bolivar Commercial*, 23 April 1982; "Redistricting 'Fallout' Continues," *Jackson Advocate*, 29 April–5 May 1982.

17. Art Harris, "Blacks, Unlikely Allies Battle Miss. Redistricting," *Washington Post*, 1 June 1982; Bill Minor, "GOP could profit from redistricting battle," *Bolivar Commercial*, 22 April 1982; *Jordan v. Winter* (1982), 1141.

18. *Jordan v. Winter* (1982), 1144; Parker, "The Mississippi Congressional Redistricting Case," *Howard Law Journal*, 405–7.

19. The six counties were Carroll, Montgomery, Webster, Choctaw, Attala, and Leake.

20. Parker, "The Mississippi Congressional Redistricting Case," 401, 406; *Jordan v. Winter* (1982), 1144–45; "Blacks To Appeal Redistrict Ruling," Commercial Appeal, 12 June 1982; Reginald Stuart, "U.S. Judges Impose Mississippi Redistricting Plan," *New York Times*, 10 June 1982; "Appeal Will Be Resumed," *Commercial Dispatch* (Columbus, Miss.), 10 June 1982; Cliff Treyens and Johanna Neuman, "High court avoids appeal, clears way for elections," *Clarion-Ledger*, 22 June 1982; "State To Stop Defending Redistricting Plan," *Starkville Daily News*, 5 April 1983.

21. *Mississippi Official and Statistical Register, 1984–1988*, 209; Lamis, *The Two-Party South*, 58; Bill Minor, "Reagan's man in Miss. ambushed," *Philadelphia Inquirer*, 30 July 1981.

22. Lamis, *The Two-Party South*, 58; "Democrat Dowdy takes victory," *Bolivar Commercial*, 8 July 1981; William Winter, interview by Jeff Broadwater, transcript, Jackson, Miss., 21 May 1991, Congressional and Political Research Center, Mississippi State University.

23. Lawson, *In Pursuit of Power*, 287–88; Herbert H. Denton, "GOP fear of black backlash led to voting rights cave-in," *Clarion-Ledger*, 6 May 1982.

24. Cliff Treyens, "Stennis backs extension of Voting Rights Act," *Clarion-Ledger*, 26 May 1982.

25. Cliff Treyens, "Stennis backs extension of Voting Rights Act," *Clarion-Ledger*, 26 May 1982; Lawson, *In Pursuit of Power*, 287; *Congressional Record–Senate*, 25 June 1981, vol. 127, part 11, 14017; *Congressional Record–Senate*, 29 October 1981, vol. 127, part 20, 25930; Thad Cochran, interview by Jeff Broadwater, transcript, Washington, D.C., 13 November 1991, Congressional and Political Research Center, Mississippi State University; *Congressional Record–Senate*, 18 June 1982, vol. 128, part 11, 14282.

26. William Winter, interview by Jeff Broadwater, 21 May 1991, 24–26; Leslie McLemore, interview by Betsey Nash, transcript, Jackson, Miss., 19 April 1991, Congressional and Political Research Center, Mississippi State University, 74–75.

27. Lamis, *The Two-Party South*, 55–56; William Winter, interview by Jeff

Broadwater, 21 May 1991; Cliff Treyens, "Stennis backs extension of Voting Rights Act," *Clarion-Ledger*, 26 May 1982; Ed Cole, interview by Betsey Nash, transcript, Jackson, Miss., 7 January 1991, Congressional and Political Research Center, Mississippi State University, 23–25; Brian Williams, "Stennis' support of Voting Rights Act may get voters to polls for primary," *Clarion-Ledger*, 26 May 1982; *Mississippi Official and Statistical Register 1984–1988*, 398–99.

28. "Irony in Mississippi," *Commercial Appeal*, 21 June 1982; *Mississippi Official and Statistical Register, 1984–1988*, 207; Webb Franklin, interview by author, tape recording, Greenwood, Miss., 18 May 2005.

29. Neilson, *Even Mississippi*, 70.

30. Fred Anklam, Jr., "Black convention nominates Clark," *Clarion-Ledger*, undated clipping; Neilson, *Even Mississippi*, 70, 76; *Mississippi Official and Statistical Register, 1984–1988*, 397.

31. "Clark Takes 2nd District With Ease," *Jackson Advocate*, August 19–25, 1982; Neilson, *Even Mississippi*, 85; "Woodcutters Endorse Clark For Congress," *Jackson Advocate*, September 2–8, 1982; Sewell and Dwight, *Mississippi Black History Makers*, 82–83.

32. Neilson, *Even Mississippi*, 95–96; Webb Franklin, interview by author, 18 May 2005.

33. Webb Franklin, interview by author, 18 May 2005; Nielsen, 89; Adam Clymer, "Race Raised as an Issue in Mississippi House Contest," *New York Times*, 14 October 1982; Parker, *Black Votes Count*, 201.

34. Adam Clymer, "Race Raised as an Issue in Mississippi House Contest," *New York Times*, 14 October 1982; Webb Franklin, interview by author, 18 May 2005; Nielsen, *Even Mississippi*, 95.

35. Webb Franklin, interview by author, 18 May 2005.

36. Sewell and Dwight, *Mississippi Black History Makers*, 67–70; Nielsen, *Even Mississippi*, 99; Gail Hall, "National Committee Hosts Tchula 7 Rally," *Jackson Advocate*, July 29-August 4, 1982.

37. Neilson, *Even Mississippi*, 99, 107–8, 116–17. Carthan was eventually acquitted of murder, but he served a sentence in a federal penitentiary in Alabama for falsifying information used to obtain funds from a federally insured bank. Sewall and Dwight, *Mississippi Black History Makers*, 71; Alice Thomas, "Fourth District Supporters Say Clark is 'People's Candidate,'" *Jackson Advocate*, September 30-October 6, 1982.

38. Campbell, *Robert G. Clark's Journey to the House*, 95–97; Neilson, *Even Mississippi*, 87.

39. Neilson, *Even Mississippi*, 117, 119; *Mississippi Official and Statistical Register, 1984–1988*, 400.

40. Charles Tisdale, "Race Still An Issue," *Jackson Advocate*, November 4–10, 1982; Sewall and Dwight, *Mississippi Black History Makers*, 83.

41. "State To Stop Defending Redistricting Plan," *Starkville Daily News*, 5 April 1983; Sewall and Dwight, 83; *Brooks v. Winter*, 461 U.S. 921 (1983); Tony Tharp, "Testimony in remap suit under way," *Clarion-Ledger*, 20 December 1983; Neilson, *Even Mississippi*, 133–34.

42. Cliff Treyens, "Judges finalize congressional districts," *Clarion-Ledger*, 8 January 1984; *Jordan v. Winter*, 604 F. Supp. 801 (1984), 818–19.

43. Lamis, *The Two-Party South*, 60. For a detailed study of the allegations against Allain during the 1983 gubernatorial race, see Howard, *Men Like That*, 278–98.

44. *Mississippi Official and Statistical Register, 1984–1988*, 450–60; Lamis, *The Two-Party South*, 61.

45. *Mississippi Official and Statistical Register, 1984–1988*, 134; Tom Oppel, "Defections threaten state Democrats' fragile coalition," *Clarion-Ledger*, 2 September 1984.

46. "Visions of a New South," *Time*, 29 October 1984.

47. "Mayor Gray Challenges Clark, Franklin In 2nd District Congressional Race," *Jackson Advocate*, 31 August 1983; Neilson, *Even Mississippi*, 139, 141.

48. "Mayor Gray Challenges Clark, Franklin In 2nd District Congressional Race," *Jackson Advocate*, 31 August 1983; Neilson, *Even Mississippi*, 135–36, 149; *Mississippi Official and Statistical Register, 1984–1988*, 495–96; "Apathy wins," *Clarksdale Press Register*, 6 June 1984.

49. Robert G. Clark, interview by Betsy Nash, 18 February 1991, 43; Webb Franklin, interview by author, 18 May 2005; Neilson, *Even Mississippi*, 175–76.

50. Mike Alexander, "Mississippi Delta," *Black Enterprise*, November 1984, 53; Simeon Booker, "The Black Man Mississippi Can Send To Congress," *Jet*, 29 October 1984, 16.

51. Simeon Booker, "The Black Man Mississippi Can Send To Congress," *Jet*, 29 October 1984, 53; Neilson, *Even Mississippi*, 172; Lamis, *The Two-Party South*, 255.

52. *Mississippi Official and Statistical Register, 1984–1988*, 500–503; Marable, *Race, Reform, and Rebellion*, 194; William Winter, interview by Jeff Broadwater, 21 May 1991, 28–29; Webb Franklin, interview by author, 18 May 2005; "Black votes help Franklin win," *Bolivar Commercial*, 7 November 1984; Neilson, 190. According to a study co-authored by Leslie McLemore, Clark lost nine percent of the vote he received in the same counties in 1982. Mary Delorse Coleman and Leslie Burl McLemore, "Continuity and Power: The Power of Traditionalism in Biracial Politics in Mississippi's Second Congressional District," in Preston, Henderson, and Puryear, eds., *The New Black Politics*, 51.

53. Leslie Burl McLemore, interview by author, 19 November 2004; Robert G. Clark, interview by Betsy Nash, 18 February 1991.

54. Parker, "The Mississippi Congressional Redistricting Case," 411–12; *Jordan v. Winter* 469 U.S. 1002 (1984), 1004, 1012–13; Tom Oppel, "State remap plans upheld by high court," *Clarion-Ledger*, 14 November 1984.

55. Webb Franklin, interview by author, 18 May 2005; Neilson, *Even Mississippi*, 183–84.

56. "The South's new grapes of wrath," *U.S. News and World Report*, 1 September 1986, 6; "Bitter Harvest," *Time*, 8 September 1986, 16–17; "Stuffing Farmers, Stiffing Peasants," *New Republic*, 11 and 18 August 1986, 5; Jay Walljasper, "Little Cell On the Prairie," *The Nation*, 25 October 1986.

57. Bob Lord, "Lyng: Better conditions coming for farmers," *Delta Democrat-Times*, 1 June 1986; "Reagan orders task force to help farmers," *Delta Democrat-Times*, 12

August 1986; Tom Brown, "Textile veto bid barely fails," *Bolivar Commercial*, 7 August 1986.

58. Sandra Camphor, "Rain brings heat relief," *Delta Democrat-Times*, 3 August 1986; "Southeast worst but not alone," Delta Democrat-Times, 3 August 1986; "Estimates Bring no surprise," *Delta Democrat-Times*, 15 August 1986; Douglas McDonald, "Mid-Delta farmers hope for better days," *Delta Democrat-Times*, 17 August 1986; "Allain seeks disaster declaration," *Delta Democrat-Times*, 8 August 1986; "Emergency declaration makes 39 counties eligible for programs," *Delta Democrat-Times*, 31 August 1986; "Many farmers harvesting final crop," *Delta Democrat-Times*, 29 September 1986.

59. Neilson, *Even Mississippi*, 191; Leslie Burl McLemore, interview by author, 19 November 2004; "Black Attorney Named Public Lands Director," *Commercial Appeal*, 19 February 1980; "Miss. Lawyer Michael Espy Runs For Seat In Congress," *Jet*, 31 March 1986; Bill Minor, "Franklin Challenged," *Clarksdale Press Register*, 9 October 1985.

60. Bill Minor, "Franklin Challenged," *Clarksdale Press Register*, 9 October 1985; "To represent all the people," *Fayette Chronicle*, 29 May-4 June 1986. "Democratic hopeful seeks to follow family footsteps," *Delta Democrat-Times*, 18 May 1986; "Congressional hopefuls cover issues at forum," *Delta Democrat-Times*, 27 May 1986; "Candidates file campaign finance statements," *Delta Democrat-Times*, 1 June 1986; "Espy attacks Franklin's performance," *Delta Democrat-Times*, 19 May 1986.

61. "Espy leads; one amendment passes, one fails," *Delta Democrat-Times*, 4 June 1986; "Espy wins; allegations to be probed," *Delta Democrat-Times*, 8 June 1986; Jane Hill, "Additional votes may nullify need for 2nd primary," *Delta Democrat-Times*, June 1986; "Johnson accuses Espy camp of election day violations," *Clarksdale Press Register*, 7 June 1986; "Johnson accuses Espy camp of election day violations," *Clarksdale Press Register*, 7 June 1986; "Rebuffed thrice, Johnson aims at Grenada," *Delta Democrat-Times*, 15 June 1986; "Johnson withdraws challenge of election," *Delta Democrat-Times*, 9 July 1986.

62. Bill Minor, "Franklin Challenged," *Clarksdale Press Register*, 9 October 1985; Carolyn Hughes, "Espy joins in the fun at festival," *Delta Democrat-Times*, 6 July 1986; Tim McWilliams, "Congressional candidate stumps Bolivar County," *Bolivar Commercial*, 17 September 1986; Fernando Del Valle, "Espy promises to represent farmers," *Delta Democrat-Times*, 23 October 1986; Carolyn Hughes, "Farmers testify of years of work with nothing to show for it," *Delta Democrat-Times*, 23 October 1986; B.N. Shaw, "Espy makes history, wins congressional seat," *Fayette Chronicle*, 6–12 November 1986.

63. "Franklin, Espy hold 1st debate," *Bolivar Commercial*, 30 September 1986; "2nd District debate takes new focus," *Bolivar Commercial*, 31 October 1986; Sandra Camphor, "Espy, Franklin bring campaign to Greenville," *Delta Democrat-Times*, 22 October 1986; Webb Franklin, interview by author, 18 May 2005.

64. Sandra Camphor, "Espy breaks racial barrier with win," *Delta Democrat-Times*, 5 November 1986; Andrea Robinson, "Evers announces support of Franklin," *Fayette Chronicle*, 30 October-5 November 1986; Leslie McLemore, interview by author, 19 November 2004; "Espy's donations outweigh Franklin's," *Bolivar Commercial*, 17 October 1986.

65. Halberstam, *The Fifties*, 455; William Winter, interview by author, 28 September 2004.

66. Sandra Camphor, 5 November 1986; "Espy credits state's maturity for victory," *Delta Democrat-Times*, 5 November 1986; Parker, *Black Votes Count*, 140.

67. *Mississippi Official and Statistical Register, 1984–1988*, 503; *Mississippi Official and Statistical Register, 1988–1992*, 432; Parker, *Black Votes Count*, 140–42; Lamis, *The Two-Party South*, 283.

68. Bill Minor, "Post-election analysis affirms Espy can attract white voters," *Biloxi Sun-Herald*, 9 April 1987; Lamis, *The Two-Party South*, 283; "Espy at work for ag committee appointment," *Clarksdale Press Register*, 6 November 1986; Simeon Booker, "Blacks Make Big Gains In November Elections," *Jet*, 24 November 1986; Webb Franklin, interview by author, 18 May 2005; Leslie McLemore, interview by author, 19 November 2004; Parker, 140; Rory Reardon, "Issues over race question in Franklin-Espy race," *Clarksdale Press Register*, 3 November 1986.

69. Rory Reardon, "Issues over race question in Franklin-Espy race," *Clarksdale Press Register*, 3 November 1986; Bill Minor, "Franklin challenged," *Clarksdale Press Register*, 9 October 85; Leslie McLemore, interview by author, 19 November 2004.

70. Leslie McLemore, interview by author, 19 November 2004.

71. Bill Minor, "Espy's stunning success," *Bolivar Commercial*, 5 November 1986.

72. See Nash and Taggart, *Mississippi Politics*, Ch. 16.

73. Civil rights organizations vigorously opposed the conservative Bork, and Stennis voted against his nomination to the surprise of many observers. Lamis, *The Two-Party South*, 300–301; Thad Cochran, interview by Jeff Broadwater, 13 November 1991, 22.

74. Lamis, *The Two-Party South*, 350; Barone and Ujifusa, *The Almanac of American Politics 1986*, 739–40. By the mid-1980s, Whitten's ratings from Americans for Democratic Action, a liberal advocacy group, reached fifty percent or higher, and the *National Journal* ranked him more liberal than conservative on economic issues.

75. Moye, *Let the People Decide*, 171–204, passim; Marable, *Race, Reform, and Rebellion*, 184.

76. Marable, 214; Barone and Ujifusa, *The Almanac of American Politics 1990*, xvii, 666–68.

Epilogue

1. J.O. Emmerich to Jack R. Reed, 25 January 1963, Jack Reed Collection, Department of Special Collection, University of Mississippi, G-3, 94–72, Box 1, Folder 12; Frank E. Smith to Jack R. Reed, 7 February 1963, Jack Reed Collection; James W. Silver to Jack Reed, 24 January 1963, Jack Reed Collection; Grisham, *Tupelo*, 152.

2. Shaffer, et al., "Mississippi" in Lamis, ed., *Southern Politics in the 1990s*, 250; Mark Leggett, "Democrats stump for Reed," *Northeast Mississippi Daily Journal*, 23 October 1987.

3. Shaffer, et al., 250.

4. Bates, "The Reagan Rhetoric," 16–17, 48–51.

5. Shaffer, et al., 254–56; Telephone interview with Gil Carmichael, 31 August 2006.

6. *Ibid*, 254–56; Bill Minor, "Fordice backs Voting Rights Act repeal, so Barrett backs Fordice," *Clarion-Ledger*, 3 November 1991.

7. Shaffer, et al., 255–56.

8. *Ibid*, 263–64.

9. Sid Salter, "Race no longer an election issue?," *Clarion-Ledger*, 6 August 2003.

10. Black and Black, *The Rise of Southern Republicans*, 205–6.

11. *Mississippi Official and Statistical Register 2000–2004*, 656–58.

12. Sid Salter, *Clarion-Ledger*, 6 August 2003; Julie Goodman, "Candidate Blackmon seen as eloquent, educated, energetic," *Clarion-Ledger*, 3 August 2003; Julie Goodman, "Blackmon to face Tuck in historic lt. gov.'s race," *Clarion-Ledger*, 6 August 2003; Julie Goodman and Patrice Sawyer, "Anderson, Reeves, win party runoffs," *Clarion-Ledger*, 27 August 2003;

13. Charlie Mitchell, "Racial politics enters race for governor," *Clarion-Ledger*, 24 August 2003; Sid Salter, "Barbour answers Musgrove with flag," *Clarion-Ledger*, 5 October 2003.

14. "Tuck has made tough stands," *Clarion-Ledger*, 2 November 2003;

15. Sid Salter, "Tight fight will show if race is key issue," *Clarion-Ledger*, 2 November 2003; "Endorsements," *Clarion-Ledger*, 3 November 2003; Pamela Berry, "Sizable turnout favors GOP," *Clarion-Ledger*, 5 November 2003; "Election: Voters energized despite the dirt," *Clarion-Ledger*, 5 November 2003; "Treasurer's Race: Unfortunately, 'race' was germane," *Clarion-Ledger*, 6 November 2003. For more information on the 2003 race, see Nash and Taggart, *Mississippi Politics*, 304–8.

16. "Bush Signs Voting Rights Act Extension," http://www.msnbc.msn.com/id/14059113/ (accessed 4/19/2009); "Senate votes to renew Voting Rights Act," http://www.msnbc.msn.com/id/13958766/ (accessed 4/19/2009).

17. Chris Joyner, "Mississippi votes for McCain," *Clarion-Ledger*, 5 November 2008; Bill Minor, "Miss. does its best to fight the tide in presidential voting," *Clarion-Ledger*, 7 November 2008; Sewell and Dwight, *Mississippi Black History Makers*, 86. For examples of columns and debate over the Bradley Effect on the 2008 election, see Patt Morrison, "The 'Bradley Effect' in 2008," http://www.latimes.com/news/opinion/la-oe-morrison2-2008oct02,0,5653453.column; Laura Smith-Spark, "Will closet racism derail Obama?," http://news.bbc.co.uk/2/hi/americas/us_elections_2008/7675551.stm; Eugene Robinson, "Echoes of Tom Bradley," http://www.washingtonpost.com/wp-dyn/content/article/2008/01/10/AR2008011003274.html?sub=new (all three accessed 20 May 2009).

Bibliography

Primary Sources

Baker v. Carr. 369 U.S. 186 (1962)

Banks, Judge Fred L. Jr.. Interview by author, tape recording, Jackson, Miss., 28 June 2005.

———. Interview by Charles Bolton, transcript, 5 March 1998. Center for Oral History and Cultural Heritage, University of Southern Mississippi.

Barnes v. Barnett. 129 So. 2d 638 (1961)

Marjorie Baroni Collection. Department of Archives and Special Collections, J.D. Williams Memorial Library, University of Mississippi.

Boyd, Henry Jr. Interview by author, tape recording, Oxford, Miss., 28 April 2004.

Brooks v. Winter. 461 U.S. 921 (1983).

Broom v. Wood. 1 F. Supp. 134, 53 S. Ct. 1 (1932).

Gilbert E. Carmichael Papers. Special Collections, Mitchell Memorial Library, Mississippi State University.

Carmichael, Gilbert. Interview by Jeff Broadwater, transcript, Washington, D.C., 18 July 1991. Congressional and Political Research Center, Mississippi State University.

Carmichael, Gilbert. Interview by author, tape recording, Meridian, Miss., 13 October 2004.

———. Interview by author, telephone, Meridian, Miss., 31 August 2006.

City of Mobile v. Bolden. 446 U.S. 55 (1980).

Clark, Robert G. Interview by Betsy Nash, transcript, Jackson, Miss., 18 February 1991. Congressional and Political Research Center, Mississippi State University.

Clark, Robert G. Interview by author, tape recording, Ebenezer, Miss., 23 July 2005.

Cochran, Senator Thad. Interview by Jeff Broadwater, transcript, Washington, D.C., 13 November 1991. Congressional and Political Research Center, Mississippi State University.

Cole, Ed. Interview by Betsy Nash, transcript, Jackson, Miss., 7 January 1991. Congressional and Political Research Center, Mississippi State University.

Conference Proceedings of Southwide Conference of Black Elected Officials. Atlanta: Voter Education Project and Southern Regional Council, 1968.

Conner v. Coleman. 96 S. Ct. 1814 (1976).

Conner v. Finch. 419 F. Supp. 1072 (1072), 419 F. Supp. 1089 (1976), 422 F. Supp. 1014 (1976), 97 S. Ct. 1828 (1977).

Conner v. Johnson. 256 F. Supp. 962 (1966), 265 F. Supp. 492 (1967), 330 F. Supp. 506 (1971), 91 S. Ct. 1760 (1971).

Conner v. Waller. 396 F. Supp. 1308 (1975), 95 S. Ct. 2003 (1975).

Conner v. Williams. 404 U.S. 549 (1972).

Harry Dent Papers. Special Collections, Robert Muldrow Cooper Library, Clemson University.

Patricia Derian Papers. Special Collections, Mitchell Memorial Library, Mississippi State University.

Franklin, Webb. Interview by author, tape recording, Greenwood, Miss., 18 May 2005.

Hamer v. Campbell. 358 F.2d 215 (1966).

Howard v. Adams County Board of Supervisors. 453 F.2d 455 (1972).

Jordan v. Winter. 541 F. Supp. 1135 (1982), 604 F. Supp. 801, 469 U.S. 1002 (1984).

Ed King Papers. Department of Archives and Special Collections, J.D. Williams Memorial Library, University of Mississippi.

Kirksey v. Board of Supervisors of Hinds County, Mississippi. 402 F. Supp. 658 (1975), 528 F.2d 536 (1976), 554 F.2d 139 (1977).

Kirksey v. City of Jackson. 552 F.2d 156 (Fifth Circuit, 1977), 461 F. Supp. 1282 (1978), 506 F. Supp. 491 (1981), 663 F.2d 659 (1981).

Kirksey v. Danks. 608 F. Supp. 1448 (D.C. Miss. 1985).

McLaurin, Griffin. Interview by Harriet Tanzman, 6 March 2000, University of Southern Mississippi Oral History Collection.

McLemore, Leslie Burl. Interview by author, tape recording, 19 November 2004, Oxford, Miss.

William F. Minor Papers. Special Collections, Mitchell Memorial Library, Mississippi State University.

Mississippi Official and Statistical Register 1952, 1968–1972, 1972–1976, 1976–1980, 1980–84. 1984–1988, 1988–1992, 2000–2004.

Mississippi Republican Party Papers. Special Collections, Mitchell Memorial Library, Mississippi State University.

Moore v. Leflore County Board of Election Commissioners. 361 F. Supp. 603 (1972), 361 F. Supp. 609 (1973), 502 F.2d 621 (1974).

NAACP v. Claiborne Hardware Co. Miss. 393 So. 2d 1290, 102 S. Ct. 3409 (1982).

National Association for the Advancement of Colored People Papers.

Papers of the President: Ronald Reagan, 1981–1988. Ronald Reagan Library, http://www.reagan.utexas.edu/resource/speeches/1983/62083b.htm.

J. Stanley Pottinger Papers. Gerald R. Ford Presidential Library, University of Michigan.

Charles Ramberg Papers. Mississippi Department of Archives and History.

Jack Reed Collection, Department of Archives and Special Collections, J.D. Williams Memorial Library, University of Mississippi.

Reynolds v. Sims. 377 U.S. 533 (1964).

Robert L. T. Smith Papers. Mississippi Department of Archives and History.

Sovereignty Commission Online. Mississippi Department of Archives and History, http://mdah.state.ms.us.

Stewart v. Waller. 404 F. Supp. 206 (1975).

Thompson, Mayor Bennie G. Interview by Chester Morgan, 13 February 1974. Center for Oral History and Cultural Heritage, University of Southern Mississippi.

United Jewish Organizations v. Carey. 430 U.S. 144 (1977).

U.S. Department of Commerce, Bureau of the Census. *Census of Population: 1960, Vol. 1 Characteristics of the Population, Part 26 Mississippi.* Washington, D.C.: GPO, 1963.

———. *1970 Census of the Population, Vol. 1 Characteristics of the Population, Part 26, Mississippi.* U.S. GPO, Washington, D.C., 1973.

———. *1980 Census of the Population, Vol. 1, General Characteristics of the Population.* Washington, D.C.: U.S. GPO, 1983.

Whitcomb v. Chavis. 403 U.S. 124 (1971).

Whitley v. Johnson. 260 F. Supp. 630 (1966).

Winter, Gov. William. Interview by author, tape recording, Jackson, Miss., 28 September 2004.

———. Interview by Jeff Broadwater, transcript, Jackson, Miss., 21 May 1991. Congressional and Political Research Center, Mississippi State University.

Secondary Sources

Alston, Lee J. *Southern Paternalism and the American Welfare State.* New York: Cambridge University Press, 1999.

Amaker, Norman. *Civil Rights and the Reagan Administration.* Washington, D.C.: Urban Institute Press, 1988.

Andrews, Kenneth T. 2004. *Freedom Is a Constant Struggle: The Mississippi Civil Rights Movement and its Legacy.* Chicago: University of Chicago Press, 2004.

Baldwin, Sidney. *Poverty and Politics: The Rise and Decline of the Farm Security Administration.* Chapel Hill: University of North Carolina Press, 1968.

Barone, Michael, and Grant Ujifusa. *The Almanac of American Politics 1978.* New York: E. P. Dutton, 1977.

———. *The Almanac of American Politics 1980.* New York: E. P. Dutton, 1979.

———. *The Almanac of American Politics 1986.* Washington, D.C.: National Journal, 1985.

———. *The Almanac of American Politics 1990.* Washington, D.C.: National Journal, 1989.

Barrow, Deborah J., and Thomas G. Walker. *A Court Divided: The Fifth Circuit Court of Appeals and the Politics of Judicial Reform.* New Haven: Yale University Press, 1988.

Bartley, Numan. *The Rise of Massive Resistance: Race and Politics in the South During the 1950s.* Baton Rouge: Louisiana State University Press, 1969.

Bass, Jack. *Unlikely Heroes: The Dramatic Story of the Southern Judges Who Translated the Supreme Court's Brown Decision into a Revolution for Equality.* New York: Simon and Shuster, 1981.

Bass, Jack, and Walter DeVries. *The Transformation of Southern Politics: Social Change and Political Consequences since 1945.* New York: Basic Books, 1976.

Bates, Toby Glen. "The Reagan Rhetoric: History and Memory in 1980s America." Ph.D. diss., University of Mississippi, 2006.

Berry, Jason. *Amazing Grace: With Charles Evers in Mississippi.* New York: Saturday Review Press, 1973.

Black, Earl and Merle Black. *The Rise of Southern Republicans.* Cambridge: Harvard University Press, 2002.

Blackwell, Unita, and JoAnne Prichard Morris. *Barefootin': Life Lessons from the Road to Freedom.* New York: Crown, 2006.

Bond, Julian. *Black Candidates: Southern Campaign Experiences.* Atlanta: Southern Regional Council, 1968.

Brauer, Carl M. *John F. Kennedy and the Second Reconstruction.* New York: Columbia University Press, 1977.

Cagin, Seth, and Phillip Dray. 1988. *We Are Not Afraid: The Story of Goodman, Schwerner, and Cheney and the Civil Rights Campaign for Mississippi.* New York: McMillan, 1988.

Campbell, Will D. *Robert G. Clark's Journey to the House: A Black Politician's Story.* Jackson: University Press of Mississippi, 2003.

Cannon, Lou. *Governor Reagan: His Rise to Power.* New York: Public Affairs, 2003.

Carson, Clayborne. *In Struggle: SNCC and the Black Awakening of the 1960s.* Cambridge: Harvard University Press, 1995.

Carter, Dan T. *From George Wallace to Newt Gingrich: Race in the Conservative Counterrevolution, 1963–1994.* Baton Rouge: Louisiana State University Press, 1996.

———. *The Politics of Rage: George Wallace, the Origins of the New Conservatism, and the Transformation of American Politics.* Baton Rouge: Louisiana State University Press, 1996.

Clark, Eric C. "Legislative Reapportionment in the 1890 Constitutional Convention." *The Journal of Mississippi History* 42 (1980): 297–315.

Cobb, James C. *The Most Southern Place on Earth: The Mississippi Delta and the Roots of Regional Identity.* New York: Oxford University Press, 1992.

Cohodas, Nadine. *And the Band Played Dixie: Race and the Liberal Conscience at Ole Miss.* New York: Free Press, 1997.

Conkin, Paul K. *Tomorrow a New World: The New Deal Community Program.* Ithaca, N.Y.: Cornell University Press, 1959.

Cortner, Richard. *The Apportionment Cases.* New York: W. W. Norton, 1970.

Crespino, Joseph. *In Search of Another Country: Mississippi and the Conservative Counterrevolution.* Princeton, N.J.: Princeton University Press, 2007.

———. "Strategic Accommodation: Civil Rights Opponents in Mississippi and Their

Impact on American Racial Politics, 1953–1972." Ph.D. diss.: Stanford University, 2003.

Crosby, Emilye. "Common Courtesy: The Civil Rights Movement in Claiborne County, Mississippi." Ph.D. diss., Indiana University, 1995.

———. *A Little Taste of Freedom: The Black Freedom Struggle in Claiborne County, Mississippi*. Chapel Hill: University of North Carolina Press, 2005.

Davidson, Chandler, and Bernard Grofman, ed. *Quiet Revolution in the South: The Impact of the Voting Rights Act, 1965–1990*. Princeton, N.J.: Princeton University Press, 1994.

Dittmer, John. *Local People: The Struggle for Civil Rights in Mississippi*. Urbana: University of Illinois Press, 1994.

Dyer, Thomas G. *Theodore Roosevelt and the Idea of Race*. Baton Rouge: Louisiana State University Press, 1980.

Evers, Charles. *Evers*. Ed. Grace Halsell. New York: World Publishing, 1971.

Evers, Charles, and Andrew Szanton. *Have No Fear: The Charles Evers Story*. New York: John Wiley and Sons, 1997.

Evers, Myrlie B., and William Peters. *For Us, the Living*. New York: Doubleday, 1967.

Foner, Eric. *Reconstruction: America's Unfinished Revolution 1863–1877*. New York: Harper and Row, 1988.

Giroux, Vincent A. Jr. "Theodore G. Bilbo: Progressive to Public Racist." Ph.D. diss., Indiana University, 1984.

Goldfield, David R. *Black, White, and Southern: Race Relations and Southern Culture, 1940 to the Present*. Baton Rouge: Louisiana State University Press, 1990.

Grisham, Vaughn L. Jr. *Tupelo: The Evolution of a Community*. Dayton, Ohio: Kettering Foundation Press, 1999.

Halberstam, David. *The Fifties*. New York: Ballantine Books, 1993.

Hall, Jacquelyn Dowd, "The Long Civil Rights Movement and the Political Uses of the Past." *Journal of American History* 91 (March 2005): 1233–63.

Harris, William. *Day of the Carpetbagger*. Baton Rouge: Louisiana State University Press, 1979.

Havard, William C., ed. *The Changing Politics of the South*. Baton Rouge: Louisiana State University Press, 1972.

Hill, Lance. *The Deacons for Defense: Armed Resistance and the Civil Rights Movement*. Chapel Hill: University of North Carolina Press, 2004.

Holmes, William F. *The White Chief*. Baton Rouge: Louisiana State University Press, 1970.

Howard, John. *Men Like That: A Southern Queer History*. Chicago: University of Chicago Press, 1999.

Howard-Pitney, David. *Martin Luther King Jr., Malcolm X, and the Civil Rights Struggle of the 1950s and 1960s: A Brief History With Documents*. Boston: Bedford/St. Martin's, 2004.

Keady, William C. *All Rise: Memoirs of a Mississippi Federal Judge*. Boston: Recollections Bound, 1988.

Key, V. O. Jr. *Southern Politics in State and Nation*. Knoxville: University of Tennessee Press, 1984.

King, Martin Luther Jr. *Stride towards Freedom: The Montgomery Story*. San Francisco: HarperSanFrancisco, 1986.

Kirby, Jack Temple. *Darkness at the Dawning: Race and Reform in the Progressive South*. Philadelphia: J. B. Lippincott, 1972.

Krane, Dale, and Stephen D. Shaffer, eds. *Mississippi Government & Politics: Modernizers versus Traditionalists*. Lincoln: University of Nebraska Press, 1992.

Kotlowski, Dean J. *Nixon's Civil Rights: Politics, Principle, and Policy*. Cambridge: Harvard University Press, 2001.

Kruse, Kevin M. *White Flight: Atlanta and the Making of Modern Conservatism*. Princeton, N.J.: Princeton University Press, 2005.

Lamis, Alexander P., ed. *Southern Politics in the 1990s*. Baton Rouge: Louisiana State University Press, 1999.

———. *The Two-Party South*, expanded edition. New York: Oxford University Press, 1988.

Landon, Michael de L. *The Challenge of Service: A History of the Mississippi Bar's Young Lawyers 1936–1986*. Fellows of the Young Mississippi Bar, 1995.

———. *The Honor and Dignity of the Profession: A History of the Mississippi State Bar, 1906–1976*. Jackson: University Press of Mississippi, 1979.

Lassiter, Matthew D. *The Silent Majority: Suburban Politics in the Sunbelt South*. Princeton, N.J.: Princeton University Press, 2006.

Lawson, Steven F. *Black Ballots: Voting Rights in the South 1944–1969*. Lanham, Md.: Lexington Books, 1999.

———. *In Pursuit of Power: Southern Blacks and Electoral Politics, 1965–1982*. New York: Columbia University Press, 1985.

Lee, Chana Kai. *For Freedom's Sake: The Life of Fannie Lou Hamer*. Urbana: University of Illinois Press, 1999.

Logue, Cal M., and Howard Dorgan. *The Oratory of Southern Demagogues*. Baton Rouge: Louisiana State University Press, 1981.

Lott, Trent. *Herding Cats: A Life in Politics*. New York: HarperCollins, 2005.

Love, Ronald. "A Community in Transition: A Study of Mound Bayou, Mississippi." Ph.D. diss.: Boston University, 1982.

Marable, Manning. *Race, Reform, and Rebellion: The Second Reconstruction and Beyond in Black America, 1945–2006*. Jackson: University Press of Mississippi, 2007.

Marsh, Charles. *God's Long Summer: Stories of Faith and Civil Rights*. Princeton, N.J., 1997.

Mayer, Jeremy D. *Running on Race: Racial Politics in Presidential Campaigns, 1960–2000*. New York: Random House, 2002.

McAdam, Doug. *Freedom Summer*. New York: Oxford University Press, 1988.

McLemore, Leslie Burl. "The Mississippi Freedom Democratic Party: A Case Study of Grass-roots Politics." Ph.D. diss., University of Massachusetts, 1971.

McMillen, Neil R. *The Citizens' Council: Organized Resistance to the Second Reconstruction, 1955–64*. Urbana: University of Illinois Press, 1994.

———. *Dark Journey: Black Mississippians in the Age of Jim Crow*. Urbana: Illini Books, 1990.

———, ed. *Remaking Dixie: The Impact of World War II on the American South*. Jackson: University of Mississippi Press, 1997.

Minchin, Timothy J. "Making Best Use of the New Laws: The NAACP and the Fight for Civil Rights in the South, 1965–1975." *Journal of Southern History* 74 (August 2008): 669–702.

Mitchell, Dennis J. *Mississippi Liberal: A Biography of Frank E. Smith*. Jackson: University Press of Mississippi, 2001.

Moran, Rachel F. *Interracial Intimacy: The Regulation of Race and Romance*. Chicago: University of Chicago Press, 2001.

Morgan, Chester M. *Redneck Liberal: Theodore G. Bilbo and the New Deal*. Baton Rouge: Louisiana State University Press, 1985.

Morrison, Minion K.C. *Black Political Mobilization: Leadership, Power and Mass Behavior*. Albany: SUNY Press, 1987.

Mounger, William D., and Joe Maxwell. *Amidst the Fray: My Life in Politics, Culture, and Mississippi*. Brandon, Miss.: Quail Ridge Press, 2006.

Moye, J. Todd. *Let the People Decide: Black Freedom and White Resistance Movements in Sunflower County, Mississippi, 1945–1986*. Chapel Hill: University of North Carolina Press, 2004.

Nash, Jere, and Andy Taggart. *Mississippi Politics: The Struggle for Power, 1976–2006*. Jackson: University Press of Mississippi, 2006.

National Roster of Black Elected Officials. Vols. 1–15. Washington, D.C.: Joint Center for Political Studies.

Neilson, Melany. *Even Mississippi*. Tuscaloosa: University of Alabama Press, 1989.

Ownby, Ted. *American Dreams in Mississippi: Consumers, Poverty, and Culture, 1830–1998*. Chapel Hill, N.C.: University of North Carolina Press, 1999.

Parker, Frank. *Black Votes Count: Political Power in Mississippi after 1965*. Chapel Hill: University of North Carolina Press, 1990.

———. "County Studies in Mississippi: Case Studies in Racial Gerrymandering." *Mississippi Law Journal* 44 (1973).

———. "The Mississippi Congressional Redistricting Case: A Case Study in Minority Vote Dilution." *Howard Law Journal* 28, no. 2 (1985).

Patterson, Ernest. *Black City Politics*. New York: Dodd, Mead, 1974.

Payne, Charles M. *I've Got the Light of Freedom: The Organizing Tradition and the Mississippi Freedom Struggle*. Berkeley: University of California Press, 1995.

Preston, Michael B., Lenneal J. Henderson Jr., and Paul L. Puryear, eds. *The New Black Politics: The Search for Black Political Power*. 2nd ed. New York: Longman, 1987.

Rice, Bradley Robert. *Progressive Cities: The Commission Government Movement in America, 1901–1920*. Austin: University of Texas Press, 1977.

Robinson, Armstead L., and Patricia Sullivan, eds. *New Directions in Civil Rights Studies*. Charlottesville: University Press of Virginia, 1991.

Robinson, Jo Ann. *The Montgomery Bus Boycott and the Women Who Started It: The Memoir of Jo Ann Gibson Robinson*. Knoxville: University of Tennessee Press, 1987.

Robnett, Belinda. *How Long? How Long? African-American Women in the Struggle for Civil Rights*. New York: Oxford University Press, 1997.

Rodgers, Harrell R. Jr., and Charles S. Bullock III. *Law and Social Change: Civil Rights Laws and their Consequences*. New York: McGraw Hill, 1972.

Rosen, Ruth. *The World Split Open: How the Modern Women's Movement Changed America*. New York: Penguin Books, 2000.

Salamon, Lester M. "Leadership and Modernization: The Emerging Black Political Elite in the American South." *Journal of Politics*, 35, no. 3 (August 1973).

———. "The Time Dimension in Policy Evaluation: The Case of the New Deal Land-Reform Experiments." *Public Policy*, 27, no. 2 (Spring 1979).

Schafer, Byron E., and Richard Johnston. *The End of Southern Exceptionalism: Class, Race, and Partisan Change in the Postwar South*. Cambridge: Harvard University Press, 2006.

Schulman, Bruce J. *From Cotton Belt to Sunbelt: Federal Policy, Economic Development, and the Transformation of the South, 1938–1980*. Durham, N.C.: Duke University Press, 1994.

———. *The Seventies: The Great Shift in American Culture, Society, and Politics*. New York: Free Press, 2001.

Sellers, Cleveland, and Robert Terrell. *The River of No Return: The Autobiography of a Black Militant and the Life and Death of SNCC*. New York: Morrow, 1973.

Sewell, George Alexander, and Margaret L. Dwight. *Mississippi Black History Makers*. Rev. ed. Jackson: University Press of Mississippi, 1984.

Sistrom, Michael Paul. "'Authors of the Liberation': The Mississippi Freedom Democrats and the Redefinition of Politics." Ph.D. diss., University of North Carolina, Chapel Hill, 2002.

Sokol, Jason. *There Goes My Everything: White Southerners in the Age of Civil Rights, 1945–1975*. New York: Alfred A. Knopf, 2006.

Thernstrom, Abigail. *Whose Votes Count? Affirmative Action and Minority Voting Rights*. Cambridge: Harvard University Press, 1987.

Wallenstein, Peter. *Tell The Court I Love My Wife: Race, Marriage, and Law, an American History*. New York: Palgrave Macmillan, 2002.

Wharton, Vernon Lane. *The Negro in Mississippi 1865–1890*. New York: Harper and Row, 1965.

White, Colleen R. "The *Jackson Advocate*: 1938–1995 A Historical Overview." Master's thesis, University of Mississippi, 1996.

Williamson, Joy Ann. *Radicalizing the Ebony Tower: Black Colleges and the Black Freedom Struggle in Mississippi*. New York: Teachers College Press, 2008.

Wolters, Raymond. *Right Turn: William Bradford Reynolds, the Reagan Administration, and Black Civil Rights*. New Brunswick, N.J.: Transaction, 1996.

Woodward, C. Vann. *The Origins of the New South, 1877–1913*. Baton Rouge: Louisiana State University Press, 1971.

Index

Aaron, Henry, 129, 130; civil rights background, 11–12, 15, 17, 147; Clarksdale municipal elections and, 67–68; close relationship with segregationists, 35, 36, 99, 101, 131, 223; Cupit affair and, 138–40; Charles Evers and, 51, 103–4, 105, 107, 108; Cliff Finch and, 79, 89, 92–93, 95; legislative races, 64, 135; opinions on black independents, 96–97, 104, 107; relations with MFDP, 15, 17, 21, 36, 42, 46, 81; Republic of New Africa and, 63; support for candidates, 26–27, 61, 102, 203; top-down "boss politics" of, 19, 45, 101, 104, 131; William Waller and, 79, 81. *See also* National Association for the Advancement of Colored People (NAACP)

Abortion: opposition to, 98–99, 102, 127, 142, 217, 222; support for, 142, 210. *See also* Women's rights

Abzug, Bella, 210

Adams County, 21, 141, 147, 156, 157, 158

Adkins, Bobby Joe, 137

Agnew, Spiro, 84

Agricultural Stabilization and Conservation Service (ASCS), 15–16, 26, 208

Alcorn State University (Alcorn A&M College), 11, 21, 41, 92

Alexander, W. B., 140, 193

Ali, Muhammad, 106

Allain, Bill, 133, 151, 152, 204, 208

Allen v. State Board of Elections, 156, 160, 161, 165, 172

Allen, Ferd, 57

American Civil Liberties Union (ACLU), 69, 115, 215

Americans for Democratic Action (ADA), 103, 215, 268n74

Ames, Adelbert, 8

Anderson, Douglas, 97, 135, 147

Anderson, Gary, 221, 222

Anderson, John, 185

AFL-CIO: endorsements, 40, 102, 196, 195, 200; MFDP and, 115; NAACP and, 17, 232–33n57. *See also* Ramsey, Claude

Armstrong, Louis, 189

Ash, J. M. "Flick," 136

At-large elections: county level, 22, 155–56, 157, 159; Jackson referendum and, 173–75; legislative, 118; municipal, 171–73, 189. *See also* Jackson; *Kirksey v. City of Jackson*

Attorney general's race, 133–34

Bailey, Howard Taft, 97

Bailey, Mrs. Thomas L., 150, 151

Baker, Ella, 12

Baker v. Carr, 109, 112–114, 116

279

Banks, Fred: at-large elections in Jackson and, 174, 176; as legislator, 77, 99, 130, 139, 147, 148; relations with other civil rights activists, 48, 107, 148;
Baptist Ministers' Union, 106
Barbour, Haley, 199, 221, 222, 223
Barbour, William, 187–88
Barefield, Stone, 130, 139
Barnes, Jimmie, 65
Barnett, Ross, 192; Cliff Finch and, 89, 95; rhetoric of, 24, 83, 94, 106
Barrett, Richard, 218–19
Bell, Osborne: coroner and ranger election and, 34, 74, 97–98; sheriff's election and, 19, 136, 137, 253n40
Berry, Jason, 59, 61
Biglane, D. A., 106
Bilbo, Theodore, 9, 93, 131, 226n6, 244n32
Black, Hugo, 118
Black and Tans, 10, 17, 24, 228–29n11
Black Economic Union, 74
Black elected officials and candidates: and election commissioners, 42–43; gender and, 148–150, 185–86; gubernatorial, 60–64, 90–91, 121, 204; as mayors, 66–67, 70–71, 131, 152–153, 202, 252n16 (see also Evers, Charles); organizations of, 99, 129, 131, 132–33; pre-1965, 7–9, 12–14, 15–16; and presidency, 222–23; "safe" candidates and, 97–98, 135–36; as school board members, 25, 42, 43, 67, 149, 153; as school superintendents, 8, 22, 73, 137, 215; second generation of, 146–49, 151–53; as sheriffs, 8, 98, 124, 135–37, 253n33; as state legislators, 121, 123, 135, 146–48, 153–54, 194 (see also Clark, Robert); 1995 and 2003 statewide elections, 219, 221–222; white intimidation and harassment of, 29, 40–41, 70, 72, 153. See also Black Republicans, Cupit affair and; Independent candidacies
—as city council members: Bolton, 69–70; Clarksdale, 67–68; Delta towns, 16, 28–29, 43–44, 65–68; Jackson, 173,

176–77, 180, 185–86, 188–89; other towns, 189
—congressional: 1960s elections; 12–14, 22–23, 25, 39–40; 1970s elections, 84, 87, 101–102, 103–108; 1980s elections, 140–43, 200–203, 205–207, 209–13, 214–15
—in county elections: county redistricting and, 156–61, 162, 166; 1967 elections, 26–27, 29–30, 32–34, 39; 1971 elections, 60, 61–62, 62–63, 64–65, 71–72, 74–75; 1975 elections, 72–73, 76–77, 96–97; 1979 elections, 131–32, 135–37; 1983 elections, 167
—women: defeated incumbents, 71–72; lower numbers in politics of black, 148–49; mayors, 148, 154; as successful candidates, 73, 75, 189; as unsuccessful candidates, 63, 73, 185–86, 101, 188, 221
Black Legislative Caucus, 140, 141, 146, 153
Black power: black candidates and elected officials and, 22, 30, 48, 63, 152; class and gender and, 35, 149; nonviolence and, 48, 50; MFDP and, 17, 19, 46–47; Republic of New Africa and, 47–48, 63. See also Republic of New Africa (RNA); Mississippi Freedom Democratic Party (MFDP)
Black Republican Council, 104, 144
Black Republicans: failed candidacies of, 135, 219; Aaron Henry and, 104; relationship with Democratic Party, 144–46; relationship with Republican Party, 23, 83, 143
Blackmon, Barbara, 221, 222
Blackwell, Unita, 71, 148, 154
Board of Corrections, 138
Bodron, Ellis, 39, 40, 87, 116
Bolden, Wiley, 180
Bolivar County: compared to Coahoma County, 65, 67, 68; elections, 33, 97, 206; generational split in black community, 131–32; municipal black

City of Mobile v. Bolden, 180–81, 183, 184, 185, 186

Claiborne County: Charles Evers's political influence in, 21, 34, 32, 64, 71, 135; Port Gibson boycott, 50, 59; Republicans and, 82, 86, 87, 107; second congressional district and, 204, 209

—black political power in: before 1969, 29, 32–33, 41, 42; before 1979, 65, 71–73, 107, 206; and 1979 elections, 135, 136, 137; since 1980, 141, 161, 166, 205

—voting patterns in: 1960s, 24, 29; 1970s: 64, 65, 86, 87, 135; 1980s, 204

Clark, Alyce, 150

Clark, Robert: apportionment and, 117, 121; black power and, 48, 63; Gil Carmichael and, 90, 92, 96; Education Reform Act and, 146, 154; election and re-election to state legislature, 30–31, 32, 39, 63, 64, 96; compared to Mike Espy, 210, 211–23; legislative career, 78, 146–47; Loyalists and, 42; MFDP and, 30–31, 32, 35; party identification and, 30–31, 63, 96, 98; relations with black politicians, 70, 98, 121, 147–48, 202, 205–206; relations with white Democrats, 105, 139, 147–48, 200, 206, 209; U.S. House races, 200–203, 205–207, 266n52; white harassment of, 41

Clark, Sylvester, 66

Clarksdale: black political power in, 65, 67–68, 99, 204; civil rights activism in, 11–12, commission government in, 171; politicians from, 129, 200, 204

Clarksdale Press Register, 68, 212

Class divisions in the black community: effects on black political campaigns, 34–35, 71, 212, 215; MFDP–NAACP feud and, 34–36; Republic of New Africa and, 47; Robert Clark and, 30–31

Clements, Jack, 77

Cleveland, 67, 68, 140, 194

Coahoma County, black political power in: before 1970, 11–12, 26, 29, 43–44;
before 1980, 65, 67, 68, 78, 135; after 1980, 166. *See also* Clarksdale

Coalition of Determined Democrats (CDD), 140

Cochran, Nielsen, 188

Cochran, Thad: aides to, 87, 135, 144; endorsements by, 91, 200; 1972 U.S. House race, 87–89, 242–43n17; 1978 U.S. Senate race, 101, 102, 103, 105–107, 130; 1984 U.S. Senate race, 205, 207; Billy Mounger and, 128–29, 146; and political fallout from 1978 victory, 130, 139; pragmatism of, 108, 127, 134, 144, 214, 255n60; voting record, 102–103, 104, 198–99, 222; Voting Rights Act of 1982 and, 198–99

Cole, Ed, 140, 142, 199, 219

Coleman, Bernard, 104

Coleman, J. P., 114, 117, 120, 121, 235n6

Colgrove v. Green, 110, 114

Collins, Alexander, 33, 71–72

Collins, Clinton, 14

Collins, Geneva, 33, 34, 41, 71–72, 73

Colom, Will, 144–46

Commission government, 16; adoption in Mississippi, 171–72, 173; Clarksdale, 67, 171; Justice Department and, 185; in other Mississippi cities, 171–72, 184; Voting Rights Act of 1982 and, 186–87. *See also Kirksey v. City of Jackson; City of Mobile v. Bolden*

—Jackson: responsiveness to black Jacksonians, 174, 178–79; in 1912, 173, 179, 180, 181–82, 183; 1977 referendum and, 173–75, unsuccessful black candidacies for, 173, 176, 180, 185–86, 188; white support for, 174–75, 181, 182

Comprehensive Planners Inc. (CPI), 156, 157, 158–59, 160

Conner, Peggy, 114

Conner v. Finch, 123, 161

Conner v. Johnson, 114–15, 117, 119, 159, 192

Conner v. Waller, 120

14, 39, 40, 69; county redistricting and, 158–59; 1977 elections, 175–76; 1977 mayor–council referendum, 173–75; 1981 elections, 185–86; 1984 mayor–council referendum, 188–89; 1984 special election, 188; 1985 elections, 189; Republicans and, 5, 84, 87, 103, 128, 134; state legislative districts in, 120, 123; school desegregation, 121. *See also Kirksey v. City of Jackson*

Jackson, Jesse: Delta visit, 162–63, 169, 183; political endorsements, 186, 209, 212; presidential campaign, 165–66, 168, 206; Tunica County and, 166. *See also* Reynolds, William Bradford

Jackson-Hinds County Community Legal Services, 118

Jacksonians for a Mayor–Council Form of Government, 182

Jackson Ministers' Union, 176

Jackson State College (University), 30, 88, 89, 97, 149

Javits, Jacob, 38, 93, 94, 101, 223

Jefferson County, 25, 55, 61, 65, 73, 132. *See also* Evers, Charles

Jenkins, Monroe, 58

Jennings, Stella, 73

Johnson, Lyndon Baines: judicial appointments, 114, 157, 160; renomination and, 41–42; voting rights and, 16, 18, 155

Johnson, Paul Jr., 14–15, 54, 116, 200

Johnson, Paul Sr., 200

Johnson, Pete, 200, 209

Jolliff, James: elections as supervisor, 33, 65; fall of, 72; legal troubles of, 40–41, 46, 50; militancy of, 33, 48, 50

Jonestown, 16, 44, 68

Jordan, Bill, 219

Keady, William, 157, 167, 204

Kelly, Tom, 174

Kennedy, Edward, 55, 91, 200

Kennedy, John Fitzgerald: civil rights and, 7, 11, 14, 15, 24, 40; judicial appointments, 114; political support for, 14, 192

Kennedy, Robert, 42, 94

Kimbrough, Lee Dorothy, 63

Kirksey v. Board of Supervisors of Hinds County, Mississippi, 158–61, 179

Kirksey v. City of Jackson: appeals, 179–81, 184–185; end of suit, 188–89; initial suit, 175; Judge Barbour's rulings, 187–88; Judge Nixon's rulings, 178–79, 183–84; testimony, 176–78, 181–183, 185; Voting Rights Act of 1982 and, 187, 188

Kirksey, Henry: apportionment cases and, 109, 114, 155, 192; at-large elections and, 174, 175, 182, 184, 188; campaigns for mayor of Jackson, 185–86, 189; compared to other black legislators, 147; county redistricting and, 158, 169–70; Delta district and, 194–95; 1975 gubernatorial race, 89–90, 94, 121, 150; 1979 state Senate race, 135, 181; 1980 U.S. House race, 140–41; 1978 U.S. Senate race, 101, 104, 107, 246n61. *See also Kirksey v. Board of Supervisors of Hinds County, Mississippi*; *Kirksey v. City of Jackson*; Kirksey plan

Kirksey plan, 194, 195, 196

King, Coretta Scott, 206, 222

King, Ed, 14, 21, 22, 39

King, Martin Luther Jr., 47, 51, 133

Klein, Joe Ann, 143

Knox, Bennie, 73

Kristofferson, Kris, 106

Kruse, Kevin, 128

Kunstler, William, 114

Labor. *See* AFL-CIO; Mississippi Labor Council; National Association for the Advancement of Colored People (NAACP), coalition with labor

Lassiter, Matthew, 128, 146

Lawson, Steven, 16, 45

Proportional representation, 156, 159, 160, 161–62, 178, 180. *See also United Jewish Organizations v. Carey*
Pryor, Estelle, 210

Quitman County, 65, 81, 166–68, 215, 258n22

Ramberg, Charles, 56, 58, 59–60
Ramsey, Burnell, 253n33
Ramsey, Claude: Charles Evers and, 40, 105; Aaron Henry and, 17, 21; Loyalists and, 115, 232–33n57; political comments and endorsements, 23, 195, 200
Rauh, Joseph, 103–104, 105
Reagan, Ronald, 82, 91, 133; county redistricting and, 155, 165, 168–69; farm crisis and, 208, 209, 211; 1976 presidential race, 126–28, 140, 143; 1980 presidential election, 139, 144, 146, 147, 204; 1984 presidential election, 204–205, 206, 207; Voting Rights Act renewal and, 162, 198. *See also* "Great White Switch"; Reynolds, William Bradford
Reaganomics, 206–207, 209
Reapportionment, 26; litigation against, 114–123; 1979 elections and, 133, 135; pre-1965, 110, 112–114. *See also Conner v. Finch; Conner v. Johnson; Conner v. Waller; Conner v. Williams*; Multimember districts; Parker, Frank; Single-member districts
Redistricting, congressional, 110, 115–16. *See also* Delta district
Redistricting, county, 156–57, 161, 162–67. *See also Kirksey vs. Board of Supervisors of Hinds County, Mississippi*
Reed, Clarke: 1975 gubernatorial race and, 90, 91, 93; 94; 1976 Republican National Convention and, 126–28; pragmatism of, 82, 143, 199; U.S. House races and, 201, 211
Reed, Jack, 217–18
Reeves, Tate, 222
Regional Council on Negro Leadership, 11

Regular Democrats, 17, 21, 52, 79–81, 89. *See also* Democratic Party; Fusion
Republican Party: black voting and ideological splits in state GOP, 36–39, 79, 81–83, 93–94, 98–99; early indifference to black voters, 14–15, 23–25; Jackson elections and, 175–76, 185–86, 188; lack of party integration in, 143, 146; open primary and, 54, 130; pre-1965, 8, 9, 10, 14–15, 17; white voters and, 102, 133–34, 139, 146, 219, 220–22; *See also* Black Republicans; Carmichael, Gil; Cochran, Thad; House races, U.S.; Gubernatorial races; Mounger, William; Reed, Clarke; Republican National Convention, 1976, Senate races, U.S.
Republic National Committee, 134
Republican National Convention: 1968, 82; 1976, 126–28
Republic of New Africa (RNA), 47–48, 63–64
Retzer, Mike, 143, 195
Revels, Hiram, 8
Reynolds v. Sims: apportionment and, 109, 114, 115–16, 117; county redistricting and, 155, 159; congressional redistricting and, 192–93, 194
Reynolds, William Bradford, 162–66, 168–69
Riddell, Tom, 95, 138
Roan, Luther, 187, 189
Robinson, Alfred "Skip," 74–77, 98, 130, 136–37, 253n40, 254n42
Russell, Dan, 115
Rust College, 22, 33, 47, 75, 231n40
Rustin, Bayard, 12

Sallis, Charles, 181, 183
Schoby, Barney, 147, 156
School board members, black, 25, 42, 43, 67, 149, 153
School superintendents, black, 8, 22, 73, 137, 215
Schweiker, Richard, 127

Chris Danielson is assistant professor of history at Montana Tech of the University of Montana.

NEW PERSPECTIVES ON THE HISTORY OF THE SOUTH
Edited by John David Smith

"In the Country of the Enemy": The Civil War Reports of a Massachusetts Corporal, edited by William C. Harris (1999)

The Wild East: A Biography of the Great Smoky Mountains, by Margaret L. Brown (2000; first paperback edition, 2001)

Crime, Sexual Violence, and Clemency: Florida's Pardon Board and Penal System in the Progressive Era, by Vivien M. L. Miller (2000)

The New South's New Frontier: A Social History of Economic Development in Southwestern North Carolina, by Stephen Wallace Taylor (2001)

Redefining the Color Line: Black Activism in Little Rock, Arkansas, 1940–1970, by John A. Kirk (2002)

The Southern Dream of a Caribbean Empire, 1854–1861, by Robert E. May (2002)

Forging a Common Bond: Labor and Environmental Activism during the BASF Lockout, by Timothy J. Minchin (2003)

Dixie's Daughters: The United Daughters of the Confederacy and the Preservation of Confederate Culture, by Karen L. Cox (2003)

The Other War of 1812: The Patriot War and the American Invasion of Spanish East Florida, by James G. Cusick (2003)

"Lives Full of Struggle and Triumph": Southern Women, Their Institutions, and Their Communities, edited by Bruce L. Clayton and John A. Salmond (2003)

German-Speaking Officers in the United States Colored Troops, 1863–1867, by Martin W. Öfele (2004)

Southern Struggles: The Southern Labor Movement and the Civil Rights Struggle, by John A. Salmond (2004)

Radio and the Struggle for Civil Rights in the South, by Brian Ward (2004; first paperback edition, 2006)

Luther P. Jackson and a Life for Civil Rights, by Michael Dennis (2004)

Southern Ladies, New Women: Race, Region, and Clubwomen in South Carolina, 1890–1930, by Joan Marie Johnson (2004)

Fighting Against the Odds: A Concise History of Southern Labor Since World War II, by Timothy J. Minchin (2004; first paperback edition, 2006)

"Don't Sleep With Stevens!": The J. P. Stevens Campaign and the Struggle to Organize the South, 1963–1980, by Timothy J. Minchin (2005)

"The Ticket to Freedom": The NAACP and the Struggle for Black Political Integration, by Manfred Berg (2005; first paperback edition, 2007)

"War Governor of the South": North Carolina's Zeb Vance in the Confederacy, by Joe A. Mobley (2005)

Planters' Progress: Modernizing Confederate Georgia, by Chad Morgan (2005)

The Officers of the CSS Shenandoah, by Angus Curry (2006)

The Rosenwald Schools of the American South, by Mary S. Hoffschwelle (2006)

Honor in Command: Lt. Freeman S. Bowley's Civil War Service in the 30th United States Colored Infantry, edited by Keith Wilson (2006)